D1551780

Consciousness and Cognition

Philosophy of Mind Series

Series Editor
David J. Chalmers, University of Arizona

Self Expressions
Minds, Morals, and the Meaning of Life
Owen Flanagan

The Conscious Mind
In Search of a Fundamental Theory
David J. Chalmers

Deconstructing the Mind
Stephen P. Stich

The Human Animal
Personal Identity Without Psychology
Eric T. Olson

Minds and Bodies
Philosophers and Their Ideas
Colin McGinn

What's Within?
Nativism Reconsidered
Fiona Cowie

Purple Haze
The Puzzle of Consciousness
Joseph Levine

Consciousness and Cognition
Michael Thau

CONSCIOUSNESS AND COGNITION

Michael Thau

OXFORD
UNIVERSITY PRESS

2002

OXFORD

UNIVERSITY PRESS

Oxford   New York

Athens   Auckland   Bangkok   Bogotá   Buenos Aires   Cape Town
Chennai   Dar es Salaam   Delhi   Florence   Hong Kong   Istanbul   Karachi
Kolkata   Kuala Lumpur   Madrid   Melbourne   Mexico City   Mumbai   Nairobi
Paris   São Paulo   Shanghai   Singapore   Taipei   Tokyo   Toronto   Warsaw

and associated companies in
Berlin   Ibadan

Library of Congress Cataloging-in-Publication Data
Thau, Michael, 1962–
Consciousness and cognition / Michael Thau.
p.   cm. — (Philosophy of mind series)
Includes bibliographical references and index.
ISBN 0-19-514181-4
1. Philosophy of mind.   2. Mental representation.   I. Title.   II. Series.
BD418.3 .T42   2001
128'.2—dc21   2001021597

1 3 5 7 9 8 6 4 2

Printed in the United States of America
on acid-free paper

This book is dedicated to Ronnie Johnson

Acknowledgments

Success depends upon luck and, to whatever extent this book sheds light on the phenomena of consciousness and cognition, it does so largely because I was lucky. First, I was lucky in having superb undergraduate philosophy teachers. I've seen many philosophy departments since my days at Temple University, and I doubt there is a better group of philosophy teachers than Mark Heller, Michael Tye, Gerald Vision, David Welker, and Bill Wisdom. I was also very fortunate to have had the late Hugues Leblanc as an undergraduate teacher. Besides being an invaluable teacher, Hugues was also something of a mentor to me and I'm one of the many people who miss him.

The influence of my undergraduate teachers shows up in one place or another in the book, but Michael Tye deserves special thanks. In various classes and seminars, Michael introduced me to the problems and issues that are treated herein, and it is because of his influence that these topics became my prime area of research. In fact, there are two papers that I tried to write for one of Michael's seminars—one on qualia and one on mental representation—on which I never managed to make any progress. I think I finally did manage to make some progress on these topics and the result is before you. Though you'll find that I disagree with Michael in a number of places, I think you'll also find that I'm enormously indebted to him throughout.

The luck reflected in the teachers I've had has continued in the students I've wound up teaching. My undergraduate students often didn't know what I was talking about, and I often found out that there was a simple explanation: namely, that I didn't know what I was talking about. Many of the fundamental ideas in this book emerged because my undergraduates were justifiably perplexed, and I thank them for continually forcing me to better understand the foundation of things. On the other conceptual end, the advanced undergraduates and graduate students I've taught have continually forced me to try to make better and more precise sense of the complexities; all of them deserve thanks but Ben Caplan, Louis Derosset, Dave Elrey, Francesco Famá, Jonathan Garthoff, Luca Struble, and Jonathan Tweedale stand out.

One of the delights of being a philosophy professor is the opportunity to travel and engage in discussion with other philosophers. Various parts of this book were presented in colloquia at Monash University, Vassar College, Reed College, Arizona State, MIT, UC Santa Cruz, UC Santa Barbara, UCLA, Simon Fraser University, NYU, the University of Calgary, Lethbridge University, and the University of Edmonton. These audiences were incredibly patient and receptive and have been invaluable in catching errors and unclarities. I thank each of these departments for their invitation and help.

I've also been incredibly lucky in the number of philosophers who've read and commented on various drafts of the book. Kent Bach, Gideon Rosen, Ali Kazmi, Jim Pryor, and Sydney Shoemaker provided detailed written comments on an earlier draft. Jeff King and other members of Kent's reading group discussed ancestors of Chapters 1, 2, and 5 with me, and these discussions have helped certain issues seem much less baffling. I had invaluable and extensive discussions with Tyler Burge on a distant ancestor of Chapter 5, and I've also received helpful written comments from Paul Benacerraf, Alex Byrne, Benj Hellie, Dave Jensen, Sean Kelsey, Harold Langsam, Robert Lurz, Jonathan Sutton, and Abe Witonsky. Kathleen Akins, Steven Davis, and Martin Hahn were kind enough to meet with me weekly to discuss an earlier draft of the book. Steven also attended a seminar I gave based on the book, and he was tremendously helpful in clarifying any number of the issues. I owe Steven a tremendous debt for both his philosophical and personal support, and I cannot thank him enough.

Though I received many helpful comments from many philosophers, I owe my biggest debt of gratitude to my philosophical A-team. This book wouldn't exist without the help of the five people mentioned below. My discussions with Mark Johnston and his comments on drafts of this book have been helpful in every possible way. Besides having an excellent eye for what's true, Mark also has an excellent eye for what's important, and I have benefitted from my association with him in innumerable ways. I was lucky to have Mark as my advisor as a graduate student at Princeton and doubly lucky that he has continued in this role. Scott Soames read and commented on every chapter, and anyone who has had Scott as a teacher will know how valuable his advice was; without him, the central ideas in the book would be, at best, completely muddled. I also count myself lucky to have Scott as a close friend; and I greatly value his support and friendship. Scott is in Princeton, but I was fortunate to have my friend Alan Hájek in Los Angeles. Al provided invaluable comments on every chapter and his continual help in nailing down elusive points have greatly improved this book. I was also lucky to have my friend Mark Kalderon in Los Angeles for a time. Mark was generous enough to read more than one draft of the manuscript, and I can't overestimate his contribution. In many places, Mark had a better understanding of what I was trying to do than I did. Ben Caplan has read more drafts of the manuscript than I could count. As unofficial editor, he caught more mistakes — from the typographical to the profoundly philosophical — than I like to think about. Thanks to Ben.

Finally, thanks to Gene McKnight and Joe Farracio for teaching me the most essential lessons of all and to Fergus Carey, Brad Kochel, and Abe Witonsky for years of friendship. And special thanks to Suzette Glasner for her love and support and for showing that my luck knows no bounds.

Contents

Consciousness and Cognition

Introduction

If we look at what philosophers of mind have been saying over the last twenty or thirty years, underneath many of the arguments and counterexamples—indeed, I think it's fair to say *underlying* most of the contention—we'll find a detailed and (at least on the surface) remarkably coherent account of the structure of mental phenomena; we'll find what has become the precise object of philosophical desire: namely, a *theory*. That is, of course, not to say that any one philosopher explicitly accepts the whole theory—though everyone wants a theory no one wants anyone else's—but it is to say that most of the major controversies in late twentieth-century philosophy of mind are intelligible only with one or another part of the theory as background. Hence, it's also to say that, if we're going to understand the debates about the mind that we've been bequeathed, it's worthwhile to bring the parts of the theory and their relations to one another completely out into the open: to, as my colleague Gavin Lawrence likes to say, "out the picture."

There are, of course, many different kinds of mental phenomena, but one important kind falls under the rubric of *cognition*; cognition involves thinking and the point of cognition is, at least in part, to yield truths, to give us true *beliefs* about the world. So, to the extent that we understand what's involved in *believing*, we'll have at least the foundation of an understanding of cognition. The theory of mental phenomena mentioned above has much to say about what believing involves and, like many philosophical theories, it can profitably be understood as arising from two obviously compelling but apparently contradictory intuitions.

Suppose two people—say, you and I—both believe something—say, that Aristotle is the most important philosopher. On the one hand, one would obviously want to say that our beliefs are the same; after all, both of us believe that Aristotle is the most important philosopher. But, on the other hand, it seems equally obvious that our beliefs are different; after all, yours is yours and mine is mine. But how

3

can both intuitions be true? How can your belief that Aristotle is the most important philosopher and mine be both identical and distinct? If the apparent inconsistency is only apparent, then it seems that the two intuitions must involve two different senses of the term *belief*: one sense of the term according to which our beliefs are the same and another quite distinct sense according to which they are different. If the term does have two distinct senses, then both intuitions might be true; but, of course, we would also face a question: if *belief* is not univocal, then what are its two senses? What does the term pick out in the sense in which our beliefs are the same, and what does it pick out in the sense in which they are distinct? But, if it's right that the two intuitions can be reconciled by appealing to different senses of the term *belief*, then we might be able to determine what these senses are by focusing on what is intuitively the same about our beliefs and what is intuitively different about them. Let's begin with difference.

One obvious difference that there might be between your belief and mine is that they might have been caused by different things; perhaps you believe that Aristotle is the most important philosopher as a result of careful study of Aristotle and other important philosophers, whereas I believe it because I've heard it said on National Public Radio. And, indeed, even if it turned out that both of our beliefs result from careful study or both result from testimony, it still seems that they will have had different causes. Your poring over the works of the great philosophers and mine are not the same event; and you might have heard of Aristotle's importance on one occasion, whereas I heard of it on another. And, even if we were both told that Aristotle is the most important philosopher by the very same person at the very same time, the sound waves that strike your ears will not be the same as those that strike mine. So it seems that, on the sense of *belief* according to which our beliefs are different things, one difference between them is that they will, in one way or another, turn out to have had different causes.

But this isn't the only way that causation appears to be relevant to their difference. It also seems that, in this sense of the term *belief* according to which our beliefs are different, they will have different effects; that is to say, they will cause different things. Your belief that Aristotle is the most important philosopher might cause you to go on the Internet and buy his complete works, whereas mine might cause me to go into a library and borrow them. And, even if we both buy or both borrow, *your* buying or borrowing is not the same event as *my* buying or borrowing; whatever actions your belief causes you to engage in will involve movements in *your* body, and whatever mine causes me to engage in will involve movements in *mine*. So it seems that, in the sense of *belief* according to which our beliefs are different, they will, in one way or another, turn out to have different effects.

We appear to have reached a result: insofar as our respective beliefs that Aristotle is the most important philosopher are different things, they have different causes and different effects. But this apparent result yields a mere *extrinsic* difference between our beliefs: it tells us that each of our beliefs bears certain kinds of relations to different things, but it does not by itself tell us anything about how our beliefs *intrinsically* differ. So it does not answer the question of what kinds of things our different beliefs actually are and what it is about them that makes them different. But, though it doesn't answer these questions, it does seem to point the way towards their answers. Suppose we both believe that Aristotle is the most important philosopher because we've both heard someone say it and each of our beliefs causes each of us to buy his complete works. If we keep following this line of thought, it appears that all we need to do is determine what kind of thing is caused in you and causes your buying behavior when you hear that Aristotle is the most important philosopher and what kind of thing is caused in me and causes my buying behavior when I hear it; for, if we've been right so far, when we find these things we will have found our respective beliefs that Aristotle is the most important philosopher. And it seems that, if we haven't exactly found these things, thanks to empirical science we know where they're to be found: they're to be found in our *brains*.

When I hear that Aristotle is the most important philosopher, some state of my brain gets caused, and it is this state of my brain that causes me to buy or to borrow or whatever other behavior the belief causes me to engage in; and, of course, likewise for you. One might even go so far as to think that *what it is* to be the belief that Aristotle is the most important philosopher is to be a state that has certain causes and effects; however, we needn't go this far. For, whatever turns out to *metaphysically make* each of our respective brain states a belief that Aristotle is the most important philosopher, it seems there can be no doubt that it is some state of your brain that is the relevant cause and has the relevant effects of your belief and some state of my brain that is the relevant cause and has the relevant effects of mine. So, whether or not these causal facts are in any way *constitutive* of what it is to be the belief that Aristotle is the most important philosopher, they do seem to tell us what kinds of things our respective beliefs are: thanks to empirical science, we know they are states of our brains.

So empirical science appears to have answered half our question: in the sense of the term *belief* according to which your belief that Aristotle is the most important philosopher and mine are different things, beliefs are brain states. But what of the other half? How are we to understand *belief* in a way that makes it true to say that your belief that Aristotle is the most important philosopher and mine are the very same thing? One answer might be that the two senses of *belief* are not so far removed and that, when we say our beliefs are the same, we're still talking about brain states, but instead of talking about brain state tokens we're talking about brain state types: just as two people can be said to drive the same car because they both drive Honda Civics—because they both drive the same *type* of car—our distinct brain states might be the same because they are both beliefs that Aristotle is the most important philosopher, because they are both the same *type* of belief. But, though this may be one reason for the intuition that our beliefs are the same, it doesn't seem to fully explain the intuition. After all, a belief (in some sense of the term) is a kind of thought; so your belief that Aristotle is the most important philosopher and my belief that he is seem to both be *thoughts*. And, insofar as they are thoughts, it doesn't seem that they are merely the same type of thought; rather, they seem to be the very same thought. And, if this is right, the sense of *belief* according to which beliefs are thoughts cannot be the sense in which they are brain states. But, if we can't find the answer to the second half of our question in the brain, where can it be found?

One obvious thing that your belief that Aristotle is the most important philosopher and mine have in common is that they both concern the very same state of affairs: namely, *Aristotle's being the most important philosopher.* So maybe the sense of *belief* according to which our beliefs are the same is a sense according to which the belief that Aristotle is the most important philosopher just is that state of affairs, just is Aristotle's being the most important philosopher; on this suggestion, our beliefs are the same (in the second sense of the term *belief*) because both are identical to this state of affairs. But, though this would give us a sense of *belief* according to which our beliefs are one and the same thing, on reflection it seems that it can't be exactly right. The state of affairs of Aristotle's being the most important philosopher exists only if Aristotle is in fact the most important philosopher; if he isn't there is no such state of affairs. For example, while Aristotle may very well be the most important philosopher, it doesn't seem likely that Parmenides is and, hence, it doesn't seem likely that there is the state of affairs of Parmenides' being the most important philosopher. But, nonetheless, someone might believe that Parmenides is the most important philosopher. Of course, what they believe would (very likely) be false, but that's precisely the problem: beliefs can be true *or* false, and identifying beliefs with states of affairs doesn't appear to allow for the possibility of false beliefs. However, though states of affairs don't appear to be what we're looking for, the reason for this points the way towards the answer. Whatever beliefs are, they must be capable of being true or false; but there are things that are capable of being both true *and false* and that seem very closely related to beliefs: namely, public-language sentences.

So maybe this second sense of *belief* is one according to which beliefs just are public-language sentences; if this is the sense of the term we're looking for, your belief that Aristotle is the most important philosopher and mine are the same because each is simply the sentence *Aristotle is the most important philosopher*. But, though this suggestion appears to be getting us closer to our answer, it's clear that it won't quite do. Obviously one needn't speak or understand any English to believe that Aristotle is the most important philosopher and, hence, it doesn't seem that we can identify the belief that Aristotle is the most important philosopher with the English sentence *Aristotle is the most important philosopher*. Someone who speaks and understands only Japanese might have the belief without knowing anything about this English sentence, so this sentence can't be the belief that Aristotle is the most important philosopher. Moreover, animals and infants seem to have beliefs and, if we're to account for this fact, we can't identify beliefs with *any* linguistic items.

But, though the linguistic answer doesn't suffice, it does appear to tell us where the answer is to be found. For it isn't as if the Japanese speaker who believes that Aristotle is the most important philosopher and the English speaker who believes the same thing have nothing at all in common. True, they do not speak the same language, but it seems obvious that both are able to believe that Aristotle is the most important philosopher because, despite speaking different languages, they share the same *concepts*; each can believe that Aristotle is the most important philosopher because each has *the concept of Aristotle* and *the concept of being the most important philosopher*. And, indeed, the sentence that each uses to express the belief that Aristotle is the most important philosopher seems to do so because the words that make up each sentence are associated with these concepts. Focusing on English, *Aristotle* seems to pick out Aristotle because it is associated with a certain thing— the concept of Aristotle—and *is the most important philosopher* seems to pick out the property of being the most important philosopher because it is associated with a certain thing, the concept of being the most important philosopher. These concepts are *the meanings* of the relevant expressions and the sentence is true because it too has a certain *meaning*; just as the sentence is composed of its constituent words, the sentence's meaning is composed of the meanings of its constituent words, of the concepts of Aristotle and being the most important philosopher. And this complex thing that is the meaning of the sentence—let's call it *the proposition that Aristotle is the most important philosopher*—looks to be the thing that you believe when you believe that Aristotle is the most important philosopher, the thing I believe when I believe that Aristotle is the most important philosopher, and the thing our Japanese speaker believes when he believes that Aristotle is the most important philosopher. Propositions are the meanings of sentences and the things we believe. And maybe you, me, and our Japanese speaker all have the same belief because we all believe the same proposition; maybe, on the sense of the term *belief* according to which our beliefs are the same, beliefs *just are* propositions.

But what sorts of things are these propositions? Well, we've already said that the meaning of a sentence is a proposition and that propositions are composed of concepts. And, once we've gone this far, it seems obvious that the proposition that Aristotle is the most important philosopher can't simply be a random collection of concepts any more than the sentence *Aristotle is the most important philosopher* is a random collection of words. The proposition that Aristotle is the most important philosopher must have a structure that is analogous to the syntactic structure of the sentence *Aristotle is the most important philosopher*; that is to say, the concepts are arranged in the proposition in a way that determines a *representational content*, in a way that determines that the proposition is true just in case the thing picked out by the concept of Aristotle has the property picked out by the concept of being the most important philosopher. Your belief, my belief, and the Japanese speaker's belief are the very same belief in the sense of the term *belief* according to which beliefs are propositions; and a proposition is a syntactically structured arrangement of concepts. And, similarly, two animals or infants can have the same belief even though they speak no language; they have the same belief if they believe the very same proposition, the very same syntactically structured collection of concepts.

But, if propositions are syntactically structured collections of concepts, what sorts of things are concepts? Well, we've already said that the meaning of a word is a concept. But it seems like a category mistake to suppose that, for example, the meaning of the word *Aristotle* could be found in someone's attic or in the course of an archeological dig or in some other galaxy. Concepts appear to be like numbers; they aren't physical objects located in space, so they must be abstract, nonphysical objects. And, since on the sense of *belief* according to which you and I believe the same thing, beliefs are composed of concepts, we also know something about what this sense of *belief* picks out: thanks to metaphysical reflection, we know it picks out a complex, syntactically structured abstract object; it picks out a proposition.

So it appears that a little empirical knowledge and a little metaphysical reflection yield the answer to the question with which we began: why does it seem that your belief that Aristotle is the most important philosopher is both different from and the same as mine? The answer seems to be that the phrase *The belief that Aristotle is the most important philosopher* is ambiguous. On the one hand, it refers to what we might call a *concrete belief*, a concrete state that is caused in individuals and causes their behavior and that we now know occurs in their brains. When someone has a belief, the sense in which his belief is his and his alone is a sense in which his belief is a belief state located in his brain. On the other hand, *The belief that Aristotle is the most important philosopher* can also refer to what we might call an *abstract belief*, an abstract object composed of concepts. When two people believe the same thing, the sense in which they share a single belief is the sense in which the belief just is the abstract belief that they both believe.

This account, besides offering an explanation of what the two senses of *belief* are, also appears to offer an explanation of what the relationship between them is; the empirical science and the metaphysical reflection seem to link up rather nicely. On the account, you have a brain state, which is your belief that Aristotle is the most important philosopher, and I have a brain state, which is mine. But what makes these distinct brain states both instances of the *belief state* that Aristotle is the most important philosopher? The obvious answer would be that they both bear a *semantic* relation to the *abstract belief*, or proposition, that Aristotle is the most important philosopher. The sentence *Aristotle is the most important philosopher* bears a semantic relation to the proposition that Aristotle is the most important philosopher: the sentence has the proposition as its meaning. And your (and mine and anyone else's) concrete belief that Aristotle is the most important philosopher bears some kind of similar semantic relation to the proposition: in some sense, brain states can also have propositions as their meanings, and the meaning of a brain state is what makes it the particular belief that it is.

We began with conflicting intuitions and wound up with a substantive theory about the basic elements of cognition and their relations to one another. According to the theory, whenever you believe, you have a concrete belief state that bears a semantic relation to an abstract belief proposition; the proposition represents the world as being a certain way and, thus, in virtue of bearing a semantic relation to the proposition your belief state has a certain representational content. Now, when you see something, it seems just plain obvious that you also have an internal state that is related to a representational content. After all, to see is to have a certain kind of thing—a *visual experience*—and visual experiences, like beliefs, have causes and effects. The visual experience you have upon seeing a ripe tomato is caused by light waves striking the retina of your eye, and it may cause you to engage in some behavior like picking up and eating the tomato.

And similar causal facts appear to be true of experiences that involve perceptual modalities other than vision; when you hear, smell, taste, or touch something, you have an auditory, olfactory, gustatory, or tactile experience. And these perceptual experiences are caused by the thing you hear, smell, taste, or touch, and they cause you to engage in certain behavior. So how could a perceptual experience be anything other than an internal state of its subject? And, given our empirical knowledge, we know that perceptual experiences, like beliefs in the first sense of the word, must be states of the brain. Moreover, if you're seeing the ripe tomato under normal circumstances, the tomato will *look red* to you. So your visual experience, besides being an internal state of yours, also represents the tomato as red: it, like your concrete belief state, bears a semantic relation to a certain representational content. And, again, likewise for other perceptual experiences: perceptual experiences, like concrete beliefs, are states of the brain that have representational content. So it appears that our theory of belief also covers perception.

However, though our theory seems to explain certain aspects of perception, there is a fundamental aspect that it doesn't seem to have the resources to explain. Perceptual experiences are *conscious* experiences: when you see, hear, smell, taste, or touch, there is a way the experience seems to you; there is—as philosophers like to say—*something it's like* to have the experience. There's something it's like to see red, and talk of representational content doesn't seem to capture this; it doesn't seem to capture the conscious aspects of perceptual experience. But how are we to account for the conscious aspect of perceptual experiences? Well, it isn't just perceptual experiences that have a conscious aspect: bodily sensations like pain and tickles are also conscious experiences—there's also something it's like to have them—and it seems that a look at the nature of sensations like pain straightforwardly provides a perfectly commonsensical account of consciousness, an account that can be straightforwardly applied to perceptual experiences.

There seems to be no distinction between *having pain* and *having the experience of pain*. If I ask you how your root canal went, it couldn't make sense for you to answer *Well, I had lots of pain, but thanks to the anesthetic I didn't experience it* or *I experienced lots of pain, but thankfully the experiences were illusory and I really didn't have any*. And the reason such answers would be nonsense seems apparent: pain *just is* a kind of experience with certain qualities; and to have a pain is *to be aware* of this kind of an experience and its qualities. But now it seems that we've explained why experiences of pain are conscious experiences. Consciousness just is the awareness of what your experiences are like, of certain qualities that your experiences have. So it appears that the reason that perception involves consciousness must be that, when you have a perceptual experience, you are *aware* of your experience and what *it's* like: the conscious aspects of perception and sensation consist in the awareness of certain qualities of your experiences. What could be more commonsensical than that?

So, by adding a bit of common sense to our empirical science and metaphysical reflection, the theory can account for consciousness as well as cognition. Cognition involves internal brain states that bear relations to representational contents; but perception involves this and something more. Perceptual experiences, like sensations, are conscious experiences, and to have a conscious experience is to know what the experience is like, to be aware of its qualities. But it isn't as if consciousness and representational content are entirely unrelated aspects of perceptual experience; it seems that the way your experience of the tomato seems to you is related to the fact that the tomato looks red to you. And our theory explains what the relation between consciousness and representational content is; the common sense and the metaphysical reflection link up rather nicely.

Return to the case of pain. Suppose I touch a stove and burn my hand. I'll be in pain and, as we've already noted, it seems that this consists in my being aware of my experience and its qualities, its painfulness. But, in some sense, my painful experience must represent the stove—after all, it was caused by the stove—and the painful quality of my experience represents the heat of the stove—after all, this quality was caused by the heat of the stove. So, in some sense, my experience of pain represents the stove as being hot: my experience of pain, like my beliefs and perceptions, appears to have a representational content, and it has the representational content it does because of its qualities and the kind of things that cause these qualities. Similarly, a visual experience is a conscious experience, so having a visual experience involves being aware of certain of its qualities. But, as we've noted, your visual experience of a ripe tomato also has a representational content: it represents the tomato as red. And what the case of touching the hot stove appears to show is that your experience has the representational content it does *because* of its qualities. Visual experiences of red have a certain quality—call it *red'*—and it's because they are red' and because red' experiences are caused by red things that they count as experiences of red; just as the experience I have when I touch the stove has a certain quality—its painfulness—and this quality represents heat because heat is what causes this quality.

It's amazing how far a little empirical science, metaphysical reflection, and common sense can take you; for they appear to have taken us to a very detailed theory that purports to explain the structure of consciousness and cognition. And this theory is at the foundation of much of late twentieth-century analytic philosophy of mind. Of course, as I've said, it isn't that many philosophers explicitly accept the whole theory; rather, it's that the theory is in one way or another what makes much of late twentieth-century philosophy of mind intelligible.

To the extent that you accept one or another part of the theory, you'll take certain questions to express the fundamental problems about consciousness and cognition that need to be solved.

Are our internal beliefs states, like sentences and propositions, complex entities with a syntactic structure?

How does a brain state come to be related to a certain proposition?

Is the representational content of perceptual experiences propositional, or does it differ from the representational content of belief?

What are concepts and how are they to be individuated?

To the extent that you have qualms about one or another part of the theory, you'll take certain questions to express ways in which the theory might have to be revised if it is to adequately account for consciousness and cognition.

Do brain states really need to bear semantic relations to propositions in order to be beliefs, or might the semantic part of the theory be dispensable?

Are propositions really complex entities with a syntactic structure or might they be less fine-grained?

Does the nature of the qualities of experience that account for its conscious aspects allow that experiences can be wholly physical brain states, or must we suppose that there's something nonphysical about them?

Do pains and other bodily sensations really have representational content, or is their lack of representational content what distinguishes them from perceptual experiences?

And denying some fundamental part of the theory needn't diminish its relevance. For a denial that some part of the theory describes reality is often a denial of the reality of the mental phenomena that part is supposed to explain.

The brain cannot be divided into states that correspond to our beliefs; hence, there are no beliefs and it is up to cognitive science to provide us with an alternative account of the mind.

We aren't aware of the qualities of our experience, so consciousness is a myth.

As you can tell by the title, this book is about consciousness and cognition. The book is organized around three philosophical puzzles. Each of the puzzles appears to provide arguments for some part of the theory of consciousness and cognition presented above. The puzzles are more similar—strikingly more similar—than has heretofore been recognized. But the puzzles do not in fact provide any reason to accept any part of the theory. And, indeed, the similarities among the puzzles show that different parts of the theory arise from the same mistakes, that most (but not entirely all) of the theory is simply wrong, and that most (but not entirely all) of the problems it appears to make intelligible are pseudo-problems. Moreover, the theory has obscured the nature of both consciousness and cognition and, in doing so, has obscured what really needs to be explained about consciousness and cognition; and the illusion of explanation the theory fosters has obscured how frighteningly little we know about these two essential aspects of our humanity. A little empirical science, metaphysical reflection, and common sense is, at least in this case, a dangerous thing.

Or so I hope to show. So without further ado . . .

1

Spectrum Inversion

0. Introduction

There is a well-known philosophical problem concerning *spectrum inversion*. One way to put the problem is roughly as follows. Suppose, as is probably the case, that you and I generally apply the same color terms to the same sorts of things: we both agree that grass is appropriately called **green**, the sky is appropriately called **blue**, etc. But suppose further that our apparent agreement about the application of color terms masks the fact that I am *spectrally inverted* with respect to you: red things look to you the way green things look to me and vice versa, yellow things look to you the way blue things look to me and vice versa, etc. There is clearly some way in which your visual experience of a ripe tomato differs from mine. But it is doubtful that our visual experiences differ with respect to what color they *represent* the tomato as being. After all, we both express our beliefs about the color of the tomato by uttering the sentence *It's red*, so it's very plausible that we both *believe* that the tomato is red. And, if our respective visual experiences of the tomato lead each of us to believe that it's red, how could either of our visual experiences fail to represent it *as* red? So spectrum inversion presents a case in which there seems to be a difference between two perceptions that can't be a difference in what they represent. Many philosophers conclude that there must be more to perceptual experiences than *what* they represent; perceptual experiences must also be individuated by *how* they represent. Though each of our visual experiences represents the tomato as red, yours represents redness by having a certain intrinsic quality, while mine represents it by having a different intrinsic quality.

There is a well-known philosophical problem called *Frege's puzzle*. One way to put the problem is roughly as follows. It seems that the belief that Superman flies and the belief that Clark Kent flies must be different beliefs. After all, Lex Luthor has the former but not the latter. Yet the belief that Superman flies seems to represent that a certain individual flies; and, since Superman is Clark Kent, the belief that Clark Kent flies seems to represent that the very same individual flies. So Frege's puzzle presents a case in which there seems to be a difference between two beliefs that can't be a difference in what they represent. Most philosophers conclude that there must be more to beliefs than *what* they represent; beliefs must also be individuated by *how* they represent. Though the belief that Superman flies and the belief that Clark Kent flies each represent that the same individual flies, they differ in their *mode of presentation* of that individual.

There is a well-known philosophical problem concerning *black-and-white Mary*. One way to put the problem is roughly as follows. Mary has never seen any colors except black, white, and shades of grey. She is looking at a ripe tomato on a black-and-white television screen, and having been told that it is red, she believes that it is red, even though her visual experience represents it as being some shade of grey. Suddenly the screen becomes colored and Mary's new visual experience represents the tomato as red. Her new visual experience and her belief both represent the same thing: namely, that the tomato is red. Yet surely Mary learns something as a result of having the new visual experience. So black-and-white Mary presents a case in which there seems to be a difference between a perceptual experience and a belief that can't be a difference in what they represent. Most philosophers conclude that there must be more to perceptual experiences than *what* they represent; perceptual experiences must also be individuated from beliefs by *how* they represent. Some claim that the difference between Mary's visual experience of the tomato and her belief is that the former represents redness by having a certain intrinsic quality, while others deny the existence of such qualities and claim that visual experiences and beliefs represent redness via different concepts of red.

So the three philosophical problems discussed above are, in a certain light, strikingly similar. Respectively, they provide arguments that facts about *what* is represented are insufficient to adequately distinguish perceptual experiences from each other, beliefs from each other, and perceptual experiences from beliefs. And, hence, they suggest that facts about *how* perceptual experiences and beliefs represent are required to properly individuate them: to adequately distinguish perceptual experiences from each other, beliefs from each other, and perceptual experiences from beliefs.

Most philosophers agree that the world is represented to subjects in belief and perception; but, as is plain from the above discussion, the view that there is more to belief and perception than what they represent is about as close to philosophical orthodoxy as anything. Indeed, as I hope will emerge, the view is, in one way or another, held by almost every philosopher of mind; it is so ubiquitous that it is often difficult to recognize its presence for lack of contrast and, even when noticed, it can appear to be a triviality rather than the substantive claim that it is. My aim in this book is to bring the view out into the open and, in doing so, to show that it is mistaken. And, as might be expected if the mistake is as pervasive as I suggest, it has had some very unfortunate consequences for our understanding of belief and perception. So I also hope to point the way toward a better understanding of these (and to some extent other) mental phenomena. On the better understanding, *belief and perception form a single class of mental phenomena marked by their representational nature and any mental difference between any two members of the class must be a difference in what they represent*. At this stage, this formulation of the better understanding is apt to seem like a slogan and many questions need to be answered in order to see what it's supposed to capture. In exactly what sense are belief and perception representational, and how exactly do two things differ when they differ in what they represent? And each of the three philosophical problems just discussed presents an apparent difference that apparently can't be a difference in what is represented. Hence, if the slogan is correct, each of the problems must be responded to in one of two ways: either the apparent difference must turn out *not* to be genuine, or the difference really *is* a difference in what is represented.

I'll begin to answer these questions by discussing two currently popular views on the nature of perception. Each of the views says something right and important, but each, I will argue, also goes astray in some important respect.

1. Two views on perception

Over the last ten years, there has been an unprecedented amount of philosophical research on consciousness and perception. As one would expect in a discipline that thrives on lack of consensus, the result is that there are at least as many views on consciousness and perception as there are researchers. Indeed, those of us responsible for keeping track of the field can only be thankful that philosophers rarely change their minds. However, though a thousand flowers have bloomed, most of them fall on one side or the other of what Ned Block (forthcoming) has called "the greatest chasm in the philosophy of mind." In order to get a rough idea of the two sides, consider the following two cases.

(SEEMSRED)   You are looking at a red object and there is nothing abnormal about the circumstances or your visual system.

(SEEMSBLUE)   You are looking at a blue object and there is nothing abnormal about the circumstances or your visual system.

Obviously, what it's like for you to be in the circumstances described in (SEEMSRED) will differ from what it's like for you to be in those described in (SEEMSBLUE). There is a difference in how the two circumstances would seem to you, a *subjective difference* between your visual experiences in these circumstances. Of course, we would ordinarily describe this difference by saying that in the one case the thing *looks red* to you, while in the other it *looks blue*. But, though this may be a correct description of the difference, it isn't an explanation of it. What is it for something to look red, or blue, or some other color to you?

The philosophers on one side of the chasm—the *intentionalists*—hold that the subjective difference between your visual experiences is fully explainable by the fact that the objects are represented to you as having different colors. In the circumstances described in (SEEMSRED), your visual experience represents the thing you are seeing as red, while in the circumstances described in (SEEMS-BLUE), it represents the thing you are seeing as blue, and that is why the two circumstances seem different to you. The fact that something looks red (or blue, or some other color) to you is completely explained by the fact that your visual experience represents the thing as being red (or blue, or the other color). Indeed, the intentionalist holds that any difference in the way things perceptually seem is fully explained by a difference in what the perceptual experiences represent; subjective differences between perceptual experiences are always explained by *representational differences* between them.

But what is it for a visual experience to represent something as being a certain color; or, more generally, what is it for one thing to represent another thing as being a certain way? Some intentionalists have much to say in answer to this question, and in Chapter 2 I will argue that they have erred in focusing on the wrong features of representation. For now it will suffice to point out one thing about the relevant notion of representation: namely, its link to the notions of truth and falsity. When X represents O as being a certain way, this implies that X represents O *truly* if O is that way and *falsely* if it is not. More specifically, when a visual experience represents something as being a certain color, the experience represents the thing truly if the thing is that color, and falsely if it isn't.

On the other side of the chasm stand the *qualia freaks*. According to them, the intentionalist's explanation of differences in how things perceptually seem may be acceptable as far as it goes, but it certainly doesn't go far enough. For the qualia freak claims that the alleged fact that two perceptual experiences represent their respective objects differently does not completely explain any subjective difference there might be between them. A full explanation must advert to intrinsic properties that the experiences *themselves* have—to what are called *qualia*—and not merely to differences in what the experiences represent. In the circumstances described in (SEEMSRED), your visual experience has some intrinsic property in virtue of which it represents the thing as red, and in the circumstances described in (SEEMSBLUE) your visual experience has some different intrinsic property in virtue of which it represents the thing as blue; and it is because the two experiences have these different qualities that the two circumstances seem different to you. To borrow a bit of terminology from Christopher Peacocke (1983, 20–21), let **red'** be shorthand for *the intrinsic quality that your visual experience has when something seems red to you*, and **blue'** be shorthand for *the intrinsic quality that your visual experience has when something seems blue to you*, and so on for the other colors. In general, the qualia freak holds that corresponding to the colors red, blue, yellow, etc., there are the *primed-colors* red', blue', yellow', etc. While colors are properties of objects in the external world, the primed-colors are intrinsic properties of visual experiences. When something looks to be some color to you this is at least in part because your visual experience has the corresponding primed-color property. And the subjective difference between your visual experience when you are seeing an object that looks one color to you and your visual experience when you are seeing one that looks another color is due to the different primed-color properties of your visual experiences.[1]

Of course, it is difficult to understand a theory without having some understanding of the reasons for and against it. And there is one particular argument for the qualia freak's view that brings out the differences between the intentionalist and the qualia freak rather nicely. The argument involves the possibility of *spectrum inversion*. Unfortunately the argument from spectrum inversion, like most arguments given on behalf of the qualia freak's view, is intended to establish two things at once: in this case, that the qualia freak's view is correct *and* that functionalism about the mental is false. And, while there may be interesting connections between the qualia freak's view and the denial of functionalism, the way in which the two positions are entangled has obscured exactly how the inverted spectrum argument motivates the qualia freak's view.

2. Spectrum inversion and functionalism

Here is a standard telling of the spectrum inversion story. Imagine two people—call them *Norm* and *Abnorm*—who both speak the same language—say, English—and have lived in the same community all of their lives. Each goes about his daily business in much the same manner as the other and in particular each uses color terminology in the same way as the other does and in the same way as the rest of his community does. They both agree that ripe tomatoes are appropriately called *red*, grass is appropriately called *green*, etc. But, despite these similarities, there is a difference between Norm and Abnorm. While Norm's perception of the world is perfectly normal, Abnorm's isn't. For when Abnorm looks at a ripe tomato (in normal circumstances), even though he calls its color *red*, the tomato in fact looks green to him. And when he looks at grass (in normal circumstances), even though he calls its color *green*, the grass in fact looks red to him. In general things look and always have looked to be their complementary color to Abnorm; he is *spectrally inverted* with respect to Norm and the rest of his community.

The possibility of spectrum inversion is often used simultaneously as an argument for the qualia freak's view and against *functionalism* about the mental. Functionalism can be seen as the combination of two ideas. The first idea is that mental state types are defined by their function, by what they do. The second idea is that what a particular mental state type does is defined by its *causal role*, by the kinds of things it causes and is caused by, where these include other mental states. For example, a functionalist might say that what it is for a particular mental state to be pain is for it to be caused by certain kinds of things like bodily damage, and to cause certain kinds of things like panic and movement away from the source of the pain.[2]

The argument against functionalism and for the qualia freak's view runs as follows. It seems as if Abnorm's inverted spectrum won't result in any behavioral differences between him and Norm. After all, things have always looked to be their complementary color to Abnorm. So, even though grass looks red to him, he has learned to apply the term *green* to grass; even though the sky looks yellow to him, he has learned to apply the term *blue* to the sky; and so on. The fact that things look to be the wrong color to him won't be revealed in his use of color terminology, and it's not obvious that there need be any other way in which it would be revealed. And, given that there are no relevant behavioral differences between Norm and Abnorm, it should be possible that there are also no relevant functional differences between them. However, there clearly is a mental difference between them and, hence, it's possible for there to be a mental difference without any corresponding functional difference. So functionalism cannot be a complete theory of the mind, and in order to explain the mental difference between Norm and Abnorm, we must suppose that their visual experiences of ripe tomatoes have different intrinsic qualities.

Gilbert Harman has responded that this argument begs the question against the functionalist account of mental representation. According to Harman, part of the functionalist definition of mental states says that, when someone has no reason to doubt the veridicality of his visual experience, the way a thing looks to him will cause him to have a belief that the thing *is* that way. So, if the ripe tomato looks green to Abnorm, then under normal circumstances he will come to believe that it is green. Hence, according to functionalism, Norm and Abnorm will have different beliefs about the color of ripe tomatoes: Norm believes that they are red, while Abnorm believes that they are green. Harman goes on to claim that, since each of them expresses his belief about the color of ripe tomatoes by saying *They're red*, they must mean different things by *red*. But Harman (1990, 48) claims that, according to functionalism and common sense, if Norm and Abnorm "use words in the same way with respect to the same things, then they mean the same things by those words (assuming also that they are members of the same linguistic community and their words are taken from the common language)." So, according to functionalism, undetectable spectrum inversion is impossible, and the argument against functionalism (to quote Harman from an earlier paper) "really comes down simply to denying the functionalist account of the content of concepts and thoughts without actually offering any reason for that denial" (Harman 1982, 250).

Now Harman's response as he presents it is rather weak. He argues that *if* functionalism is true, then undetectable spectrum inversion is impossible and concludes from this that undetectable spectrum inversion is impossible. But, as the saying goes, one man's *modus ponens* is another's *modus tollens*, and one wonders why it isn't at least equally legitimate to conclude that, since undetectable spectrum inversion seems possible, functionalism must be false. Which conclusion should be drawn depends upon whether there's a better case to be made for functionalism or for the possibility of undetectable spectrum inversion. And it is a bit unfair to claim that no reason has been given to think that undetectable spectrum inversion is possible. After all, there is no reason for the functionalist to deny that *I* might wake up tomorrow and find that what it's like for me to see red things is what it used to be like for me to see green things, etc. But, as Sydney Shoemaker (1982) has pointed out, this seems to give me some idea of what it would be like for you to have been spectrally inverted with respect to me all along and thus gives me some reason to believe that it's possible.

Indeed, suppose that we found out that the activity in your brain that is correlated with your seeing something red (under normal circumstances) is the same as the activity in my brain that is correlated with my seeing something green (under normal circumstances), and likewise for our experiences of the other colors. Wouldn't this provide good evidence that our spectra are inverted with respect to each other? After all, isn't it plausible that there's something about what it's like for someone to see colors that depends entirely on physical facts about his brain and central nervous system? And why couldn't the brain state of Norm's that is correlated with seeing something red be the brain state of Abnorm's that is correlated with seeing something green, etc.?

So there are good reasons to think that lifelong undetectable spectrum inversion is possible. And thus, if we are to choose between *modus ponens* and *modus tollens*, the latter has a good deal going for it. However, with this said, Harman's response is much weaker than it could have been. For, though he presents his reasons for rejecting the possibility of spectrum inversion as consequences of functionalism, they don't really depend upon functionalism at all.

Recall that Harman claims that the functionalist definition of mental state types will include the following:

(1) When something looks red (or some other color) to someone, if he has no reason to doubt that his experience is veridical then he comes to believe that the thing is red (or the other color).

and that functionalism also implies the following:

(2) If two people apply the same color terminology to the same objects and belong to the same linguistic community, then they mean the same things by their use of color terminology.

Since Norm and Abnorm belong to the same linguistic community and since both of them use *red* to refer to red things, (2) implies that each means that the tomato is red when he says *It's red*. But, provided that each expresses his belief about the tomato's color by uttering *It's red*, this in conjunction with (1) implies that each of their experiences of the tomato represents it as red. So, Harman concludes, if functionalism is true, then spectrum inversion is impossible. However, whether or not (1) turns out to be partly *definitive* of something's looking red, it does seem that (1) must be true. Suppose that Abnorm is looking at a ripe tomato and that he has no reason at all to suppose that his experience of the tomato is in any way misleading (for example, he doesn't believe that he is on LSD, or that the lighting is odd, or that he's dreaming). Then surely whatever color the tomato looks to him will be the color he comes to believe it is. Otherwise, how things seem to Abnorm would be inexplicably severed from how he believes them to be. So, contrary to Harman's presentation, the truth of (1) doesn't depend at all on functionalism. And likewise for (2): since by hypothesis they both speak English, one doesn't have to be a functionalist to believe that Norm and Abnorm both mean red by *red*. I am not sure that Harman is right to claim that this is just common sense, but one of the great advances of recent philosophy of mind is to bring out its plausibility.[3] The upshot is that Harman's argument that undetectable spectrum inversion is impossible doesn't really depend on any functionalist assumptions.

So it seems that Harman's response has more going for it than his presentation suggests. However, there are still problems for functionalism. For, as we saw above, it seems as if I can imagine what it would be like to wake up and find that my spectrum is inverted. And this seems to give me a way to imagine what it would be like for you if yours has always been inverted with respect to mine. When properly formulated, Harman's response gives us a reason to think that what I seem to be imagining is impossible, but it doesn't tell me what mistake I'm making when I think I can imagine behaviorally undetectable spectrum inversion. Even if the argument against spectrum inversion shows that I'm not imagining that red things look green to you and blue things look yellow to you, etc., still I do seem to be imagining *something*. So perhaps the lesson of Harman's response is not that spectrum inversion is impossible, but rather that one needs to be careful about how it is described.

In fact, in the argument that undetectable spectrum inversion *is* possible, I didn't say that I could imagine that red things *look green*, etc. Rather, I said that I could imagine that *what it's like* for me to see red things is *what it's like for you* to see green things, etc. So, rather than supposing that things that *look red* to Norm *look green* to Abnorm, etc., we should suppose that *what it's like for Norm to see red* is *what it's like for Abnorm to see green*, etc. Or alternatively we might describe the case by saying that *the way red things look to Norm* is *the way green things look to Abnorm*, etc. Either of these descriptions seems to get at what we wanted to describe in the original description of spectrum inversion, and both are immune to Harman's response. To see that they're immune, recall that the response depends on the fact that, if the tomato looks green to Abnorm (and he has no reason to doubt his perception), then he'll come to believe that the tomato is green. But, if spectrum inversion is described in terms of *what it's like*, rather than in terms of the colors things look to have, then instead of saying that the tomato looks green to Abnorm we will say that what it's like for Abnorm to see the tomato is what it's like for Norm to see green things. But this doesn't imply anything about Abnorm's beliefs about the tomato's color. Similarly, the claim that the tomato looks to Abnorm the way that green things look to Norm also seems to have no such implication. Hence, rather than showing that undetectable spectrum inversion is impossible, Harman's response merely shows that it isn't properly described in terms of the colors things look to have. Or, to put the point another way, what Harman's response shows is that *even if Abnorm's spectrum is inverted with respect to Norm's, things still look to be the same color to them*. Does this mean that we still have a good argument against functionalism?

The issues concerning functionalism and spectrum inversion seem to me to be far more murky than the participants in the debate take them to be and, hence, I think that it is far from clear what the answer to the above question is. Recall that the argument depends on the claim that the possibility of lifelong undetectable spectrum inversion implies that there can be mental differences without functional differences. But this claim is a bit puzzling. Why should the absence of *behavioral* differences between Norm and Abnorm imply that it is possible that there are no *functional* differences between them? After all, one reason that functionalism is supposed to be an improvement on behaviorism is that *there can be functional differences without there being behavioral differences* and, hence, unlike behaviorism, it allows that there can be mental differences without any corresponding behavioral differences. And why doesn't the alleged fact that Norm and Abnorm's visual experiences of ripe tomatoes have different primed-color properties imply that there is a functional difference between them? After all, since the primed-color properties account for differences in the way things seem, it would appear that they must have some kind of a causal impact on belief and, hence, that primed-color property differences must imply functional differences. So, as far as I can tell, the issues concerning functionalism are far more complex than they initially seem, and since they are not central to my concerns I will ignore them. However, once we separate off the concerns about functionalism, we do have the beginnings of an interesting argument against intentionalism and for the qualia freak's view.

3. Spectrum inversion sans functionalism

In the last section we saw that the proper conclusion to draw from Harman's response is that, even if Abnorm's spectrum is inverted with respect to Norm's, things will still look to be the same color to them. So, if Norm and Abnorm are looking at a ripe tomato, it looks red to both of them. Recall that the reasons for believing that the tomato must look the same color to them are as follows.

(i) If someone doesn't doubt that his visual experience is veridical, then when something looks red to him he'll come to believe that it is red.

(ii) If Norm and Abnorm apply color terminology in the same way and belong to the same linguistic community, then they mean the same thing by their use of color terminology. Hence, since they both express their belief about the color of the tomato by saying *It's red*, they both believe that it is red.

Now, it is important to note that (ii) reflects a more general truth. One of the truly great discoveries in philosophy of mind is that the content of someone's belief depends upon both his causal connections to things in the environment and the practices of his linguistic community. On a planet where there is no water, there are no beliefs about water even if there is some substance indistinguishable from water (Putnam 1975 and Burge 1982); in a community where *arthritis* has a different meaning, the belief someone expresses by saying *Arthritis is a painful disease* is different from the belief that members of our linguistic community express by it (Burge 1979a). And, if Norm and Abnorm have been reared in the same environment and linguistic community and agree in their application of color terms, then each expresses the same belief when he says *The tomato is red*. The content of someone's belief about the color of an object depends on the sort of things he has causal connections to and upon facts about his linguistic community; that is to say, *externalism* is true of beliefs about the colors of things. And the conclusion that the tomato looks the same way to both Norm and Abnorm amounts to the recognition that externalism is also true about the colors things look to have. For (i) says that beliefs about an object's color will generally reflect the color the thing looks to have, and this means that externalism about color-beliefs implies externalism about the colors things *look* to have.

But notice that the point in (i) is equally plausible when applied to visual experiences that represent something as being red; that is to say, it's equally plausible that, if someone doesn't doubt that his visual experience is veridical, then when his visual experience *represents something as being red* he will come to believe that the thing is red.[4] After all, how could Abnorm come to believe that the tomato is red if his visual experience represented it as green?

One might be tempted to answer this question by saying that Abnorm is deceived about what color his visual experience represents the tomato as having. Although his visual experience represents it as green, he *believes* that it represents it as red, and this is why he comes to believe that the tomato is red (see Tye 1991, 126). But notice that, if this answer is correct, what perceptual experiences actually represent is irrelevant to the beliefs that we form based upon them. It is Abnorm's *belief* about what his experience represents rather than what his experience actually represents that forms the basis for his belief about the tomato, and the same should be true for normal perceivers. Of course, normal perceivers aren't deceived about what their perceptual experiences represent and, hence, their beliefs will reflect what their experiences represent. But, still, it is their beliefs about what their experiences represent rather than what their experiences actually represent that determine what they come to believe about the objects of their perceptions.

But surely it is what our perceptions represent and not our beliefs about what they represent that is the basis for our judgments about the things we perceive. You don't consciously think about what properties your visual experience represents the tomato as having and then infer that it has these properties; rather, the tomato visually seems to be a certain way to you, *is visually represented as being* a certain way, and you immediately judge it to be that way. And there is no reason to maintain that your beliefs about the objects of your perceptions are *unconsciously* determined by your beliefs about what properties these perceptions represent their objects as having. Indeed, if it is your beliefs about perceptual representations rather than perceptual representations themselves that are relevant to what you come to believe, why shouldn't it be higher-order beliefs about what your beliefs represent that are actually relevant to what you believe? Perceptual belief-formation isn't a process of thinking about mental representations; it is a process of thinking about the world *by means of* mental representations. To claim that in the normal course of things it is the *representations themselves* that are the objects of thought is to return to the worst errors of sense-data theory.

So, if Abnorm comes to believe that the tomato is red, his visual experience must represent it as being red. Hence, experiential *representation* of a thing's color is linked to belief about its color in the same way that the color the thing *looks* to have is linked to belief about its color. And this means that externalism about color-beliefs implies externalism about experiential representation of color.

But recall that one reason for thinking that spectrum inversion is possible is that it seems that what it's like for a person to see a particular color is determined entirely by his physical constitution; if we found out that the activity in your brain that is correlated with your seeing something red (under normal circumstances) is the same as the activity in my brain that is correlated with my seeing something green (in normal circumstances), and likewise for our experiences of the other colors, we would have good reason to think that we are spectrally inverted with respect to each other. And this gives us an argument against intentionalism and for the qualia freak's position.

If the fact that a visual experience represents its object as being red is externally determined, but what it's like to see red is internally determined, then—contrary to the intentionalist's view—the former can't entirely explain the latter; and likewise for the other colors. Moreover, the qualia freak *does* seem to have a way of explaining the internally determined aspect of what it's like to see particular colors. Whenever your experience represents something as red, it does so in virtue of having the intrinsic property red'. Which primed-color property a particular visual experience has is determined internally, and it is the primed-color properties that are inverted in cases of spectrum inversion. Spectrum inversion can't be explained in terms of representational features of experience because it doesn't involve inversion of representational features of experience.

In short, *the argument from spectrum inversion ultimately involves a clash between internalist and externalist intuitions.* If Norm and Abnorm are in the same brain state, then it seems that there must be something about their perception of the tomato that seems the same to them; but, given that representation of color is externally determined, each of their visual experiences must represent the tomato as being red. Hence, the subjective difference between their visual experiences of the tomato must be explained by nonrepresentational features of their visual experiences.

4. The irrelevance of behavioral undetectability: Extending the argument

The fact that the argument from spectrum inversion ultimately involves a clash of internalist and externalist intuitions has important consequences. When the possibility of spectrum inversion is used as an argument against functionalism, it is important that the inversion be behaviorally undetectable. For, if there are behavioral differences between Norm and Abnorm that reveal their relative spectral inversion, then there clearly are functional differences between Norm and Abnorm. Some have responded to the argument against functionalism by pointing out that certain asymmetries between the colors make it doubtful that spectrum inversion could be undetectable (see Harrison 1967, and Hilbert and Kalderon 2000). For example, people tend to say that red things look warm, while blue things look cold; and the brightest shade of yellow is brighter than the brightest shade of blue. But, once the argument for the qualia freak's position is separated off from the argument against functionalism, it's clear that the issues concerning color asymmetries have no bearing on the former. Even if there would have to be some asymmetries in how Norm and Abnorm report on the tomato's color, this doesn't mean that their experiences represent the tomato as being different colors. This is obviously so since many of these asymmetries don't in fact obtain universally; for example, while many people do report that red looks warm, it's also true that many people don't report this. But the fact that you fall into one of these groups as opposed to the other is no reason to deny that your visual experiences of ripe tomatoes represent them as red. Indeed, rather than undermining the qualia freak's argument, the fact that many of these asymmetries in color perception aren't universal offers another argument for his position. The fact that you report that red looks warm while I don't is evidence that there is a subjective difference between our visual experiences of ripe tomatoes. But no one is inclined to think that it is evidence that our respective visual experiences of the tomato represent it as being different colors.

The fact that the argument for the qualia freak's view doesn't depend upon the possibility that spectrum inversion is undetectable is important. For, although undetectable spectrum inversion may be possible, cases of undetectable inverted shape, inverted size, or other properties plausibly represented in visual experience clearly aren't. If the way that square things look to you is the way that triangular things look to me, then there would certainly be differences in our behavior. Color is remarkable among the properties that visual experience seems to represent in that color properties are the only ones for which undetectable inversion is even remotely plausible. Hence, so long as one thinks that undetectability plays a role in the argument, one won't be inclined to think that there is likely to be any argument that there are primed-shape properties, primed-distance relations, etc. However, once we realize that undetectability plays no role in the argument, it is far less clear that there isn't an equally good argument for primed-shape properties, primed-distance relations, etc. After all, as in the case of color, it seems that there must be something about a person's experiential representation of shape, distance, etc. that depends entirely on the physical facts about the person, something about what it's like to see squares, triangles, distances, etc. that is internally determined. But *square*, *nearer than* etc. are public-language predicates that should have the same meaning in everyone's mouth, and we should expect that the content of beliefs that we express using this terminology is externally determined.[5] But, as in the case of color, this implies that perceptual representation of these properties is externally determined. Hence, there is an argument for the existence of primed-shape properties, primed-distance relations, etc.[6]

And, indeed, one should *expect* that the qualia freak's view does extend beyond the colors to other properties that are plausibly represented in perception. After all, the qualia freak's view is a descendant of seventeenth-century views of perception according to which perceptible properties are properties of ideas: seeing something as green involves having an idea that is itself green. And, of course, the seventeenth-century theory of ideas is not restricted to color properties: seeing some object in the external world as green and square is supposed to involve having an idea that is square as well as green. Contemporary qualia freaks generally have enough sense to eschew the more unsettling aspects of the seventeenth-century view. They realize that, whatever cognitive relation we bear to our perceptual ideas, it isn't a perceptual relation; we *see* tables and chairs, not ideas of tables and chairs. And most realize that if anything in the world is colored, it is material objects, not ideas of material objects. So, rather than saying that perceptual experiences have color properties, they generally say they have *primed*-color properties. There are, of course, good reasons for these emendations of the seventeenth-century view of perception since the unamended claims strain plausibility. However, it's not at all clear what reason there would be to amend the view so that it applies only to color.

Of course, in the seventeenth century a distinction was made between *primary* qualities and *secondary* qualities: between those properties of ideas that, according to Locke (1690/1975), resemble properties of objects in the world and those that don't. And shape properties were thought to be primary qualities while color properties were thought to be secondary properties. But the distinction as characterized in the seventeenth century, rather than suggesting that ideas have color properties but not shape properties, *requires* that ideas have the latter; after all, if the primary qualities of ideas are going to resemble qualities of objects in the world, then ideas have to have primary qualities. So nothing about the seventeenth-century division of qualities into the primary and secondary gives any reason to think that the qualia freak view would hold only for colors.[7]

Though the qualia freak's view is intended to avoid some of the more unfortunate consequences of the seventeenth-century theory of ideas, there doesn't seem to be any reason to suppose that it should differ from the latter in being restricted to the colors. But this has been obscured by the focus on undetectable spectrum inversion and the fact that there isn't any corresponding hypothetical case of undetectable shape, distance, etc. inversion. The focus on spectrum inversion has also had another unfortunate consequence. Spectrum inversion is, to put it mildly, a fanciful possibility. And, though much of contemporary analytic philosophy seems to take the positing of fanciful possibilities as a (and perhaps *the*) method of doing philosophy, it is still very difficult to take such cases, or any view that rests entirely on such cases, seriously. And it isn't just nonphilosophers who have difficulty taking unfettered imagination seriously as a method of doing philosophy; many working philosophers are inclined to think that no serious person could rest much on it. Moreover, those inside and outside philosophy who are skeptical about reliance on the absurd surely have a point. Even in the absence of any positive reasons to doubt the cogency of spectrum inversion, the apparent conceivability of far-out science fiction possibilities is a slim reed on which to rest an account of perception. Who in the end knows whether such strange possibilities really are conceivable? And, even if they are, who knows if this means they are possible? However, some of the absurd counterfactual cases that occur in philosophy are merely ways to make a plausible point vivid. For example, the twin-earth cases are a way of bringing out how difficult it is to conceive of someone having a thought about something without having some causal contact with it and the difficulties with the (at first blush plausible) idea that what one thinks about depends solely on what one is like internally. Similarly, once we separate off the concerns about functionalism, spectrum inversion is just a way to bring out conflicting internalist and externalist intuitions about perception.

5. Qualia and Fregean senses

As I mentioned at the beginning of this chapter, there is an unnoticed similarity between the qualia freak's view and the view that beliefs are individuated by senses. Given that representation of colors, shapes, etc. is plausibly externally determined and given that there is something else about perception of these properties that is internally determined, the qualia freak argues that the internally determined aspects of experience just are certain of their intrinsic properties or, as these intrinsic properties are called, their *qualia*. Moreover, qualia provide a means for distinguishing experiences that have the same externally determined representational features— that represent the same color, shape, etc.—but that differ in their internally determined features—that seem different to their respective subjects; for example,

Norm's and Abnorm's visual experiences of the tomato might both represent it as red even though Norm's experience does so in virtue of being red' while Abnorm's does so in virtue of being green'. Similarly, according to *Fregean* theories of belief content, two thoughts might represent the same individual but nonetheless be distinct in virtue of containing different modes of presentation of that individual. These modes of presentation that figure into beliefs are called *senses*, and qualia are modes of presentation that figure into perception rather than belief. However, despite the fact that senses and qualia are intended to play the same role, there is an important dissimilarity in exactly how each is supposed to play it; but, once this dissimilarity is brought out, it becomes less clear that qualia can in fact play it.

To bring out this dissimilarity we need to make explicit the picture of mental phenomena on which the debates between qualia freaks and intentionalists, on the one hand, and Fregeans and non-Fregeans, on the other, rely. I list both parties in both debates because the picture is common to all; at issue is how it is to be filled out. According to this picture, at least *three* kinds of things are involved in any instance of mental representation. Take as an example my belief that Hesperus is a planet. The first thing involved is me, the subject of the belief. Besides the subject, there is a second kind of thing involved: namely, the thought that Hesperus is a planet. And the thought is the thing that determines the *representational content* of the belief. When I believe that Hesperus is a planet, a subject—me—bears a relation to a thought with a certain representational content—the content that Hesperus is a planet. However, there is also a third element to the picture of mental phenomena: some state or event that occurs, in some sense, *in* me and is related to the thought in something like the way a sentence is related to the thought it expresses. To believe something *just is* to be in some belief state that bears the appropriate relation to the relevant thought. The so-called *mind-body problem* as it applies to beliefs is the problem of what the nature of these belief states is: are they physical states of my brain, or are they nonphysical states of my soul? The materialist gives the first answer while the dualist gives the second.

This picture is also supposed to apply to perception. When I perceive an apple as red, there are again three things involved: the subject (namely, me), the representational content[8] (namely, that the apple is red), and some state or event occurring in my body or soul. And, again, the relation between the perceptual state and its representational content is supposed to be something like the relation between a sentence and its content. So, in the case of both belief and perception, the picture has three components: a subject, a belief or perceptual state, and a representational content. And, though both qualia and senses are supposed to individuate mental phenomena that represent the same things, they occupy different places in the picture. To see this, let's first consider how senses are supposed to individuate thoughts.

The belief that Hesperus is a planet and the belief that Phosphorus is a planet appear to be different beliefs; after all, it seems perfectly possible for someone to believe the one and not believe the other. But Hesperus is Phosphorus, and each belief attributes the property of being a planet to the object that it represents, so the thoughts are not individuated by what they represent. Hence, it is argued, the thoughts must represent their respective objects differently; that is to say, each contains a different mode of presentation of the same object. Just what exactly these modes of presentation are supposed to be will be discussed in Chapter 2. But, whatever modes of presentation turn out to be, they are features of the thoughts, *not* of the belief states.

When I believe that Hesperus is a planet and you believe that Hesperus is a planet, we appear to believe the same thing. So, since our thoughts are identical, the mode of presentation that figures into your thought that Hesperus is a planet and mine are the same thing. And, of course, there is nothing special here about the mode of presentation associated with the name *Hesperus*; anytime you and I believe the same thing, the same modes of presentations will figure into our thoughts. Frege ([1918] 1977) puts this point by saying that thoughts and their constituent senses are neither material objects nor token mental episodes in the lives of subjects; that is to say, they are not mental states. Rather, they are abstract inhabitants of what he calls *the third realm*. Two thoughts that contain distinct senses are supposed to also have distinct representational content; and this is so even if their respective senses pick out the same object. Now, though qualia are like Fregean senses in that they are intended to individuate mental phenomena that represent the same things, qualia don't play this role by being constituents of the representational content of perception; rather, qualia individuate experiences by being properties of those very experiences. What distinguishes Norm's visual experience of the tomato from Abnorm's is the character of the experiences themselves: Norm's is red¹ while Abnorm's is green¹. Qualia, unlike senses, are not supposed to be features of the representational content of perception; rather, they are supposed to be features of perceptual states.

According to the qualia freak, the red¹ quale that your experience has when you are seeing a ripe tomato is a property of a particular token mental event, namely, your visual experience of the tomato. Qualia, to use Frege's terminology, are properties of things in the *second realm*, the realm of token mental events. So, though qualia and senses are supposed to serve the same general function, they do so in entirely different ways. While philosophers do hold that there are belief states that occur in the subject, senses are neither parts nor properties of such states; they are constituents of thoughts and they determine representational content. So two thoughts that differ in sense are thereby supposed to differ in content, whereas two perceptions that differ in their qualia are not thereby supposed to differ in content. And, importantly, this difference between senses and qualia helps to clarify some puzzling ways in which the qualia freak's view tends to be characterized.

Recall that *my* initial characterization of the qualia freak's view in Section 1 was that, in contrast with the intentionalist, the qualia freak holds that, at least sometimes, when things perceptually seem different to two subjects, this will have to be explained by appealing to the intrinsic qualities of their experiences. And, though any qualia freak would certainly accept this characterization of the view, it is not generally the way the view is characterized. Usually, the view is presented as the view that there is more to a perceptual experience than its representational (or *intentional*) properties. Now, on the face of it, this characterization is a bit odd. After all, anyone who accepts the picture of experience according to which perceptual states are what relate subjects to the representational content of perception (and this seems to be pretty much everyone) agrees that there is more to a perception than its representational content. For the perceptual state that carries the content will have to have nonrepresentational features that distinguish it from other perceptual states. However, the distinction between qualia and senses helps to explain what the standard characterization is attempting to get at.

On the picture of mental phenomena under discussion, two belief-state tokens are of the same belief-state type if they relate their subjects to the same thought; your belief that 7 is a prime number and my belief that 7 is a prime number count as the *same* belief because both relate us to the same thought, namely, the thought that 7 is a prime number. Now, our belief state tokens may differ in their intrinsic properties; for example, if materialism is true, yours may be a token of one kind of brain state while mine is a token of another. But such differences do not make them tokens of different belief-state types. It is the thought a belief state relates its subject to and not the intrinsic features of the state itself that determines what kind of *belief* state it is. But, if different thoughts always have different representational content, then belief states are individuated by their representational properties; two token belief states are of the same belief-state type when and only when they relate their subjects to thoughts with the same representational content. The fact that two belief-state tokens have different intrinsic properties doesn't make them different kinds of beliefs. But the fact that two distinct perceptual-state tokens have different qualia *is* supposed to make them different kinds of perceptions; for differences in qualia are supposed to account for differences in how things seem, and differences in how things seem are clearly perceptual differences. And, since a difference in qualia does not by itself imply a difference in representational content, on the qualia freak's view representational features do *not* exhaust the *perceptual* features of perceptual experience.

So the distinction between the different ways in which qualia and senses are supposed to fulfill their roles as individuators of mental states—senses, unlike qualia, do so by changing representational content—helps to explain the standard characterization of the qualia freak's view. Unlike senses, qualia are supposed to account for perceptual differences without thereby implying differences in representational content. But recall that the reason that qualia are supposed to account for mental differences is that they are supposed to account for the way things seem to subjects. If, for vividness, we focus on spectrum inversion, the claim that Norm's and Abnorm's respective visual experiences of the tomato have different qualia is supposed to account for the subjective difference between their visual experiences, the difference in how things seem to Norm and Abnorm. So differences in the qualia two experiences have are supposed to account for subjective differences between them without thereby implying that there are any differences in representational content between them. But, once these features of the qualia freak's view are clearly brought out, an incoherence in the qualia freak's view also emerges. For, as we'll see in the next section, it simply isn't possible to account for subjective differences between perceptual experiences without positing representational differences between them.

6. Phenomenology and representational content

Let's assume that perceptual representation of properties expressible via public-language shape predicates, color predicates, distance predicates, etc., is externally determined. Let's also assume that the way things perceptually seem to us is internally determined. As we've seen, the qualia freak can use these assumptions in his argument for the existence of the primed properties of experience. These primed properties are supposed to account for the internally determined aspect of how things perceptually seem; however, as we saw in the previous section, since they are properties of perceptual states, they do not affect the representational content of perception.

Focus again on spectrum inversion. The qualia freak accounts for the subjective difference between Norm's and Abnorm's respective visual experiences of ripe tomatoes by claiming that there is no difference in representational content between their visual experiences; rather, their experiences have different intrinsic properties: Norm's is red' while Abnorm's is green'. The first point that needs to be made is that merely adverting to differences in their visual experiences clearly won't be enough to account for the subjective difference between them. The subjective difference between Norm's and Abnorm's visual experiences is a difference in the way things *seem* to them; hence, besides the fact that their visual experiences have different properties, the qualia freak will also have to maintain that Norm and Abnorm are in some sense *aware* of their respective visual experiences. After all, how could the fact that Norm's and Abnorm's respective visual experiences of the tomato have different properties account for a difference in how things seem to them if each is not at all aware of his experience? Now, many qualia freaks will accept this point and, by itself, it doesn't threaten the qualia freak's view. After all, the mere fact that you are aware of an object of a certain type doesn't imply anything about the representational content of your experience of it. The fact that Janet is aware of an object that happens to be a red convertible says nothing about the way her awareness presents the object to her; the object may seem to her to be an orange convertible, or a green sedan, or a giant box, or what have you, but she is still aware of a red convertible. Being aware of something that is an F does not at all imply that you are aware of it *as* being an F. So the fact that using qualia to account for subjective differences requires that we be aware of our experiences does not threaten the idea that differences in qualia do not amount to differences in representational content. However, the discussion of why this is so brings out that it isn't sufficient for the qualia freak to claim that we are aware of our experiences if qualia are to account for the way things seem to perceivers.

Suppose that you and I are both seeing a square object, but (for whatever reason) the object looks circular to me. Notice that both of us are aware of a square object because we are each seeing an object that is square. Hence, the different ways the object appears to us can't be explained by the features that the object we are aware of actually has. The qualities that the object actually has are entirely irrelevant to the explanation of the subjective difference between our experiences. In order to explain the difference in how the object appears to us, one must advert to a difference in the way the object seems. More generally, to say that you are aware of something that is x has no implications concerning the way the object seems to you. But a similar point holds for the alleged primed properties of visual experience. The fact that Norm is aware of a red' experience while Abnorm is aware of a green' experience implies nothing about the way their experiences of the tomato seem to them. If the qualia freak is to account for the subjective difference between their experiences of the tomato, it is insufficient to note that the experiences have different qualities and that each is aware of his experience; each of them will also have to be aware of his experiences *as having* the relevant quality. Abnorm's experience of the tomato must seem green' to him, and Norm's must seem red' to him.

Now, it is unlikely that a qualia freak would have qualms about this conclusion; since the primed-color properties are often alleged to be introspectively accessible, he should hold that Norm's experience of the tomato will seem to be green' to him. But what has gone unnoticed is that this requires that his experience be *represented* as being green' to him. For suppose he has an experience that seems green' to him. We can ask whether the experience *really is* green'. If it is, his experience is represented to him accurately; if it is not, it is represented to him inaccurately. Many proponents of sense-data theory made the mistake of thinking that experiences of sense-data could not be subject to truth or falsity and yet still be an inferential ground for propositional knowledge.[9] Though the contemporary qualia freaks tend to eschew many of the implausible features of sense-data theory, they make a similar mistake. For they assume that one can account for the way things seem to someone without any appeal to the way things are represented as being.

My point so far is that you can't account for the way things seem to a subject without adverting to how things are represented to him. So the fact that Abnorm's experience is green' while Norm's is red' can account for the subjective difference between their experiences only if Abnorm's experience is represented to him as being green' and Norm's is represented to him as being red'. Both sides of the chasm have missed this point, but once it is acknowledged a stronger point emerges. *All that's required to account for the subjective difference between our experiences is that they be represented differently to us.* So long as Abnorm's experience seems green' to him and Norm's seems red' to him, there will be a subjective difference.

It is entirely irrelevant whether their respective experiences actually have these properties.

There is an essential weakness in the argument from spectrum inversion. As we have seen, at the heart of the argument is the idea that, since the representation of properties expressible via public-language color, shape, distance, etc. predicates is externally determined, the intentionalist cannot account for the internally determined aspects of the way things seem and, hence, there must be some nonrepresentational aspect of perceptual experience. But the way things seem to a perceiver cannot be explained by nonrepresentational features of his experience. Hence, the qualia freak has no argument that there is some nonrepresentational difference. The most he can claim to have established is that differences in *how the external world is represented* can't account for the internally determined features of perceptual experience and, hence, that these features of perceptual experience must be explained in terms of the way that perceptual experiences *themselves* are represented to subjects. When Norm sees the tomato, his visual experience is represented to him as being red', but when Abnorm sees it, his visual experience is represented to him as being green'.

My claim is that it is incoherent to attempt to account for the way things seem to a subject without bringing in representational content; whenever there is seeming, there is the question of whether the seeming reflects the way things really are, of whether it represents them accurately. Hence, the qualia freak's view will have to be revised so that experiences are represented to subjects as having certain qualities. There are, however, a few points that it is crucial to be clear on.

First, I am not claiming that if something seems a certain way to someone there is always the question of whether it in fact does *seem* that way. If someone kicks a ball, then they have in fact kicked a ball; if something falls off the shelf, then something has in fact fallen off the shelf; and if something seems some way to someone then, of course, it does seem that way to him. In general, I think that it is safe to assume that sentences of the form *if P then P* express truths. My claim is that if something seems some way to someone, then there is the question of whether it *is* that way, not whether it *seems* that way.

Second, it is bound to be objected that I am ignoring a crucial aspect of the qualia freak's view. For, if one holds that qualia account for the way things perceptually seem to us, it is quite natural to hold that the way in which an experience seems to its subject is in fact always the way that it really is, that you can't be in error about the qualia your experience seems to have. And, if this is right, doesn't this suggest that there simply is no distinction between seeming and being in the case of qualia and, hence, that the qualia freak needn't maintain that an experience is *represented* to its subject *as* having some quale?

Well, no, it doesn't. And indeed the tendency to think that we have some kind of privileged access to properties of our experiences that are alleged to account for perceptual seeming, rather than undermining my point, actually strengthens it. If it is true that one can't be mistaken about the qualia that one's experience has, this is not to say that there is no question of whether they seem to be the way they are; rather, it is to say that the answer to the question is always yes. The alleged fact that experiences always have the qualia they are represented as having amounts to the fact that they are always represented accurately, not to the fact that they aren't represented at all. The point here is quite important. If one is a qualia freak, there is a strong inclination to think that our experiences are always represented to us the way they actually are; *but this is just to say that they are always represented the way they are.* The common claim that a subject can't be wrong about the qualia his experience has *requires* that his experience be represented to him. For, if it is not represented to him, what possible sense can be made of the idea that the way it seems is the way it is? The privileged access claim is not the denial that there is a seems/is distinction in the case of qualia; rather, it's the claim that the two sides of the distinction always go together, that the way an experience seems with respect to its qualia is always the way it is. Hence, the privileged-access claim, rather than obviating the need for representation of qualia, implies it.

7. An alternative view of perception

We have seen that, since subjective differences can't be explained in terms of nonrepresentational differences, the qualia freak's view must be revised. Since he must admit that the intentionalist is correct in thinking that all subjective differences are explained in terms of representational differences, his only disagreement with the intentionalist can be over exactly what sort of representational differences explain subjective differences. The intentionalist claims that the only difference that there could be between Norm's and Abnorm's visual experiences of the tomato is a difference in what color it is represented as being. Hence—given that perceptual representation of color is externally determined—he is forced to deny that spectrum inversion is possible. But the revised qualia freak view claims that, while Norm's and Abnorm's experiences of the tomato represent it as the same color, there is another representational difference between them. Norm's experience is represented to him as being red', while Abnorm's is represented to him as being green'. In general, the revised qualia freak position will maintain that the primed properties an experience is represented as having is internally determined and that the internally determined features of perceptual experience just are representations of the experiences themselves as having primed properties.

But now that we see how the qualia freak's position needs to be revised another view emerges. Since representation of color, shape, distance, etc. can't account for the internally determined aspect of visual experience, the revised qualia freak position claims that visual experience must also represent other properties. But the revised qualia freak position goes farther and claims that these other properties aren't represented as properties of objects in the external world; rather, they are represented as properties of visual experience itself. However, the fact that representation of color, shape, distance, etc. properties can't account for the internally determined aspects of experience implies only that some other properties must be represented in visual experience; *it does not imply that these properties aren't represented as properties of objects in the external world.*

One objection to an ancestor of the qualia freak's view was first given by G. E. Moore (1922, 22) when he pointed out, against sense-data theory, that perception is *diaphanous*. Though Moore was a proponent of sense-data theory, he recognized that the theory is not true to the phenomenology of perception. When looking at, say, a ripe tomato, if you try to focus on the sense-datum that the theory alleges is the immediate object of your visual experience, the only thing there for you to focus on seems to be the tomato. In the context of spectrum inversion, Moore's objection can be put as follows: the subjective difference between Norm's and Abnorm's visual experiences is a difference in the way objects in the world seem to them, not a difference in the way their respective experiences seem. When both Norm and Abnorm look at the tomato, it is the *tomato itself* that seems different to them. And their respective experiences seem different to them only insofar as the tomato is presented differently by those experiences. The intentionalist claims that experience merely represents objects as being colored, shaped, etc., and given externalism about representation of color it seems that he can't account for the subjective difference between experiences that represent objects as having the same properties of that sort. So the qualia freak posits awareness of intrinsic mental properties to account for the difference. But, given that this requires that these mental properties be represented to us by experience, and given Moore's point, another view suggests itself. The revised qualia freak view is right that representation of properties distinct from the colors is required to account for the possibility of spectrum inversion; and, more generally, it is right that representation of properties distinct from shape, distance, etc. properties is required in order to account for the internally determined features of experience. But the view is wrong in supposing that our perceptual experiences themselves are represented as having these properties; rather, perceptual experiences represent objects in the world as having them. Though the properties represented must be distinct from the color, shape, distance, etc. properties, they are properties that objects in the world are represented as having.

The qualia freak claims that the internally determined aspects of perceptual experience are intrinsic qualities of perceptual experience itself and uses primed-color, primed-shape, etc. terms to pick out these qualities. However, according to the view I am suggesting, there are no such properties. Hence, strictly speaking *red'*, *square'*, etc. don't pick out anything. I have argued that the internally determined aspects of experience must be explained in terms of properties that experience represents objects in the world as having. But which properties are these? Well, they will be the properties whose representation is inverted by Abnorm's experience.

Focus on some red thing: you see that there is a way that it looks, an intrinsic surface property it appears to have in virtue of which it also appears to be more similar to orange things than it is to blue things. And similarly there is a way that green things look, a way that blue things look, etc. Now, the phrase *the way red things look* (in this context) picks out an intrinsic property that red things appear to have; and, if a particular object appears to have this property to you, then your visual experience represents the object truly if it really does have that property.[10] But recall that one way to describe spectrum inversion is to say that the way red things look to Norm is the way green things look to Abnorm, and so on. So it is representation of these properties that is inverted in cases of spectrum inversion and that is internally determined. We ordinarily think that these properties *just are* the color properties, that this way that red things look *just is* red, etc. But if spectrum inversion is possible, then these properties cannot be the color properties; rather, they are properties that are distinct from the colors and that visual experience represents objects as having.[11] Likewise, if you focus on some square thing you will see that there is a way that it looks, a property it appears to have in virtue of which it is more similar to a (nonsquare but otherwise) rectangular thing than it is to a circular thing, and likewise for other shapes. Again, it is representation of these properties rather than representation of shape properties that is internally determined. And likewise for all properties and relations that are expressed via public-language predicates and that we take to be represented in visual experience.

The qualia freak is right that there is a property distinct from redness represented in visual experiences of red objects. But it isn't a property of an experience; rather, it's a property that your visual experience represents the tomato as having. According to this view of perception, there is something right about both the intentionalist's and the qualia freak's views. The intentionalist is right that visual experience only represents objects in the external world as having certain properties. But the qualia freak is right that visual experience represents properties distinct from but corresponding to the colors. However, these properties are not properties of experience; rather, visual experience represents objects in the material world as having these properties.

8. Generalized use-mention confusion

The qualia freak mistakenly assumes that merely positing that Norm's and Abnorm's experiences have different intrinsic qualities will account for the subjective difference between their experiences. And it is very plausible that—as Gilbert Harman (1990) and Michael Tye (1994) have claimed—the qualia freak errs in confusing properties that are represented with properties of the representation, that he is engaging in a kind of *generalized use-mention confusion*. When the charge is put this way, however, it seems as if the qualia freak is being accused of making some kind of elementary mistake that only beginning philosophy students make. But here it is important to take note of a point made by (ironically enough) Ned Block (1983,

516–17): namely, that in much of our ordinary talk we simply don't distinguish between what is represented and what represents; for example, Block points out that "[p]eople who work routinely with graphical representations of sounds (e.g., oscilloscope readings) often speak of them as if they had the properties of the sounds they represent—for example, being loud or high pitched."[12]

We aren't very good at distinguishing representations from what they represent, and the distinction between them, in some sense, constitutes a complex and important philosophical discovery. It is now almost universally granted that even if we are aware of intrinsic properties of our experiences these properties are not color or shape properties. It is little emphasized that despite their philosophical genius none of the great early modern philosophers seems to pay much explicit respect to this distinction. Descartes, Locke, Berkeley, and Hume seem to take it for granted that ideas are the bearers of the color and shape properties, never once explicitly recognizing that this might involve generalized use-mention confusion. And, as Frege ([1894] 1952) pointed out, one crucial error that the psychologists about logic were making was uncritically assuming that the logical relations held between mental entities like judgements. Frege points out what the psychologists missed: that there is a distinction between the *acts* of thinking and the *objects* of thinking and that the logical relations clearly hold between the latter. The distinction between a representation and what is represented is not some obvious distinction that only the philosophically untutored can miss. Rather, the distinction is an important theoretical discovery, and if it is not carefully kept in mind, even the best of us will confuse the two. Indeed, our tendency to confuse representations with what they represent has the status of Old Testament sin. We are enjoined not to make images of God; for, if we do, despite the fact that there can be no greater distinction than that between the creator of the universe and a piece of stone that represents the creator, we are still bound to mistakenly worship the stone.

The qualia freak makes just this kind of error. For, while he recognizes that there must be qualities distinct from the colors, shapes, etc. to account for the internally determined aspect of perceptual experience, he mistakenly takes these qualities to be qualities of perceptual experience rather than qualities that perceptual experience represents things in the external world as having. Indeed, given certain features of the qualia freak's view, it is apparent that it rests upon just such a confusion.

According to the view, in the ordinary course of perception we are aware of properties of our experiences. So, when I see a black piano, under normal circumstances, I am aware of my perceptual experience of the black piano, where the perceptual experience of the black piano is some event or state that carries the representational content of my perception. But my awareness of this state or event is clearly some kind of an experience of that state or event and, hence, there is something more than a bit puzzling about the view. If being aware of a black piano requires having a second awareness of one's awareness of the black piano, shouldn't being aware of one's awareness require a third awareness that is the awareness of the awareness of the initial awareness? If being aware of an object requires being aware of your experience of the object, then being aware of the experience should require being aware of your experience of the experience. The qualia freak's view appears to require that every experience of an ordinary material object requires an infinite number of experiences of experiences. Now, obviously, no one would accept this view, but how is the qualia freak to avoid it?

The answer seems to be something that is implicit in the qualia freak's view: namely, that my experience of the piano is not distinct from my experience of my experience of it. I clearly do not undergo an infinite number of visual experiences when I see a piano, and I do not even undergo two. Rather, the visual experience of the piano and the experience of that experience will have to be one and the same event. But, once this feature of the qualia freak's view is made explicit, it is hard to see how to make any sense of it. How could one and the same thing constitute my awareness of the piano as well as my awareness of that awareness? No doubt some will be inclined to think this is what one should expect since perception is pretty mysterious. But there is a difference between a mystery and a confusion, and the claim that an awareness of an object can also be an awareness of itself seems a lot more like the latter. For my experience of the piano is supposed to be something that represents the piano to me, so to think that it also represents itself to me appears to be, as Harman and Tye have claimed, to confuse it with the piano.

9. Pain and other sensations

Consciousness is the what-it's-like aspect of our mental lives. Part of what constitutes a subject's consciousness is his perceptions: what it's like to see, hear, taste, smell, and touch his environment. But another important aspect of consciousness is bodily sensation: pains, tickles, tinglings, etc. As we have seen, qualia are meant to account for subjective differences in perception, for the difference in what it's like to have different kinds of perceptual experiences. According to the qualia freak the reason, for example, that the experience of a red thing seems different than the experience of a blue thing is that one is aware of the different qualia that the experiences have. However, qualia are not merely supposed to account for the perceptual aspect of our conscious experience; they are also supposed to account for that aspect of our conscious experience that includes bodily sensation. And, indeed, it is useful to think of the qualia freak's view as coming in two stages: first, there is a somewhat natural view of bodily sensation; and, second, there is an assimilation of perception to bodily sensation.

The somewhat natural view of bodily sensation is what Sydney Shoemaker (1994a) has called *the inner sense model*. Take pain as an example; on the inner sense model, a pain is a mental object or event that occurs in its subject, and to experience pain is to be aware of the intrinsic properties—that is to say, the *qualia*—of the mental object or event. So, when you cut yourself while slicing bread, the knife slashing against your skin causes a mental event or object—your pain—and what it's like for you to feel the pain is due to your awareness of its intrinsic qualities. As I say, this is a somewhat natural view of pain and other bodily sensations, and the qualia freak assimilates perception to sensation, as viewed in this way. When you *see* the bread knife, the light reflecting off the knife and into your eyes causes a mental object or event: your experience or *visual* sensation of the bread knife. And what it's like for you to see the knife is due to your awareness of the visual sensation's intrinsic properties.

As in the case of perception, the qualia freak will maintain that your awareness of the qualia of sensation is nonrepresentational. But, as in the case of perception, this is one way in which the view goes wrong. If you are aware of your pain as having certain qualities then your pain is as it seems if it does have these qualities and isn't as it seems if it doesn't; that is to say, your pain is represented to you as having these qualities. And, once again, the tendency to claim that you can't be mistaken about the qualities of your bodily sensations entails, rather than falsifies, this point. If there were no representation, no notion of accuracy would even be applicable. To say that you can't be mistaken about the qualities of your pain is to say that they are always represented as they are.

Moreover, as in the case of perception, there is an incoherence in the qualia freak's view of sensation that shows that the view results from generalized use-mention confusion. The qualia freak's account of perception requires that in order to have a perceptual experience of something you must be aware of your experience and, as we saw in Section 8, this means that the account requires that your awareness of your experience of, say, the tomato is not distinct from your experience of the tomato. For, if they are distinct, then it seems that you will have to have a third experience—namely, the awareness of your awareness of your experience of the tomato—distinct from the other two. And your awareness of the third experience will require a fourth, which will require a fifth and a sixth, etc. The only way to avoid this absurdity is to hold that your awareness of your experience of the tomato just is your experience of the tomato. Now, the same will hold on the qualia freak's conception of sensation; your awareness of your experience of pain cannot be distinct from your experience of pain.

Now, in some ways, this doesn't seem quite as bad as the analogous claim that the qualia freak has to make in the case of perception: namely, that your awareness of your perceptual experience isn't distinct from that experience. For, in the case of pain, it's somewhat natural to think that your experience of the pain and the pain itself are one and the same thing (see, for example, Tye 1995, 112) and, if this is so, why shouldn't the experience of the pain be identical to the experience of the experience? In the case of perception, however, it is ludicrous to think that your experience of the tomato is identical to the tomato; that is, after all, more or less the much-derided view of Berkeley ([1710] 1957).

However, there are ways in which Berkeley's view doesn't deserve the derision it gets. Certainly, Berkeley's view that material objects like tomatoes are just ideas (or congeries of ideas) is too ridiculous to be believed. However, Berkeley starts with Locke's assumption that the immediate objects of perception are ideas: that, for example, in the case of seeing the tomato, the thing that you are immediately aware of is a red and spherical idea of the tomato. Now, it is, I think, undeniable that, if Locke's claim is meant to be taken literally, it results from generalized use-mention confusion; the only way to think that, when looking at the tomato, the thing you directly see is your idea of the tomato and that idea is the thing that is red and spherical is to confuse the tomato with the idea. As emphasized above, in whatever way an idea of the tomato is implicated in your seeing the tomato, and whatever it is that an idea of the tomato turns out to be exactly, you see objects in the material world, not ideas of those objects; and it is objects in the material world, not ideas of those objects, that have color and shape. However, if you are going to begin by confusing the idea of the tomato with the tomato, Berkeley's conclusions seem to be the right ones to draw. The round and red thing you see is the tomato and it's the only relevant thing that you see; so, if the thing you see turns out to be an idea, the tomato had better turn out to be an idea. Berkeley's view is ridiculous, but it results from taking the presuppositions that most of his contemporaries shared seriously. Samuel Johnson's much-quoted remark while kicking a stone: "Thus I refute you Berkeley" could have just as rightly been "Thus I refute you Locke." For the thing he sees his foot strike isn't an idea; it's a material object.

My point here is not to defend Berkeley against Locke; rather, it is that it isn't so unnatural to think that the idea of the tomato just is the tomato. To the extent that it is natural to think that the thing you are seeing is a red and round idea of a tomato, it will be natural to think that the tomato just is the idea. Now the suggestion that the pain and the experience of pain are one and the same thing, like the suggestion that the idea of the tomato and the tomato are one and the same thing, is difficult to make sense of. How could an object or event be identical to an experience of that object or event? But, though it's harder to see that the pain and the experience of the pain might be distinct, the idea that they aren't distinct is very hard to make sense of. How could your awareness of some event or object, which is at least in part a relation between you and the object, be identical to the object? Of course, this view of pain goes hand in hand with the idea that pains cannot exist unless they are the objects of some subject's awareness. However, even if this were right, it doesn't really help to make sense of the awareness and the pain being one and the same thing. A valley cannot exist without bearing a certain relationship to a mountain, but this doesn't mean that the valley is identical to the mountain, much less to the relation it bears to the mountain; the relation between a mountain and a valley, on the one hand, and the valley itself, on the other, are of completely different ontological categories. And perhaps Kripke ([1972] 1980, 110–15) is right that I couldn't have existed without having been conceived by my parents; but this doesn't mean that I'm identical to my parents, much less that I'm identical to the relation of *being conceived by*. Again, I am of a completely different ontological category than the relation. However, though it's hard to make sense of how the awareness of an event or object could be identical to the object, it isn't at all hard to make sense of how someone could think they are. As emphasized above, the distinction between a representation and what it represents is not a natural distinction to make and, even once one is aware of the distinction, it's extremely difficult to keep the two things separate. And there are obvious reasons that it would be easier to see the distinction in the case of visual perception (where the history of philosophy itself shows how difficult it is to see it) than it would be in the case of sensations like pain.

Suppose it looks to you as if there is a tiger about to attack. You have ways of checking whether there really is a tiger. You can ask others if they see a tiger, you can wave your hands around and see if it feels like there's a tiger out there, you can check to see if you're hearing the sounds of a tiger. Because objects in the material world can be detected by many individuals and many perceptual senses, it isn't so hard to think of cases where you'll have a visual perception qualitatively identical to one that you would have if you were actually seeing a material object, but where there is no object present. The distinction between undergoing a perceptual representation according to which there is some object in your environment, on the one hand, and some actual object in your environment, on the other, is thus easy to see. But, in the case of pain, these ways of checking aren't nearly as relevant. Since other people don't experience your pain, their testimony can't be much help in telling whether or not the experience is veridical. And, since you can't detect pain by any of your other senses, they also can't be that much help.

As stated above, the qualia freak's view of perception can be seen as the adoption of a quite natural view of sensation and an assimilation of perception to sensation. But, despite its naturalness, the view of sensation is incoherent in the same way that assimilating perception to it is. Moreover, there is an explanation of why an incoherent view should be natural: namely, the naturalness—and, indeed, almost un-avoidability—of generalized use-mention confusion. And there is also a reason this confusion should be harder to detect than in the case of perception: after all, none of your perceptual senses represent pain to you, and other people cannot detect your pains. However, though the qualia freak's account of perception and sensation is wrong, his assimilation of the two phenomena isn't. The correct view of perception is that objects, and not our own perceptual experiences, are represented to us as having certain properties. And the correct account of sensation is similar, except that sensation represents parts of our bodies as having certain properties. What Shoemaker calls *the inner sense model*, according to which sensation involves a perception of some internal mental thing, is wrong. However, the term *inner sense* itself isn't such a bad description of sensation. Sensation does involve a kind of inner sense. But, when you have a pain, you are not sensing your own experience as being a certain way: to think that is to confuse the sensation with the experience of its object. Rather, you are sensing some part of your body as being a certain way.

To see that this is so, smash your hand with a hammer (or at least pretend that you have). Notice that it feels as if something is going on in your hand. If we take *pain* to refer to the kind of quality that seems to be instantiated in your hand, then one of your current experiences represents pain. It is obvious that pain is being represented, since your experience is veridical just in case what seems to be going on in your hand really is going on in your hand, and it is nonveridical just in case what seems to be going on in your hand isn't. And, though it isn't as easy to see how pain could be nonveridical as it is to see how perception could be, it isn't impossible either. For it could be the case that your experience is nonveridical: maybe you have no hand and are experiencing phantom limb pain. In this case you are hallucinating that there is pain in your hand.[13] Alternatively, pain is sometimes taken to be an experience that represents a certain quality as being instantiated in your hand. If we use *pain* in this way, then you are in pain whether or not you have a hand. Our use of the term *pain* is itself equivocal and this is a reflection of our tendency toward generalized use-mention confusion in this case. Moreover, that our use of the term is equivocal makes it even harder to see that the natural view of sensation is confused.

However, even pain is not entirely immune to evidence that there is a distinction between the experience and what the experience represents as going on in some part of your body. Phantom limb pain is one clear case where the sensation of pain is nonveridical. But, as Gilbert Harman (1990, 39–40) has pointed out, there are other cases that seem to count as evidence of nonveridical pain. Sciatica is a disease in which a ruptured disk presses against the sciatic nerve. Since the nerve runs from the lower back to the foot, sciatica causes a feeling of agonizing pain down the length of the leg even though there is nothing wrong with the leg. I was unfortunate enough to have suffered from sciatica, and the knowledge that there was nothing wrong with my leg seemed to be some evidence that the painful feelings that seemed to run up and down my leg were nonveridical.

10. Shoemaker's view

So far, I have suggested that an adequate account of perceptual representation should have two features. First, it should agree with the intentionalist that all subjective differences between perceptions are explainable in terms of representational differences. The intentionalist has to be right about this, since whenever something perceptually seems some way to someone, there is always a question of whether things really are that way, always a question of whether the perception represents its object truly or falsely. But, second, an adequate account of perceptual representation should agree with the qualia freak that there are properties distinct from but corresponding to colors, shapes, distances, etc. involved in visual representation. However, the qualia freak is wrong in thinking that these properties are properties of visual experience; rather, they are properties that visual experience represents material objects as having.

Sydney Shoemaker (1994a) offers a view of perception that meets both of the above desiderata. Shoemaker agrees that the subjective difference between Norm's and Abnorm's visual experiences of the tomato must be explained by the fact that their experiences represent the tomato as having different properties; and he also agrees that it is implausible that these turn out to be different *color* properties. Hence, he agrees that visual experience must represent objects as having properties distinct from but corresponding to the colors. However, there are two ways in which Shoemaker's account of perceptual representation fails. The less important of the two involves its scope; since Shoemaker is not explicitly motivated by a clash between internalist and externalist intuitions, he does not hold that there must also be properties represented in experience distinct from but corresponding to shape, distance, and other properties and relations expressible via public-language predicates. But the more important inadequacy arises from Shoemaker's account of what the properties distinct from but corresponding to the colors turn out to be.

According to Shoemaker, the property distinct from redness that Norm's visual experience represents the ripe tomato as having is roughly the property of *causing an R-experience*, where R is some property that is intrinsic to Norm's visual experience of the tomato; whereas the property distinct from redness that Abnorm's visual experience represents it as having is roughly the property of *causing a G-experience*, where G is a property that is intrinsic to Abnorm's experience of the tomato and that is distinct from R. So, while Shoemaker doesn't claim that we are *aware* of intrinsic properties of visual experience, the alleged fact that Norm's and Abnorm's respective visual experiences of the tomato have different intrinsic properties does play a role.

Now, one objection that Shoemaker considers is that the property of causing an R-experience in Norm is a relational property, yet Norm's experience won't seem to him to represent the tomato as having a relational property. Shoemaker responds to this objection by pointing out that the fact that Norm's visual experience fails to represent the property as relational does *not* imply that the experience represents the property as not being relational. Shoemaker is certainly right that the objection is confused. The sentence *It's raining* does not represent that it's windy; but it does not represent that it's *not* windy. However, there is a related worry that Shoemaker does not consider and that is not confused.

According to Shoemaker, the property distinct from redness that Norm's visual experience represents the tomato as having is the property of causing an R-experience in him. But it seems clear that Norm's visual experience of the tomato doesn't represent the tomato *as* causing an R-experience in him. After all, unless Norm has read Shoemaker's paper, he will have no idea that the tomato has this property. And R is just a place-holder for whatever property it is that normal perceivers' visual experiences of red objects are supposed to have. This means that, even if he has read Shoemaker's paper, Norm still won't know which relational property the tomato has. So, on Shoemaker's view, Norm's visual experience of the tomato represents that it has a some particular property, and that property *just is* the property of causing an R-experience in him, but his experience doesn't represent the tomato as having the property of causing an R-experience in him. How can this be?

In answering this question it is important to note that Shoemaker claims that the relevant property *is identical to* the property of causing R-experiences in Norm. According to Shoemaker, these apparently distinct properties are in fact *one and the same* property. Hence, Shoemaker needs to tell some story about how Norm's visual experience can represent that the tomato has the one property without representing that it has the other. Now the important point here is that this problem for Shoemaker's view is just an instance of Frege's puzzle.

To return to the example of the puzzle from the beginning of this chapter, Lex Luthor believes that Superman can fly but does not believe that Clark Kent can fly. But Superman is identical to Clark Kent, so how can this be? Given that Superman just is Clark Kent, how could someone believe that Superman has some characteristic without thereby believing that Clark Kent does? Recall that the common answer to this question is that believing that Superman can fly is not merely a matter of having a belief that represents a certain individual. For, if it did merely amount to this, the two beliefs would be the same. When you have a belief that represents an individual, besides the individual, there is a way that the individual is represented to you by your belief: there is a *mode of presentation* of the individual. And, though Lex's belief that Superman flies does represent Clark Kent to him (they are, after all, the same person), it does not represent him *as* Clark Kent. So, the story goes, the belief that Superman can fly and the belief that Clark Kent can fly, though they represent the same individual, contain distinct modes of presentation of that individual and, hence, are themselves distinct. And the problem just raised for Shoemaker's account of spectrum inversion is just another instance of Frege's puzzle, though it differs in two ways from the standard examples. First, rather than concerning belief, it concerns perceptual seemings: the worry is that the tomato *perceptually seems* to have a certain property to Norm, and according to Shoemaker this property just is the property of causing an R-experience, but the tomato doesn't seem to have the property of causing an R-experience to Norm (and similarly, *mutatis mutandis,* for Abnorm). Second, rather than concerning the *object* that the relevant mental phenomenon is about—namely, the tomato—it concerns a property the subject's perceptual state *ascribes* to that object.

Given that the problem raised for Shoemaker's account is just an instance of Frege's puzzle, the solution, if there is one, would seem to be that properties are not merely ascribed to objects by perception; rather, perception ascribes properties to objects via modes of presentation. Norm's visual experience of the tomato represents the property of causing R-experiences in him, but it does not represent it as the property of causing an R-experience; rather it represents it in some other way.

The fact that Shoemaker must ultimately advert to modes of presentation creates problems for his view. First, we are owed some account of what these modes of presentation are. But, more importantly, it turns out that Shoemaker will have to invoke differences in modes of presentation to explain the subjective difference between Norm's and Abnorm's visual experience.

Shoemaker's reason for claiming that Norm's visual experience of the tomato represents it as having a property distinct from but corresponding to redness is that he thinks that each of Norm's and Abnorm's visual experiences should represent the tomato's color veridically and, hence, that they should both represent it as red. So the subjective difference between them can't be explained by a difference in the color that they represent the tomato as being. Shoemaker concludes that the subjective difference must be explained in terms of representational differences with respect to some properties other than colors, properties of causing certain kinds of visual experience.[14]

But, as noted above, Norm's experience of the tomato won't represent it *as* causing an R-experience in him, and Abnorm's experience of the tomato won't represent it *as* causing a G-experience in him. It doesn't seem to Norm that the tomato has the property of causing an R-experience in him, and it doesn't seem to Abnorm that the tomato has the property of causing a G-experience in him. So these properties themselves are irrelevant to the explanation of the subjective difference between them. And, hence, it must be *how* these properties are represented rather than *what* properties are represented that explains the subjective difference between Norm's and Abnorm's visual experience. That is to say, it is the modes of presentation of the properties rather than the properties represented that explain the difference. In Section 6 of this chapter, we saw that merely positing that Norm's and Abnorm's respective visual experiences of the tomato have different properties can't account for the subjective difference between them. Shoemaker's view turns out to have a similar defect; for the representational differences that he claims obtain between Norm's and Abnorm's respective experiences *also* can't account for the subjective difference between them.

I have argued that Shoemaker winds up having to explain subjective differences in terms of nonrepresentational differences.[15] But, given this, he might as well abandon the idea that experience represents properties distinct from but corresponding to the colors and just say that Norm's visual experience of the tomato and Abnorm's visual experience of it each represent the tomato as red, but that the subjective difference between them is a difference in the mode of presentation of redness. Since the properties distinct from but corresponding to the colors don't do any explanatory work with regard to the subjective difference between Norm's and Abnorm's visual experiences, there is no need to claim that visual experience represents any such properties.

So Shoemaker's attempt to identify the properties distinct from but corresponding to the colors with certain relational properties makes his view unstable; since things don't *seem* to have these properties, representation of them can't explain subjective differences. But, assuming that the clash of internalist and externalist intuitions that motivates spectrum inversion really does require that there be properties distinct from but corresponding to the colors represented in perception, if these properties turn out not to be Shoemaker's relational properties, what are they? I think that some answer can be given to this question, though rather than being some account of the metaphysical nature of these properties the answer is an imperative: namely, use your eyes and focus on some red thing. You see that it appears to have some *intrinsic* property in virtue of which it is more similar to an orange thing than it is to a blue thing. If the thing you are looking at really does have this property, then your perception of the object is veridical; otherwise, it is not. So your perception of the thing represents it as having this intrinsic property. We ordinarily take this property to be redness, but it isn't. Nor is it identical to any relational property. It is exactly as it seems to be.

11. Conclusion

I have argued that an adequate account of perceptual representation should have two commitments. First, like intentionalism, it should explain all subjective differences between perceptions in terms of representational differences between them. The intentionalist is right about this because subjective differences just are differences in how things seem. And, whenever something perceptually seems some way to someone, there is always a question of whether the thing really is that way and, hence, always a question of truth or falsity. But, second, an adequate account of perceptual representation should also respect a genuine insight of the qualia freak's: namely, that properties distinct from but corresponding to the colors play a crucial role in perceptual representation. However, the qualia freak errs in thinking that these properties are properties of visual experience; rather, they are properties that vision represents objects in the world as having.

I have also argued against Shoemaker's attempt to identify these properties with certain relational properties. However, the upshot of the argument against Shoemaker doesn't merely raise trouble for his account of what these properties are; it also somewhat undercuts the motivation for holding that they exist. Recall that the problem with Shoemaker's account is that it requires that there be modes of presentation of the relevant properties. However, once the properties turn out to be presented via modes of presentation, there is no reason not to say that Norm's and Abnorm's visual perceptions represent objects as being the same color; it's just that their respective visual perceptions represent particular colors via distinct modes of presentation. Norm's perceptions represent redness via some mode of presentation, while that mode of presentation presents greenness to Abnorm, and so on for the other colors; and, moreover, it is these modes of presentation, rather than the properties that they present, that will wind up accounting for the subjective difference between Norm's and Abnorm's visual experience. To put the point in terms of the more general considerations that underlie the argument from spectrum inversion, Shoemaker should say that the internally determined aspects of perception result from how the properties it ascribes to objects are presented rather than from the properties themselves.

Now, if we reject Shoemaker's identification of the properties that ground spectrum inversion with relational properties, there is no need to invoke modes of presentation in our account. However, even though modes of presentation aren't required by the account, why not abandon the account and use them to explain spectrum inversion anyway? That is, why not get rid of the idea that there are heretofore unrecognized properties distinct from but corresponding to colors represented in perception and just say that the subjective difference between Norm's and Abnorm's visual experience—and more generally the internally determined aspect of how things perceptually seem to subjects—is due to the modes of presentation that present the colors? Both Norm's and Abnorm's perceptions represent the tomato as red but the subjective difference between them resides in their respective perceptions presenting red differently to Norm and Abnorm. Shoemaker's account seems to require this possibility but the point here is that, even if it is not required, isn't it still more plausible than the suggestion that the perceptually presented property we take to be redness is in fact some other property?

Now, if the modes of presentation of the colors are identified with qualia, we have already seen one reason why this account won't work. The difference between Norm and Abnorm is a difference in how things seem to them and, hence, it must involve a difference in representational content. So merely positing distinct qualia won't do the trick unless we also posit that they are aware of their experiences as having distinct qualia. But this account winds up having no advantage over the account that I'm suggesting since, as we saw in Section 6, it too claims that there are properties distinct from but corresponding to the colors represented in visual perception; it's just that the properties turn out to be represented as being properties of experiences rather than properties of objects in the world. So nothing at all is gained by claiming that the modes of presentation of colors are qualia and, given Moore's point about the diaphanousness of perception, a plausible account of the phenomenology of perception is in fact lost.

However, recall that, though differences in qualia don't imply differences in representational content, there are other kinds of modes of presentation that are alleged to affect representational content. The senses that are posited to solve Frege's puzzle concerning belief *are* supposed to be constituents of the thoughts themselves and, hence, unlike qualia, are supposed to contribute to representational content. So, while the fact that differences in perceptual seeming must involve differences in representational content does rule out qualia as perceptual modes of presentation, it does not rule out accounting for spectrum inversion in terms of modes of presentation. It's just that these modes of presentation will have to be like the senses that are alleged by the Fregean to be constituents of belief, insofar as they will have to directly contribute to representational content.

Now, though nothing said so far rules out the idea that sense-like modes of presentation might account for the internally determined aspects of perception, the reader should be a bit uneasy as to the level of generality of the suggestion. It's all well and good to suggest that there might be a kind of mode of presentation that can do the job here—that is, that can directly affect representational content and, hence, account for the internally determined way things perceptually seem to subjects—but, if it is to amount to more than just a suggestion, some account of what these modes of presentation are like must be given. But, still, unless there is some reason to think that such an account cannot be given, the argument for the view of perception suggested in this chapter is less than completely convincing.

Moreover, there are other reasons that the argument of this chapter might reasonably be resisted. In short form, the argument runs as follows. Perceptual representation of color, shape, distance, etc. is externally determined, but there is something about perceptual experience that is internally determined. Hence, this internally determined aspect of perception can't be accounted for by representation of color, shape, distance, etc. But, since the way things seem to someone must be explained by the way they are represented as being, this internally determined aspect of experience must be representational. And, given Moore's point that perception is diaphanous, this internally determined aspect of perception involves ways in which things in the world are represented as being.

But this argument depends upon some assumptions that might seem dubious. On the one hand, if you are convinced that mental representation of color, shape, distance, etc. is externally determined, then there is reason to doubt that there is some aspect of the way things seem that is internally determined. After all, the recent discovery that the content of at least some mental states is externally determined was surprising, and I think that the philosophical community is still digesting the lessons of externalism. So, though it seems plausible that something about perception is internally determined, perhaps this plausibility is a result of incomplete digestion. (See Dretske 1995, 130–41 for an argument that phenomenology is externally determined.) On the other hand, if you are convinced that there is some aspect of how things seem that is internally determined, there is reason to doubt that mental representation of color, shape, distance, etc., is externally determined. After all, if it turns out that some aspects of conscious experience are internally determined, then there is reason to think that Norm and Abnorm needn't mean the same thing by their color, shape, distance, etc. terminology.

In Chapter 5 I will present an argument for the view advocated in this chapter that doesn't depend upon any internalist or externalist assumptions. And this argument will reveal a further defect in Shoemaker's view. As we have seen, Shoemaker holds that visual experience represents objects as having color properties *and* properties distinct from but corresponding to the colors. But, as we will see, visual experience represents *only* the properties that are distinct from but correspond to the colors, and likewise for shape, distance, etc. On the basis of visual representation of properties distinct from but corresponding to the colors, shapes, etc., one comes to believe that objects in the world have certain colors, shapes, etc. But visual experience doesn't represent objects as having color, shape, etc.

The full account of perception that I will argue for is, at this stage, bound to seem fantastic. There would be reason enough to resist the idea, suggested in this chapter, that perception represents objects as having properties distinct from but corresponding to colors and shapes. But how could it be that perception *doesn't* represent objects as having colors or shapes or any of the other properties and relations that we manifestly see? If we know anything at all about the colors don't we know that they are represented in vision? However, though I can see the force that such questions will have at this stage, the claims I wish to make about perception are far more tenable that they first appear. The argument in Chapter 5 and the considerations that surround it explain both why these claims seem so absurd and why they in fact aren't.

However, the discussion in Chapter 5 depends crucially on settling whether there could be perceptual modes of presentation that, unlike qualia, contribute to the representational content of mental states. And, more generally, understanding both the argument itself and the general issues it is meant to resolve will require that we achieve a better understanding of mental representation. So, before turning to the other argument, more needs to be said about the notion of representation.

In this chapter, an account of perception was introduced that differs from intentionalism in the following respect. The intentionalist claims that the subjective differences between color experiences must be explained by differences in what colors are represented. Whereas I have argued that the subjective difference between color experiences is explained by differences in representation of properties distinct from but corresponding to the colors. But the view introduced in this chapter differs from intentionalism in another, perhaps more important, way. At least a few intentionalists have adopted some of Franz Brentano's ideas about representation. Brentano focuses on the fact that representation involves *aboutness*. However, Brentano's focus, rather than clarifying the notion, has further obscured it. So in the next chapter I argue against taking Brentano's line on representation. The lesson will be that in focusing on aboutness Brentano and his followers have focused on the wrong aspect of representation and that it is better to focus on the link between representation and truth.

2

The Structure of Belief and Perceptual Representation

0. Introduction

In this chapter I turn to belief and perceptual representation. Some intentionalists have much to say about this topic. As their name suggests, many adopt Franz Brentano's view that one defining characteristic of mental representation is its *intentionality*.[1] I begin by discussing the alleged intentionality of mental representation for several reasons. First, I think that the view is both wrong and on the wrong track, so it must be set aside if we are to get a clear picture of belief and perceptual representation. But, second, the view that mental representation has intentionality arises from certain natural assumptions about mental representation and is sometimes used to solve a particular problem about perception. And any adequate account of mental representation must account for the natural assumptions and solve the problem. Finally, and perhaps most importantly, the account of mental representation in terms of intentionality turns out to be strikingly similar to views it is often designed to counter; and the mistaken presuppositions that ground this similarity crop up in one way or another in a surprising number of other places relevant to both consciousness and cognition.

1. Intentionality and paradox

As we have already noted, one obvious feature of belief and perceptual representation seems to be that objects are represented as being certain ways. Brentano's view emerges from considering something that seems equally obvious. When a belief or perception represents some thing as being a certain way, the belief or perception bears a certain relation to the thing: namely, it is *about* the thing. But, once we grant this seemingly obvious point, it turns out that the aboutness relation has some very peculiar features.

Suppose I come to believe that there is an Irish pub in Philadelphia without believing of any particular Irish pub that it is in Philadelphia. Then it seems that my belief is about an Irish pub even though there is no particular Irish pub that it is about. So apparently a belief can stand in the aboutness relation to a thing of a certain kind (in this case an Irish pub) without there being any particular thing of that kind to which it stands in the relation. So one strange feature of the aboutness relation would seem to be

(A1) A belief can bear the aboutness relation to an F without there being some particular F to which it bears the relation.

But the strangeness doesn't stop there. For I might come to have a more particular belief that *the Irish pub at 1214 Sansom Street* is a good pub. In this case my belief does seem to be about a particular Irish pub. But suppose that, unbeknownst to me, this is the pub owned by the waterslide champion of Wildwood. Since this is not known to me, my belief isn't about the pub owned by the waterslide champion of Wildwood, even though it *is* about the Irish pub at 1214 Sansom Street, and that is the pub owned by the waterslide champion of Wildwood. So another rather strange feature of the aboutness relation would seem to be

(A2) A belief can bear the aboutness relation to the F without bearing the aboutness relation to the G *even though* the F *is* the G.[2]

Finally, I might come to believe that *the Irish pub at 1214 Sansom Street* is good, even though there never have existed and never will exist any Irish pubs at that address. In this case, my belief is about the Irish pub at 1214 Sansom Street even though no such Irish pub ever exists. So the final strange feature of the aboutness relation would seem to be

(A3) A belief can bear the aboutness relation to an F though no F's ever exist.

Brentano calls the thing that a belief or perception is about its **intentional object**, and (A1), (A2), and (A3) imply some rather strange things about intentional objects. First, an intentional object needn't be a particular thing; second, an intentional object can be the F without being the G, even though the F is the G; and, third, there can be intentional objects that never exist.[3]

The aboutness relation and the intentional objects to which it relates beliefs and perceptions are strange. And I think that philosophers have tended to accept this strangeness because, after all, everybody knows that there's something funny about the mental anyway. However, this attitude is more than a bit cavalier. For to say that the aboutness relation is strange is an understatement. The aboutness relation isn't just strange; it's downright paradoxical. If there really is a good argument that you can bear a certain relation to a thing without there being any particular thing that you bear the relation to, then this argument presents a paradox; for plainly if you're related to a thing, then there must be some particular thing to which you are related! And, if there really is a good argument that you can bear a certain relation to something and at the same time not bear that relation to it, then this argument presents a paradox; for plainly, if you bear some relation to something, then you bear that relation to it! And, if there really is a good argument that you can be related to a thing even though that thing never exists, then this argument presents a paradox; for plainly you can't be related to something that never exists! No one is inclined to quietly accept the paradoxes of set theory because, after all, sets are funny things anyway, and no one should be inclined to quietly accept these paradoxes of the mental.[4]

Gilbert Harman uses the alleged fact that intentional objects needn't exist in his response to the so-called *argument from illusion* for sense-data theory, and he considers the objection that his appeal to nonexistent objects is paradoxical. The version of the argument from illusion that Harman attempts to rebut asks us to consider Eloise, who is hallucinating some brown and green object, and it runs as follows:

(1) Eloise is seeing something brown and green.
(2) But there is nothing in the material world that is a brown and green thing that she sees.
Therefore,
(3) There exists some mental brown and green thing that she sees.

Harman's response is that perception has intentional objects, and there are two senses of *S is seeing x*: one sense in which *x* must pick out an actually existing object and another sense in which *x* picks out an intentional object. Harman claims that (1) is true only if we take *seeing* to be used in the second sense. Hence, the brown and green thing that Eloise is seeing is the intentional object of her visual perception and, since she is hallucinating, it doesn't exist. So we shouldn't infer that what she sees is mental from the fact that there's nothing physical before her: what she sees doesn't exist at all. To make all of this palatable, Harman draws an analogy to searching. Ponce de Leon was searching for the fountain of youth; hence, according to Harman, he was searching for something. But there is no fountain of youth, so searches have intentional objects: the thing that Ponce de Leon was searching for was a nonexistent intentional object.

Harman (1990, 37) recognizes the peculiarity of his appeal to intentional objects when he considers the following response:

> You agree that there is a sense in which Eloise sees something green and brown when there is nothing green and brown before her in the external world. You are able to deny that this brown and green thing is mental by taking it to be a nonexistent and merely in-

tentional object. But it is surely more reasonable to suppose that one is in this case aware of something mental than to suppose that one is aware of something that does not exist. How can there be anything that doesn't exist? The very suggestion is a contradiction in terms, since "be" simply means "exist," so that you are really saying that there exists something that does not exist. There are no such things as nonexistent objects!

In response, Harman concedes that ultimately something does need to be said about how there can be nonexistent things. However, Harman (1990, 37–38) claims:

> I do not see that it is my job to resolve this issue. However this issue is resolved, the theory that results had better end up agreeing that Ponce de Leon was looking for something when he was looking for the fountain of youth, even though there is no fountain of youth, and the theory had better *not* have the consequence that Ponce de Leon was looking for something mental.

Harman then goes on to say that any theory that is able to meet these criteria for searching will provide the resources to meet them for seeing as well.

But, as I pointed out above, the claim that there are nonexistent intentional objects is paradoxical. And, prior to the resolution of a paradox, one is not in a position to put constraints on the way things should stand upon resolution. Imagine an ancient Greek saying of Zeno's paradox *I don't care how the paradox is resolved, but it had better turn out that the sum of infinitely many numbers is not a finite number.* This response isn't wrong simply because it denies what's crucial to the resolution of Zeno's paradox. It's wrong because it is in the nature of resolving a paradox that certain apparently undeniable facts aren't really facts at all. And an acceptable resolution of a paradox helps us see why the apparently undeniable facts aren't as compelling as they initially seem. Prior to an acceptable resolution, one simply isn't in any position to say which putative facts are non-negotiable.

Given the paradoxical nature of intentional objects, and in the absence of a resolution to the paradoxes, it is difficult to see how accepting Brentano's view is better than accepting sense-data theory. Moreover, though the claim that there are intentional objects is supposed to provide a plausible alternative to sense-data theory, on a closer look the two views turn out to be more similar than they are different; and the view that there are intentional objects merely adds the above paradoxes without eliminating the fundamental problem of sense-data theory.

2. Intentionality and sense-data theory

On Harman's account of things, the view that perceptual relations have intentional objects is supposed to provide a sensible alternative to the ludicrous claim of sense-data theory that we perceive our own ideas. However, in exactly what way does Harman's account differ from sense-data theory? Let's begin by looking at the case of hallucination.

According to sense-data theory, when someone hallucinates, for example, a pink elephant, since by hypothesis there's no pink elephant for him to see, he must be seeing something else; and, since whatever it is that he is seeing is pink and elephant-shaped, this something else that he sees is also pink and elephant-shaped. But, at this stage, we should be struck by the fact that Harman's account of hallucination is so far exactly the same as the sense-data theorist's; since there's no pink elephant to be seen, according to Harman, there's something else that the person is seeing. And, since what the person sees is pink and elephant-shaped, this something else that he sees is also pink and elephant-shaped. The difference is that Harman claims the thing doesn't exist, whereas the sense-data theorist claims it is mental. But, on both theories, hallucination involves perceiving some object to be exactly the way it is. And, importantly, on neither theory is this unique to hallucination.

In cases of hallucination, there is no object in the material world that the subject sees. And, though hallucination is a kind of nonveridical perception, it is not the only kind. Another kind of nonveridical perception is what Austin (1962, 22–24) calls *illusion*, cases in which the subject *does* see something in the material world but in which his perception misrepresents the thing.[5] Suppose that you are undergoing some kind of illusion—say you're looking at an actual grey elephant—but for whatever reason your perception misrepresents its color as pink. In whatever sense in which hallucinating a pink elephant involves *seeing* something pink, it seems that, in the illusory case, you are also *seeing* something pink. But, although unlike the case of hallucination there actually *is* an elephant in front of you if you are undergoing a mere illusion, the elephant in front of you isn't pink; by hypothesis it's grey. So, like cases of hallucination, in cases of illusion the subject also appears to see some object that doesn't exist: namely, in the example we're considering, a pink elephant. And this means that the person who thinks that hallucination involves seeing nonexistent intentional objects should also think that illusion involves seeing nonexistent intentional objects. What makes a perceptual episode count as an illusion will be that, as in the case of hallucination, the material world doesn't match up to the intentional object that the subject sees; in hallucination this is because there is no object in the material world, whereas in illusion this is because the object in the material world doesn't have some of the properties that the intentional object has. But this makes the account of illusion—like the account of hallucination—almost identical to the account given by the sense-data theorist. On both views, illusion involves seeing a certain type of object that has properties that the relevant object in the material world fails to have. It's just that the intentional-object theorist claims the thing seen doesn't exist, whereas the sense-data theorist claims it's mental.

Intentional-object theorists have tended to focus on cases of hallucination; but, insofar as hallucination and illusion are both cases of perceptual misrepresentation, it's hard to see why there shouldn't turn out to be nonexistent intentional objects in both cases. And, indeed, once this is noticed it's hard to see why subjects shouldn't turn out to see nonexistent intentional objects in veridical cases of perception as well. After all, what you see in the hallucination and illusion cases needn't seem any different to you from what you see in the veridical cases, so there's at least an argument that even veridical cases of perception should turn out to involve seeing intentional objects that are distinct from the material object seen. Moreover, the intentional-object theorist's account of what makes nonveridical cases of perception nonveridical seems to imply that veridical cases also involve intentional objects. For, if instances of perceptual misrepresentation occur when there is no relevant object in the material world that has all of the properties that the intentional object has, the natural account would be that instances of accurate perceptual representation occur when there is a relevant object in the material world that *does* have all of the properties that the intentional object has; if misrepresentation involves mismatch, then accurate representation would seem to involve match. Hence, it seems that even in the case of veridical perception, there should be an intentional object that is distinct from the object in the material world that the subject sees; and, if these objects don't exist in the case of nonveridical perception, it isn't easy to see why they should turn out to exist in the case of veridical perception. The fact that veridical perception of a grey elephant *does* involve seeing an existent grey and elephant-shaped thing can't be a reason for thinking that the intentional object exists, if that thing isn't the intentional object. But now the account is looking even more like sense-data theory; every case of visual perception involves seeing a certain kind of object exactly as it is and the perception is accurate just in case there is something in the material world that matches this object. Again, the only difference is that the intentional-object theorist claims the objects don't exist while the sense-data theorist claims they are mental.

So far, I am claiming that there are good reasons to extend the intentional-object theorist's views to apply to instances of perception that are illusory or veridical as well as hallucinatory, and that the resulting theory turns out to not be very different from sense-data theory. However, good reasons are not always decisive reasons and there may be other reasons that weigh in favor of *not* extending the theory beyond cases of hallucination. But, in this regard, the view is also on a par with sense-data theory. One of Austin's (1962, 44–54) important points is that, even if the hallucinatory case were to establish the existence of sense-data, it's not clear that there are any grounds to extend the account to illusion and veridical perception. And, given that intentional objects turn out to serve precisely the same role as sense-data in accounting for hallucination, they are likely to be on a par with regard to the justification for their extension to other cases of perception. But, more importantly, whatever the balance of reasons finally favors, there is a more general point here. Insofar as both views are motivated by considering cases of hallucination, both views make precisely the same general assumption about the hallucinatory case; for *both assume that in cases of hallucination there must be some object of your perception that is exactly the way it seems to be.* Since there is no guarantee that there is any such physical object, the sense-data theorist concludes that there must be a nonphysical object of your perception. Brentano and his followers make the same mistake; but, instead of claiming that the object that is exactly as it seems is merely nonphysical, they claim that it is nonexistent. To my mind, this can hardly be claimed an improvement.

Indeed, the fact that intentional objects are supposed to be exactly as they seem leads to another problem with the claim that perception has intentionality. For, when Eloise hallucinates a brown and green object, her visual perception may be indistinguishable from a veridical perception of a brown and green object. But, then, besides seeming to be brown and green, the alleged intentional object of her perception will seem to her to exist. Though the object of Eloise's visual perception doesn't exist, she is not hallucinating that there is a nonexistent object before her; she's hallucinating that there's an existing object before her. Hence, the alleged intentional object of her perception should be taken to actually exist, because intentional objects are always as they appear to be. We can get at the same point with the analogy that Harman uses against sense-data theory. Harman points out that Ponce de Leon didn't want to find an idea of the fountain of youth. Fair enough, but neither did he want a *nonexistent* fountain of youth. After all, only a fountain that actually exists would provide eternal youth. So, whatever reason there is to think that the object of Ponce de Leon's search wasn't an idea, there is equal reason to think that it was something that existed.

But of course it's still true that the fountain of youth doesn't exist and, in the case of Eloise's hallucination, it's still true that what she sees doesn't exist. So it isn't just that *there are* intentional objects that don't exist; it's also true that some nonexistent intentional objects exist. Notice that the proponent of nonexistent intentional objects cannot block the conclusion that they sometimes also exist by citing Kant's ([1787] 1922, 478–86) idea that existence isn't a property of particulars like redness or squareness is but is rather a precondition for having such properties. For the main feature of intentional-object theory is that intentional objects can have properties even though they don't exist.

So, rather than helping to explain belief and perceptual representation, positing intentional objects makes them paradoxical.[6] More importantly, the view that there are intentional objects seems to arise from the same mistaken assumptions as sense-data theory. But, besides its being paradoxical, there are other important reasons to think that intentionality is the wrong way to go in attempting to explain belief and perceptual representation. For, as we will see, intentionality has nothing to do with belief and perceptual representation and, hence, is not the defining feature of either.

3. The link to truth and falsity

In Chapter 1 we saw one important feature of belief and perceptual representation, namely, their link to the notions of truth and falsity: when a belief or perception represents O as being P, it represents O truly if O is P and falsely if it isn't. So there is something about perceptions and beliefs that makes them capable of being true

or false, that makes them—to borrow a phrase of Crispin Wright's (1992, 12)—
truth-apt.[7] We are now attempting to find out a bit more about representation.
But—as Harman's example of searching brings out—*intentionality doesn't really
have anything in particular to do with the link between representation and truth-
aptness.*

Searches don't have truth-values, yet searches are alleged to have intentionality.
And other common putative examples of intentionality involve mental phenomena
that don't seem to be truth-apt. Tye (1995, 94) uses the example of thinking about
a golden mountain to show that one can think about things that don't exist. But, if
I merely think about a golden mountain without actually believing or disbelieving
that there is such a thing and without thinking anything else about it, then it isn't
at all clear that my thought has any truth-value. The paradoxical aboutness relation
is alleged to be a feature of practically all mental phenomena, but *our* concern is belief and perceptual representation. Hence, our concern might be better served if we
began by considering something that is unique to belief and perceptual representation: namely, their link to truth and falsity.

It might be responded that the link to truth and falsity *isn't* unique to belief and
perceptual representation. For there does seem to be a way in which even thoughts
about golden mountains can be considered true or false. If a golden mountain doesn't
exist, then why not say that my thought about a golden mountain is false? After all,
if the thought were true, there would have to be a golden mountain. One might even
go farther and suggest that when the object of a search doesn't exist there is no reason not to say that the search is false. So it seems that we do have some understanding of how truth and falsity might be applied to the range of mental phenomena that are alleged to have intentionality.

Now I think that there is something right about these objections. What's right is
that there are many mental phenomena to which we can (perhaps) make sense of
applying the notions of truth and falsity, even if it is unnatural to apply those notions to them. For example, consider desires. While it's not at all natural to think of
a desire as true or false, there is an easy way to apply such notions to desires. We
can say that a desire that P is true just in case it's true that P and false otherwise.
But our ability to coherently apply truth and falsity to desires, imaginings, etc.
masks an important difference between these mental phenomena and the phenomena of belief and perception.

When a belief is false, it is *flawed*; there is something *wrong* with it. Of course
it may not turn out to be very important that it's false and there may be other features of it (say, its usefulness) that more than make up for its falsity. But, still, falseness in belief is a vice and truth a virtue. Likewise for perception: if you perceive
something to be the case that isn't in fact the case, then something is wrong with
your perception. And a perception that accurately reflects the way the world is has
at least one thing going for it. Besides being truth-apt, perceptions and beliefs are
also *truth-normed*.

Kripke (1982) has claimed (more or less on behalf of Wittgenstein) that there is something normative about linguistic meaning. If I ask you what 2+2 is, then it seems incorrect for you to say anything but *4*. Kripke's claims about the normativity of language are a bit puzzling; for there is only something wrong with an answer other than *4 if you want to speak the truth*. And it is important to note that not speaking the truth in this context needn't mean lying or misleading. It would be perfectly acceptable for you to answer *5* if you were clearly being sarcastic and the situation warranted sarcasm, or if we were spies and answering *5* were part of our code, or for innumerably many other reasons. But then there is nothing at all mysterious about the normativity of language. For that normativity derives entirely from — to borrow a bit of Kantian terminology — *hypothetical imperatives*: *if you want to speak the truth* you should answer *4*. Thus any account of reference that explains why *5* refers to the number 5, together with the fact that 2+2=4, completely explains the alleged normativity. If *5* refers to the number 5 and you want to speak the truth, then *5* is the wrong answer, because 2+2 isn't 5. However, while the normativity of language rests entirely on hypothetical imperatives, the normativity of belief rests on — to borrow the complementary bit of Kantian terminology — *categorical imperatives*. There is something wrong with a false belief or a nonveridical perception regardless of the desires of the person who has them. The essence of beliefs and perceptions is to aim at truth and away from falsity.

Even though it may be possible to consider desires, imaginings, etc. as truth-apt, they are not truth-normed. If I imagine a golden mountain, there may be a sense in which my imagining is false, but it is certainly not the case that the lack of a golden mountain makes my imagining in any way deficient. You can call the desire for food of a man destined to starve *false* if you want, but without food he will die; and the fact that his desire will go unsatisfied doesn't mean that there is anything deficient about it. Perhaps his *need* for food constitutes a falling away from some ideal of extreme self-sufficiency, but given that he needs the food, his desire for it is beyond reproach.

It is because perception and belief are obviously and essentially truth-normed that they are also obviously and essentially truth-apt. Since it is of their nature to aim at truth and away from falsity, they must be *subject to* truth and falsity. Hence, it makes sense to begin an investigation into the nature of belief and perceptual representation by considering what they would have to be like in order to be truth-apt. But since desires, imaginings, etc. are not truth-normed, it is far less obvious that they are truth-apt. And, even if there is some trivial way to apply the notions of truth and falsity to desires, imaginings, etc., since they are not truth-normed, it is far from obvious that this sense in which they may be truth-apt gives us any clue to their essential nature. To draw a parallel, utterances of declarative sentences are clearly truth-apt, but as pointed out above, they are not truth-normed. And utterances are not truth-normed at least partly because false utterances can be perfectly good ways of getting information across (as in the case of sarcasm). But this suggests that utterances of declarative sentences are better viewed as falling under norms of *communication* and, hence, that focusing strictly on their truth or falsity is liable to yield a false picture.[8]

Many contemporary philosophers say that mental representation is intentional without explicitly advocating Brentano's views on intentional objects. However, they do follow Brentano in holding that the crucial fact about belief and perceptual representation is that beliefs and perceptions are *about* things. But the crucial fact about belief and perceptual representation is that they are essentially truth-normed and, hence, essentially truth-apt. And this doesn't hold for the rest of the range of mental phenomena alleged to be intentional. Since the truth-aptness of belief and perception are also crucial to their being representational, it is doubtful that focusing on aboutness can shed any light on belief and perceptual representation.

Indeed, the recognition that belief and perceptual representation are truth-normed brings into sharper focus the error at the heart of both sense-data theory and the intentional-object theory. Since belief and perceptual representation are truth-normed, a belief or perception has the potential to be either successful or unsuccessful: successful if it represents its object truly and unsuccessful if it represents its object falsely. But, as we saw above, even when a perception misrepresents some object in the world, the alleged intentional object of the perception is supposed to be exactly the way it seems to be. And the same is true for the alleged sense-datum: it too is supposed to be exactly the way it appears to be. If a ripe tomato seems blue to me, then my perception of it is nonveridical. But the alleged intentional object of my perception *is* blue and, hence, is successfully represented. So both Brentano's view and sense-data theory can be seen as an attempt to understand unsuccessful mental representation as a special kind of successful representation: namely, a kind that is successful only with respect to an intentional object or a sense-datum.[9] But assimilating *all* representation to the case of successful representation is unlikely to yield a correct account of the phenomenon.[10]

A better strategy is to focus on what belief and perceptual representation must be like in order to be truth-apt. As we will see, the result of following this strategy will shed light on aboutness and the paradoxes of intentionality as well as explaining where the argument from illusion goes wrong. These issues concerning representation are clearer in the case of belief than they are in the case of perception. Hence, I begin by focusing on belief representation and return to perceptual representation once we have a better understanding of belief representation.

4. The relational nature of belief

Before turning to what beliefs must be like in order to be truth-apt, it is important to notice that belief is relational: when Marie believes that vitamin C prevents colds, *the thing that she believes* is that vitamin C prevents colds; and, when Sally believes that summers in New Jersey are unbearable, *the thing that she believes* is that summers in New Jersey are unbearable. In general, whenever someone believes that P, *the thing that he believes* is that P. Let's call the relevant relation *the belief relation*, and—adopting the standard contemporary terminology—let's call the things (whatever they may be) that we bear the belief relation to **propositions**. When you have a belief, it is the proposition, the thing that you believe, that determines the representational content of your belief.

Now, as we saw in Chapter 1, on the standard philosophical picture of belief there is more to any instance of the belief relation than merely the subject and the proposition he believes. On the standard picture, besides these two elements, there is some state or proper part of the subject that relates him to the proposition. We're considering what a belief would have to be like in order to be truth-normed and, hence, truth-apt. The relational nature of belief and the standard philosophical account of the elements involved in that relation are important, because there is a prior question that must be settled before turning to our question: namely, which of the elements in the picture *is* the belief? Which thing is the thing that is truth-normed and, hence, truth-apt? Now, of course, one element of the picture—namely, the subject—isn't a candidate. When Gene believes that good posture is important, it isn't Gene himself that is true or false. However, in the case of the other elements, it isn't so easy to say which is our primary concern. For both the state of the subject and the proposition seem to be, in some sense, beliefs. Moreover, as we will see, there is actually another element, distinct from both the state of the subject and the proposition he believes, that is a candidate.

Once the elements involved in the belief relation are brought to light, it's pretty obvious that propositions—the things we believe—are, in some sense of the term, themselves *beliefs*. When Sally believes that snow is white, what she believes is that snow is white; and, when Hank believes that vitamin C prevents colds, what he believes is that vitamin C prevents colds. But it is also true that, when Sally believes that snow is white, her belief *is* that snow is white; and, when Hank believes that vitamin C prevents colds, his belief *is* that vitamin C prevents colds. That is to say, it's natural to think that a subject's belief just is the thing that he believes, that his belief just is the proposition that he bears the belief relation to. Moreover, when both Sally and Hank believe that snow is white, they believe the same proposition, and they also have the same belief. But, on the picture, the only thing common to Sally and Hank in this case will be that they bear the belief relation to the same proposition, so their having the very same belief means that, in at least one sense of the term, *beliefs* are propositions; in this sense of the term, beliefs are very much like thoughts (or at least very much like thoughts as Frege [(1918) 1977] understood them to be).[11]

Few will disagree with the characterization of beliefs as propositions. However, most philosophers will claim that there is another sense of the word **belief** according to which it refers to the state of the subject that relates him to the proposition. Now, if all that were at issue here were whether the word **belief** is ambiguous, there would be nothing of much interest here at all. But, behind the tiresome linguistic question concerning the word **belief**, there is an important question concerning beliefs: is the state of the subject that relates him to what he believes the thing that is essentially truth-normed and, hence, truth-apt, or is it the proposition that has these features? Or do both states *and* propositions have these features? I think the answer—or at least, as we will see, part of it—is that it is propositions rather than states that are truth-apt. And the reason that this is the answer is at least as important as the answer itself. For the reason that propositions rather than belief states are the proper subject of our concern is that the standard philosophical picture is wrong in supposing that believing requires belief states. Denying the accuracy of this part of the orthodox picture is bound to seem absurd to most philosophers—indeed, it's liable to seem absurd enough as to also seem like the kind of claim whose sole purpose is to shock and draw attention. After all, that believing essentially involves belief states seems to be an utterly undeniable triviality. And can I really mean to be denying it? Well, not exactly. But I do think that the orthodox picture has run together the undeniable triviality with a substantive claim that is decidedly deniable.

5. Instantial states vs. internal states

Part of the orthodox picture is that belief is a relation between subjects and propositions. And one way in which the claim that there are belief states is trivial is that whenever you have a relation there does seem to be a trivial sense in which you have a state: namely, the state of being in that relation. For example, marriage is a relation and, if Ben and Marie are in that relation (that is, are *married*), there is the state of their being married. Similarly, being the same height as is a relation and, if Joe and Mike are in that relation (that is, are *the same height*), there is the state of their being the same height. And this is not a special feature of relations; relations are abstract entities that groups of particulars instantiate, but at the same ontological level there are also properties: abstract entities like redness and squareness that single particulars instantiate. And just as, whenever a and b instantiate some relation, there is the state of their being in that relation, whenever a has some property, there is the state of its having that property. If the tomato is red, there is the state of its being red; if the tomato is in front of you, there is the state of its being in front of you; and, coming back to belief, if Scott bears the belief relation to the proposition that diets high in soy protein reduce cholesterol (that is, if he *believes that diets high in soy protein reduce cholesterol*), there is in the same sense the state of Scott's believing this.

However, in this sense of *state*, there is trivially a state whenever something has a property or whenever two (or more) things bear a relation to one another because there being a state, in one sense of the term, just amounts to the thing's or things' instantiating the property or relation. The state of the tomato's being red is not some second thing distinct from the tomato in virtue of which it is red; rather, it's nothing more than the tomato's being red. The state of Ben and Marie being married is not some third thing distinct from Ben and Marie in virtue of which they are married; rather, it's nothing more than their being married. And the state of Joe and Mike's being the same height isn't some third thing distinct from Joe and Mike in virtue of which they are the same height; rather, it's nothing more than their being the same height. The same goes for belief. In the trivial sense in which there are belief states, the state of Scott's believing that diets high in soy protein reduce cholesterol isn't some third thing distinct from Scott and the proposition that diets high in soy protein reduce cholesterol; rather, it's nothing more than his believing that proposition. Let's call those states that are nothing over and above some thing's or things' instantiating a property or relation *instantial states*.

However, there is a more robust sense of *state* according to which a state isn't merely the instantiation of some property or relation. On the more robust sense, a state is something like a proper part, or the condition of a some proper part, of an individual. A state of a (physically realized) Turing machine isn't some relation the machine bears to some other thing; it's a proper part, or the condition of some proper part, of the machine. And similarly a state of the brain isn't some relation the brain bears to some other thing; it's something like a proper part, or the condition of some proper part, of the brain. On this sense, the existence of a state requires more than the instantiation of some property or relation; it requires that there be some particular that *is* the state. Let's call these particulars *internal states*.

On the sense in which it is trivial that there are belief states, these states are instantial states: they are nothing over and above the actual belief relations that obtain between subjects and propositions. However, on the orthodox picture according to which there are belief states, the existence of these states amounts to more than the triviality. On the orthodox picture, these states are supposed to be internal states that relate subjects to the propositions they believe. For example, Scott's state of believing that diets high in soy protein reduce cholesterol doesn't simply consist in his believing that proposition; rather, the belief state is supposed to be some event or proper part of Scott in virtue of which he believes that proposition. Indeed, the traditional construal of the mind-body problem (applied to beliefs) *depends* upon thinking of belief states as internal states. At issue is the nature of the alleged internal state: is Scott's belief that diets high in soy protein reduce cholesterol just some physical internal state of his brain (or, more generally, of his body), or is it some immaterial state of his soul? If a belief state were meant only to be a instantial state—if Scott's belief state merely consisted of his bearing a relation to the relevant proposition—there would be no such question, just as there is no question concerning whether the state of Ben and Marie's being married, or the state of Joe and Mike's being the same height, is a material or immaterial thing. In some sense, neither is a thing at all; both are instantiations of *relations*.

Now, of course it is true—and I am not denying—that there is something about a subject in virtue of which he believes what he does and, indeed, it is safe to go a bit farther than this. We know empirically that the brain has a particular relevance to the mental life of a subject and, more particularly, that what propositions someone believes is in part dependent on what's going on in his brain. And it's important to realize that I am absolutely not denying this. However, the orthodox philosophical view that there are internal belief states amounts to a lot more than the claim that the brain is the organ of cognition. On the orthodoxy, for each proposition that a subject believes there is supposed to be a distinct internal state corresponding to this proposition and in virtue of which the subject bears the belief relation to that proposition; for every proposition you believe there is supposed to be some distinct internal state of you that bears a relation to it that is similar to the one that holds between a sentence and the proposition it expresses. Indeed, Ramsey, Stitch, and Garon (1990) have argued that if certain models of the brain are correct there simply are no beliefs, since (according to them) on these models not every belief the subject has corresponds to some state of his brain. And Ramsey et al. simply assume what most philosophers of mind assume: namely, that if there aren't discrete internal states corresponding to each belief then there are no belief states and, hence, no beliefs.

However, once the distinction between instantial states and internal states is made clear, it becomes equally clear that some argument needs to be given for the claim that believing involves internal belief states. And, though it's clear that there's something about the subject in virtue of which he believes what he does, this doesn't imply that for each of his beliefs there is an internal state of him in virtue of which he believes it, just as the fact that there's something about Mike that makes him the same height as Joe and something about him that makes him the same height as Mark doesn't imply that there are distinct internal states of Mike in virtue of which he bears these relations. The assumption that beliefs are internal states depends upon what I'll call the *particularizing fallacy*: the fallacy of confusing the instantiation of some property or relation with a particular, of confusing an instantial state with an internal state. And, once the fallacy is exposed, some argument is needed for the claim that believing involves having an internal belief state.

6. Against internal belief states

The philosophical conception of belief according to which beliefs (in one sense of the term) are internal states of subjects is usually assumed to be an utter triviality with nary a thought that it might be a substantive claim for which argument is needed. Some of this is no doubt due to the particularizing fallacy. Talk of belief states is trivial because there are trivially instantial states; but, if the distinction is not made explicit, it is easy to think that the trivial talk concerns internal states. However, once the trivial is distinguished from the substantive, an apparent reason for thinking that there are internal belief states quickly comes to mind. And, besides the fact that *state* can mean something trivial or something substantive, this reason, I think, also plays a role in why it is assumed that beliefs must be internal states.

The apparent reason is that beliefs seem to have causal powers. For example, your belief that you are late for a meeting can cause you to walk faster. So, the line of thought goes, since beliefs play a causal role in the production of behavior, they had better turn out to be states of subjects. After all, propositions are abstract entities that don't cause anything; so, to the extent that beliefs are causally productive in behavior, they can't merely be propositions.

However, when we consider other relations that subjects can bear to abstract entities, this reason for supposing that beliefs have causal powers seems pretty dubious. Suppose Bob's score on the GRE was 2400. It seems right to say *Bob's GRE score caused the admissions officer to take his application very seriously*. But it would be wrong to infer from this that the number 2400 caused the admissions officer to take Bob's application very seriously. And it would be even more wrong to infer that there is some use of *Bob's GRE score* according to which it refers to some state or proper part of Bob or his application. Rather, though the sentence seems to attribute causal powers to the thing referred to by *Bob's GRE score*, it's really used as an attribution of causal powers to Bob's *having* a score of 2400 on the GRE: that is, to a relation that obtains between Bob and the number 2400. Likewise, mutatis mutandis, for sentences like *Liz's weight caused the floor to collapse*, *Steve's height gave him an inferiority complex*, *the color of his jacket caused everyone to stare*, etc. In each case, the sentence appears to be saying that some abstract entity causes something. But in each case it would be absurd to suggest that this means that there is some internal state of the person or thing the sentence is about that is really doing the causing. Rather, though the sentences appear to attribute causal powers to abstract entities, each is really used to convey that the instantiation of some relation—a relation between the person or thing that the sentence is about and an abstract entity—causes something. And likewise for sentences that seem to attribute causal powers to beliefs. There is no difference between saying *His belief that he was running late caused him to walk faster* and *His believing that he was running late caused him to walk faster*. Notice that there are two points here. First, we often use sentences that appear to attribute causal powers to abstract entities to convey that something's bearing some relation to an abstract entity has causal powers. Hence, nothing about our ordinary belief talk suggests that beliefs must be internal states. But, second and more importantly, bearing a relation to an abstract entity is a perfectly normal way for a thing to have a causal power. That is not to say that there is no legitimate question of how this can be so, but it is to say that there's nothing particularly suspect about the idea that bearing a relation to *a proposition* could be a way of having a causal power. If your *weighing* 300 pounds can cause the floor to collapse, then there's no particular reason that your *believing* that you are late for a meeting shouldn't cause you to walk faster.

Indeed, when we consider the nature of intentional behavior, the demand for a causal explanation in terms of internal states turns out to be somewhat puzzling. When you, for example, kick a ball, though your behavior is *constituted* by a movement of your leg, insofar as what you're doing is intentional you are *not* moving your leg at such and such velocity and in such and such direction; what you are doing is *kicking a ball*. And, while an internal state may be the *prima facie* more appropriate candidate for explaining the leg movement that constitutes your behavior, a relation to a proposition is *the prima facie* more appropriate candidate for explaining the behavior itself. Your believing that, for example, if you kick the ball it will go in the opposing team's goal might be one of the causes of your behavior. Now the proposition that if you kick the ball it will go in the opposing team's goal should turn out to bear some interesting relation to the ball it is intuitively about. So, in virtue of bearing a relation to this proposition you will bear some relation to the ball. But something that involves a relation *to the ball* would seem to be a better candidate for a cause of your *kicking the ball* than would some internal state of yours. I don't mean to suggest here that I've established that a relation to a proposition could be the cause of your behavior but an internal state couldn't; I mean to point out only that much of our intentional behavior is itself essentially relational, so it is strange to start by assuming that the causes of this behavior couldn't be relational. To kick the ball is to get in a certain relation with the ball, so one might expect that the causes of kicking the ball should also involve relations to the ball. And, given that this expectation is reasonable, considerations about the proper causes of behavior give no reason to start an investigation of beliefs by assuming that they must, in some sense of the term, be internal states.

It might seem that another reason for thinking that beliefs are internal states is provided by arguments for the so-called *language of thought hypothesis* (see, for example, Fodor 1975). According to this hypothesis, beliefs (and other propositional attitudes) are internal states of subjects that have a sentence-like structure: for example, my belief that snow is white is some state of my brain that has a constituent that represents snow and a constituent that represents whiteness. Since the language of thought hypothesis *includes* the claim that beliefs are internal states of subjects, arguments for the hypothesis should be arguments for this claim. However, the main reasons that the language of thought hypothesis is supposed to be plausible are that there are certain ways in which beliefs appear to be like language.

(i)   Beliefs are systematic. For example, in general, if a subject is capable of believing that a bears relation R to b, then he is capable of believing that b bears relation R to a.
(ii) In principle we have the capacity to think infinitely many thoughts.
(iii) Beliefs are fine-grained. For example, it appears that a subject can believe that a is F without thereby believing that b is F even though a is b.
(iv) Beliefs are truth-apt.

Proponents of the language of thought hypothesis argue that (i)-(iv) would be explained if the hypothesis were true and, hence, that we should accept that it is. But the language of thought hypothesis can explain (i)-(iii) merely in virtue of its claim that *beliefs are structured*; that is to say, the claim that they are also internal states of subjects does no work in the explanation. (The ways in which beliefs seem to be fine-grained and what is required to account for this will be discussed at length later in this chapter and in the next one.) The fact that if I can believe that Farid kicked

Joe then I can believe that Joe kicked Farid is fully explained if the propositions—that is, the things I believe—have something like the syntactic structure of sentences. As we will see in this chapter, the proponents of the language of thought hypothesis are right to think that beliefs are structured. However, they need an *additional* argument for the claim that beliefs are internal states of subjects.

Moreover, it's important to realize the precise role this argument for the language of thought hypothesis is intended to play. The argument claims that, because beliefs are like language in certain ways, they are structured like language. That is, it is *not* an argument that there are internal belief states; rather, it's an argument that beliefs, whatever they turn out to be, are not simple entities but rather are complex entities with something like the syntactic structures we find in natural languages. Of course, if there are no internal belief states at all, then there are no syntactically structured internal belief states. But most philosophers of mind simply assume that there are internal belief states, and the language of thought hypothesis is not meant to address skepticism about whether there even are such things. It is, rather, meant to tell us something about their nature: namely, that they are complex entities with syntactic structure. Indeed, Jerry Fodor is explicit about all of this. He takes it as a matter of common sense that beliefs are essentially states of subjects (see, for example, Fodor 1987, 136) and the arguments for the language of thought hypothesis are not meant to buttress his take on common sense. Fodor (ibid.) also says: "Practically everybody thinks that the objects of intentional states [i.e. propositions] are in some way complex." And, hence, his arguments for the language of thought hypothesis aren't meant to establish that propositions are structured. Rather, the arguments are supposed to establish that "*mental states—and not just their propositional objects—typically have constituent structure*" (ibid.). That there are internal belief states is presupposed by these arguments and, hence, once the distinction between instantial and internal states is made clear, they provide no reason to think that believing involves the latter.

Most contemporary philosophers of mind begin by assuming that beliefs must be internal belief states; indeed the assumption might better be said to occur before they begin, since it is rarely even articulated. And I think that, if we are careful to distinguish instantial states from internal states, the assumption is completely unwarranted. But, besides being unwarranted, it is also fantastically speculative. The existence of internal belief states requires that there be some as yet undiscovered taxonomy of your brain such that elements of this taxonomy can be put in one-to-one correspondence with your beliefs. Indeed, even this understates how speculative the hypothesis is since it assumes that we know what the proper taxonomy of beliefs is. But, of course, there are any number of questions on this side of the problem: for example, is your belief that snow is white and grass is green distinct from your belief that grass is green and snow is white? Is your belief that you'll be alive an hour from now distinct from your belief that you'll be alive sixty minutes from now? Is your belief that smoke causes fire distinct from your belief that fire is caused by smoke? And, of course, there are any number of similar questions.

Now if we did enough poking around in the brain we might find that it has some taxonomy that is close to isomorphic to some natural taxonomy of beliefs and this might settle the hard questions about the latter. But, currently, we haven't the faintest idea how this might go. And, prior to doing a lot of poking around in the brain and discovering at least the beginnings of how it will go, how could we be at all entitled to think that the proper taxonomy of the brain will match up with some taxonomy of beliefs? The view that there are internal states is at best a gesture towards a research strategy and at worst wild empirical speculation.

Daniel Dennett (1977, 1981, 1983, 1987) is one philosopher who has recognized that there's no good reason to believe that the relevant taxonomy exists. But we need to distinguish two questions here. One is whether there actually are internal belief states and, with regard to this question, Dennett is on the side of the angels. But another question is whether the reality of believing depends upon there being internal belief states: that is to say, whether talk about belief just is talk about belief states. If the answer to this second question is *yes*, then the absence of internal belief states will imply that there are no beliefs. And it is answering the second question *yes*, rather than the first, that involves the particularizing fallacy. The fallacy is that talk of belief just is talk of internal states and, for all his clarity on the first question, Dennett hasn't escaped the grip of the particularizing fallacy.

Dennett (1987, 72) thinks that, in the absence of internal belief states, statements about beliefs turn out "true only if we exempt them from a certain familiar standard of literality." It is notoriously difficult to get at exactly what Dennett means (see Byrne 1998 for an attempt), but the point is something like this: it is useful in predicting and explaining people's behavior to talk as if they have beliefs (and desires, etc.) and thus to adopt what Dennett calls *the intentional stance*. Indeed, it's so useful that such talk can even be said to be true. But (in the absence of internal belief states) the truth of a statement about beliefs doesn't consist in anything other than the extreme usefulness of such talk. Whereas there is more to the truth of statements about, say, electrons; these statements are made true by the actual existence of electrons. Most philosophers think that, if there are no internal belief states, there are no beliefs; Dennett thinks that, if there are no internal belief states, then there are beliefs, but their existence is in some way the result of theoretical idealizations and, hence, in some way less robust. But once you see that beliefs are propositions and believing is nothing more than a relation to a proposition, there's no reason to think that the absence of internal belief states would make the existence of beliefs in any way less robust. Dennett considers a case in which three people each come to believe that a Frenchman has committed murder in Trafalgar Square but come to believe it in radically different ways. He says:

> [T]hey all believe that a Frenchman committed murder in Trafalgar square. . . . This is a shared property that is visible, as it were, only from one very limited point of view — the point of view of folk psychology. Ordinary folk psychologists have no difficulty imputing such useful but elusive commonalities to people. (1981, 54–55)

But there is something elusive about the commonality among the three people only if you think that their having the same belief means that they must be in the same internal state. If you recognize the relational nature of belief and don't commit the particularizing fallacy, then it's easy to say what they have in common: they each believe the same proposition.

The mistake in the particularizing fallacy about belief isn't the thought that there are internal belief states. The fallacy is thinking that, *if there aren't*, then the reality of belief is in some way called into question: the thought that a robust realism about belief requires that there be internal belief states. And one reason it's important to see the relational nature of belief is that, in doing so, one sees that the reality of cognition isn't held hostage to the existence of internal belief states. But there is another reason that the relational nature of belief is important. Earlier, we noted that the essential fact about belief is that it is truth-normed; a true instance of belief is, at least in part, a successful instance, and a false one is, at least in part, an unsuccessful one. So long as we are tacitly in the grips of the particularizing fallacy, this way of getting at the truth-normativity of beliefs seems acceptable. If your belief that bees can sting is some internal state of yours, then your belief can count as successful, in part, because *it* is true. But, once we explicitly see that believing is a relation to a proposition, this way of putting the point is obviously wrong.

It can't be your *belief* that bees can sting that is successful. For that belief, just like mine, is a proposition; indeed, they are the very same proposition. And it isn't as if the proposition itself, independently of anyone's believing it, is successful. After all, there are other mental phenomena besides belief and perception that are very plausibly relations to propositions. For example, if we can come to believe what we previously only supposed, then supposing must also be a relation to a proposition. And it is a philosophical commonplace that desire is also a relation to propositions. But, as pointed out in Section 3, belief and perception are the only mental phenomena that are truth-normed; there is nothing inappropriate about making a false supposition for the purpose of *reductio*, nor does the fact that a desire will go unsatisfied imply that it is in anyway inappropriate. If we commit the particularizing fallacy, there seems to be nothing wrong with saying that the belief itself is successful if true, for the supposition that there is a largest prime and the belief that there is will be distinct internal states and, hence, the latter can be flawed even though the former isn't. But, once we recognize the relational nature of belief, given that supposing has the same nature, there is no distinct object involved in your believing that there's a largest prime and your supposing that there is. The difference between the two is that they are different relations to the very same proposition. And one important difference between the relations is that the *belief relation*, unlike the supposing relation, is truth-normed. By mislocating the ontological nature of belief, the particularizing fallacy also mislocates its normativity. Beliefs—that is to say, propositions—are truth-apt, but the belief relation is truth-normed: successful when borne to a true proposition and unsuccessful when borne to a false one. Because believing is truth-normed, the things we believe must be truth-apt and, hence, propositions must be truth-apt.

To believe is to believe *something* and, insofar as you believe something that is true, you believe successfully. One would expect that philosophers, above all, would see these trivialities. But, precisely because these are, in some sense, trivialities, it is easy to overlook them and to fail to see their importance.

7. The possible worlds account of propositions

As we saw in the previous section, the arguments for the language of thought hypothesis do not establish the existence of structured internal belief states but at most establish that propositions are structured. But what is it to say that propositions are structured? The best way to see the answer to this question is to first consider what it would be like for a proposition to be *unstructured*. And, more importantly, the conception of propositions according to which they are unstructured can be seen as arising from the most minimal requirements that their truth-aptness places on them.

If we begin our investigation into belief representation with the obvious fact that propositions are truth-apt, another related obvious fact immediately emerges: whether a particular proposition is true or false does not depend entirely on the nature of the proposition itself; rather, it depends on its nature *and* the way that the world actually is. Besides the way that the world actually is, there are other ways that the world might have been; and, if the world had been some other way, then some beliefs would have had different truth-values than they actually have. If we take (the unfortunately named) possible worlds to be ways that the world might have been, then these observations can be expressed as follows: each proposition must determine a function from possible worlds to truth-values, where the function determined by a proposition takes a possible world to the truth-value of the proposition at that world.[12] But, then, a natural proposal to start with is that a proposition *just is* the function from worlds to truth-values that it determines. Call this view *the possible worlds account* of propositions.

Robert Stalnaker (1984) is one proponent of the possible worlds account.[13] As he recognizes, the account faces a grave difficulty, which he calls *the problem of equivalence*. The possible worlds account implies that if P and Q are *necessarily equivalent* propositions—that is, if they have the same truth-value at any possible world—then they are in fact one and the same proposition: in particular, if P and Q are both necessarily true—that is, true at all possible worlds—they are in fact one and the same proposition. Consider, for example, the proposition that 2 is even and the proposition that ZF is incomplete. As mathematical truths, both are necessarily true; but this means that, on the possible worlds account, each is identical to a constant function from possible worlds to the truth-value true. And, since there is only one such function, this means they are the same proposition. To quote Stalnaker (ibid., 72), "The problem is that the possible worlds analysis seems to have the following paradoxical consequence: if a person believes that P, then if P is necessarily equivalent to Q, he believes that Q." For example, the account seems to imply that anyone who believes that 2 is even also believes that ZF is incomplete, since it implies that the proposition that 2 is even is the proposition that ZF is incomplete. But it seems obvious that lots of people who believe that 2 is even do not believe that ZF is incomplete and, hence, the account seems to conflict with the obvious.

Stalnaker's solution to the problem is to claim that, where P is a necessary truth, sentences of the form *S believes that P* do not express that S bears the belief relation to the proposition that P. Rather, what such a sentence expresses is that S bears the belief relation to the proposition that *the sentence P* expresses a necessary truth. For example, according to Stalnaker, the sentence *Abe believes that ZF is incomplete* does not express that Abe bears the belief relation to the proposition that ZF is incomplete. Rather it expresses that he bears the belief relation to the proposition that *the sentence ZF is incomplete* expresses the one necessarily true proposition. And, in the case where *Abe believes that ZF is incomplete* is false, Abe fails to believe that the sentence *ZF is incomplete* expresses the one necessarily true proposition, because he doesn't know which proposition the sentence expresses. Since it is perfectly possible that the sentence *ZF is incomplete* might not have expressed the proposition that it does, that it does express this proposition is only a contingent truth and, hence, the possible worlds analysis doesn't imply that Abe must believe it, even if he does believe other necessary truths, or, rather, even if he does believe the one necessary truth. Stalnaker's solution is, in short, that a sentence that appears to ascribe a necessarily true mathematical belief in fact ascribes a contingently true metalinguistic belief about the meaning of the relevant mathematical sentence.

While this response does allow Stalnaker to distinguish the belief that ZF is incomplete from the belief that 2 is even, it creates some obvious difficulties for the individuation of other seemingly distinct beliefs. Someone can believe that ZF is incomplete without knowing what the English sentence *ZF is incomplete* means and, hence, without believing that the sentence expresses the necessarily true proposition. And someone can believe that the sentence *ZF is incomplete* expresses a necessary truth while not understanding the sentence and, hence, without believing that ZF is incomplete. So the sentence *Abe believes that ZF is incomplete* doesn't appear to say anything like that Abe believes that the sentence *ZF is incomplete* expresses a necessary truth. Stalnaker (1984, 74) says that his account requires "more complexity and more context dependence than is usually recognized" in the semantics of belief ascription, and he would likely respond to the above worries by appealing to the context-dependence of belief attribution. Until we know how Stalnaker's story about the context-dependence of belief attributions would go, we don't know whether he can meet these objections.

However, I don't think we need to worry about whether there is some plausible description of context-dependence that can save the possible worlds account, for there are other worries in the neighborhood of the problem of equivalence that are fatal.

8. Saying and believing

The problem of equivalence begins with the observation that if the possible worlds account is correct, there is only one necessarily true proposition. That much is undeniable, and it seems equally undeniable that the propositions that ZF is incomplete and that 2 is even are both necessarily true. But this latter claim isn't as straightforward as it appears to be. A true mathematical sentence *P* does bear *some* important relation to a necessarily true proposition, and it's natural to think this necessarily true proposition is simply the proposition that P, but what is the relationship between the sentence *P* and this necessarily true proposition that makes *it* the proposition that P? The answer to this question may seem trivial: what makes it the proposition that P is that the sentence *P expresses* it, where a sentence expresses a proposition when the proposition is what a speaker *says* by uttering the sentence. But the question persists in a slightly different form: why do you wind up saying one proposition as opposed to another by uttering some sentence?

One obvious criterion to apply here is that what someone says by assertively uttering a sentence should generally be something that the utterance *conveys* to his listeners. Of course, what you convey by uttering a sentence can go beyond what you literally say (your listener might have to *get your drift*), and the reverse can also be true: sometimes it's clear that you don't convey what you've literally said (for example, you might be engaging in sarcasm). But it's natural to think that, if *P* expresses some proposition, someone who utters *P* will generally have conveyed the proposition that P to his listeners. This criterion is somewhat vague (we'll have occasion to make it more precise in Chapter 4), but it needn't be any more precise to see that it's not a criterion that Stalnaker can use. For, on Stalnaker's view, someone who utters a mathematical sentence *P* will rarely, if ever, convey the proposition that P. Remember, if *P* is a mathematical sentence, Stalnaker thinks that the proposition that P is the one and only necessarily true proposition. But this means that if your listeners believe any necessary truth, they *already* believe the proposition that P. And, since most, and probably even everyone, will believe *some* necessary truth (for example, the proposition that 1=1, or the proposition that all men are men), your utterance of some mathematical sentence *P* will rarely, if ever, convey to anyone that P. On the possible worlds account the proposition expressed by a mathematical sentence turns out to be a triviality—something that everyone already believes—and, hence, something that you won't generally convey by *any* utterance, including the utterance of a mathematical sentence. But, given this, how is it that, for example, the sentence *ZF is incomplete* comes to express the proposition that ZF is incomplete?

Stalnaker can't answer the question by appealing to what is generally conveyed by someone who utters the sentence, but notice that he also can't appeal to the role the sentence plays in *belief ascriptions*. Besides using sentences to convey information, we also use them to pick out the beliefs that we want to say someone has. In a sentence of the form *S believes that P* the phrase *that P* picks out some proposition that the sentence ascribes to S. Throughout this chapter, I've been calling this proposition *the belief that P* and let's explicitly adopt this terminology.[14] Now it seems that the belief that P just is the proposition that P: that it's what you say when you assertively utter the sentence *P*. For example, in *Abe believes that ZF is incomplete*, the phrase *that ZF is incomplete* refers to a proposition that the belief ascription relates Abe to, and it seems that this—what we're calling *the belief that ZF is incomplete*—is what you say by uttering the sentence *ZF is incomplete* and, hence, is the proposition that ZF is incomplete. But Stalnaker's solution to the problem of equivalence is that the proposition that the belief ascription relates Abe to is some contingent metalinguistic proposition. Hence, the belief that ZF is incomplete can't be the necessarily true proposition that ZF is incomplete. This means that Stalnaker can't explain which proposition a sentence *P* expresses by saying it's just the belief that P—the proposition to which *S believes that P* relates S—but it also points to an essential, and ultimately indefensible, arbitrariness that pervades the possible worlds account.

Notice first that, though I've *stipulated* that the phrase *the belief that P* refers to the proposition the phrase *that P* picks out in *S believes that P*, there's a good argument that even Stalnaker should take this to be how the phrase is used in ordinary language. Stalnaker tries to make the possible worlds account consistent with the intuition that, for example, *Abe believes that 2 is even* can be true while *Abe believes that ZF is incomplete* is false by claiming that, even though the proposition that 2 is even just is the proposition that ZF is incomplete, these aren't the propositions the sentences ascribe to Abe. But just as it seems that two ascriptions of true mathematical belief can, nonetheless, have distinct truth-values, it also seems that true mathematical beliefs can *themselves* be distinct: for example, there would be little point in capturing the intuition that *Abe believes that 2 is even* can be true even though *Abe believes that ZF is incomplete* is false if you wind up having to deny the intuition that *The belief that 2 is even is distinct from the belief that ZF is incomplete* is true. And, while it may be possible to account for the truth of this sentence without assuming that *the belief that P* picks out the same proposition that *that P* does when embedded in a belief ascription, with this assumption Stalnaker's account implies that the sentence is true. But there's a more general point here. Stalnaker, like most philosophers who have focused on our belief talk, only treats belief *ascriptions*. But there are a variety of other kinds of phrases in which *believes* or some cognate appears and, presumably, what's wanted is a unified treatment of all such phrases; for example, *the belief that P* should turn out to refer to whatever it is that S bears the belief relation to when *S believes that P* is true. But some very puzzling aspects of Stalnaker's account come on the heels of this observation.

Suppose that you are the world's leading expert on set theory and logic and Abe's mathematical education stopped at high-school algebra. Intuitively, each of the following sentences is true

(1) *You believe that ZF is incomplete and Abe doesn't believe that ZF is incomplete.*

(2) *You have the belief that ZF is incomplete and Abe doesn't have the belief that ZF is incomplete.*

(3) *You and Abe have different beliefs.*

(4) *You have beliefs about ZF that Abe doesn't have.*

(5) *You have some mathematical beliefs that Abe doesn't have.*

And of course, one could go on and on. Now, so far, I've argued that since Stalnaker wants to respect intuitions about (1), he should also respect intuitions about (2)–(5) and any other relevant sentences that contain *believes* or a cognate. But it isn't just that we have intuitions about *believes* and its cognates. We also have intuitions about what it is people *say* by uttering certain sentences.[15]

Suppose Abe assertively utters the sentence *2 is even* and you assertively utter the sentence *ZF is incomplete*; intuitively, each of the following is true:

(6) *Your utterance expresses the proposition that ZF is incomplete and Abe's doesn't.*

(7) *Your utterance and Abe's express different propositions.*

(8) *Neither you nor Abe has expressed every mathematical proposition.*

(9) *You have said that ZF is incomplete and Abe hasn't.*

(10) *You and Abe have not said the same thing.*

(11) *Neither you nor Abe has said every mathematical truth.*

Stalnaker thinks that (6), (7), and (8) are false and, assuming that what someone says by uttering a sentence is just the proposition his utterance expresses, he should also say that (9), (10), and (11) are false. But what motivation could there be for respecting intuitions about sentences containing *believes* while denying intuitions about sentences that contain terms like *expresses* and *says*? Stalnaker gives an object-language argument that the proposition that ZF is incomplete and the proposition that 2 is even are identical and then attempts to preserve the relevant intuitions about what people do and don't believe by giving a metalanguage analysis of belief ascriptions. But, if proceeding in this way makes sense, so would beginning with belief: that is, he equally well could have given an object-language argument that anyone who believes any necessary truth believes that ZF is incomplete and then given a metalinguistic defense of our intuitions about what propositions are and aren't expressed by utterances. It's not uncommon for philosophers to suppose that what one says by uttering a sentence differs from the proposition it expresses when embedded in belief ascriptions or other linguistic contexts (see Dummett 1981a, 446–47 and 1981b, 572–73; Evans [1979] 1985, 181–82, 199–208, and

[1982] 1995, 73–76; and Stanley 1997, 574–78). But the general point here is that our intuitions about (i) what proposition a sentence expresses, (ii) what someone says by uttering the sentence, (iii) what belief the sentence expresses, and (iv) what someone believes when the sentence can be used to truly ascribe a belief to him are all going to be the same; and any argument against one of these intuitions is almost certain to provide an equally good argument against all the others. So it's hard to see how there could be any non-arbitrary way to decide when to wheel in the object-language argument and when to wheel in the metalinguistic defense.

The proponent of the possible worlds account can't avoid all of its counter-intuitive consequences by drawing a distinction between the proposition that P and the belief that P. And, even if he draws the distinction to avoid some of them, there will be no principled way to decide whether to preserve intuitions about what we say or what we believe. I think the way in which any decision on the matter would be completely arbitrary shows that we really don't have a grasp on what it would mean to claim that the proposition that P is distinct from the belief that P. But recall that we began by asking, on the possible worlds account, what could make it the case that a mathematical sentence expresses the one necessarily true proposition? And we've seen that it can't be answered in terms of the information conveyed by a mathematical sentence or the role it plays in belief ascriptions. There is, however, one other answer available, but its availability completely undermines the account.

The only way for the proponent of the possible worlds account to explain how mathematical sentences come to express the propositions they do will be by appealing to the *semantic structure* of mathematical sentences. Since *2* refers to 2, *is even* attributes the property of being even, and 2 has the property of being even in every possible world, the sentence expresses a necessary truth. But, given that we need 2 and the property of being even to determine that *2 is even* expresses a necessarily true proposition, why shouldn't we reject the possible worlds account and take the proposition that 2 is even to be a complex entity consisting of a part that determines 2 and a part that determines the property of being even in such a way as to ascribe the property of being even to 2? Of course it's possible to distinguish between what's *pre-semantic* and what's *semantic*: that is, about what goes into determining which proposition a sentence expresses and what goes into the proposition itself. But, given that *not* drawing such a distinction provides an easy solution to the problem of equivalence, what point is there in drawing it? Restricting our attention to propositions that ascribe a property to an object, we can represent the proposition that a is F by the ordered pair

<*a*, *F-ness*>,

where *a* is something that determines a and *F-ness* something that determines F-ness. The proposition is true just in case the thing determined by the first member of the ordered pair has the property determined by the second member.[16] Call this the **structured account** of propositions.[17]

One of Stalnaker's main motivations for the possible worlds account is that it obviates the need for explaining how our beliefs relate us to the objects they are intuitively about. Since a function from possible worlds to truth-values won't determine any such object, if this is what propositions turn out to be, we don't need to account for the way belief relates us to such objects. But, be that as it may, we will still need an account of how *language* relates us to such objects. As Stalnaker (1984, 3) notes, on the possible worlds account "propositions lack structure of a kind that reflects the semantic structure of the sentences that express them." But, as the fact that mathematical truths are necessarily true brings out, we will still need some account of how it is that sentences have such semantic structure and, in part, this will involve explaining how words relate us to the objects and properties they stand for. And, given that we need such an explanation in the case of language, it is difficult to see how we gain anything by eliminating the need in the case of belief. Indeed, if belief turns out to be as coarse-grained as the possible world account suggests, it's difficult to see how the semantics of language could be as fine-grained as it is.

The structured account of propositions explains the truth-aptness of propositions by adverting to the objects and properties determined by their constituents. Unlike the possible worlds account, it avoids the problem of equivalence without severing the link between saying and believing. Apparently different necessary propositions can be distinguished by their different constituents, and when someone assertively utters the sentence *2 is even* what he says is what he believes when he believes that 2 is even.[18] Taking structured propositions to be the things that we believe gives a plausible account of belief representation. However, structured propositions are also crucial to a proper understanding of perceptual representation.

9. Perceptual representation

Perception, like belief, is truth-normed and, hence, truth-apt. However, in the case of belief, it is the things that we believe—namely, propositions—that are the bearers of truth-value. Hence, there is a disanalogy between perception and belief, since it's clear that the things that we perceive aren't the bearers of truth-values: when you look at a table what you perceive is the table; but, if your perception is non-veridical, it isn't the table that's false. The qualia freak assumes that there is some state of the subject—namely, *his experience*—that bears the truth-value and that intrinsic features of this state figure into the individuation of perceptions. In Chapter 1 I argued that the latter claim is false, but I also want to argue that the former claim is false as well: a perception isn't a state of a subject. Rather, like belief, perception is a relation between subjects and propositions.

If we suppose that a perception is a state of the perceiver and that this state bears the truth-value, then we have a question: how could this state come to bear a truth-value? It seems to me that we know of only one answer to this question: namely, that the state comes to have a truth-value by being related to a proposition that is the primary bearer of the truth-value. Beliefs have truth-values, but they have truth-values simply by being propositions, and sentences have truth-values by expressing propositions. Since the only way that we know of that something can come to bear a truth-value is directly by being a proposition or derivatively by being related to one, we must conclude that perceptions have truth-values in one of these ways. And, since a perception is not a proposition, it can have a truth-value only derivatively by being related to one. Indeed, Sellars's ([1956] 1997) attack on *the myth of the given* can be seen as imposing the requirement that perceptions relate individuals to propositions. Many of our beliefs are based on our perceptions. If perception relates subjects to propositions, then this process is no more mysterious than the process of beliefs leading us to other beliefs. However, if perception isn't a relation to a proposition, it is hard to see how there could be inferential relations between perception and belief.

Still, many philosophers will find the claim that perception is a relation to a proposition fantastic. After all, propositions are what sentences express and, as we have seen, they have a kind of syntactic structure that mirrors (or is mirrored by) the syntactic structure of sentences. But, the line of argument continues, it's obvious that nothing about perception has this kind of syntactic structure and, in particular, visual perception is clearly more pictorial than it is sentential. Such philosophers will likely have related worries about my earlier claim that perception is truth-apt: that perceptions are capable of being true or false. While it's true that truth is a species of accuracy, they will say, truth is a *special kind of accuracy*: a kind that applies only to propositions and, derivatively, to things like sentences that express propositions. Since perceptions are clearly not sentential but rather are pictorial, they will insist, truth and falsity cannot be applied to them. Rather, it is the more general notions of accuracy and inaccuracy that apply to perception. These doubts about the propositional nature of perception depend upon an alleged disanalogy between propositions and perceptions, but the analogies that are meant to reveal the disanalogy—between propositions and sentences, on the one hand, and between perceptions and pictures, on the other—cannot sustain the doubts. The first analogy turns out to be too thin, whereas the second is simply mistaken.

To begin with the first, in what way are propositions analogous to sentences? Well, the common answer is that, like sentences, propositions have a syntactic structure. For example, as we've seen, the proposition that 2 is even contains something that determines 2 and something that determines evenness; but, on the way of cashing out the analogy we're considering, it also has a structure that determines that the property of evenness is being *ascribed* to 2. So the syntactic structure of the proposition explains why it ascribes evenness to 2; and, for example, the syntactic structure of the proposition that Farid kicked Joe determines that it is Farid who (according to the proposition) kicked Joe rather than the other way around. In general something about propositions determines particulars, properties, relations, etc., and it is the syntactic structure of the proposition that—like the syntactic structure of sentences—determines the way these are related. On the surface, this seems all very clear, but one doesn't have to look too deep before it gets murky.

The way in which sentences are syntactically structured is pretty familiar. For example, in simple English subject-predicate sentences, the subject comes before the predicate. Since English is read left to right, in written English a word is before another when it is to the left of it, whereas in spoken English a word is before another when it is spoken temporally before it. So, in general, natural-language syntactic relations are *realized* by temporal relations in spoken language and spatial relations in written language. But, if syntactic relations between *2* and *evenness* are supposed to explain why the proposition that 2 is even ascribes evenness to 2, there is a question of what realizes these syntactic relations in the proposition.

We have been representing the proposition that 2 is even—the proposition whose structure determines that evenness is ascribed to 2—as <*2*, *evenness*>. That is to say, we have been using the same notation used to represent ordered pairs to represent simple object-property propositions, where the property determined by the property-determining thing that would be the second member of the pair is ascribed to the object determined by the object-determining thing that would be the first member of the pair. But propositions are not ordered pairs, and the fact that it is convenient to use this notation to represent them gives no more reason to think they are ordered pairs than the fact that it is convenient for a coach to represent the opposing players by *0* means that the opposing quarterback is the number 0. If there really are propositions (and if there aren't we are obviously making a big mistake talking about them) and if they really are structured, then the question of what their structures consist in is a substantive one. And, so long as we don't confuse propositions with the sentences that we use to express them or the notation we use to represent them, it is apparent that the relations that obtain between the constituents of propositions can be nothing like the well-understood relations of temporal and spatial priority that realize the syntactic structure of sentences.

But, wait, here's an intriguing thought: maybe what distinguishes the syntactic structure of sentences from that of propositions is that in the latter case this structure is *not* realized by any other structure. What gives a sentence its syntactic structure is the spatial or temporal structure of its tokens, but the syntactic structure of a proposition is simply a brute fact about it not explicable in terms of, or in any way parasitic on, any other kind of structure. Now, something like this may be possible, but it's hard to know what to make of it. How are we to understand something's having parts that bear syntactic relations to one another but *not* in virtue of bearing some other relation to one another? What exactly are these *sui generis* syntactic relations? Think of it this way: a token of a spoken-language word consists of certain sounds in a certain order; and the *phonological* structure of some word depends entirely on the sounds that compose a token utterance of the word and the temporal ordering of those sounds. Now, the basic units of phonology needn't be sounds (for example, Perlmutter (1992) gives a phonology for American Sign Language) and the ordering that determines phonological structure needn't be temporal (if the phonology of written language is distinct from, rather than parasitic on, the phonology of spoken language, it will be spatial rather than temporal), but it doesn't seem to make sense to talk of phonological structures that are brute: ones that don't depend on being realized in some other kind of structure. At a minimum, a lot would need to be said to show how something like this could be so in the case of phonological structure. And the same is true for syntactic structure; we can only understand something's having either kind of sructure if it's realized in some other well-understood structure and, if the structure of propositions is syntactic, one needs either to say what kind of structure realizes it or to explain how it could exist without any realization.[19]

But, with this said, one might think that the phenomenon of syntactic ambiguity shows that the syntactic structure of language goes beyond its spatial or temporal realization and, hence, that we do have a grip on how something can have a syntactic structure that isn't realized in some other structure. For example, the sentence **Visiting relatives can be boring** is syntactically ambiguous; **Visiting relatives** might be a verb phrase (in which case *the activity* of visiting one's relatives is what can be boring) or it might be a noun phrase (in which case *people* who are one's visiting relatives are what can be boring). So in cases of syntactic ambiguity we have syntactical differences without any corresponding differences in the realizing structure; and why aren't such cases straightforward examples of unrealized syntactic relations?

Well, the reason they aren't is that the existence of syntactic differences that cannot be accounted for by differences in realizing structure is not the same thing as the existence of unrealized syntactic structure. In fact, quite the opposite is true: cases of syntactic ambiguity are cases in which two distinct syntactic structures are *realized* in a single temporal or spatial structure—it's the written or spoken realization that's ambiguous—and this means that the phenomenon requires that *there be* a written or spoken realization. So rather than showing that there can be unrealized syntax, the phenomenon of syntactic ambiguity *depends* upon the syntax being realized in some structure.

But, given that we haven't the slightest clue as to what the structure of propositions really consists in, it is a mistake to think that we can appeal to the structure of a proposition in order to explain, for example, why the proposition that 2 is even ascribes the property of evenness to 2.[20] Our talk of the structure of the proposition is no more than the recognition that there must be *something* about it that determines that the property is ascribed to the object; it is not even a first stab at an explanation of what that something is. And indeed the talk of structure is itself metaphorical, since we have no idea of a kind of structure—be it temporal, spatial, or set-theoretic—that by itself ascribes a property to an object. But once the thinness of the metaphor at the root of the analogy between sentences and propositions is recognized—once we recognize that all we can say by way of cashing out the metaphor is that the "structure" that the proposition in which 2 is even places *2* and *evenness* is such that the proposition ascribes evenness to 2—perception looks to be propositional. After all, perception clearly does ascribe properties to objects—things perceptually appear to be certain ways—and, given that talk of the structure of simple object-property propositions is merely a way to redescribe property ascriptions, perception seems to be a propositional relation *par excellence.*

I have been speaking as if, as in the case of the syntax of natural language, there must be some relations that realize the analogous syntax of propositions. But it may be that this assumption itself results from reading features of the sentences we use to express propositions into the propositions themselves. Perhaps there is no relation distinct from property ascription in virtue of which the proposition that 2 is even ascribes evenness to 2. But this is just to say that *all there is* to the so-called structure of the proposition is that it ascribes the property determined by *evenness* to the thing determined by *2*. And, if this is so, since perception does ascribe properties to objects, perception is certainly propositional. At a minimum, we don't know anything about the structure of propositions except that it involves relations in virtue of which properties and relations are ascribed to objects and groups of objects. In this case, the only thing we know about propositions indicates that perception is propositional. At a maximum, there are no relations between the constituents of propositions that realize the syntactic-like relations between the constituents of propositions: all there is, for example, to the structure of the proposition that 2 is even is that the property is ascribed to the object. In this case, perception is certainly propositional.

It is important to recognize that the reason that I think that perception is a relation to a proposition is *not* that I have some well-worked out conception of what a proposition is. On the contrary, it seems to me that the difficulty here is realizing how little we really know about propositions and their so-called structure. Because we have a familiar notation that to some extent represents them and the relations that obtain between their constituents, and because we can say a lot about, to take one example, the semantics of language, without knowing their nature or what these relations are, it is tempting to think that they are familiar entities, as familiar as the notation we use to represent them. But once we realize that the familiarity of the notation obscures a complete lack of familiarity with what it represents—that the analogy between sentences and propositions isn't really even informative enough to deserve to be called an analogy—perception seems to have one feature that makes something a proposition: namely, it ascribes properties to objects.

And likewise for the claim that there is a distinction between the accuracy and inaccuracy of perception and the truth and falsity of belief. Once we see how thin a metaphor our talk of propositional structure is, it is hard to see in what sense truth is a special kind of accuracy. In ordinary talk there is little to distinguish truth from accuracy. We speak of representations as being more accurate or less accurate, but we also speak of them as being more true or less true. It does no more violence to ordinary usage to call a sentence *accurate* than it does to call it *true*, nor is ordinary usage more abused when pictures are described as truly representing their subjects rather than accurately representing them.

But what of the other analogy that seems to make it implausible that perception involves a relation to a proposition? Granted that the sense in which propositions are sentence-like is thin enough that perception looks propositional, isn't there something pictorial about perception that casts doubt on the idea that it could be like belief? Here, rather than suffering from thinness, the metaphor is simply confused. It's true that *seeing* a flower can be very much like *seeing* a picture of a flower; but this is a reason to think that the picture and the flower are similar rather than a reason for thinking that seeing is like a picture. *Petting* a dog can be very much like *petting* a cat, but no one would infer from this that petting is like a cat.

Of course, as pointed out in the beginning of this section, we see tables and chairs, not propositions. And, even though we can talk of seeing *that* the tomato is red or seeing *that* the table isn't level—that is, even though sometimes perceptual verbs take *that*-clauses, which name propositions, as their objects—in such cases one still can't be said to *see* the proposition; seeing that the tomato is red involves seeing the tomato, not the proposition that it's red. Moreover, most of the time that a perceptual verb takes a *that*-clause, the *that*-clause *doesn't* pick out a proposition that the subject is, to introduce a phrase, *perceptually related to*, the one that gives the representational content of his perception. Consider sentences like *I see that you're tired, You can see he's no snappy dresser, She's sees that there's no food in the refrigerator*, and so on *ad infinitum*. It's not at all plausible that the properties of being tired, not being a snappy dresser, and not containing food are represented in perception. Indeed, in Chapter 5 we'll see that a phrase of the form *that P* almost never picks out a proposition that someone is perceptually related to. But these linguistic facts say nothing about whether perception involves a relation to a proposition; just as the fact that the sentence **Bob threw the ball** doesn't contain any reference to Bob's arm or hand doesn't show that arms or hands aren't essential to the throwing relation. It's uncontroversial that perception involves relations to representational content and, hence, it should be uncontroversial that it involves relations to propositions. And, insofar as these propositions ascribe properties to objects, perception also involves a relation to objects; to *see some object* is for that object to be represented as being some way by your visual experience: that is, it is for some proposition you are *visually related to* to ascribe a property to that object.

However, if belief and perception are both truth-normed relations to propositions, there is a question of why it is objects that are seen, while it is propositions that are believed. But there is a ready answer to this question. Unlike belief, perception—besides being truth-normed, as belief is—seems to be what we might call *object-detecting*-normed. The function of perception isn't merely to relate us to true propositions; it is also to detect objects in the perceiver's environment. If you see something as having some property it doesn't have, then your perception is inaccurate and, hence, flawed; but it's also true that if you fail to see something right before your eyes, something has gone wrong with your perception. Perception isn't just supposed to relate us to true propositions; it is also supposed to relate us to propositions that have constituents that determine some of the things in our immediate environment. When you don't see an object, you aren't thereby perceptually related to a false proposition; nonetheless, in some cases failure to see an object counts as perceptual failure. Because a crucial function of perception is object-detection, it is objects that we talk of as being perceived. But, because another function of perception is to represent those objects accurately, perception must be a relation to a proposition.

10. Perception and the particularizing fallacy

But, once we acknowledge that perception relates subjects to propositions, what reason do we have to think that the relation is mediated by some state of the subject? One reason might be that we seem to attribute causal powers to perceptions. However, we have already looked at and rejected this as a reason for thinking that beliefs must be states of subjects, and these same grounds for rejecting it apply to perception.

I think many will respond that the assumption that perceptions are states of subjects is on a par with the assumption that when someone has a belief there's something that he believes. That is to say, both are ordinary, commonsense views. After all, we do talk of our experiences, and what are experiences if not perceptual states of subjects? But the notion that an experience is some state of the subject is, as in the case of belief, a result of the particularizing fallacy. An experience is a relation—an interaction between a subject and the world—not a particular that mediates that relation. The experience of being a bank teller isn't some mental state shared by all and only bank tellers; rather, to have had a bank teller's experience is to have done and lived through the things that bank tellers do and live through. And visual experiences are likewise experiences of seeing. The way in which philosophers have hijacked the term *experience* to refer to alleged perceptual intermediaries makes the qualia freak's view seem as if it simply derives from common sense. After all, it *is* a matter of common sense that people have experiences. But, of course, it *isn't* at all a matter of common sense that people have *experiences* in the sense of the term that the qualia freak uses. It is not a matter of common sense that there are perceptual intermediaries, let alone that experiences are perceptual intermediaries. And the most plausible view is that perception—like belief—is a relation between a subject and a proposition.

Of course there are differences between perception and belief. In Chapter 1 we saw that it's plausible that perceptual contents are internally determined, whereas most belief contents aren't. And, as pointed out in the previous section, perception, unlike belief, is object-detecting-normed. In Chapter 5, I will argue that the propositions that belief relates us to are typically unavailable in perception. But there is no reason to think that perception isn't like belief in being a relation between subjects and propositions. This is the best explanation of the fact that perception is truth-normed and the only explanation of how many of our beliefs can derive from perception.

That experiences are not particulars has bearing on the notion of subjective difference that is central to much of the discussion in Chapter 1. Subjective differences are differences in how things seem to subjects, and the qualia freak tries to explain these differences by appealing to differences in how the experiences of those subjects seem to them. Now, it's certainly true that two visual experiences can seem different; your experience of a red thing and your experience of an otherwise identical blue thing will seem different to you. But this is not to say that the experiences are particulars that seem different to you. The experiences are instantiations of a relation between you and the object seen; they are seeing events. And these events seem different to you because the objects seen seem different to you. Touching a hot object will seem different than touching a cold object; but, of course, this isn't to say that there are objects called *touches* that seem hot and cold to you. The touches are touching events, and they seem different to you because the object touched seems hot in the one case and cold in the other.

11. Intentionality revisited

The fact that perception is a relation between subjects and propositions also indicates what's wrong with the argument from illusion. Perception relates subjects to propositions that ascribe properties to objects: when you look at a ripe tomato, it perceptually seems to have certain properties, and this is best explained by the fact that you are related to a proposition that ascribes these properties to the tomato. But perceptual representation doesn't merely ascribe properties to the objects one sees; it also ascribes properties to the bit of the world that is before your eyes. Perception relates a subject to propositions that there are objects with such-and-such qualities and bearing such-and-such relations to each other in the place before his eyes. The obvious way to account for this is to say that, besides relating subjects to propositions that the objects seen seem to have such-and-such properties, it also relates subjects to existential propositions: propositions that there are such-and-such things with such-and-such properties and bearing such-and-such relations to each other. When Eloise hallucinates a brown and green object, there is no brown and green object—intentional or otherwise—that she sees. Rather, to say that Eloise is seeing something brown and green is to say that her perception relates her to an existential proposition that there is an object that is brown and green (and has whatever other properties the thing she seems to see seems to have) before her.[21]

So, if we take perception to be a relation between subjects and propositions, we needn't invoke intentional objects to explain nonveridical perception. But the fact that belief, like perception, is a relation to structured propositions yields a solution to the puzzles of intentionality which is a more-or-less well-known application of ideas from Frege's "On Sense and Reference."

Recall the first puzzle of intentionality considered in Section 1:

Suppose I come to believe that there is an Irish pub in Philadelphia without believing of any particular Irish pub that it is in Philadelphia. Then it seems that my belief is about an Irish pub even though there is no particular Irish pub that it is about. So apparently a belief can stand in the aboutness relation to a thing of a certain kind (in this case an Irish pub) without there being any particular thing of that kind to which it is related.

But to believe that there is an Irish pub in Philadelphia is to bear the belief relation to the existential proposition that there is an Irish pub in Philadelphia. This proposition has no particular Irish pub as a constituent, nor does it have any constituent that serves to pick out some Irish pub as the object of my belief. So my belief needn't relate me to any particular Irish pub. Rather, to say that my belief is about an Irish pub is to say that my belief is the existential proposition that there is an Irish pub in Philadelphia. This proposition will contain things that determine the property of being an Irish pub, the property of being in Philadelphia, and a constituent corresponding to the existential quantifier.

Recall the second puzzle of intentionality considered in Section 1:

> Suppose I come to believe that *the Irish pub at 1214 Sansom Street* is a good pub. In this case my belief does seem to be about a particular Irish pub. But suppose that, unbeknownst to me, this is the pub owned by the waterslide champion of Wildwood. Since this is not known to me, my belief isn't about the pub owned by the waterslide champion of Wildwood even though it *is* about the pub at 1214 Sansom Street, and that is the pub owned by the waterslide champion of Wildwood.

The proposition that the Irish pub at 1214 Sansom Street is a good pub does relate me to an Irish pub. It relates me to the Irish pub at 1214 Sansom Street because the property of being the Irish pub at 1214 Sansom Street is the constituent of the proposition that determines the thing that is relevant to the belief's truth-value: that thing (if such there be) *is* the unique thing that has the property, and the belief is true if that thing is indeed a good pub.[22] But, since the Irish pub at 1214 Sansom Street *just is* the pub owned by the waterslide champion of Wildwood, my belief does relate me to the pub owned by the waterslide champion of Wildwood. Hence, in any sense in which my belief relates me to the Irish pub at 1214 Sansom Street, it relates me to the pub owned by the waterslide champion of Wildwood. So to say that my belief is *about* the Irish pub at 1214 Sansom Street, but not *about* the pub owned by the waterslide champion of Wildwood, can only be to say that the property of being the Irish pub at 1214 Sansom Street picks out the object of the belief, whereas the property of being owned by the waterslide champion of Wildwood doesn't. If, as some proponents of the view that mental representation has intentionality claim, there is a sense of ***about*** according to which ***My belief is about the Irish pub at 1214 Sansom Street*** is true, but ***My belief is about the pub owned by the waterslide champion of Wildwood*** is false, then this sense of ***about*** must pick out the properties that determine a belief's object, rather than the object itself.

Recall the final puzzle of intentionality considered in Section 1:

> I might come to believe that *the Irish pub at 1214 Sansom Street* is good, even though there never have existed and never will exist any Irish pubs at that address. In this case

my belief is about the Irish Pub at 1214 Sansom Street even though no such Irish pub ever exists.

If no such Irish pub ever exists, then my belief can't relate me to any such Irish pubs. So to say that my belief that the Irish pub at 1214 Sansom Street is good is about the Irish pub at 1214 Sansom Street must be to say that my belief's object (if such there be) is the unique thing that has the property of being the Irish pub at 1214 Sansom Street. Again, this sense of *about* must pick out the properties that determine the belief's object, rather than the belief's object itself.[23]

12. The Fregean/Millian distinction
and the what/how distinction

So far we have seen that belief and perception relate subjects to propositions and that a proposition is a structured entity that contains things that determine which object it represents and which properties that object is represented as having. Once again, restricting our attention to propositions that ascribe a property to an object, we can represent the proposition that a is F by the ordered pair

<*a*, *F-ness*>,

where *a* is something that determines a, *F-ness* something that determines F-ness, and the proposition ascribes the property determined by the second member of the ordered pair to the object determined by the first member. But what are the constituents of propositions? The philosophical terrain is normally divided into two positions: Millianism and Fregeanism. However, I want to argue that, contrary to prevailing philosophical opinion, the dispute between Fregeans and Millians *is not a dispute about any fundamental issues in the philosophy of mind*. And, unfortunately, the Fregean/Millian distinction has obscured another distinction, a distinction between two views that do differ on fundamental issues in the philosophy of mind. This other distinction involves the distinction between *what a belief or perception represents* and *how it represents*—the *what/how* distinction—that was mentioned at the beginning of Chapter 1. But what is the Fregean/Millian distinction, and in what way does it differ from the what/how distinction?

Some of the constituents of a proposition must determine objects and properties and, according to Millianism, the constituents of a proposition determine objects and properties by *being* the relevant object or property: *a* just is a, and *F-ness* just is F-ness. But, according to Fregeanism, the constituents of propositions aren't simply the objects and properties that they determine. The constituents of propositions determine objects and properties by being *modes of presentation* of them.

Recall that at the beginning of Chapter 1 I gave the following account of the Fregean/Millian debate:

There is a well-known philosophical problem called *Frege's puzzle.* One way to put the problem is roughly as follows. It seems as if the belief that Superman flies and the belief that Clark Kent flies must be different beliefs. After all, Lex Luthor has the former but not the latter. Yet the belief that Superman flies seems to represent that a certain individual flies; and, since Superman is Clark Kent, the belief that Clark Kent flies seems to represent that the very same individual flies. So Frege's puzzle presents a case in which there seems to be a difference between two beliefs that can't be a difference in what they represent. Most philosophers conclude that there must be more to beliefs than *what* they represent; beliefs must also be individuated by *how* they represent. Though the belief that Superman flies and the belief that Clark Kent flies both represent that the same individual flies, they differ in their *mode of presentation* of that individual.

Since a belief is the thing believed—the proposition to which the subject bears the belief relation—the distinction between what a belief represents and how it represents is the distinction between what a proposition represents and how it represents. And, hence, the lesson that I have claimed that most philosophers draw from Frege's puzzle would seem to be that propositions must be individuated by how they represent: that they must contain modes of presentation of the things that they represent. Given this, it would be natural to assume that the what/how distinction marks off the Millian/Fregean distinction: that to hold that propositions are individuated only by what they represent is to be a Millian about belief, and to hold that they must also be individuated by how they represent is to be a Fregean.

As natural as this assumption would be, the Millian/Fregean distinction in fact cuts across the what/how distinction. In order to see this, we need to divide each of the Millian and Fregean views into two. Once each view is divided, it will emerge that one of the Fregean positions has much in common with one of the Millian positions and that the other Fregean position has much in common with the other Millian position. We will then be in a position to see why the Fregean/Millian distinction cuts across the what/how distinction and why the latter distinction marks a far more important division on the nature of the mind than the former does.

13. Descriptive Fregeanism and non-descriptive Fregeanism

It seems that Lex Luthor believes that Superman flies but doesn't believe that Clark Kent flies, and Fregeans draw the conclusion that the proposition that Superman flies must be distinct from the proposition that Clark Kent flies.[24] However, since Superman is Clark Kent, the two beliefs cannot be distinguished by the individual that each represents as flying. Hence, the Fregean holds that the beliefs must be distinguished by their mode of presentation of that individual. But there are two different Fregean proposals for exactly what a mode of presentation is.

The naive reading of Frege's "On Sense and Reference" (1892) suggests that a mode of presentation of an object is something like the content of a description that the object uniquely satisfies: that is to say, it is a property (or collection of properties) that the object uniquely satisfies. So the mode of presentation of Superman in the proposition that Superman flies will be something like the property of being the super-powered protector of Metropolis, and the mode of presentation of Superman in the proposition that Clark Kent flies will be something like the property of being the bespectacled *Daily Planet* reporter. Call this view *descriptive Fregeanism.*[25]

Of course, the Fregean may wish to say that, rather than containing the property of F-ness, the proposition that the G is F contains some mode of presentation of F-ness.[26] For, just as it's possible not to know that two names co-refer, it's also possible not to know that two predicates pick out the same property. However, the discussion will be unnecessarily complicated if modes of presentation of properties are included. So, for now, let's ignore this complication and represent the descriptive Fregean's proposal for the proposition that a is F as

<[G-ness], F-ness>,

where G-ness is the mode of presentation of a, and the brackets indicate that the unique thing that has G-ness, rather than G-ness itself, is the object of the proposition. Call a proposition whose first term is [G-ness] for some property G-ness a *descriptive proposition.*

Now, there are well-known reasons to think that a mode of presentation can't be anything like the content of a definite description. After all, if the proposition that Clark Kent flies is the proposition that the bespectacled *Daily Planet* reporter flies, then, if Jimmy Olsen rather than Clark Kent were the bespectacled *Daily Planet* reporter, the proposition that Clark Kent flies would represent Jimmy Olsen as flying rather than Clark Kent as flying; and, if no one at the *Daily Planet* wore glasses, the proposition that Clark Kent flies wouldn't represent any particular person as flying. However, even in counterfactual circumstances in which Clark Kent isn't the bespectacled *Daily Planet* reporter, the belief that Clark Kent flies should turn out to be about Clark Kent (see Kripke [1972] 1980). These sorts of considerations have led many philosophers to abandon descriptive Fregeanism and to accept in its place what I will call *non-descriptive Fregeanism.*

According to non-descriptive Fregeanism, the modes of presentation that individuate the belief that Superman flies from the belief that Clark Kent flies aren't collections of properties that Superman uniquely satisfies. Modes of presentation do pick out individuals, but they don't do so by uniquely, as it were, describing the individual. There are various proposals for what non-descriptive modes of presentation are. Sometimes they are taken to be linguistic or quasi-linguistic entities (see, for example, Richard 1990), and sometimes they are taken to be abilities to discriminate (see, for example, Evans [1982] 1995).[27] Regardless of the exact nature of non-descriptive modes of presentation, each determines an individual, but not by means of properties that the individual uniquely satisfies. Of course, it is likely that the non-descriptive Fregean needs to say that, rather than containing the property of F-ness, the proposition that the G is F contains some non-descriptive mode of presentation of F-ness. However, as in the case of descriptive Fregeanism, let's ignore this complication for expositional ease. So, if we let *Superman* stand for the non-descriptive mode of presentation of Superman associated with the name **Superman**, and likewise for other names, then according to the non-descriptive Fregean, the proposition that Superman flies should be represented as

<*Superman*, flying>.[28]

14. Guise Millianism and pure Millianism

The Millian holds that although it seems as if Lex believes that Clark Kent flies but doesn't believe that Superman flies, in fact he does believe both. According to the Millian, the proposition that Superman flies attributes the property of flying to Superman, but there is no mode of presentation (descriptive or non-descriptive) that is a component of the proposition. Hence, according to the Millian, the proposition that Superman flies should be represented as

<Superman (the individual), flying>

and the proposition that Clark Kent flies should be represented as

<Clark Kent (the individual), flying>.

Call a proposition whose first term is an object rather than a (descriptive or non-descriptive) mode of presentation of an object a *singular proposition*. Since Superman is Clark Kent, the two singular propositions are in fact one and the same; hence, since Lex believes the first, he must believe the second.

However, the Millian must still account for why it seems that the two propositions are distinct: that is to say, why it seems that Lex believes that Superman flies but doesn't believe that Clark Kent flies. And contemporary Millians use non-descriptive modes of presentation to account for this. According to Nathan Salmon (1986), although non-descriptive modes of presentation aren't part of the proposition believed, the belief relation between individuals and propositions is mediated by them. On Salmon's view, non-descriptive modes of presentation are quasi-linguistic entities. And Salmon claims that the reason it seems wrong to say that Lex believes that Clark Kent flies is that the sentence suggests to listeners that Lex bears the belief relation to the proposition that Clark Kent flies via a mode of presentation of that proposition that includes the mode of presentation *Clark Kent*. But, on Salmon's view, while Lex does bear the belief relation to that proposition, he doesn't bear it via the mode of presentation that includes *Clark Kent* — rather, he bears it via the mode of presentation that includes **Superman** — and, hence, the belief ascription *Lex believes that Clark Kent flies* is misleading. So, although Salmon does not believe that non-descriptive modes of presentation are part of the proposition believed, he does hold that they are an essential part of the ontology of belief: the belief relation between subjects and propositions is mediated by non-descriptive modes of presentation. Let's call his view *guise Millianism*.

However, the Millian needn't accept that modes of presentation are an essential part of the belief relation.[29] One might hold that Salmon is right that the proposition that Superman flies merely ascribes the property of flying to Superman, but wrong that the belief relation between subjects and propositions is mediated by modes of presentation. Rather, another form of Millianism would claim that belief involves only subjects and the propositions they believe. Let's call this view *pure Millianism*.[30]

So we have four positions: descriptive Fregeanism, non-descriptive Fregeanism, guise Millianism, and pure Millianism. And the traditional way of dividing the philosophical terrain places the two Fregean positions on one side and the two Millian positions on the other.

Traditional Division

| descriptive Fregeanism | pure Millianism |
| non-descriptive Fregeanism | guise Millianism |

However, we are now in a position to see that the following, different way of dividing the terrain marks a very important distinction in the philosophy of mind.

New Division

| descriptive Fregeanism | non-descriptive Fregeanism |
| pure Millianism | guise Millianism |

There is a natural and obvious reason to group non-descriptive Fregeanism and guise Millianism together. For, though the views differ on the nature of propositions (since the former holds that modes of presentation are constituents of the things we believe, but the latter doesn't), they agree that non-descriptive modes of presentation are essential to the belief relation. On non-descriptive Fregeanism the non-descriptive modes of presentation enter into the belief relation by being part of the proposition, while on guise Millianism they mediate the belief relation. But, on both views, whenever someone believes something, a non-descriptive mode of presentation is involved.

But what reason is there to group descriptive Fregeanism and pure Millianism together? In order to answer this question, let's consider what distinguishes the views. One distinction between the two views concerns propositions expressed by sentences containing names. Where *a* is a name, descriptive Fregeanism and pure Millianism differ in their account of the proposition that a is F. The former claims that it is a descriptive proposition, whereas the latter claims it is a singular proposition. However, this difference doesn't decide two more general issues. The pure Millian denies that the proposition that a is F is descriptive, but should he make the much stronger claim that *no* proposition is descriptive? And the descriptive Fregean denies that the proposition that a is F is singular, but should he make the stronger claim that *no* proposition is singular?

The answer to the first question is clearly no: though the pure Millian claims that the proposition that a is F isn't descriptive, it would be ludicrous to claim that no propositions are descriptive. For, clearly, the object of the proposition that the G is F will be determined by the property of G-ness. That much is obvious. However, what of the second question: should the descriptive Fregean deny that any propositions are singular?

15. Singular propositions

The phenomenon of *de re* belief gives one reason for the descriptive Fregean to accept that at least some propositions are singular. When I say that Abe believes of Dave that he's a dangerous maniac, I seem to be attributing a belief to Abe. Moreover, in attributing the belief I am—to quote Nathan Salmon (1986, 4)—"declining to specify the way in which the subject of the attribution thinks or conceives of the *res* in question," and my attempt would be thwarted if "the variable or pronoun had, in addition to its referent, something like a Fregean *sense*" (original emphasis). Of course, the descriptive Fregean might claim that *de re* belief attributions don't really attribute a particular belief to a subject. Rather, to say that Abe believes of Dave that he's a dangerous maniac is to say that, for some description *the F*, Dave is the F and Abe believes that the F is a dangerous maniac. On this proposal, *de re* belief attributions say that the subject has some descriptive belief or other. Perhaps some such proposal could be made to work, but what reason is there for the descriptive Fregean to deny the mere possibility of someone believing a singular proposition?[31]

The descriptive Fregean might have a reason to deny the possibility of believing a singular proposition if he accepted Gareth Evans' ([1982] 1995, 89) claim that a person cannot have a thought about an object unless he has discriminating knowledge of it, where someone has discriminating knowledge of an object when either (i) he is perceiving it, (ii) he can recognize it if it is presented to him, or (iii) he knows distinguishing facts about it. This is Evans' elucidation of what he calls *Russell's Principle*. If we assume that when someone perceives an object there must be some definite description of the object available to him (*the object I am currently perceiving*, or *the object that seems to me to be such-and-such*), then Russell's Principle would seem to require that, whenever someone has a thought about an object, he must know of some description that it uniquely satisfies (although this requirement is not part of Evans' view).

Evans does give plausible reasons for thinking that Russell's Principle is true. Evans (ibid., 90) asks us to suppose that "on a certain day in the past, a subject briefly observed two indistinguishable steel balls suspended from the same point and rotating about it. He now believes nothing about one ball which he does not believe about the other." It is very implausible that the subject can now have a thought about one of the balls in the absence of his knowing any facts that would distinguish it from the other ball. Cases like this make Russell's Principle very plausible.

It seems to me that something like Russell's Principle may be correct and that it implies that whenever someone has a belief about an object he must know of some description that it uniquely satisfies. However, it is important to notice that *it doesn't give any grounds for claiming that there aren't any singular beliefs*. The most the principle implies is that if I believe that a is F, I must know of some definite description *the G* that picks out a, but *it doesn't imply that the definite description is part of the proposition that a is F*. For all the principle says, my knowledge that a is the G may constitute no part of the proposition that a is F. Hence, Russell's Principle gives no reason to deny that *de re* belief attribution is singular belief attribution.

There is a similar objection to the idea that there are any singular thoughts. Nathan Salmon (1986, 2) puts the objection as follows:

> Suppose Tom, Dick, and Harry, who have never met one another, agree to think some simple thought. Their instructions are ***Think to yourself that Ted Kennedy is tall***, and each complies. Surely what goes on in each thinker's mind will differ considerably from one thinker to the next, varying with the thinker's political ideology, and his familiarity with Kennedy's physical appearance, achievements, deeds, and so on. Tom thinks something along the lines of *That famous senator from Massachusetts is tall*, while Dick thinks *That handsome brother of Jack and Bobby is tall*, while Harry thinks *That good-for-nothing !@%!@ is tall*. As each apprehends the words ***Ted Kennedy is tall***, the content of his thought is something much richer, in structure and thought-stuff, than the crude singular proposition.[32]

Now I think that Salmon puts the point here a bit too strongly; if Dick has strong negative feelings about Ted Kennedy, he *may* think *that good-for-nothing !@%!@ is tall* when asked to think that Ted Kennedy is tall, but he also might simply think of Ted Kennedy that he's tall. But, more to the point, even if it turns out that the subject will always think of Kennedy in some particular way, this doesn't show that "his thought is something much richer . . . than the crude singular proposition"; it merely shows that all of the thoughts he's thinking taken together are much richer than that. And, of course, a subject never has a single belief without having any other beliefs. When a subject is asked to think a thought about Ted Kennedy, what he thinks may involve many of his beliefs about Kennedy's political ideology, Kennedy's physical appearance, achievements, deeds, and so on. In any sense of ***thought*** on which it's plausible that a thought about Ted Kennedy is always much richer than a singular proposition, a thought will be a collection of beliefs about him, one of which may be a singular proposition. So the claim that subjects always think of an object under some description or another, however true it turns out to be, isn't a good reason to deny that there are singular propositions.

There is a final reason that the descriptive Fregean might deny that singular propositions can be objects of belief. Many philosophers hold that the nature of belief is given by the role it plays in behavior and rationality, and this view provides another possible reason to deny that anyone ever bears the belief relation to a singular proposition. For singular propositions appear to be irrelevant to behavior and rationality. (Burge [1982] offers something like this argument.) Consider the relationship between beliefs and behavior. I use my knowledge of other people's beliefs to predict their behavior, and my own beliefs help determine what my behavior is. But it is difficult to see how belief in a singular proposition could have any effect on someone's behavior. After all, if a particular belief doesn't present its object in any (descriptive or non-descriptive) way, then how could the belief lead me to engage in any behavior toward the object? Engaging in behavior toward a particular object would seem to require that I identify it, and if my belief merely presents its object *as itself* how *could* I identify it? With regard to rationality, I might have a *de re* belief of a particular thing that it is F, and also have a *de re* belief of the very same thing that it is not F, without thereby being irrational. For example, I might believe of *that guy* that he's smart, and of *this guy* that he's an idiot, without knowing that I'm pointing to the same guy. So, given that what we believe when we have a *de re* belief is a singular proposition, singular propositions appear to be irrelevant to criticisms of rationality. And, hence, if the nature of belief is given by its role in rational reasoning and the determination of behavior, singular propositions wouldn't reflect the nature of belief at all.

I will have more to say about belief and behavior in the next chapter. However, for now suffice it to say that it may be that singular propositions are irrelevant to explanations of behavior and to criticisms of rationality. However, the idea that the nature of belief is completely given by its role in behavior and rationality seems to me to be too restrictive. Besides using my beliefs to guide my behavior and my formation of new beliefs, I also want my beliefs to be true. And it isn't just that I want them to be true because they'll serve as better guides to behavior and rationality; I want my beliefs to be true independently of these concerns. My desire for true beliefs reflects my understanding that belief is essentially truth-normed; not to care whether my beliefs are true would reflect a misunderstanding of their nature. Indeed, we want our beliefs not only to be true but also to reflect the way objects are *in themselves* rather than merely the way that we conceive of them. And, though singular propositions may be irrelevant to belief insofar as it guides behavior and rationality, they appear to be required insofar as we want our beliefs to reflect how objects are in themselves.

I have argued that there is no good reason for the descriptive Fregean to deny that singular propositions are sometimes believed. And, quite independently of the details of the argument, this conclusion is bound to strike many philosophers as impossible. For it is quite natural to think that *what it is* to be a Fregean is to deny the existence of singular propositions or at least to deny that they can be believed. But part of my point is that the standard conception of Frege's puzzle and of the Fregean position that is its putative solution runs two quite distinct things together. Frege's puzzle is a puzzle about the nature of certain beliefs; where *a* and *b* are co-referring names, the puzzle is how to account for the apparently distinct propositions expressed by sentences that differ only by substitution of one name for the other. But this is all the puzzle is. In particular it is *not* a general puzzle about what it takes for a subject to think about something in the world and solving it does not require or imply an answer to this general question.

It can seem, and has seemed to many, that the puzzle *is* about what it takes to think about things in the world. This is at least in part because the most famous putative solution to the puzzle—namely, descriptive Fregeanism—sounds a lot like a putative answer to the general question. As we've seen, descriptivism Fregeanism is the view that names pick out their referents by being associated with a mode of presentation, which consists in a collection of properties, and the referent of the name is the unique thing (if such there be) that has the properties. Descriptive Fregeanism counts as a solution to Frege's puzzle because it allows that sentences containing distinct but co-referring names express different propositions because the names are associated with different collections of properties. One among the many points that Saul Kripke ([1972] 1980) makes in *Naming and Necessity* is that the modes of presentation that the descriptive Fregean takes to be associated with names are performing two distinct functions. On the one hand, a mode of presentation is the *semantic value* of a name—what the name contributes to the propositions expressed by sentences containing it—and, on the other hand, the mode of presentation determines the name's referent. It is the first function of modes of presentation that allows them to provide a putative solution to Frege's puzzle—that allows them to individuate the proposition that a is F from the proposition that b is F when *a* and *b* co-refer; and, though descriptive modes of presentation might also serve the second function, there is no general reason that distinguishing the proposition that a is F from the proposition that b is F should also explain the way in which a name gets its referent. Although descriptive Fregeanism offers the possibility of such an explanation, a solution to Frege's puzzle needn't offer such an account.

Now, a descriptive Fregean might go farther than this. Besides using property collections to account for the distinct semantic values of co-referring names, and besides using property collections to explain how a name gets its referent, the descriptive Fregean might also use property collections to answer the general question of how it is that we think about things in the world: he might say that in order to think about some thing one must get onto the thing by knowing of a collection of properties that the thing uniquely has. This answer is far less satisfying that it first appears, since it provides no account of how we manage to think about property collections, but my aim here is not to argue for or against this account. My point here —and, indeed, in this whole section—is that, despite its similarities to descriptive Fregeanism, the account has nothing in particular to do with descriptive Fregeanism or Frege's puzzle. One might distinguish the belief that a is F from the belief that b is F by claiming that the names are associated with distinct property collections, but offer an entirely different account of what it takes to think of an object. The fact that property collections might solve Frege's puzzle and explain the way that names get their referents makes it easy to run these problems together. And, similarly, the fact that property collections might solve Frege's puzzle and account for what it takes to think about something in the world makes it easy to run these questions together. But the question of what it takes to think about an object in the world is the question of what is required to think about an object, whereas Frege's puzzle is a puzzle about the nature of particular thoughts, namely, those expressed by sentences containing names. Even if it turned out that thinking about an object requires knowing of properties that it uniquely satisfies, this does not mean that we never think of an object by believing a singular proposition. At most, it would place a requirement on what it takes to believe a singular proposition.

So there doesn't seem to be any reason for the descriptive Fregean to deny that subjects can believe singular propositions, and he should accept the apparent fact that a singular proposition is attributed when a *de re* belief attribution is made. And, hence, both the pure Millian and the descriptive Fregean should hold that some propositions are descriptive and some are singular. So they differ only with respect to their accounts of particular propositions: namely, those expressed by sentences containing names.[33] And, while this is a dispute, it is not about the nature of belief. *Rather it's about the nature of particular beliefs.* Put another way, it's not a dispute in the philosophy of mind. Rather, it's a dispute in the philosophy of language, particularly about which propositions are expressed by sentences containing names.

So the dispute between the descriptive Fregean and the pure Millian isn't a dispute about the nature of belief. However, both these views do differ with non-descriptive Fregeanism and guise Millianism over the nature of belief. For, as we will see, both descriptive Fregeanism and pure Millianism hold that there is nothing more to the belief relation than what the belief represents, whereas both the non-descriptive Fregean and the guise Millian hold that how a belief represents is an essential part of the ontology of belief.

I have used thousands of words to justify and explain a certain taxonomy of views, and we are now in a position where a few pictures may help. Continuing to ignore the issue of how propositions determine the properties that they ascribe to objects, the descriptive Fregean and pure Millian positions can be represented in the following diagrams.

As Figures 2.1 and 2.2 indicate, the descriptive Fregean and the pure Millian disagree about what the belief that a is F is; however, they agree that the belief relation relates subjects to entities consisting of objects and properties and that there are no non-descriptive modes of presentation in the belief relation.

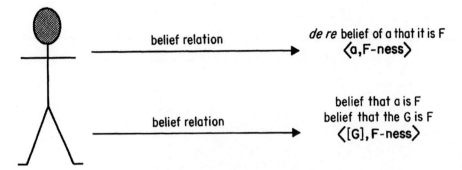

Figure 2.1 Descriptive Fregeanism

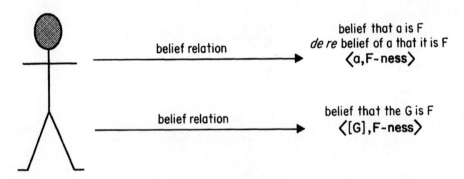

Figure 2.2 Pure Millianism

The non-descriptive Fregean and guise Millian positions are represented in Figures 2.3 and 2.4 (again ignoring issues about the mode of presentation of properties ascribed).

As Figures 2.3 and 2.4 show, the non-descriptive Fregean and the guise Millian are in complete agreement on the ontology of belief. Both agree that the belief relation involves non-descriptive modes of presentation that determine objects. They merely disagree about which items in the ontology of belief are the things believed.

In *Naming and Necessity*, Kripke ([1972] 1980) argues that the semantic value of a name is not the semantic value of some definite description. But Gareth Evans ([1982] 1995, 73–76) has claimed that Kripke's observations are about the propositions expressed by sentences containing names—about what we *say* by uttering, for example, *Hesperus is a planet*—and do not necessarily tell us anything about what we believe when we, to continue the example, *believe* that Hesperus is a planet. But it is important to see that my claim that Frege's puzzle is a puzzle in philosophy of language rather than a puzzle in philosophy of mind is not at all the same as Evans' claim. In fact, as discussed in Section 8, I take it that Evans' claim

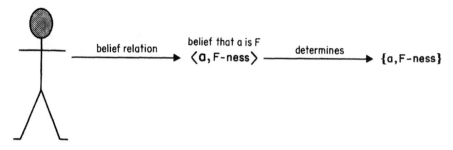

Figure 2.3 Non-descriptive Fregeanism

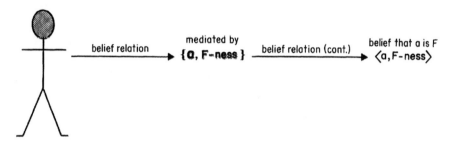

Figure 2.4 Guise Millianisn

is wrong: whatever it is I say when I utter the sentence *Hesperus is a planet* is exactly what I believe when I believe it's a planet. True, Kripke frames his arguments in terms of sentences: he points out, for example, that *Aristotle* couldn't mean the same thing as *The teacher of Alexander*, since, if it did, the sentence *Aristotle taught Alexander* would be a necessary truth rather than a contingent one. But the point could equally well be put in terms of belief: if the *belief* that Aristotle taught Alexander picked out Aristotle by containing the property of being the teacher of Alexander, then the *belief* would be necessary rather than contingent. I take it that conclusions about what we *say* by means of our sentences will have direct consequences for belief, since we say and believe the same kind of things—namely, propositions—and (ignoring context-sensitive terms), if *P* expresses a proposition, then the belief that P just is that proposition. My claim is that Frege's puzzle is primarily a puzzle in the philosophy of language rather than in the philosophy of mind; it is a puzzle about the propositions expressed by *sentences that contain names*. As such, a putative solution may have interesting consequences for beliefs that are expressed by sentences containing names; but, as such, it is not a general puzzle about the nature of belief. The puzzle does provide some motivation for thinking that sentences containing names do not express singular propositions, but it provides no motivation for thinking that there are no singular propositions. More generally, Fregeanism and Millianism are competing accounts of what the semantic value of a proper name is; according to the latter it's the name's referent, whereas according to the former it's something that determines the referent. But the distinction between Fregeanism and Millianism does not mark any distinction concerning the ontology of belief. With regard to the ontology of belief, the important distinction is between *what* beliefs represent and *how* they represent.

16. Explaining the what/how distinction

It might seem that there isn't really any distinction between what a belief represents and how it represents. After all, consider the belief that Superman flies. If we ask the question, *What does it represent Superman as being?* the answer is, *It represents him as being a flyer*; and, if we ask, *How does it represent Superman as being?*, the answer is the same.

However, the distinction I want isn't a distinction between what the belief represents *Superman as being* and how the belief represents *Superman as being*. Rather it is a distinction between what the belief represents and how it represents.

In order to see what the distinction is, consider the sentence *Superman flies*. Notice that the question *How does the sentence represent Superman?* can be taken in two ways. First, one might answer that the sentence represents Superman as flying. But, second, one might answer that the sentence represents Superman by containing the word *Superman*. It is this second sense of *how* that I mean to be getting at in the what/how distinction. In the second sense, how something is represented isn't a question about what properties it is represented as having. Rather, it is the question, In virtue of what feature of the representation is the individual represented? And notice the answer to such a how question doesn't affect the truth-conditions of the representation. Whether Superman is represented by the name *Superman* or not doesn't affect the truth-conditions of a sentence that represents him as flying.

On the other hand, I mean the phrase *what a belief represents* to pick out something that affects truth-conditions. In the case of beliefs that ascribe a property to an object, what is represented is the object as having a certain property. But notice that if the object is picked out by a definite description (in a sentence), the content of the description *is* being attributed to the object (in the proposition expressed); that is to say, the object is represented as having the collection of properties that constitute the content of the description.

We have already seen that both descriptive Fregeanism and pure Millianism agree that there are no non-descriptive modes of presentation. But notice that in so doing they also agree that beliefs are individuated only by what they represent.[34] By contrast, the non-descriptive Fregean believes that they should also be individuated by how they represent: by modes of presentation that do not affect what properties the object of the belief is represented as having. Now, strictly speaking, the guise Millian doesn't believe that beliefs are individuated by how they represent, but he does hold that how they represent is an essential aspect of the belief relation.

So both the descriptive Fregean and the pure Millian hold that the belief relation involves only what is represented, whereas both the non-descriptive Fregean and the guise Millian hold that how the things the belief is about are represented is essential to the ontology of belief. By not distinguishing between descriptive and non-descriptive modes of presentation, and by focusing exclusively on whether the mode of presentation is a constituent of the thing believed, the Fregean/Millian distinction washes over the distinction between holding that how things are represented is essential to the ontology of belief and denying that it is. Let's call the thesis that the belief relation is merely a relation between subjects and what their beliefs represent *dyadism* about belief, and let's call the view that non-descriptive modes of presentation are essential components of believing *triadism* about belief.

The distinction between dyadism and triadism about belief depends upon the distinction between descriptive and non-descriptive modes of presentation. For dyadism about belief *just is* the view that the only kinds of modes of presentation that enter into the belief relation are descriptive, and triadism about belief *just is* the view that non-descriptive modes of presentation enter into the belief relation. We have already seen one important difference between descriptive and non-descriptive modes of presentation: the former attribute properties to the objects they pick out, whereas the latter do not. And this is one reason that the former involve only what is represented, whereas the latter involve how things are represented. But there is another related difference between the two kinds of modes of presentation. In order to see this difference, we need to take another look at what we've seen so far.

First, we saw that in order to explain belief and perception we will need at least two sorts of things: subjects and things that they are related to. Second, it's clear that the things to which subjects are related must be true or false. Third, it's clear that they can't be individuated merely by their truth and falsity in different possible worlds. Fourth, it seems as if they need to be individuated in terms of the existing objects that they are about and the properties that they ascribe to these objects. Thus, so far our story of belief and perception involves only two sorts of things: *subjects* (the sorts of things that have beliefs and perceptions) and *stuff in the world* (the existing things that beliefs and perceptions are about, and the properties that beliefs and perceptions ascribe to these things). While it is true that belief relates subjects to propositions, at this point we have no reason to suppose that propositions are composed of anything beyond stuff in the world. So at this point our account of belief and perception includes only two sorts of things: subjects and stuff in the world.

Now, most philosophers hold that belief and perception essentially involve a third sort of thing, a sort of thing that stands between the subject and the world.[35] In the case of perception, sometimes this third sort of thing is taken to be a perceptual intermediary and its intrinsic properties, sometimes this third sort of thing is taken to be an intentional object, and sometimes this third sort of thing is taken to be a sense-datum. What each of these views has in common is that the perceptual relation between subjects and propositions is taken to be mediated by some third sort of thing. But notice that the explanation of descriptive modes of presentation doesn't require one to go beyond the category of stuff in the world: we can account for descriptive modes of presentation in terms of properties that beliefs clearly do ascribe to objects. But non-descriptive modes of presentation are a third kind of thing, a thing that stands between the subject and the stuff in the world—they are *how* stuff in the world is represented and, hence, go beyond *what* stuff is represented—whereas descriptive modes of presentation involve only a commitment to *what* stuff is represented.[36] According to triadism, our cognitive relation to stuff in the world is mediated by non-descriptive modes of presentation whereas according to dyadism it isn't.

It is well known that descriptivism has fallen out of favor, largely due to the work of Kripke ([1972] 1980) and Kaplan (1989). However, the fact that philosophers have focused exclusively on the Fregean/Millian distinction has obscured the fact that, besides descriptivism, dyadism is another casualty of (forgive the barbarism) *the new theory of reference*. Russell's account of belief is a dyadist account, and the naive interpretation of Frege's view is that he's a descriptivist about belief ascriptions involving names and, hence, also a dyadist. But most contemporary Fregeans and Millians agree that there is more to the belief relation than what is represented. So dyadism about belief is an unknown casualty of the new theory of reference.

17. Conclusion

Now that we know what dyadism about belief is, it may seem as if it couldn't possibly be true. After all, surely the belief that Superman flies must be distinct from the belief that Clark Kent flies. Yet, as we have seen, it is grossly implausible that either belief picks out its object by means of a description and, hence, grossly implausible that they can be distinguished by what they represent Superman as being. And, even if Salmon is correct and the beliefs aren't in fact distinct, then surely he is also correct in thinking that how Superman is represented plays a role in explaining why the beliefs *seem* to be distinct.

But why does it seem as if the belief that Superman flies must be distinct from the belief that Clark Kent flies? We have already seen one reason: it seems as if Lex has the former belief but lacks the latter. However, this is only one of many reasons that have been given for claiming that (where *a* and *b* are co-referential names) the belief that a is F must be distinct from the belief that b is F. And, as we will see in the next chapter, there are important connections between the many reasons. Moreover, once these connections are brought out, it becomes apparent that *how individuals are represented can play no role in explaining why the beliefs seem different.*

3

Frege's Puzzle

0. Introduction

In the last chapter we saw that many Fregeans and Millians are *triadists* about beliefs: they account for the apparent difference between, for example, the belief that Superman flies and the belief that Clark Kent flies by claiming that there is always more to the belief relation than believers and *what* their beliefs represent. According to non-descriptive Fregeans, the apparent difference is genuine; *how* a particular belief represents *what* it does is part of the belief itself, and the two beliefs differ because they contain distinct *non-descriptive modes of presentation* of their object. According to guise Millians, the difference is only apparent; a belief itself contains only *what* it represents, but the relation between believers and what they believe is always mediated by non-descriptive modes of presentation. The important point is that on both versions of triadism a complete account of the belief relation involves a believer and two other kinds of things: the stuff in the world that constitutes *what* his belief represents and the non-descriptive modes of presentation that constitute *how* this stuff is represented.

In the last chapter I presented diagrams that depict what the two versions of triadism have in common. However, in order to make some difficult distinctions more manageable, I explicitly ignored the fact that the triadist must posit non-descriptive modes of presentation for the properties (and relations) *ascribed* to objects by beliefs as well as for the objects themselves. Throughout this chapter, I will continue to focus on the triadist's claims about how the *objects* represented by beliefs are determined. But everything said below easily generalizes to the properties (and relations) ascribed to objects, and it is important to note the complete triadist view of the belief relation, which is depicted in Figure 3.1.

In the last chapter I argued that, if beliefs are to be adequately distinguished from

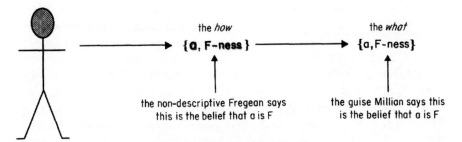

the *how*
{a, F-ness}

the *what*
{a,F-ness}

the non-descriptive Fregean says
this is the belief that a is F

the guise Millian says this
is the belief that a is F

Figure 3.1 Triadism about belief

one another, then they must determine objects and properties; for example, the belief that 2 is even must determine 2 and the property of being even if it is to be distinct from other necessarily true beliefs. As the above diagram indicates, both the
non-descriptive Fregean and the guise Millian accept that beliefs determine objects
and properties.[1] For example, on both views, the belief that Superman flies and the
belief that Clark Kent flies each determine the person Superman and the property
of flying. The question I want to take up in this chapter is whether the triadist is
right that the apparent difference between these beliefs requires that there be distinct non-descriptive modes of presentation corresponding to the names *Superman*
and *Clark Kent*: that is, more generally, whether the apparent difference between
certain beliefs that are identical with respect to their *what* requires that *how* objects
and properties are represented is an essential component of the belief relation.

1. Four ways of generating Frege's puzzle

Before we can decide whether non-descriptive modes of presentation are required
to account for the apparent difference between certain beliefs, we need to know why
the beliefs appear to be different. In fact, there are at least four different reasons and
we might think of each as providing a *way of generating Frege's puzzle*, where the
puzzle is how to account for the apparent difference. The first three ways of generating the puzzle are not always adequately distinguished from one another and,
more importantly, it's sometimes alleged that the fourth way of generating the puzzle is radically different from the others in virtue of being immune to a certain kind
of solution. However, as we will see, the fourth way of generating the puzzle places
no special limits on how it can be solved. Indeed, there are connections between
each of the ways of generating the puzzle and, because of these connections, an adequate solution to any of the ways should imply a solution to all the others. Moreover, these connections will have important consequences later in our discussion.

  The intuitions that motivate the first way of generating Frege's puzzle were mentioned in the previous chapter: namely, it seems that *S believes that a is F* can be

true and *S believes that b is F* false even when the names *a* and *b* co-refer. If such belief ascriptions really can have different truth-values, then they must express different propositions. And, since they each ascribe a belief to the very same individual, this means the sentences embedded in their respective *that*-clauses pick out different beliefs. So the belief that a is F must be distinct from the belief that b is F.

In "On Sense and Reference," Frege ([1892] 1984a) gives a different reason for thinking that the two beliefs differ. Rather than appealing to the truth-value of belief ascriptions, Frege appeals to the information conveyed by simple sentences: sentences that don't contain the word *believes* or any other mental terminology. Frege observed that, even when *a* and *b* co-refer, sentences of the form *a=b* are (or at least can be) informative while sentences of the form *a=a* are not, and he concludes that the sentences must express different propositions (or, in Frege's terminology, different *Gedanken*; the term is usually translated as *thoughts*). Now the fact that the sentences *a=a* and *a=b* convey different information does suggest that what is said by assertive utterances of the them—that is, the propositions expressed by them—are different. However, this doesn't yet show that the *beliefs* that a=a and a=b are distinct. Recall that, besides believing propositions, we also *say* them by assertively uttering sentences that express them. Recall also that *the proposition that P* is what a subject S says when he assertively utters the sentence *P*, whereas *the belief that P* is what he believes when *S believes that P* is true. And, while it is appears to be trivial that the proposition that P just is the belief that P— that what you say by assertively uttering *P* is exactly what you believe when you believe that P—it is possible, as Robert Stalnaker does (see Chapter 2, Section 7), to deny this apparent triviality. And, if the apparent triviality is false, nothing about the propositions that a=a and that a=b will imply anything about the beliefs that a=a and a=b. Hence, if Frege's observation is going to provide an argument that the relevant beliefs are distinct—that believing that a=a and believing that a=b involve relations to distinct propositions—the apparent triviality is required.

Now, although Frege seems to have thought that the puzzle arises from special problems concerning the identity relation, Nathan Salmon has pointed out that identity plays no special role and that the puzzle really concerns the substitution of co-referring names.[2] Salmon observes that there are uninformative sentences that *don't* make any reference to identity but that nonetheless differ from informative sentences only in the substitution of co-referring names. For example, the sentence *Hesperus is a planet if Phosphorus is* is informative while the sentence *Phosphorus is a planet if Phosphorus is* is not (see Salmon 1986, 12). Such examples clearly do show that identity isn't the source of the problem, but we don't really need to consider any particular examples to see this. For, upon reflection, it is clear that the distinction between informative and uninformative sentences itself plays no crucial role in generating the puzzle.

To say that *a=b* is informative while *a=a* is not is to say that the first sentence can convey *new information* to someone while the second cannot. Thus the difference that Frege points out can be seen, from a more general perspective, as a difference in *information conveyed*. And the more general fact that two sentences convey different information gives us as much reason to suppose they express different propositions as does the more specific fact that one conveys new information while the other doesn't. So, since *a is F* conveys different information from *b is F* even when *a* and *b* co-refer, again the problem seems to concern co-referring names rather than identity. Moreover, even if the distinction between informativeness and uninformativeness were essential to generating the puzzle, informativeness is a relative notion: sentences aren't informative or uninformative *tout court*; rather, they are informative or uninformative *to individuals*. But *a is F* can be informative to someone though *b is F* isn't even when the two names co-refer. So, again, the second way of generating the puzzle has nothing in particular to do with identity; rather, it involves the information conveyed by sentences containing names (or indexicals).

So far, we have two reasons for thinking that the belief that a is F can be distinct from the belief that b is F even when the names co-refer: the first appeals directly to intuitions about the truth-value of belief ascriptions, while the second appeals to intuitions about the different information conveyed by simple sentences and concludes that the relevant sentences convey different information because they express different propositions. Now presenting the second way of generating the puzzle as an *inference* from the fact that *a is F* and *b is F* convey different information to the conclusion that they express different propositions is bound to strike some as making the argument unnecessarily weak. To some philosophers (and you know who you are) it's just obvious that sentences convey different information by expressing different propositions; it's just obvious that we *say* different things by uttering them. And to non-philosophers (if there are any out there) it's also likely to seem obvious; after all, how else could the sentences convey different information if we don't say different things by uttering them?

Well, the information a sentence conveys isn't always a result of what's said by someone who utters it. If, for example, I assertively utter the sentence *Fergie was sober today* I will probably convey that Fergie's often not sober. But, of course, though I've suggested that he's often not sober, I haven't actually *said* it. And, since the Millian thinks that, where *a* and *b* are co-referring names, the sentences *a is F* and *b is F* express the very same proposition, he'll try to account for the differences in the information they convey in terms of *pragmatic* factors: that is, in the way that *Fergie was sober* today conveys that he's often not sober. Exactly how information is conveyed via pragmatic factors will be discussed in the next chapter. For now it will suffice to understand a sentence as conveying information *via pragmatic factors* when the information isn't part of the proposition expressed by the sentence.

Now, at this stage, it may seem implausible that the different information conveyed by *Superman flies* and *Clark Kent flies* can be accounted for along the lines of the *Fergie was sober today* example; that is to say, it may seem doubtful whether anything like the Millian's account can be made to work. This is a question that will be taken up at the end of this chapter and it will occupy our attention into the next. For now, however, we want to be neutral between the Fregean and Millian positions, since, as will emerge, the Fregean account is itself not without serious difficulties and the Millian account is less problematic than it may first appear. So, when I say that two sentences convey different information, I'm being neutral as to whether this results from their expressing different propositions and I'm presenting the second way of generating Frege's puzzle as an inference from a difference in information conveyed to a difference in proposition expressed.[3]

The possible distinction between the information a sentence conveys and the proposition it expresses isn't important only for the second way of generating Frege's puzzle just mentioned; it's also important because the third way of generating the puzzle involves the fact that two sentences convey different information as well. But, rather than focusing on the information conveyed by simple sentences, it focuses on the information conveyed by belief ascriptions. *S believes that a is F* and *S believes that b is F* convey different information even when the names *a* and *b* co-refer and, hence, they seem to express different propositions. But, since they both ascribe a belief to the same subject, the only way they can express different propositions is if they ascribe different beliefs. So, again, the beliefs that a is F and b is F must be distinct.

The appeal to the different information conveyed by the belief ascriptions is important; for, besides providing a way of generating Frege's puzzle, it's also related to the other ways of generating it and, indeed, shows how these ways are related to one another. The way of generating Frege's puzzle that appeals to the *information* conveyed by belief ascriptions is obviously related to the way that appeals to the *truth-value* of belief ascriptions: the former way of generating the puzzle assumes that the two belief ascriptions convey different information because they *express different propositions* and, with regard to the latter way of generating the puzzle, the intuitions that the two belief ascriptions have different truth-values result from our idea about what *proposition each expresses*. The way of generating the puzzle that appeals to the *information conveyed* by belief ascriptions is also related to the way that appeals to the *information conveyed* by simple sentences: if, as the latter way of generating the puzzle claims, *a is F* and *b is F* express different propositions, then, given that the proposition that P is identical to the belief that P, *S believes that a is F* relates S to a different belief than *S believes that b is F* does; hence, as the former way of generating the puzzle claims, the two belief ascriptions must express different propositions. So, even though the three ways of generating Frege's puzzle discussed above are distinct, they bear a close relation to one another. And, importantly, the relations among them imply that any solution to one way of generating the puzzle should provide a solution to the others: they imply that there should be a *unified solution* to the three ways of generating Frege's puzzle discussed so far.[4]

In order to see that there should be a unified solution, consider the way of generating Frege's puzzle that appeals to the information conveyed by simple sentences. It starts with the observation that the sentences *a is F* and *b is F* can convey different information even when the names co-refer. Hence, an adequate solution to this way of generating the puzzle must tell us two things: (i) whether the two sentences convey different information because they express different propositions (the Fregean will take this line) or whether they express the same proposition and, hence, convey different information because of pragmatic factors (the Millian will take this line); and (ii) what information each of the sentences conveys. So, regardless of how some proposed solution stands with respect to (i) (that is, whether it's Fregean or Millian), it must imply that the sentence *a is F* conveys some piece of information I_a while the sentence *b is F* conveys some distinct piece of information I_b; and this is enough to provide a solution to the way of generating Frege's puzzle that appeals to the information conveyed by belief ascriptions. For, if *a is F* conveys I_a and *b is F* conveys I_b, then *S believes that a is F* should convey the information that S bears the belief relation to I_a while *S believes that b is F* should convey that he bears it to I_b. Because we intuitively accept that the proposition that P just is the belief that P, to the extent that *a is F* seems to express one proposition while *b is F* seems to express another, *S believes that a is F* will seem to express that S bears the belief relation to the former proposition while *S believes that b is F* will seem to express that he bears it to the latter. To put the point more generally, intuitions that a sentence expresses some proposition will go along with intuitions that belief ascriptions containing that sentence relate their subject to that proposition. So, if the way of generating Frege's puzzle that appeals to the information conveyed by simple sentences is adequately addressed, then the way of generating the puzzle that appeals to the information conveyed by belief ascriptions should thereby also be adequately addressed.[5]

Likewise, regardless of whether it is Fregean or Millian, an adequate account of the intuitions behind the way of generating the puzzle that appeals to the information conveyed by belief ascriptions should provide an adequate account of those behind the way that appeals to the truth-value of belief ascriptions. The latter way of generating the puzzle starts with the observation that *S believes that a is F* can seem true and *S believes that b is F* can seem false even when *a* and *b* co-refer. But this means that if we account for the former way of generating the puzzle by saying that the first sentence conveys that S bears the belief relation to I_a while the second conveys that he bears it to I_b, it should turn out that S *really does* bear the belief relation to I_a but *fails* to bear it to I_b. To put the point in a slightly different way, the way of generating the puzzle that appeals to the information conveyed by belief ascriptions tells us that the two belief ascriptions convey different information, while the way that appeals to the truth-value of belief ascriptions tells us that the one piece of information can seem true while the other seems false. So the differences in information featured in the former way should explain the apparent differences in truth-value featured in the latter.

Finally, an adequate account of the intuitions behind the way of generating the puzzle that appeals to the truth-value of belief ascriptions should provide an adequate account of those behind the way that appeals to the information conveyed by simple sentences. The intuitions behind the former way of generating the puzzle imply that *S believes that a is F* can convey true information, even though *S believes that b is F* conveys information that is false; so the two sentences must convey *different information*. Moreover, the difference in information conveyed had better concern what S believes, so the first belief ascription conveys that S bears the belief relation to some piece of information I_a, while the second conveys that he bears it to some distinct piece of information I_b. And this difference is sufficient to account for the intuitions behind the way of generating the puzzle that appeals to the information conveyed by simple sentences: since the first belief ascription conveys that S bears the belief relation to I_a, the embedded sentence *a is F* should convey the information I_a; and, since the second belief ascription conveys that he bears it to I_b, the embedded sentence *b is F* should convey I_b. To put the point more generally, intuitions that two belief ascriptions with the same subject express different propositions will be accompanied by intuitions that their respective embedded sentences pick out different beliefs.

As we have just seen, a solution to the way of generating Frege's puzzle that appeals to the information conveyed by simple sentences should provide a solution to the way that appeals to the information conveyed by belief ascriptions; a solution to the latter way of generating the puzzle should provide a solution to the way that appeals to the truth-value of belief ascriptions; and a solution to that way of generating the puzzle should provide a solution to the way that appeals to the information conveyed by simple sentences. So a solution to *any* of the above three ways of generating Frege's puzzle should provide a solution to the other two ways; that is, there should be a unified solution to these ways of generating the puzzle. However, there is a fourth way of generating the puzzle, and some have claimed that it raises special worries for the Millian. In particular, it has been claimed that, while the Millian may be able to solve the puzzle when it is generated in one of the first three ways, his resources aren't sufficient to handle the fourth way.

2. The way that appeals to reasons for behavior

To see what the fourth way of generating Frege's puzzle is, suppose that Lex Luthor is lurking behind a door clutching some kryptonite. What might Lex's reason for engaging in this behavior be? One answer might be that he believes that Superman is coming. But, even if he also believes that Clark Kent is coming (say, he has an interview with Clark Kent scheduled), the latter belief is *not* a reason for his behavior. And, if one belief is a reason for his behavior while the other isn't, they can't be the same belief. More generally, even when a is b, there seem to be cases in which S's belief that a is F is his reason for engaging in some behavior while his belief that b is F isn't. And, of course, if there are such cases, the relevant beliefs must be distinct.

The fourth way of generating the puzzle obviously presents no special problems for the Fregean. His solution to the first three ways of generating the puzzle is to accept that the beliefs are distinct and to explain what distinguishes them. And, of course, if the beliefs really are distinct, there is no worry about how the first explains Lex's behavior even though the second doesn't. However, the Millian denies that the beliefs are distinct; on his view, *a is F* and *b is F* express the *very same* proposition and the different information they convey results from pragmatic factors. And likewise for the belief ascriptions: the Millian explains our intuitions that they have distinct truth-values by claiming that they convey different information and that we confuse the information conveyed by each with the proposition it expresses. Because pragmatic factors are crucial to the Millian's explanation of the intuitions cited in the first three ways of generating Frege's puzzle, some philosophers have denied that the Millian has the resources to solve the puzzle when it is generated in the fourth way. After all, unlike the other ways, the fourth way of generating the puzzle doesn't *seem* to involve information conveyed by sentences. To quote Richard Heck (1995, 80n.4): "the problem does not only concern intuitions about belief reports—which might be susceptible of pragmatic explanation—but the status of everyday explanations of behavior." How, then, can the Millian provide a unified solution to Frege's puzzle? The answer is that there is nothing special about the fourth way of generating the puzzle; it too is related to each of other ways in a manner that implies that a solution to one should be a solution to all. To see how, let's take a look at the Millian's solution to the way of generating the puzzle that appeals to the information conveyed by simple sentences.

According to the Millian, the sentences *Superman is coming* and *Clark Kent is coming* express the very same proposition but convey different information because of pragmatic factors: the first pragmatically imparts to listeners some piece of information I_{SM} while the second pragmatically imparts some distinct piece of information I_{CK}. As we have seen, if these claims are correct, they straightforwardly provide a solution to the way of generating Frege's puzzle that appeals to the information conveyed by belief ascriptions: the difference between the information conveyed by *Lex believes that Superman is coming* and *Lex believes that Clark Kent is coming* should turn out to be that the former pragmatically imparts to listeners that Lex bears the belief relation to I_{SM} while the latter pragmatically imparts that he bears it to I_{CK}.

Now, according to the Millian, the two belief ascriptions express the very same proposition and, of course, this *seems* wrong. However, according to the Millian, the apparent wrongness is due to a confusion: namely, we confuse information each belief ascription conveys with the proposition it expresses, when in fact each only *pragmatically imparts* the relevant information. This explanation is deeply counterintuitive, since it appears to imply that we—that is, *perfectly competent speakers*—don't know the meaning of many perfectly ordinary sentences. Be that as it may, *if* the Millian is correct, he straightforwardly has a solution to the way of generating Frege's puzzle that appeals to reasons for behavior. If we mistakenly think that the information that Lex believes, I_{SM}, is part of the proposition expressed by the sentence *Lex believes that Superman is coming*, and if we also mistakenly think that the information that Lex believes, I_{CK}, is part of the proposition expressed by the sentence *Lex believes that Clark Kent is coming*, then it follows that we'll think that the proposition expressed by the former sentence gives a reason for Lex's behavior while the proposition expressed by the latter doesn't; for the fact *that Lex bears the belief relation to* I_{SM} explains his behavior and the fact *that he bears it to* I_{CK} doesn't. And this alleged confusion about which propositions the belief ascriptions express is sufficient to address Heck's worry. Recall that Heck claims the way of generating Frege's puzzle that appeals to reasons for behavior doesn't involve intuitions about belief ascriptions; rather, it involves "the status of everyday explanations of behavior." But, of course, we give everyday explanations of behavior by uttering attitude ascriptions; and, hence, to the extent that we are confused about which propositions the sentences *Lex believes that Superman is coming* and *Lex believes that Clark Kent is coming* express, we will be confused about whether the propositions they express explain Lex's behavior.

So, contrary to Heck, a Millian solution to the way of generating Frege's puzzle that appeals to simple sentences—and, hence, a Millian solution to *any* of the first three ways of generating the puzzle—*should* provide a solution to the way of generating the puzzle that appeals to reasons for behavior. Moreover, a Millian solution to the latter way of generating the puzzle should provide a solution to the first three ways of generating it. For, if, as the Millian claims, the information conveyed by the first belief ascription counts as an explanation of Lex's behavior while the information conveyed by the second doesn't, then the two belief ascriptions must convey that Lex has *different* beliefs; and, obviously, if they convey that Lex has different beliefs, then the intuitions behind the way that appeals to the information conveyed by belief ascriptions—and, hence, the intuitions behind all of the other ways of generating Frege's puzzle—are explained. Since a *Fregean* solution to any of the first three ways of generating the puzzle should also provide a solution to the way that appeals to reasons for behavior and *vice versa*, on either view there should be a unified solution to all of the ways of generating Frege's puzzle.

In order to be completely clear about the response to Heck, two points need to be made. First, the fourth way of generating Frege's puzzle *does* put constraints on what I_{SM} and I_{CK} can be. Since *Lex believes that Superman is coming* counts as an explanation of his behavior and since the Millian claims that we mistakenly think that it expresses the proposition that Lex bears the belief relation to I_{SM}, the fact that Lex bears the belief relation to I_{SM} had better explain his behavior. And, similarly, the fact that he bears the belief relation to I_{CK} had better *not* explain his behavior. However, the Millian is no worse off in this regard than the Fregean. Remember, everyone thinks that the relevant sentences convey different information; the Fregean and the Millian disagree only about whether the sentences do so because they express different propositions. So, the Fregean also needs distinct pieces of information corresponding to the sentences *Superman is coming* and *Clark Kent is coming*, and they will do the same work in addressing the four ways of generating Frege's puzzle as they do for the Millian. In short, the Fregean also needs the fact that Lex believes I_{SM} to explain his behavior and the fact that he believes I_{CK} *not* to explain it.

Second, as noted above, the Millian is forced to claim that our intuitions about the propositions expressed by belief ascriptions are sometimes radically unreliable. And at this stage of our discussion you may find it very hard to believe that competent speakers can be so wrong about the meanings of such very ordinary sentences. Be that as it may, my point thus far has been only that, *if* the Millian has a solution to any of the first three ways of generating Frege's puzzle, he should have a solution to the way that appeals to reasons for behavior. The Millian's claims about the propositions expressed by belief ascriptions may be hard to swallow, but they are no more harder to swallow in the context of the fourth way of generating the puzzle then they are in the context of the others.

Now that we have seen the four ways of generating Frege's puzzle and seen that the puzzle should have a unified solution, we can take a look at how the triadist about belief might use non-descriptive modes of presentation to solve it. Clearly the notion of two sentences *conveying different information* is crucial to the ensuing discussion. But there are *two* distinct ways that non-descriptive modes of presentation might explain the relevant information conveyed and, though both ways occur in the literature, that they are distinct has been missed. Once they are clearly distinguished, it's apparent that, while one explanation is available to any triadist, the other is available only to the non-descriptive Fregean.

3. Two ways the triadist can explain the differences in information conveyed: Differences-in-the-how and differences-about-the-how

Obviously two sentences will convey different information if *what* they represent is different. If two sentences express propositions that ascribe different properties to the same individual, or the same properties to different individuals, or different properties to different individuals, then they will convey different information. As pointed out in Chapter 2, the descriptive Fregean offers this kind of account of the different information conveyed by the relevant sentences. On his view *Superman flies* and *Clark Kent flies* express different propositions and the different propositions count as different pieces of information because *what* they represent is different: the first sentence expresses (something like) the proposition that the super-powered protector of Metropolis flies, while the second expresses (something like) the proposition that the bespectacled *Daily Planet* reporter flies. So the proposition expressed by the first sentence ascribes the property of being the super-powered protector of Metropolis to its subject, while the proposition expressed by the second ascribes the property of being the bespectacled *Daily Planet* reporter to its subject; hence, *what* they represent is different. And this means that the belief ascriptions

S believes that Superman flies and *S believes that Clark Kent flies* relate S to different beliefs and, hence, also differ with respect to *what* they represent.

One serious problem with descriptive Fregeanism—as Saul Kripke ([1972] 1980) famously brought out—is that it gets the modal status of propositions expressed by sentences containing names entirely wrong.[6] If the name *Clark Kent* expresses the content of the description *the bespectacled 'Daily Planet' reporter*, then the proposition that Clark Kent is the bespectacled *Daily Planet* reporter is true in any world in which there is a unique bespectacled *Daily Planet* reporter. However, clearly someone other than Clark Kent might have been the bespectacled *Daily Planet* reporter and, hence, the proposition is false at some such worlds. And, since any plausible candidate for the descriptive sense of the name *Clark Kent* is satisfied by Clark Kent only contingently, there is no acceptable candidate for the descriptive sense of the name. Moreover, as Kripke ([1972] 1980) points out, a genuine proper name designates the same thing in every possible world. So, if *Superman* and *Clark Kent* are genuine proper names, then the proposition that Superman flies and the proposition that Clark Kent flies have identical truth-values in any possible world; and this means that they do not present their object via *distinct* descriptions. The only conclusion to draw is that *what* the two propositions represent is the same: namely, each represents that the same individual flies.[7]

According to the non-descriptive Fregean, the proposition that Superman flies and the proposition that Clark Kent flies differ insofar as they contain distinct non-descriptive modes of presentation of their object. So, on his view, one way that the sentences *Superman flies* and *Clark Kent flies* might convey different information is if *any* difference between two propositions constitutes a difference in information: two propositions don't merely constitute different information if *what* they represent is different; they also constitute different information if *how* they represent is different. On this *differences*-in-*the-how* proposal, *Superman flies* and *Clark Kent flies* convey different information *merely in virtue* of expressing propositions that differ in how they represent Superman. And, if Lex Luthor were to come to believe that Clark Kent flies, he would have new information *merely in virtue* of coming to believe this proposition; the new belief counts as new information even though *what* it represents is identical to *what* is represented by a proposition that Lex already believes (namely, that Superman flies).

Since the guise Millian holds that the propositions *don't* contain non-descriptive modes of presentation and, hence, that two propositions *never* differ in their *how*, he cannot use a differences-*in*-the-how proposal. However, there is another proposal that might account for the difference in information conveyed, and it is open to both the non-descriptive Fregean and the guise Millian. On the proposal described above, the propositions that Superman flies and that Clark Kent flies constitute different information merely in virtue of containing distinct non-descriptive modes of presentation; and, hence, Lex gets new information upon hearing the sentence *Clark Kent flies* simply by coming to believe the proposition it expresses. But, on the proposal that is open to both versions of triadism, even if there are differences in the *how*—and the guise Millian claims that there aren't any *hows* in propositions at all—they don't by themselves constitute differences in information and, hence, Lex doesn't get new information upon hearing the sentence *Clark Kent flies* merely by coming to believe the proposition it expresses; rather, on a *differences-about-the-how* proposal, he gets new information by also coming to believe a *different proposition*, a proposition that concerns *how* the speaker *apprehends* what is represented by the proposition that Clark Kent flies.

If the non-descriptive Fregean adopts such a proposal, then he denies that a difference in *how* two propositions represent *by itself* constitutes a difference in information conveyed; rather, the sentences *Superman flies* and *Clark Kent flies* convey different information because the first conveys that the person who uttered the sentences believes a proposition containing the non-descriptive mode of presentation **Superman** while the second conveys that he believes a proposition containing the non-descriptive mode of presentation **Clark Kent**. The guise Millian does *not* accept that propositions contain any non-descriptive modes of presentation and, hence, on his view two propositions never differ in their *how*. However, he does hold that when an individual believes a proposition his relation to it is *mediated* by some non-descriptive mode of presentation. Hence, he can adopt a differences-*about*-the-how proposal by saying that an utterance of *Superman flies* conveys different information from an utterance of *Clark Kent flies* in virtue of the first's conveying to listeners that the non-descriptive mode of presentation **Superman** *mediates* the speaker's relationship to the proposition that Superman flies and the second's conveying that the non-descriptive mode of presentation **Clark Kent** mediates it.

The distinction between the two ways that non-descriptive modes of presentation might figure into an account of the relevant differences in information conveyed is subtle; however, it is important to note that there really is a difference. On the first way—available only to the non-descriptive Fregean—any difference in how two propositions represent by itself constitutes a difference in information. On the second way—available to both the non-descriptive Fregean and the guise Millian—a difference in how two propositions represent does not by itself constitute a difference in information conveyed; rather, two sentences that are identical with respect to what the propositions they express represent can convey different information because, besides the fact that each conveys to listeners the proposition it expresses, each also conveys some additional piece of information concerning how some subject apprehends what is represented by the proposition.

Suppose that I utter the sentence *Clark Kent flies* to Lex Luthor and that he believes me. If, as a way of fixing ideas, we assume that non-descriptive modes of presentation are merely public-language sentences and that a sentence mediates a believer's relation to some proposition just in case the sentence expresses that proposition and the believer accepts the sentence, then Figures 3.2 and 3.3 depict the non-descriptive Fregean versions of the two proposals.

The non-descriptive Fregean versions of the two proposals

(assuming that non-descriptive modes of presentation are public-language sentences)

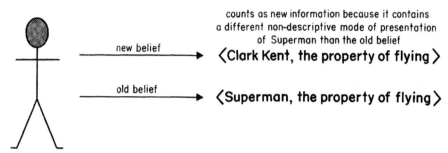

Figure 3.2 Differences-*in*-the-how

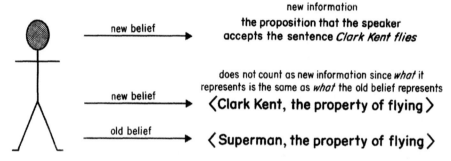

Figure 3.3 Differences-*about*-the-how

As the diagrams indicate, on a differences-*in*-the-how proposal, if two beliefs differ with respect to *how* they represent, then they constitute different information; hence, Lex's new belief that Clark Kent flies counts as new information even though it represents the same individual as having the same property as does his old belief that Superman flies. On a differences-*about*-the-how proposal, by contrast, *only* a difference in *what* two beliefs represent implies that they constitute different information. So, although Lex's belief that Clark Kent flies is new, it still doesn't count as new information, since *what* it represents is the same as what his old belief that Superman flies does. Lex gets new information upon hearing the sentence *Clark Kent flies* because, in addition to coming to believe that Clark Kent flies, he also comes to believe that the speaker accepts the sentence.

The above diagrams depict how both proposals work on the non-descriptive Fregean's view (on the assumption that non-descriptive modes of presentation are merely public-language expressions). As stated above, the guise Millian cannot adopt a differences-*in*-the-how proposal. However, Figure 3.4 depicts how a differ-

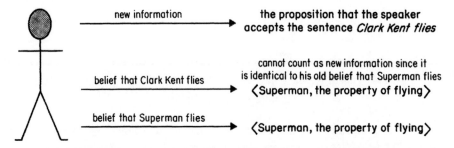

Figure 3.4 The Guise Millian version of a differences-*about*-the-how proposal

ences-*about*-the-how proposal works on the guise Millian's view (again, to fix ideas, assuming that non-descriptive modes of presentation are public-language expressions).

As the diagram indicates, the guise Millian cannot say that upon hearing the sentence *Clark Kent flies* Lex gets new information in virtue of coming to believe the proposition it expresses because, on his view, that proposition *just is* the proposition that Superman flies and, hence, Lex already believes it. So, instead, the guise Millian claims that the new information that Lex gets upon hearing the sentence is that the speaker accepts it.

Once the distinction between the two proposals is clear, it's understandable why a guise Millian should adopt a differences-*about*-the-how proposal. Since the guise Millian doesn't think that the relevant propositions contain non-descriptive modes of presentation, he obviously can't explain the difference between *a is F* and *b is F* by saying they contain *different* non-descriptive modes of presentation. Since he, so to speak, doesn't believe that propositions contain any *hows* in the first place, he can't adopt a differences-*in*-the-how proposal; all that's left is to adopt a differences-*about*-the-how proposal. However, at this point it's bound to seem a bit odd that any non-descriptive Fregean would adopt a differences-*about*-the-how proposal. After all, if you're a non-descriptive Fregean, you think that non-descriptive modes of presentation are constituents of propositions, so why wouldn't you just say that two propositions that contain distinct non-descriptive modes of presentation thereby constitute different information? Why bother to explain the difference in informativeness between *Superman flies* and *Clark Kent flies* by appealing to collateral propositions, when you think the sentences themselves express different propositions?

Well, despite the apparent oddity, some non-descriptive Fregeans have adopted a differences-*about*-the-how proposal.[8] And, more importantly, though they haven't recognized it there is a good reason that they've done so. For, despite the fact that non-descriptive Fregeanism posits that the modes of presentation are constituents of propositions, certain versions of the view cannot avail themselves of a differences-*in*-the-how proposal. Bringing this out has important consequences in its own right, but it also helps to cast the distinction between the two proposals in a sharper light: namely, the light of representational content.

4. Representational content, qualia, and non-descriptive modes of presentation

Recall that in Chapter 1 we discussed two distinct ways in which *experiences* might be distinguished from one another. On the one hand, you might distinguish them by appealing to a difference in their representational content while, on the other, you might appeal to some other kind of difference. For example, if you thought that there are internal perceptual states, you might try to distinguish two perceptions by appealing to the properties of such states. Recall also that this is precisely what the qualia freak does; an experience is supposed to be an internal state of its subject that mediates his relation to its representational content, and the qualia freak attempts to distinguish, for example, a visual experience of an object that seems red from an otherwise identical visual experience of an object that seems blue by appealing to the intrinsic qualities of the respective experiences: by appealing to their qualia. But, given that an experience is supposed to *mediate* its subject's relation to its representational content, the fact that your experience has a particular quale is not a part of its representational content. That is to say, the qualia freak tries to account for subjective differences between experiences without appealing to differences in representational content. And, as we saw in Chapter 1, this is one major reason that his view fails; differences in how things seem *just are* differences in representational content.

By contrast, recall the way in which Fregean senses are supposed to individuate beliefs. If two beliefs contain distinct Fregean senses, then they *are* thereby supposed to differ in representational content. Hence, positing Fregean senses to explain the difference between, for example, the belief that Superman flies and the belief that Clark Kent flies doesn't involve the same mistake as does positing qualia to explain the subjective differences between experiences. Qualia are supposed to be properties of, in Frege's terminology mentioned in the first chapter, *second-realm* entities, properties of token internal mental states; and that two experiences have different qualia does not by itself imply that they have different representational content. Whereas Fregean senses are *third-realm* entities that *are* supposed to affect representational content; and, as such, the latter might do the job of individuating the relevant beliefs. But what does all this have to do with the distinction between a differences-*in*-the-how proposal and a differences-*about*-the-how proposal?

Well, we need to begin by making some facts about our terminology explicit. As the last paragraph makes clear, I have been using the term *Fregean sense* for a belief-individuator that *does* directly affect representational content: when two beliefs contain distinct Fregean senses, they must have distinct representational contents. However, though I haven't been explicit about it, I've been using *mode of presentation* neutrally, as a term for a belief-individuator that *might or might not* directly affect representational content: two beliefs might contain distinct modes of presentation yet not differ in their representational content. The non-descriptive Fregean claims that, where *a* and *b* are co-referring names, the belief that a is F is distinct from the belief that b is F because they contain distinct non-descriptive modes of presentation. Now, assuming that these non-descriptive modes of presentation do directly affect representational content, this explanation might work; but, if they don't directly affect representational content, it has an immediate problem. We're supposed to think that the beliefs are distinct because the sentences *a is F* and *b is F* convey different information, and the non-descriptive Fregean takes them to convey different information because they express different propositions; that is to say, he thinks the relevant information conveyed just is a part of the proposition that each expresses. But, if the proposition expressed by each sentence amounts to different information, then it would seem that the propositions have to differ in their representational content; if there's no difference in representational content, how could there possibly be a difference in information? So, if non-descriptive modes of presentation turn out not to directly affect representational content, it appears that the non-descriptive Fregean is making the same mistake as the qualia freak does in his account of perception: he is, so to speak, trying to make second-realm differences do the work of third-realm differences. And, hence, contrary to his intention, it seems that he can't account for the fact that *a is F* and *b is F* convey different information. However, recall that the qualia freak can revise his view so that it avoids this error by saying that it's the *representation* of the experiences *as having* qualia that explains the subjective differences between experiences. And there is a similar move available to the non-descriptive Fregean.

Suppose that non-descriptive Fregeanism is true but that non-descriptive modes of presentation contained in a proposition don't directly affect representational content. Now suppose that Ronnie assertively utters the sentence *Superman flies* and Gene assertively utters the sentence *Clark Kent flies*. Ronnie's utterance expresses the proposition <Superman, flying> whereas Gene's utterance expresses the proposition <Clark Kent, flying>; but, since the modes of presentation Superman and Clark Kent don't directly affect the representational content of these propositions, they can't explain the different information the two sentences convey. However, the difference could be due to some other proposition that is conveyed but that *isn't* expressed by each sentence. Upon hearing Ronnie's utterance, you come to believe that Superman flies, but you might also come to believe something about Ronnie: namely, *that Superman and flying are constituents of one of Ronnie's beliefs*. And, likewise, upon hearing Gene's utterance, you come to believe that Clark Kent flies, but you might also come to believe something about Gene: namely, *that Clark Kent and flying are constituents of one of Gene's beliefs*. Non-descriptive modes of presentation that don't directly affect representational content can figure into an explanation of the different information conveyed by the sentences, but only if the information turns out to be *about* the relevant non-descriptive modes of presentation; that is to say, only if the non-descriptive Fregean adopts a differences-*about*-the-how proposal.

If the non-descriptive modes of presentation contained in a proposition do directly affect its representational content, then the mere fact that the belief that a is F contains one non-descriptive mode of presentation and the belief that b is F contains another will explain why the sentences *a is F* and *b is F* convey different information. They will do so in virtue of expressing propositions that, so to speak, contain different *hows*; that is to say, a differences-*in*-the-how proposal can be adopted. However, if the non-descriptive modes of presentation contained in a proposition don't directly affect its representational content, the fact that the two sentences express propositions that contain different non-descriptive modes of presentation cannot by itself explain why they convey different information. But this fact can figure into such an explanation. Though the propositions expressed by the two sentences won't themselves count as different information, each sentence can convey a collateral proposition about, so to speak, the *how* of the proposition it expresses; that is, a differences-*about*-the-how proposal can be adopted.

We saw in Chapter 1 that if the qualia freak is to explain subjective differences between perceptions by appealing to qualia, then, since the mere instantiation of a quale doesn't directly affect the representational content of an experience, he must maintain that these qualia are represented in perception and that the representational content of a perception is, in part, *about* its qualia. Similarly, if the non-descriptive Fregean is to explain the differences in information conveyed between two sentences in terms of non-descriptive modes of presentation that don't affect representational content, he must adopt a differences-*about*-the-how proposal: he must say that the difference in information conveyed is about the non-descriptive modes of presentation.

The distinction between the two proposals is subtle, but it does have important consequences for Fregeanism. As we've seen, a non-descriptive Fregeanism that posits modes of presentation that don't directly affect representational content is forced to adopt a differences-*about*-the-how proposal. But, in doing so, it loses one of the main virtues associated with Fregeanism. On the non-descriptive Fregean version of a differences-*in*-the-how proposal, the sentences *S believes that a is F* and *S believes that b is F* convey different information (even when the names co-refer) merely because they express propositions that constitute different information. And, since the non-descriptive Fregean's view captures the Fregean intuition that such belief ascriptions can have different truth-values, it is tempting to think that even if he adopts a differences-*about*-the-how proposal the sentences convey different information merely because the propositions they express constitute different information. For example, Mark Richard (1990, 127) is a non-descriptive Fregean who adopts a differences-*about*-the-how proposal, and he believes that his view makes "the relevant information a part of the semantic content of a sentence." (A version of Richard's view is discussed in the next section.)

However, as tempting as this thought may be, it isn't in fact correct. For, even though the non-descriptive Fregean captures the Fregean intuitions about the truth-value of belief ascriptions, if he adopts a differences-*about*-the-how proposal, the relevant information conveyed by each belief ascription isn't part of the proposition it expresses. For a belief ascription merely expresses that its subject believes some proposition, whereas the relevant information conveyed is that a certain non-descriptive mode of presentation is a *constituent* of the proposition he believes; and clearly the proposition *that S believes that a is F* is distinct from the proposition *that the non-descriptive mode of presentation ɑ is a constituent of the proposition that S believes*. To get at the difference in a more intuitive way, the second proposition is *about* the non-descriptive mode of presentation ɑ while the first isn't. On a guise Millian version of a differences-*about*-the-how proposal, the relevant information is not part of the proposition expressed by the belief ascription but rather is pragmatically conveyed by it. And, on a non-descriptive Fregean version of a differences-*about*-the-how proposal, the relevant information isn't a part of the proposition expressed by the sentence either; rather, it is also pragmatically conveyed. The only difference is that a guise Millian like Salmon explains how the information is conveyed in terms of what we might call *conversational pragmatics*: rules that govern conversational exchanges (and which will be discussed in the next chapter). Whereas the non-descriptive Fregean will explain it in terms of different pragmatic factors; for example, when I utter the sentence *S believes that a is F* you might get the relevant information in virtue of your knowledge that the truth of the sentence *implies* that the non-descriptive mode of presentation ɑ is a constituent of the proposition that S believes.

Richard believes that one of the important advantages of his view over Millianism is that, unlike Millianism, it explains the different information conveyed by *S believes that a is F* and *S believes that b is F* semantically; that is, it explains it in terms of the propositions expressed by the belief ascriptions. But, in fact, it doesn't. Though, on his view, the ascriptions relate S to different propositions, this is not the different information that they convey. Rather, like Salmon's guise Millianism, Richard's view explains the different information in terms of collateral propositions about the relevant non-descriptive modes of presentation. *S believes that a is F* does express the proposition that S bears the belief relation to the belief that a is F, but it also conveys that S accepts the sentence *a is F* and, on Richard's view, it's *the latter* that explains why the belief ascription conveys different information from *S believes that b is F*. And, indeed, because his modes of presentation are linguistic items and, hence, don't directly affect the representational content of propositions that contain them, he cannot explain the differences semantically. For, as pointed out in Section 1, the difference in information conveyed between the belief ascriptions is that they convey that S believes different propositions; the first conveys that S believes what's conveyed by *a is F*, while the second conveys that S believes what's conveyed by *b is F*. But, since Richard's modes of presentation don't directly affect representational content, the propositions expressed by *a is F* and *b is F*, different though they may be, can't differ in information. So, contrary to his intentions, Richard's explanation of the difference in information conveyed by the belief ascriptions isn't a semantic explanation of how they relate S to different information.

For the above reasons, any non-descriptive Fregean who posits modes of presentation that don't directly affect representational content has to adopt a differences-*about*-the-how approach to solving the puzzle. And that's why this type of non-descriptive Fregeanism loses one virtue it's supposed to have over Millianism in accounting for how the information by the relevant belief ascriptions is conveyed. Both views will have to claim that the different information conveyed by *S believes that a is F* and *S believes that b is F* results from collateral propositions that each conveys. To focus again on Richard's view, he might as well say that the belief ascriptions ascribe Millian propositions to their subjects but that they convey different information because each conveys that S accepts the sentence embedded in its *that*-clause; that is, he might as well be a guise Millian. If the goal is to make the difference between the belief ascriptions semantic, then nothing at all is gained by adding that the sentences are constituents of propositions they express. It might *seem* that something is gained, since putting the modes of presentation in the propositions makes it turn out that the two belief ascriptions really can differ in truth-value. However, given that our intuitions that their truth-values can differ arise from the different information they convey, and given that, on the view under discussion, this difference is not in fact a semantic difference, there's no reason for the view to respect these intuitions; that is to say, its account of the information differences completely undermines the intuitions about possible divergence in truth-value. So a non-descriptive Fregeanism according to which modes of presentation don't affect representational content loses one advantage Fregeanism is supposed to have over Millianism since, appearances to the contrary, it can't give a semantic explanation of the different information conveyed by the relevant belief ascriptions.

Now it may seem that this defect is peculiar to Richard's version of non-descriptive Fregeansim and that there are other versions of the view according to which the different information conveyed by *S believes that a is F* and *S believes that b is F* does result from semantics rather than pragmatics. For example, one might claim that belief is a three-place relation between subjects, Millian propositions, and non-descriptive modes of presentation (rather than a two-place relation between subjects and Fregean propositions that *contain* non-descriptive modes of presentation). On such a view, *S believes that a is F* turns out to express something like: S bears the belief relation to the (Millian) proposition that a is F via the non-descriptive mode of presentation a. The belief ascription *S believes that a is F* is, so to speak, *semantically about* a, whereas *S believes that b is F* turns out to be semantically about b (for views of this sort, see Crimmins and Perry 1989, Schiffer 1992, and Crimmins 1992). However, though such a view posits a semantic difference between the belief ascriptions, it's not at all clear that it should count as a species of *Fregeanism*.

If, as the view under discussion claims, non-descriptive modes of presentation are not constituents of propositions, then the proposition that a is F just is the proposition that b is F (where the names co-refer) and hence—assuming that the belief that a is F just is the proposition that a is F (see Chapter 2, Section 8)—*the belief that a is F* just is the *belief that b is F*. Hence, on the classificatory scheme I've adopted, the views under discussion turn out to be guise Millian views in which the relevant belief ascriptions convey different information because of semantics rather than pragmatics. This no doubt seems odd, but it's important to see that the oddness here is that there are two natural ways to characterize Fregeanism that turn out not to be equivalent: one in terms of whether distinct but co-refering names must contribute the same thing to the beliefs named by expressions containing them (that is, whether *the belief that a is F* and *the belief that b is F* must co-refer when the names do) and another in terms of whether substitution of co-refering names in belief ascriptions preserves truth-value (that is, whether *S believes that a is F* and *S believes that b is F* must have the same truth-value when the names co-refer). Philosophers of language have tended to focus on belief ascriptions rather than other kinds of phrases in which the word *belief* or one of its cognates appears; but, if your concern is what the semantic value of a name tells you about the nature of beliefs, it's natural to focus on the second (as I have). But, of course, as discussed in Chapter 2, Section 8, in the end both kinds of cases (as well as other uses of *belief* and cognate terms) must be accounted for.

To approach the same point from a slightly different direction, the view we're discussing says that belief is a three-place relation among subjects, non-descriptive modes of presentation, and (Millian) propositions; but Salmon's view is the same except that belief reports *quantify over* the non-descriptive modes of presentation. If you're worried about the nature of propositions picked out by sentences containing names, you'll count both views as Millian; but, if you're worried about the truth-value of belief reports containing names, only Salmon's counts as Millian. However, the important point here is the one emphasized in Chapter 2, Sections 14–16: namely, if your primary worry is about the ontology of mind rather than the semantics of names, there is no interesting difference between these two views; both hold that our cognitive relation to stuff in the world is mediated by non-descriptive modes of presentation and, hence, both are triadist views of belief that should be classified together. And likewise for a view like Richard's, according to which belief is a two-place relation between subjects and propositions that contain non-descriptive modes of presentation. So far as philosophy of mind goes, it doesn't matter whether this view is Fregean or Millian; what's important is that it involves a triadist proposal. And, as we'll now see, no such proposal can solve Frege's puzzle.

5. Against differences-about-the-how

As we saw in the previous section, according to a differences-*about*-the-how proposal, the sentences *Superman flies* and *Clark Kent flies* convey different information because the first conveys that Superman mediates the speaker's relation to what the proposition expressed by the sentence represents, while the second conveys that Clark Kent is the mediator. However, it is important to note that those who adopt a differences-*about*-the-how proposal claim that the relevant information conveyed by the belief ascriptions concerns which non-descriptive modes of presentation mediate *the subject's* relation to the relevant proposition rather than which mediate the *speaker's* relation to it. Nathan Salmon is a guise Millian and Mark Richard is a non-descriptive Fregean, but both offer a differences-*about*-the-how proposal and claim that, where belief ascriptions are concerned, the differences in information conveyed concern which non-descriptive modes of presentation mediate the *subject's* relation to what the belief represents. According to Salmon (1986, 116), "our purpose in belief attribution is to specify how the believer stands with respect to a proposition." And, according to Richard (1990, 126), "[b]y and large, the point of attitude ascription is to get across some information about the how of the attitude as well as its what."

According to both Salmon and Richard, when I utter the sentence *Lex believes that Superman flies* I convey to listeners that the non-descriptive modes of presentation Superman and the property of flying mediate Lex's relation to *what* the belief that Superman flies represents. And on both of their views Superman and the property of flying *do* mediate this relation: on Richard's view, they do so by being part of the belief <Superman, the property of flying> that the ascription attributes to Lex, where the belief *determines what* it represents;[9] and, on Salmon's view, they do so by mediating Lex's relation to the belief, where the belief *itself* consists of *what* it represents. Hence, on both of their views an utterance of the sentence *Lex believes that Superman flies* conveys *true* information. Furthermore, according to Salmon and Richard, the sentence *Lex believes that Clark Kent flies* conveys to listeners that the non-descriptive modes of presentation Clark Kent and the property of flying mediate Lex's relation to what the belief that Clark Kent flies represents. And on both of their views Clark Kent does *not* in fact mediate the relation: according to Richard, this is because Lex does not bear the belief relation to the proposition <Clark Kent, the property of flying>; and, according to Salmon, this is because the non-descriptive mode of presentation Clark Kent does not mediate Lex's apprehension of the proposition that Superman flies.[10]

The first point that needs to be made is that if you adopt a differences-*about*-the-how proposal, then you'd better claim that non-descriptive modes of presentation are *public-language expressions*. For, otherwise, it is ludicrous to claim that information about non-descriptive modes of presentation is generally conveyed by utterances. There is a tendency to think that solving Frege's puzzle just means coming up with some way to distinguish the relevant belief ascriptions. But, though the puzzle is an argument that the belief ascriptions are distinct, it results from the observation that the relevant sentences convey different information. Hence, any solution to the puzzle had better have some plausible account of the information conveyed by the sentences. But when someone utters a sentence in my presence it's patently obvious that I don't get any information about their brain states, or about any entities that mediate their or anyone else's relation to what they believe other than bits of public language. David Braun (1998, 567–68) also makes this point. Hence, we've got to assume that, on a differences-*about*-the-how proposal, non-descriptive modes of presentation simply are public-language expressions and the information that distinguishes two sentences that express propositions identical with respect to their *what* concerns which sentences mediate some subject's belief relation to that *what*: that is, which among the sentences that express a proposition with that *what* some subject accepts.[11] However, it should be noted that the points below apply with equal force if non-descriptive modes of presentation turn out to be something other than public-language expressions.

So a differences-*about*-the-how proposal claims that, for example, the sentences **Superman flies** and **Clark Kent flies** convey different information insofar as each conveys that the *speaker* accepts it; whereas, for example, the sentences **Lex believes that Superman flies** and **Lex believes that Clark Kent flies** convey different information insofar as each conveys that *Lex* accepts its embedded sentence. However, a little reflection reveals that this account can't solve Frege's puzzle. There are three related reasons for this and the first is that the account can't provide a unified solution to the puzzle.

To see this, consider how the account explains the differences in information conveyed by the two simple sentences **Superman flies** and **Clark Kent flies**. These sentences aren't themselves belief ascriptions and, hence, as we have seen, if the relevant information each conveys concerns which sentences someone accepts, then the only person available is the one who utters the sentence: someone who utters **Superman flies** conveys the information that *he*, the speaker, accepts that very sentence; whereas someone who utters **Clark Kent flies** conveys the information that *he* accepts *that* very sentence. But then, when I utter the sentence **Superman flies** I convey one bit of information—that *I* accept the sentence **Superman flies**—and when I utter the sentence **Lex believes that Superman flies** I *don't* convey that Lex bears the belief relation to this information; for the information that I convey by uttering the belief attribution concerns which sentence *Lex* accepts. Thus a differences-*about*-the-how proposal must deny the very plausible idea that the information conveyed by the belief ascriptions involves the *very same* information that is conveyed by the simple sentences; that is to say, the proposal doesn't provide a unified solution to Frege's puzzle. Moreover, this fact implies worse troubles for the proposal's response to the way of generating Frege's puzzle that appeals to reasons for behavior.

Recall that, on the way of generating Frege's puzzle that appeals to reasons for behavior, the relevant beliefs are alleged to be different because the information conveyed by the sentence **Lex believes that Superman is coming** gives a reason for his lurking behind the door clutching a piece of kryptonite, whereas the information conveyed by the sentence **Lex believes that Clark Kent is coming** doesn't. But, on a differences-*about*-the-how proposal, the first sentence conveys different information from the second because the first conveys that Lex accepts the sentence *Superman flies*, whereas the second conveys that he accepts the sentence *Clark Kent flies*. And the fact that Lex accepts a certain sentence cannot be a *reason* for his behavior. Lex's reasons for engaging in this behavior clearly must involve what *beliefs* (or desires, or intentions, etc.) he has and not what sentences he accepts.

I think that the above point has been lost on many philosophers because of an ambiguity in the way of generating Frege's puzzle that appeals to reasons for behavior. As my name for this way of generating the puzzle suggests, I have been careful to construe the explanation of behavior as one that provides *reasons* for the relevant behavior. However, what I call *the way of generating Frege's puzzle that appeals to reasons for behavior* is usually put simply in terms of what counts as a good *explanation* of someone's behavior. And when we ask for an explanation of someone's behavior, the demand is ambiguous between a demand for a mere *causal* explanation and a demand for his *reasons* for behaving as he did.[12] If the demand is construed in the former way, someone's acceptance of a sentence *might* explain his behavior, since accepting a sentence *might* be causally relevant to the production of behavior; at a minimum, it isn't incoherent to suppose that this is so. However, if the demand for an explanation is a demand for the subject's *reasons*, then it can't be answered by citing a mere cause. It *is* incoherent to suppose that someone's acceptance of a sentence could be a reason for his behavior, since a subject's reason must be a belief, a desire, or some other attitude of his. Of course, I do not mean to suggest that a demand for reasons is in general preferable to a demand for mere causes; in different circumstances one or the other might be the appropriate explanation for someone's behavior, and in some circumstances either might do. What I am pointing out is that sometimes we do ask for an explanation in terms of reasons, and under these circumstances a differences-*about*-the-how proposal doesn't provide a coherent explanation.

So a differences-*about*-the-how proposal gives an unacceptable response to the way of generating Frege's puzzle that appeals to reasons for behavior. However, the proposal is also committed to *another response* to this way of generating Frege's puzzle and, unfortunately, it is no better than the first. Suppose I utter the sentence *Superman is coming* in Lex Luthor's presence and upon hearing the sentence he begins to lurk behind the door clutching some kryptonite. Clearly the information that I conveyed to Lex by uttering the sentence constitutes his reason for lurking behind the door. But, on a differences-*about*-the-how proposal, the information I convey to Lex by uttering the sentence is information that *I* accept a certain sentence. So, if we consider the information conveyed by belief ascriptions, a differences-*about*-the-how proposal explains Lex's behavior in terms of sentences *he* accepts; but, if we consider the information conveyed by simple sentences, the proposal explains Lex's behavior in terms of *his beliefs* about sentences *the speaker* accepts. And, importantly, neither explanation of Lex's behavior is even close to correct. His reasons for doing what he does don't involve sentences he accepts, and they certainly don't involve sentences I accept. Any proposal that implies two distinct reasons for Lex's behavior is suspect and, if neither is the sort of thing that can be a reason, the proposal must simply be wrong. And, of course, these criticisms have nothing in particular to do with the Lex Luthor case; a differences-*about*-the-how proposal will have the same unacceptable consequences for any such case.

So far, we have seen three problems with a differences-*about*-the-how proposal: first, it fails to provide a unified solution to all of the ways of generating Frege's puzzle; second, because of the first problem, it winds up implying two distinct solutions to the way of generating Frege's puzzle that appeals to reasons for behavior; finally, neither of these solutions is even close to correct. However, these problems result from specific features of Richard's and Salmon's proposals. Because they take the collateral information conveyed by the relevant belief ascriptions to concern *what sentences its subject accepts* rather than some *belief its subject has*, their solution to the problem of belief ascriptions doesn't provide a solution to the problem posed by the sentences embedded in those belief asciptions. Hence, they have to advert to information about the sentences the speaker accepts to solve the problem posed by the embedded sentences. And, as a result, they wind up without a unified solution to the puzzle. Moreover, since the collateral information in both cases concerns the sentences someone accepts, neither is even a candidate to explain the problem posed by reasons for behavior.

But there is a way of revising the proposal so that it avoids these problems. You could claim that, for example, *Superman is coming* and *Clark Kent is coming* convey different information because each sentence conveys that *it* is true (rather than that the speaker accepts it). This would provide a unified solution to Frege's puzzle if one also claimed that, for example, *Lex believes that Superman is coming* and *Lex believes that Clark Kent is coming* convey different information because each conveys that Lex believes that its embedded sentence *is true* (rather than that Lex accepts its embedded sentence). Since Lex's acceptance of the sentence *Superman is coming* more or less amounts to his believing that it's true, the revised proposal is in the spirit of Richard's and Salmon's. But, unlike their initial proposal, saying that the collateral information conveyed by *Lex believes that Superman is coming* is that he believes that the sentence *Superman is coming* is true entails a solution to the problem posed by the embedded sentence *Superman is coming*. The information conveyed by assertive utterances of *Superman is coming* will just be the belief that the collateral information conveyed by *Lex believes that Superman is coming* attributes to Lex: namely, the belief that the sentence *Superman is coming* is true. Similarly, the collateral information conveyed by *Lex believes that Clark Kent is coming* attributes to Lex the belief that the sentence *Clark Kent is coming* is true. And, since this difference in the information conveyed by the belief ascriptions concerns what Lex *believes*, it isn't incoherent to claim that the difference explains why the first but not the second gives the reason for Lex's behavior. This very slight revision to Richard's and Salmon's kind of proposal is necessary if it is to provide a unified solution to Frege's puzzle and, hence, avoid the serious problems that result from not providing such a solution.

However, the revised proposal is not without problems of its own and, unfortunately, these problems are fatal. Although on this proposal the different information conveyed by the belief ascriptions does concern Lex's beliefs, the relevant belief *still* isn't his reason for lurking behind the door. Lex doesn't lurk behind the door merely because he believes some sentence to be true; his reason for engaging in this behavior must ultimately involve beliefs he has about Superman and not beliefs he has about sentences. For example, suppose that Lex believes *Superman is coming* expresses the proposition that snow is white or has no idea what proposition it expresses; in either case his belief that it's true won't be a reason for him to behave as he does. The fact that he believes that the sentence is true can't be a reason for his behavior unless he also thinks it expresses a proposition that would provide a reason for his behavior. So, if the revised proposal is going to work, the proposition that Lex takes the sentence *Superman is coming* to express will have to provide a reason for him to lurk. But on neither the guise Millian nor the non-desciptive Fregean proposal does Lex take the sentence to express a proposition that would provide a reason for his behavior.

According to the guise Millian, Lex (mistakenly) thinks the proposition *Superman is coming* includes the information it conveys; that is, Lex will mistakenly take it to express a different proposition than the sentence *Clark Kent is coming* does only because he thinks the proposition expressed by each sentence includes the collateral information it conveys. But, on the revised proposal, the relevant collateral information that each sentence conveys is that it is true, so Lex will take the sentence *Superman is coming* to express the proposition that Superman is coming and that the sentence *Superman is coming* is true. And this takes us right back to the initial problem: his belief that Superman is coming can't (on the Millian's story) provide a reason for his lurking behind the door because it's identical to his belief that Clark Kent is coming, which doesn't provide any such reason; and his belief that the sentence is true can't provide a reason unless he takes it to express a proposition that provides a reason. The point here is that on the guise Millian view Lex *doesn't* take the sentence to express a proposition that would give him a reason to lurk behind the door with the kryptonite since he takes it to express the unhelpful singular proposition that Superman (that is, Clark Kent) is coming and the proposition that the sentence is true. Given that this is what he takes the sentence to express, his belief that the sentence is true just amounts to his believing the unhelpful singular proposition that it does in fact express and the unhelpful proposition that the sentence is true. So the revised proposal doesn't help the guise Millian to explain Lex's behavior.

And the non-descriptive Fregean version of the revised proposal doesn't fare much better. On the revised proposal, the collateral information conveyed by *Lex believes that Superman is coming* is that Lex believes that the embedded sentence *Superman is coming* is true, and my point is that this belief will provide a reason for Lex's behavior only if Lex takes the sentence to express a proposition that would provide a reason for his behavior. Now, unlike the guise Millian, the non-descriptive Fregean does take the sentences *Superman is coming* and *Clark Kent is coming* to express different propositions; the proposition that Superman is coming contains the non-descriptive mode of presentation **Superman** while the proposition that Clark Kent is coming contains the non-descriptive mode of presentation **Clark Kent**. So, given that Lex takes the sentence *Superman is coming* to express the proposition that Superman is coming and takes the sentence *Clark Kent is coming* to express the proposition that Clark Kent is coming, he will take them to express propositions that are distinct from one another. But now the question is: how could the proposition <**Superman, is coming**> provide a reason for Lex's behavior when the proposition <**Clark Kent, is coming**> doesn't? Lex's belief that the sentence *Superman is coming* is true is, on the proposal under consideration, supposed to provide a reason for his behavior. But since he takes it to express the proposition that Superman is coming—that is, the proposition <**Superman, is coming**>—his belief that the sentence is true will provide a reason for his behavior only if that proposition would provide such a reason.

But this means that the proposal under consideration is really a differences-*in*-the-how proposal. For, according to the proposal under consideration, the fact that the proposition that Superman is coming contains a distinct non-descriptive mode of presentation from the proposition that Clark Kent is coming will by itself have to explain how the first can provide a reason for Lex to lurk while the second doesn't. And, of course, if one provides a reason and the other doesn't, they had better constitute different information; that is to say, mere differences *in* non-descriptive modes of presentation will have to result in differences in information. And this means that what is really being offered is a differences-*in*-the-how proposal.

As we saw at the end of the previous section, if modes of presentation don't affect representational content, they can't ground differences in information; and this is precisely why someone like Richard, who claims that non-descriptive modes of presentation are the kinds of things that don't affect representational content, is forced to adopt a differences-*about*-the-how proposal and explain the relevant differences in information conveyed in terms of collateral propositions. And, as we saw at the beginning of this section, on such a proposal the only plausible candidates for the non-descriptive modes of presentation are sentences, since these are the only things that don't affect representational content that our ordinary utterances convey anything about. Finally, we saw in this section that the only kind of collateral information about a sentence that can provide a unified solution to Frege's puzzle is information that the sentence is true. What the considerations in the last paragraph show is that, in order for the Fregean to account for reasons for behavior, the modes of presentation he posits will *have* to affect representational content. For he's going to wind up saying that Lex's belief that the sentence *Superman is coming* is true is the reason for his lurking behind the door and, hence, he's going to have to say how the proposition that Superman is coming by itself could explain Lex's behavior.

A Fregean solution to the puzzle that appeals to modes of presentation that don't affect representational content can't possibly work and, ultimately, the Fregean has to posit modes of presentation that do affect representational content and offer a differences-*in*-the-how proposal. We've also seen that guise Millianism cannot offer a solution to the puzzle either. Hence, the only possible triadist solution left is a Fregeanism according to which modes of presentation *do* affect representational content: a Fregeanism that explains the differences in information that ground the puzzle by appealing to a differences-*in*-the-how proposal.

And, indeed, it shouldn't be surprising that the differences-*about*-the-how proposal can't be made to work, for the proposal rests on some false assumptions. The motivation behind a differences-*about*-the-how proposal is the thought that we care not only about *what* a subject believes, but also about *how* he believes it; that is to say, we care about which sentences he would use to express his belief. But, as a matter of fact, we generally don't care very much at all about which sentences the subject of a belief report would accept; and this is reflected by the fact that *such information is rarely conveyed by belief ascriptions*. The fact that you generally can use an English sentence to ascribe a belief to a subject who speaks no English *without* giving any indication that he doesn't speak English or of what language he does speak shows that in such cases information about which sentence the subject accepts isn't communicated. However, such information isn't even normally communicated when it's clear to listeners that the subject of the belief ascriptions *does* speak the language in question.

To see this, consider, once again, the belief ascription *Lex believes that Superman flies*. It's quite natural to think that, when I utter the sentence, I convey to listeners that Lex would accept the sentence *Superman flies*. However, as natural as this thought is, it is in fact false. For suppose that on several occasions Lex has seen Superman flying about the city saving various citizens from harm. Suppose further that Lex has no idea what this individual is called but that on one occasion or another he has pointed to him and said *He flies*. Knowing these facts, it would clearly be appropriate for me to utter the sentence *Lex believes that Superman flies*. Or suppose that, rather than having no idea as to what the individual is called, Lex mistakenly believes that he is called *Fred* (or *Bill*, or *Susan*) and, hence, he utters the sentence *Fred* (or *Bill*, or *Susan*) *flies*. In either of these cases it would *still* be perfectly appropriate for me to utter the sentence *Lex believes that Superman flies*. But, if uttering the belief ascription is appropriate even when Lex refers to Superman only by an indexical or by some name that does not in fact refer to Superman, how can it be that the belief ascription normally conveys information that Lex would accept the sentence *Superman flies*? Indeed, given the various circumstances in which it would be appropriate for me to utter the belief ascription, how can it be that it normally conveys *any information whatsoever* about which sentences Lex would or would not accept?

To drive the point home, suppose that Lex has the proper uses of the names *Superman* and *Clark Kent* reversed: he thinks that the former name is used to refer to the bespectacled *Daily Planet* reporter and that the latter name is used to refer to the super-powered individual whom he has seen flying about the city. Assuming that the listener doesn't have the proper use of the names reversed, it would *still* be appropriate to utter the sentence *Lex believes that Superman flies* and inappropriate to utter the sentence *Lex believes that Clark Kent flies* even though, in these circumstances, the sentence Lex would in fact accept is the one embedded in the latter belief ascription. This point is even clearer in the case of belief ascriptions in which the embedded sentence contains indexicals. If I am pointing at Superman while he is dressed in his Superman outfit, I can utter the sentence *Lex believes that he flies* even if Lex doesn't know what Superman looks like and, hence, *wouldn't* accept an utterance of the embedded sentence; and under these circumstances I can also utter the sentence *Lex believes that you fly* to Superman. Indeed, if I am talking to Superman it will usually be inappropriate for me to use any term that refers to Superman besides *you* in the *that*-clause of the belief ascription; and this will be true even if Lex doesn't know what he looks like and, hence, wouldn't accept an utterance of the embedded sentence.[13]

Now, of course, in certain contexts my assertive utterance of the belief ascription *might* convey information about what sentences Lex does or doesn't accept. For example, if my listeners know that Lex has no beliefs about what Superman's name is and they know that he knows what Superman looks like, then the belief ascription might convey that Lex would only accept the sentence (uttered while pointing to Superman in his Superman outfit) *He flies* or the sentence (uttered while pointing at Superman in the outfit) *You fly*, etc. Or, if my listeners know that Lex mistakenly thinks that Superman is called *Batman*, my utterance of the belief attribution might convey to them that Lex would accept the sentence *Batman flies*. But the point is that no such background conditions need be in place for the belief ascription to be perfectly appropriate and that, in general, no *such background conditions are in place.*

I have been emphasizing that a belief ascription doesn't usually convey any information concerning what sentences its subject does or doesn't accept. And it is a bit ironic that the reason for this was essentially given by Frege. In "On Sense and Reference," Frege ([1892] 1984a) recognizes that the significance of an identity statement usually doesn't concern language: for example, Frege points out that the discovery that Hesperus is Phosphorus was a significant astronomical discovery and not just a discovery about names.[14] But a differences-*about*-the-how proposal claims that the different information conveyed by the sentences *Superman flies* and *Clark Kent flies* concerns *sentences*, and likewise for the difference in information conveyed by belief ascriptions involving these sentences. And, as Frege noted, it is a mistake to think that, in general, the different information conveyed by two sentences that are identical with respect to their *what* concerns linguistic expressions. Insofar as the non-descriptive Fregean adopts a differences-*about*-the-how proposal as a solution to Frege's puzzle, he attempts to capture Frege's views on the individuation of belief by ignoring one of Frege's important insights about what the difference in significance between the relevant sentences *isn't.*[15]

6. Against differences-in-the-how

In the last section we saw that a differences-*about*-the-how proposal comes nowhere near to adequately addressing Frege's puzzle, so the non-descriptive Fregean must suppose that modes of presentation do affect representational content and adopt a differences-*in*-the-how proposal. And, as we've seen, unlike a differences-*about*-the-how proposal, a differences-*in*-the-how proposal is open only to the non-descriptive Fregean. If, as the non-descriptive Fregean claims, non-descriptive modes of presentation are constituents of propositions, then **Superman flies** and **Clark Kent** flies might convey different information *merely in virtue* of expressing propositions that contain different non-descriptive modes of presentation; differences in non-descriptive modes of presentation might by themselves imply differences in information conveyed. Indeed, some philosophers of mind seem to assume that a differences-*in*-the-how proposal is correct when they respond to Frank Jackson's famous *knowledge argument*, which was mentioned at the beginning of Chapter 1.

The knowledge argument asks us to consider Mary, a brilliant neuroscientist and psychologist who has spent her whole life in a room in which everything is either black, white, or some shade of grey. We are to suppose that Mary has learned all of the physical facts about vision—where the physical facts include the chemical, biological, and functional facts—but that she has learned these facts from a black-and-white television and equally colorless books. The point is that, while Mary knows all of the physical facts about vision, she has never seen any colors besides black, white, and shades of grey. We are next asked to suppose that Mary is set free from her prison and that the first object she sees is red: say, it's a fire engine. Jackson claims that upon seeing the fire engine Mary will learn a new fact: namely, what it is like to see red. Jackson concludes that since Mary already knew all of the physical facts, the fact that she learns must be *non-physical*.

Many philosophers have responded to Jackson with the claim that what it's like to see red *is* a physical fact and, hence, is, in some sense, a fact Mary already knew. When she learns what it's like to see red, she apprehends this fact via a new *non-descriptive mode of presentation*. Thus, although Mary's new belief has the same *what* as one of her old beliefs, she gets new information because the belief is new with respect to its *how*.[16] In other words, a differences-*in*-the-how proposal is correct. I will have much more to say about the Mary case in Chapter 5, but for now it suffices to note that, despite the prevalence of the thought that differences in information conveyed might just amount to differences in non-descriptive modes of presentation, the thought is in fact very dubious. The first reason to be suspicious is that new information is always accompanied by a belief that is new with respect to its *what*.

Suppose you sometimes hear Steven talking about someone whom he calls *Ed* and Sam talking about someone whom he calls *Bill* but that you don't hear what either says about the person he is discussing. Suppose further that someone utters the sentence *Ed is Bill* to you and that you believe him. If Ed really is Bill, *what* your new belief represents is the same as *what* is represented by the belief that Ed is Ed. But when you accept the sentence *Ed is Bill* you also learn that the person Steven calls *Ed* is the person Sam calls *Bill*; and, since, by hypothesis, you haven't heard what either says about Ed or Bill, this is the only other thing you learn. Notice that *what* this new belief represents is different from *what* the belief that Ed is Ed represents and, hence, upon hearing the sentence *Ed is Bill*, you acquire a new belief that differs from any of your old beliefs with respect to its *what*. And it seems to me that there's nothing special about this case, and, hence, I want to suggest the following principle.

The New Information Principle
Whenever someone gets new information in virtue of accepting some sentence, he also gains a belief that differs from any of his old beliefs with respect to its *what*.

According to the New Information Principle, new information is always accompanied by information that is new with respect to its *what,* and it's hard to see how this could be false. After all, whenever some sentence *S* conveys new information to you, you will at least come to believe *that S is true*; and the belief that *S* is true will differ from any of your old beliefs with respect to its *what*. However, it has been suggested to me that there is a counterexample to the principle: that it is possible that someone—call her *Lisa*—could use some name—say, *Ellen*—to refer to what she takes to be two distinct individuals and yet she could *have absolutely no beliefs* about either that would individuate them. Suppose, however, that Ellen is in fact Ellen. Upon hearing someone utter the sentence *Ellen is Ellen* (and understanding how each occurrence of *Ellen* was being used), Lisa would get new information. But since, by hypothesis, Lisa has no beliefs that distinguish the individuals she mistakenly thought were distinct, and since her name for the individuals is the same, what new belief could she have that differs from any of her old beliefs with respect to its *what*? There seems to be no candidate; so, if the Lisa case is cogent, then it appears that the New Information Principle is false.

I think that it is doubtful that the Lisa case is in fact cogent because I have serious doubts that someone could believe that a and b are distinct if she didn't have any way at all to distinguish them. To be clear, I, of course, do not doubt that Lisa could believe that *there are* two individuals named *Ellen*; what I doubt is that Lisa could have any *de re* beliefs about Ellen.[17] However, whether or not the case is cogent really doesn't matter; for, even though the names are the same, Lisa *still* gains a new belief that differs from any of her old beliefs with respect to its *what*. Upon hearing the sentence *Ellen is Ellen*, Lisa will clearly come to believe that the two occurrences of *Ellen* in the sentence refer to the same individual. And this belief differs from any of her prior beliefs with regard to what it represents.

It is important to notice that the new information that Lisa gets upon hearing

Ellen is Ellen is not going to be significant information; and the information that the two occurrences of *Ellen* refer to the same individual will also lack any significance. But notice that the same holds in the *Ed is Bill* case. Under the circumstances described in that case, whatever information you gain by hearing the sentence *Ed is Bill* is not going to be very significant, and the belief that the person Steven calls *Bill* is the person Sam calls *Ed* will be equally insignificant. Suppose, however, that you've heard Steven say *Ed is building a nuclear weapon* and you've heard Sam say *Bill would like to destroy the city*, and that you believed both of them. Now the information you gain upon hearing *Ed is Bill* is *very significant*; but you also gain a belief whose *what* differs from what is represented by the belief that Ed is Bill: namely, that someone who wants to destroy the city is building a nuclear bomb! Again it seems to me that there's nothing special about this case and, hence, I want to suggest that the following principle is also true.

The Significance of New Information Principle
Whatever the significance of the new information that someone gets in virtue of accepting a sentence, he will get information that is new with respect to its *what* that is equally significant.

The above two principles strongly suggest that differences in information conveyed cannot be accounted for by mere differences in non-descriptive modes of presentation and, hence, that a differences-*in*-the-how proposal must be wrong. Since getting new information via some sentence always involves getting a belief that differs from any of your prior beliefs with respect to its *what*, and since the new information will always be equal in significance to one of these new beliefs, the most plausible supposition is that when a sentence conveys new information it does so *by* conveying information that is new with respect to its *what*. At a minimum, a proponent of a differences-*in*-the-how proposal must explain how it facilitates the truth of the New Information Principle and the Significance of New Information Principle; that is to say, he must explain the role that non-descriptive modes of presentation play in getting the information that is new with respect to its *what* and in making this information as significant as the new belief that merely differs with respect to its *how*. Moreover, there is a very plausible explanation of how a sentence can convey information to a listener that is new with respect to its *what* even though he already believes *what* it represents: when conversational participants believe that the thing named *a* is D and each knows that the other does, an utterance of the sentence *a is F* can be used to convey the information that the thing that is D is F;[18] hence, *a is F* can convey information that is new with respect to its what even when *a* and *b* co-refer and the listener already believes that b is F. And, since this explanation *doesn't* claim that non-descriptive modes of presentation are constituents of beliefs, there is no reason to think that they are.

One reason I think that the Significance of New Information Principle is true is that it doesn't seem to have any counterexamples. However, the way of generating Frege's puzzle that appeals to reasons for behavior yields another motivation for the principle; moreover, it also shows another way in which differences-*in*-the-how proposals go wrong. To see this, suppose that Lex already believes the information conveyed by the sentence **Clark Kent is coming** and that I utter the sentence **Superman is coming** in Lex's presence and he believes me. What do the two principles of this section imply about this case? According to the New Information Principle, since Lex gains information upon hearing my utterance, he must also acquire a new belief that differs from any of his prior beliefs with respect to its *what*. And indeed this is so: for, upon hearing the sentence, Lex will come to believe that the super-powered protector of Metropolis who is his mortal enemy and who is vulnerable to kryptonite is coming; and *what* this belief represents differs from *what* any of his prior beliefs represents. The information Lex gains upon hearing the sentence is pretty significant to him, and the Significance of New Information Principle implies that one of his beliefs that is new with respect to its *what* must be equally signifi-cant. And indeed this is also so: for Lex's belief that his mortal enemy who is vul-nerable to kryptonite is coming is just as significant to him as whatever the new in-formation is that he gets upon hearing the sentence **Superman is coming**.

Now, clearly, the reason that Lex lurks behind the door clutching the kryptonite is some belief he gains in virtue of hearing the sentence **Superman is coming**. But, just as clearly, Lex's reason for engaging in this behavior is that he believes *that his mortal enemy who is vulnerable to kryptonite is coming*. For, even if we accept that the non-descriptive mode of presentation Superman is a constituent of the belief that Superman is coming, the fact that Lex has this belief doesn't give him a rea-son to behave as he does. After all, even if the belief that Superman is coming is <Superman, the property of coming>, the belief won't be a reason to lurk be-hind the door clutching kryptonite if he doesn't believe that Superman is vulnerable to kryptonite; nor will it be a reason if he believes that Superman is a Girl Scout selling cookies rather than his mortal enemy. And, even if Superman is presented to him via some non-descriptive mode of presentation other than Superman, he'll *still* have a reason to lurk behind the door clutching kryptonite as long as he be-lieves that the person coming is *his mortal enemy who is vulnerable to kryptonite*. So the non-descriptive mode of presentation Superman appears to be entirely ir-relevant to Lex's reason for behaving as he does.

Note that my point isn't merely that Lex's believing the (alleged) proposition <Superman, the property of coming> needn't result in any behavior on his part. Any behavior a subject engages in results from many of his attitudes and, hence, the fact that Lex *could* believe the proposition and not lurk behind the door wouldn't show that it isn't his reason for behaving in this way. But a belief can be a reason for some behavior even if its subject doesn't engage in the behavior; for ex-ample, if I believe that you are the criminal the police are looking for, and I desire to see justice done, then I have reasons to turn you in; but, even if my belief that you're my wife trumps these reasons, they are nonetheless reasons to turn you in.

Because of this, the way of generating Frege's puzzle that appeals to reasons for behavior doesn't require that the subject engage in the relevant behavior: whether or not Lex decides to lurk behind the door clutching the kryptonite, the information he gains upon hearing the sentence *Clark Kent is coming* isn't a reason to lurk, while the information he gains upon hearing *Superman is coming* is. But the (alleged) proposition <𝔖𝔲𝔭𝔢𝔯𝔪𝔞𝔫, 𝔱𝔥𝔢 𝔭𝔯𝔬𝔭𝔢𝔯𝔱𝔶 𝔬𝔣 𝔠𝔬𝔪𝔦𝔫𝔤> *isn't* a reason for him to lurk behind the door. It isn't that his belief that Superman is a Girl Scout selling cookies trumps his reason for lurking in the way that my belief that you're my wife trumps my reason for turning you in; rather, Lex's believing the proposition <𝔖𝔲𝔭𝔢𝔯𝔪𝔞𝔫, 𝔱𝔥𝔢 𝔭𝔯𝔬𝔭𝔢𝔯𝔱𝔶 𝔬𝔣 𝔠𝔬𝔪𝔦𝔫𝔤> by itself isn't *any* reason to lurk behind the door. If he *does* lurk behind the door clutching the kryptonite, he does so because he believes that *his mortal enemy who is vulnerable* to *kryptonite* is coming, and the (alleged) proposition <𝔖𝔲𝔭𝔢𝔯𝔪𝔞𝔫, 𝔱𝔥𝔢 𝔭𝔯𝔬𝔭𝔢𝔯𝔱𝔶 𝔬𝔣 𝔠𝔬𝔪𝔦𝔫𝔤> is entirely irrelevant to his behavior.

Notice that it won't do to respond that in order to think of Superman via the mode of presentation 𝔖𝔲𝔭𝔢𝔯𝔪𝔞𝔫 you have to think of him in a certain way, say, as the superhero who is vulnerable to kryptonite. One reason this won't do is that the mode of presentation does no work in the explanation of Lex's behavior; it's the way of thinking about Superman that necessarily goes along with the mode of presentation that does all the work in explaining why Lex does what he does and, hence, short of stubbornness, there's no reason whatsoever to insist that there is any such thing. But the more important reason is precisely Kripke's point that ordinary names don't have any particular descriptive content associated with them. Lex doesn't need to think of Superman in any particular way in order to express some belief of his by using a sentence that contains the name *Superman*. It is the fact that the sentences *Superman is coming* and *Clark Kent is coming* contain different names that makes it seem that the first but not the second counts as an explanation of Lex's behavior and, hence, any mode of presentation that rationalizes Lex's behavior will have to be tied to the name *Superman*. But it is a particular descriptive content that rationalizes Lex's behavior and, since no particular descriptive content is tied to any name, one can't save non-descriptive Fregeanism by claiming that thinking about an individual by means of some mode of presentation requires thinking about him as the thing that satisfies some descriptive content.

So a differences-*in*-the-how proposal can't provide a reason for Lex's behavior and, hence, the proposal can't be correct. Moreover, one important mark of the significance of a piece of information to someone is the behavior it gives him a reason to engage in. If one belief is a reason for someone to engage in a certain behavior while another isn't, then the beliefs can't be equally significant to the subject. Hence, since non-descriptive modes of presentation are irrelevant to the reasons for a subject's behavior, the Significance of New Information Principle must be true.

The above points are perfectly general. If you come to believe that a thing that has certain properties has certain other properties, it is clear how this might give you a reason to behave in a certain way: if you have an aversion to things that have the first set of properties, and the fact that the thing has the second set of properties makes a certain behavior a means for avoiding or destroying the thing, you have a reason to engage in that behavior; or if you love anything that has the first set of properties, and the fact that it has the second set makes a certain behavior a means for promoting the thing's well-being, then you have a reason to engage in that behavior. But how could the fact that you apprehend the thing via one non-descriptive mode of presentation rather than another give you any reason to engage in any behavior? And, given that it can't give you such a reason, how can it account for any significance that your belief about the thing has? Once again, as long as we are careful to construe the demand for an explanation of the relevant behavior as a demand for the subject's reasons for engaging in the behavior, the answer to both questions is that it can't.

As we saw in the previous chapter, one crucial aspect of belief and perceptual representation is their relation to truth and falsity: when a belief or perception represents that some state of affairs obtains, it is true if that state of affairs does obtain and false if it doesn't. But we do not have any perceptual contact with beliefs or perceptions, and there are some kinds of representations that we do perceive and, hence, that are more familiar to us. For example, we perceive sentences and photographs, and a sentence or photograph is true (or veridical) if the state of affairs it represents obtains and false (or non-veridical) if it doesn't. Now for all of these familiar kinds of things that represent, there is a distinction between the representation and *what* it represents: a sentence represents some state of affairs because it contains words that are distinct from the objects and properties in the state of affairs, and a photograph represents some state of affairs because of features of the paper that constitutes it that are distinct from the objects and properties in the state of affairs.[19] And I think that one mistake that the non-descriptive Fregean (like any other triadist) makes is assimilating belief to these more familiar forms of representation. Because the kinds of representation that we know the most about represent *what* they do in virtue of containing things distinct from what they represent, it is natural to assume that belief (and perception) are the same. The guise Millian makes the same mistake insofar as he assumes—as is true in the familiar forms of representation—that a subject's relation to what his belief represents must be mediated by some entity that is distinct from the objects that his belief represents.

Our discussion thus far has shown a reason why it is wrong to assimilate the way beliefs represent to the way sentences and other more familiar forms of representation represent. When two distinct sentences represent the same state of affairs, they differ in *how* they represent it. But such a difference can't mean that *what* one sentence represents is new information while *what* the other represents isn't; nor can it mean that *what* one sentence represents constitutes a reason for some behavior while *what* the other represents doesn't. When someone learns that the German for **snow is white** is **Schnee ist weiss** he doesn't learn any new information about snow or whiteness; upon learning what the German sentence says, no one thinks: *My God, that's interesting; Schnee ist weiss!*[20] And learning what is represented by some sentence in a language foreign to you also generates no new reasons for behavior that concerns what the sentence represents.

In the case of linguistic representation, differences in *how* two sentences represent don't correspond to differences in their informational content or to differences in the reasons they provide. And what we have seen in this section is that these are general features of differences in *how* two things represent. The brand of non-descriptive Fregeanism discussed in this section attempts to ground a difference in representational content between beliefs without positing a difference in the objects they concern and the relations and properties they ascribe to these objects; that is to say, it attempts to ground a difference in representational content without positing a difference in *what* is represented. But the lesson is that a belief's representational content *just is* what it represents. So differences in how two beliefs represent cannot amount to differences in representational content.

In the previous chapter, we saw that some have claimed that the nature of a belief is given by its role in practical and theoretical reasoning; but, insofar as this is correct, a belief's nature can't be that it contains a certain non-descriptive mode of presentation. For that two beliefs differ in the non-descriptive modes of presentation they contain can't constitute differences in their representational content and, hence, can't constitute a difference in the reasons they provide. In these regards, the significance of a belief resides not at all in its *how* and entirely in its *what*.

7. Two false assumptions

So far, we have seen that

(1) Whenever someone gets new information in virtue of accepting some sentence, he also gains a belief that differs from any of his old beliefs with respect to its *what*.

(2) Whatever the significance of the new information that someone gets in virtue of accepting a sentence, he will get information that is new with respect to its *what* that is equally significant.

(3) Only information that is new with respect to its *what* can constitute a new reason for the person to engage in some behavior.

And, as we have also seen, there is an obvious explanation of how a sentence that expresses a proposition that doesn't constitute information that is new with respect to its *what*, can convey information that *is* new with respect to its *what* because conversational participants associate the description D with the name a—that is to say, because they believe that the thing named a is D—an utterance of the sentence a *is F* can be used to convey the information that the thing that is D is F. The general point is that it is descriptive information that is relevant to Frege's puzzle rather than non-descriptive modes of presentation and, hence, non-descriptive modes of presentation don't provide a solution to the puzzle. I think that the fact that it is descriptive information that is relevant to the puzzle has been obscured by some assumptions that philosophers tend to make, whose plausibility, as we will see, depends upon a poor diet of examples.

The first false assumption is that, for any two co-referring names or demonstratives *a* and *b*, *S believes a is F* conveys something different from *S believes that b is F*. Now when a particular example is given, it is usually from a comic book or it is the *Hesperus/Phosphorus* case, and this is not accidental. For there aren't many pairs of co-referring names for which the assumption holds. *Olga believes that Grice wrote 'Logic and Conversation'* doesn't seem to convey anything different from *Olga believes that Paul Grice wrote 'Logic and Conversation'* or from the second conjunct of *Grice is coming and Olga believes that he wrote 'Logic and Conversation'*. Indeed, it is important to note that actual cases of Frege's puzzle are quite rare, and thus the epicyclical attempts to formulate a theory in accordance with our intuitions concerning such cases are to some extent undercut.

However, when I claim that actual cases of Frege's puzzle are rare, I don't mean to say that Fregean intuitions about belief ascriptions are so rare. There are pairs of actually co-referring names besides *Hesperus* and *Phosphorus* for which it seems appropriate to say that *S believes that a is F* can be true while *S believes that b is F* is false. For example, prior to taking my first philosophy of language class, I had never heard the name *Tully*, and the sentence *Mike didn't believe that Tully was a Roman orator even though he did believe that Cicero was one* seems to be an appropriate description of my situation; and there are plenty of people who don't know that Cary Grant's original name was *Archie Leach*, and the sentence *They don't believe that Archie Leach was an actor even though they do believe that Cary Grant was one* is an appropriate description of their situation. However, it is often not recognized that in these cases *the Millian intuitions seem equally correct*. One could say *Mike didn't believe that Tully was a Roman orator* or *Mike believed that Tully was a Roman orator but didn't know that he was called 'Tully'*, and no ordinary English speaker would balk at either way of describing my ignorance. Similarly, one could say *Most people don't believe that Archie Leach was an actor* or *Most people believe that Archie Leach is an actor but they don't know that he's called 'Archie Leach'*, and again no ordinary speaker would balk. When philosophers consider these kinds of examples, they rightly claim that the Fregean intuitions seem correct; but they generally don't realize that the Millian intuitions seem equally correct and, hence, that intuitions about these cases don't favor either view. The *Superman/Clark Kent* and *Hesperus/Phosphorus* cases are cases in which *only* the Fregean intuitions seem correct. As such, they do present arguments for Fregeanism; however, as such they are also extremely rare. And what they have in common is that almost everyone competent to use one of these names associates some descriptive content with it. There are many cases in which neither Fregeanism nor Millianism seems counterintuitive; what these cases have in common is that they are cases in which it isn't widely known that the relevant individual has two names, although there aren't any descriptive contents that most speakers associate with both names. But the vast majority of co-referring names are like *Grice* and *Paul Grice* in that they seem to be universally substitutable *salva veritate* in belief ascriptions. And the false idea that most names are like *Hesperus* and *Phosphorus* has obscured how crucial descriptive information is to the generation and solution of Frege's puzzle.

Now it might be replied that, even though *Grice* and *Paul Grice* are interchangeable in most belief ascriptions, it's still possible for someone not to believe that *Grice is Paul Grice*. This brings us to the second false assumption that philosophers tend to make: that, even if two co-referring names *a* and *b* are often substitutable in belief reports *salva veritate*, someone who believes that a is a could always fail to believe that a is b and, hence, they aren't substitutable *salva veritate* when the embedded sentence is of the form *a=b*. But, even though it is common, the assumption that someone could always fail to believe that a is b is a bit curious. Suppose I now utter the sentence *Suzette doesn't believe that Grice is Paul Grice* to you. Suppose further that you trust me and thus want to believe what I tell you; is there anything here for you to believe? The answer is: no, if I were to utter the above sentence, you wouldn't know what information I meant to get across. In general, understanding what information someone wants to get across by uttering a sentence of the form *S doesn't believe that a=b* requires a mutual understanding between speaker and hearer of some description associated with each name. And when there is no such mutual understanding *S doesn't believe that a=b* isn't at all informative.

Consider the claim that someone perfectly familiar with George Orwell could still not believe that Orwell is Blair. Suppose I said to you, *Abe doesn't believe that Orwell is Blair.* Do you have any idea exactly what information I mean to convey? We *can* think of a context where it is clear what information I mean to convey: perhaps you and I both associate some description *D* with the name *Orwell* and some distinct description *D'* with the name *Blair* and we both know that the other does; then I might convey that Abe doesn't believe that the person who's D is D' or even that Abe *does* believe that the person who's D *isn't* D'. But in the absence of any such background knowledge you *wouldn't* know what I meant to convey. Notice that the belief ascription doesn't even convey that Abe doesn't believe that the *person called Orwell* is the *person called Blair*. For I might make these belief ascriptions even if Abe is completely unaware of the names *Blair* and *Orwell*. For example, suppose that in his private life Orwell goes by the name *Blair* and that he is Abe's next door neighbor. Suppose further that Orwell is giving a reading at Borders under the name *Orwell*, that he always gives readings under this name, and that one day Abe points to Orwell while he is reading and, failing to recognize him as his neighbor, says, *I don't believe he's my next door neighbor*. Even though Abe is unaware of the two names, it *still* might be correct to say *Abe doesn't believe that Orwell is Blair*. It would be correct so long as it conveyed the information that he doesn't believe that the reader at Borders is his neighbor.

Likewise for identity statements that aren't embedded in belief ascriptions. Suppose I utter the sentence *Brad Kochel isn't Fergus Carey*. What information have I conveyed to you? Well, not much besides that the person whom I call *Brad Kochel* isn't the same person as the one I call *Fergus Carey*. But, if you come to associate with the names the descriptive content that I do, then the non-identity statement will have a more substantive significance to you.

The lesson is that the significance of identity statements containing co-referring names *a* and *b* and belief ascriptions involving such statements also depends upon the descriptive content that speakers and listeners associate with the names; and the relevant descriptions are rarely just *the referent of 'a'* and *the referent of 'b'*. The false idea that *S doesn't believe that a=b* is informative independently of such descriptive content has obscured the importance of descriptive content.

Recall that both Richard and Salmon attempt to explain the difference in information conveyed by belief ascriptions that are identical with respect to their *what* by saying that, besides caring about what a person believes, we also care about which sentences he would use to express his belief. In Section 5 of this chapter, we saw that such information isn't generally communicated by a belief ascription and that Richard and Salmon are wrong to think that *we care* about it. In general we don't care very much at all about what names someone uses to refer to the object of his belief. But we often do care about what properties the believer thinks the name's referent has. And, besides pointing to an error in Richard's and Salmon's differences-*about*-the-how proposal, this fact also points to an error in a differences-*in*-the-how proposal. Since our concern in the Frege's puzzle cases is with *descriptive information* (even putting aside the criticism in Section 6), it is doubtful that such a proposal can succeed.

As noted above, Frege himself saw that the relevant information isn't information about public-language names; but he also saw that the relevant information conveyed *does* concern descriptive content that is associated with the name. For, even though he never says that modes of presentation are the contents of definite descriptions, in every example he gives they are the content of some definite description.[21] Thus, both of the proposals according to which *non-descriptive* modes of presentation account for the relevant differences in information conveyed attempt to get the letter of Frege's theory right by violating the spirit behind it.

8. Conclusion

I have argued that the significance of a sentence involving a name depends upon descriptions associated with the name and not on non-descriptive modes of presentation and, hence, that Frege's puzzle doesn't provide a motivation for either triadist position. So, given that descriptive Fregeanism itself is false, it would seem that pure Millianism must be the correct account of belief. But isn't any brand of Millianism simply absurd? How could it be true that the sentences *Lex believes that*

Superman is coming and ***Lex believes that Clark Kent is coming*** mean the very same thing? It seems that we just couldn't be as deceived about the meanings of belief ascriptions as the Millian claims we are. However, as we will see in the next chapter, this way of expressing the consequences of Millianism depends upon a confusion about the structure of linguistic communication.

4

The Structure of Linguistic Communication

0. Introduction

In the last chapter, we saw that the information relevant to solving Frege's puzzle is *descriptive* information and, hence, that the puzzle provides no motivation for the triadist's view that non-descriptive modes of presentation are essential to the belief relation. This eliminates triadism from the consideration; and, since descriptive Fregeanism is also false, the argument has led us to pure Millianism. However, it's one thing to know where you've been led and quite another to believe that you can live there. As we have seen, *any* version of Millianism seems to have the fantastic consequence that competent speakers don't know the meaning of many perfectly ordinary sentences. In this chapter, we'll see that this way of putting the point against Millianism depends upon a misunderstanding about the structure of linguistic communication and that, once the misunderstanding is cleared up, the consequences of Millianism turn out to be entirely agreeable. The misunderstandings can best be brought out by examining some remarks of Paul Grice concerning what I will call *the Gricean paradox*.[1] The misunderstanding and the paradox both revolve around Grice's notion of *implicature*.

1. What's implicated and what's said

Grice introduces the notion of implicature in the following passage.

> Suppose that A and B are talking about a mutual friend, C, who is now working in a bank. A asks B how C is getting on in his job, and B replies, *Oh quite well, I think; he likes his colleagues, and he hasn't been to prison yet*. At this point A might well inquire what B was implying, what he was suggesting, or even what he meant by saying

137

that C had not yet been to prison. The answer might be any one of such things as that C is the sort of person likely to yield to the temptation provided by his occupation, that C's colleagues are really very unpleasant and treacherous people, and so forth. It might, of course, be quite unnecessary for A to make such an enquiry of B, the answer to it being, in the context, clear in advance. It is clear that whatever B implied, suggested, meant in this example, is distinct from what B said, which was simply that C had not been to prison yet. I wish to introduce as terms of art, the verb *implicate* and the related nouns *implicature* (cf. *implying*) and *implicatum* (cf. *what is implied*). (1989, 24)[2]

So we have a distinction between what someone *says* by uttering a sentence and what he *implicates* by uttering it. Given what Grice says about the distinction, in certain cases it is clear how it applies. For example, if you ask how Fergie is doing, and I reply *Well, he's sober today*, in most contexts I would be implicating that Fergie is often drunk, but I have only said that he is sober today.

Grice spends most of the rest of the chapter trying to explicate maxims that govern conversational exchanges in accordance with

The Cooperative Principle
Make your conversational contribution such as is required, at the stage at which it occurs, by the accepted purpose or direction of the talk exchange in which you are engaged. (Grice 1989, 26)

And it is conversational participants' *mutual knowledge* of these maxims—each participant's knowledge of the maxims, his knowledge that the others know them, his knowledge that the others know that he knows that they know them, and so on—that allows a sentence to be used to communicate more than what it says. For example, two of the maxims concern what Grice calls *quantity*, the amount of information that a cooperative speaker must give. The first maxim of quantity is, "Make your contribution as informative as is required (for the current purposes of the exchange)" (Grice 1989, 26). And, in the above example, given that you asked how Fergie was doing, my remark that he was sober today is responsive to your question only if there is some reason to suppose that he's usually not sober; that is, if it turns out that Fergie's usually sober, then I haven't given the information required to answer your question. Hence, according to Grice, your knowledge of the maxim allows you to infer from what I said that he is often drunk, and my knowledge that you know the maxim allows me to use the remark to convey this information. Grice takes there to be at least nine maxims that plausibly follow from the Cooperative Principle, other examples of which are, *Do not make your contribution more informative than is required* (the second maxim of quantity), and *Do not say what you believe to be false* or *that for which you lack adequate evidence* (the two maxims of *quality*).

Although the notion of what is said by an utterance is an essential part of his account of implicature, he never gives an explicit characterization of *what someone says by uttering a sentence*; rather, he relies on the reader having "an intuitive un-derstanding of the meaning of *say* in such contexts" (Grice 1989, 24–25). In Chap-ter 2, Section 7, I also relied on an intuitive understanding of *say* when I called what someone says (or *expresses*) by assertively uttering a sentence *P the proposition that P*. Part of what was relied upon is the intuitive idea that what someone says by as-sertively uttering a sentence (together with the way the world is) determines whether his utterance is true or false. And, though Grice is not explicit about this, it's pretty clear that he's relying on the very same intuitive idea.

Grice distinguishes between two different kinds of implicatures: *conversational implicatures*—those that, like in the *Fergie is sober* example, depend on the con-versational participants' mutual knowledge of the conversational maxims—and *conventional implicatures*—those that depend upon their mutual knowledge of the conventional meanings of words. And, in his discussion of the latter, it becomes clear that, for Grice, *what is said* by an utterance is what we're calling *the propo-sition it expresses*. To quote:

> In some cases the conventional meaning of the words used will determine what is im-plicated, besides helping to determine what is said. If I say (smugly), *He is an Eng-lishman; he is, therefore, brave*, I have certainly committed myself, by virtue of the meaning of my words, to its being the case that his being brave is a consequence of (follows from) his being an Englishman. But while I have said that he is an English-man, and said that he is brave, I do not want to say that I have *said* (in the favored sense) that it follows from his being an Englishman that he is brave, though I have cer-tainly indicated, and so implicated, that this is so. I do not want to say that my utterance of this sentence would be, *strictly speaking*, false should the consequence in question fail to hold. So *some* implicatures are conventional, unlike the one with which I intro-duced this discussion of implicature. (1989, 25–26; original emphases)

So, in some cases, the conventional meanings of the words in a sentence *them-selves* determine what the sentence implicates as well as what it says.[3] But notice that Grice's reason for claiming that he hasn't *said* that, if one is an Englishman, then one is brave by uttering *He is an Englishman; he is, therefore brave* is that the utterance *would not be false* should the conditional fail to hold; that is to say, it would not be false in virtue of the conditional's being false. And this strongly sug-gests that Grice means *what is said* by an assertive utterance of a sentence to be what it is that (together with the way the world is) makes the utterance true or false; that is to say, it suggests that he's relying on the very same intuitive understanding that we relied on in Chapter 2 and that for Grice *what is said* by an assertive utter-ance of a sentence *P* is what we're calling *the proposition that P*.[4]

Now the proposition expressed by a sentence definitely isn't a brute fact about the sentence as a whole; rather, which proposition some sentence expresses is a func-tion of the words that make up the sentence together with its syntactic structure. The intuitive way to put this idea would be in terms of *meaning*: what is said by a sentence is its meaning, and the meaning of the sentence is determined by the meanings and syntactic arrangement of its constituent words. However, though this intuitive idea is important to understanding what Grice means to be doing, that way of putting it won't quite do.

We have various intuitive ideas about linguistic meaning. Some of these ideas are that words have meaning and that the meaning of a sentence is determined by the meanings of its constituent words. But some of our intuitive ideas about meaning are inconsistent with others; for we intuitively believe both that the sentence *I am tired* means the same thing no matter who utters it *and* that whether an utterance of a sentence is true or false is determined solely by what it means and the way the world is. Now, if the word *I* just meant *the speaker*, there would be no inconsistency in these intuitions. But, as David Kaplan (1989) has observed, *I* cannot mean *the speaker* if a sentence's *meaning* is what (together with the way the world is) determines its truth-value. For my utterance of *I am tired* is true at some possible world just in case *Mike Thau* is tired in that world, regardless of whether Mike Thau happens to be speaking in that world.[5] So, if all of our intuitions about meaning are to be correct, then there must be distinct notions of meaning corresponding to the intuitions that the meaning of an utterance (together with the way the world is) determines whether it's true or false and that each word always means the same thing.

Let's call the notion of meaning according to which the meaning of a sentence is a function of its constituent words and determines its truth-value *semantic value*. Because my utterance of *I am tired* is true at a possible world just in case *Mike Thau* is tired in that world, the semantic value of the word *I* in my utterance of *I am tired* is simply me (or at least something that determines me at all possible worlds). And the semantic values of the words in the utterance (together with their syntactic arrangement) determines its semantic value, where the utterance's semantic value is the proposition it expresses. More generally, each word in an utterance has a semantic value, the semantic value of an uttered sentence is a function of the semantic value of its constituent words (and its structure), and the semantic value of an uttered sentence is what determines (together with the way the world is) its truth-value; that is, the semantic value of an uttered sentence is the proposition that it expresses.

2. The philosophical importance of implicature

It is important to note that Grice does not intend *implicature* merely to be a discovery in the philosophy of language; it is supposed to be a discovery in the philosophy of language that sheds light on many debates in other areas of philosophy. Once upon a time the slogan *Meaning is use* inspired many philosophers to draw metaphysical conclusions on the basis of when it is or isn't appropriate to use certain sentences. One example of this strategy concerns the question of whether someone's performance of an action is always accompanied by his *trying* to perform that action. To quote Grice (1989, 6–7):

Is it always correct, or only sometimes correct, to speak of a man who has done something as having *eo ipso* tried to do it? Wittgenstein and others adopt the second view.
Their suggestion is that if, say, I now perform some totally unspectacular act, like
scratching my head or putting my hand into my trouser pocket to get my handkerchief
out, it would be inappropriate and incorrect to say that I tried to scratch my head or
tried to put my hand into my pocket. It would similarly be inappropriate to speak of me
as *not* having tried to do each of these things. From these considerations there emerges
the idea that for *A tried to do x* to be correctly used, it is required that A should not
have done x (should have been prevented).[6]

So, according to "Wittgenstein and others," reflection on how the word *tried* is appropriately used shows that it *isn't* true that whenever someone performs an action
he also tries to perform that action.

Grice uses the notion of conversational implicature to point out that the proper
application of the meaning-is-use strategy is far more limited than its proponents
sometimes took it to be. His point is that sometimes it is incorrect to use a sentence
because of what is normally implicated by it rather than because of its semantic
value. For example, Grice suggests that the reason that it seems incorrect to utter
the sentence *A tried to do x* when the action was totally unspectacular is not that
the sentence's semantic value includes that A failed to do x; rather, the reason is that
the sentence usually carries the *conversational implicature* that A failed to do x.
Thus, even when a subject's performance of an action was totally unspectacular, it
may be *true* that he tried to perform the action, although it would be misleading to
say that he did. When a sentence usually carries some conversational implicature,
Grice calls its implicature a ***generalized conversational implicature***.

Grice's point is that heavy-handed application of the meaning-is-use strategy is
apt to lead us astray because when some sentence carries a generalized conversational implicature, we are apt to confuse the implicature with its semantic value.
However, he cites one feature of conversational implicatures that can help dispel
such confusion.[7] To quote:

> Since, to assume the presence of a conversational implicature, we have to assume that
> at least the Cooperative Principle is being observed, and since it is possible to opt out
> of the observation of the principle, it follows that a generalized conversational impli-
> cature can be canceled in a particular case. It may be explicitly canceled, by the addi-
> tion of a clause that states or implies that the speaker has opted out, or it may be con-
> textually canceled, if the form of the utterance that usually carries it is used in a context
> that makes it clear that the speaker is opting out. (1989, 39)

So a piece of information that speakers normally intend a particular sentence to
convey is *canceled* in some context just in case the sentence isn't used to convey it
in that context. Grice's point is that a sentence's conversational implicature is more
easily canceled than its semantic value is and, hence, the cancelability of an implicature can be used to determine that it is merely an implicature.[8] And Grice uses
cancelability to demonstrate that the semantic value of *A tried to do x* does not include that A failed to do x. To quote:

A doctor may tell a patient whose leg has been damaged to try to move his toes tomorrow, and the patient may agree to try; but neither is committed to holding that the patient will fail to move his toes . . . . Moreover, someone else who has not been connected in any way with, or even was not at the time aware of, the damage to the patient's leg may correctly say, at a later date, *On the third day after the injury the patient tried to move his toes (when the plaster was removed), though whether he succeeded I do not know.* (1989, 7)[9]

Normally *A tried to do x* is used to suggest that A failed to do x; but, in Grice's example, it does not suggest this. Hence, the example provides evidence that the suggestion is a generalized conversational implicature rather than a part of the sentence's semantic value. However, the mere fact that there are contexts in which the relevant information is canceled is not, by itself, supposed to decisively demonstrate that the information is not part of the sentence's semantic value. In order to demonstrate this, Grice claims that one must be able to explain how conversational participants' mutual knowledge of the conversational maxims implies that, in general, the sentence *should* implicate the information. And, in the case of *tried*, there appears to be such an explanation. As we've seen, one of the conversational maxims (the first maxim of quantity) requires that a speaker makes his contribution as informative as is required. But suppose that the speaker believes that A simply did x. In these circumstances an utterance of *A tried to do x* wouldn't be as informative as an utterance of *A did x*. For, in most conversations that include such a sentence, the listeners will be concerned with whether or not A did x and not merely with whether he tried to do it. So, if A managed to do x, and the speaker is observing the first maxim of quantity, then he would have simply said *A did x*. Hence, if the speaker instead utters *A tried to do x*, listeners will generally infer that his reason must be that he takes the more informative *A did x* to be false and, hence, they will infer that A didn't do x. And, since the conversational participants have common knowledge of these facts, the speaker can justifiably intend his use of the sentence to convey the implicated information.

The above account of Grice's work on implicature is incomplete: I have not given a complete list of the nine maxims that Grice claims govern conversational exchanges (and even Grice [1989, 27] says that "one might need others"), nor have I given a complete list of the philosophical disputes that Grice hopes his work will help adjudicate. Moreover, though Grice's work on conversational implicature is one of the best and most important works of twentieth-century philosophy, there is much in it that is vague or underdeveloped.[10] However, it should be clear that many of Grice's observations presented above are *obviously correct*.

First, it is obviously correct that there is sometimes a distinction between the semantic value of an utterance and the information it is used to convey. If it turns out that Fergie has never had a drink in his life, then *Fergie was sober today* is *true*; so the semantic value of the sentence doesn't include the information that Fergie is often drunk. Nonetheless, in many contexts the sentence can be used to convey this information.

Second, it is obvious that something like Grice's account of how implicatures are carried is correct. It's just obvious that the way in which you get the information that Fergie is often drunk from my claim that he was sober today involves the fact that, if he *isn't* often drunk, then there is some way in which I am being uncooperative. And it's obvious that there's something about how we understand what it takes to cooperate that allows me to intend to use the sentence to convey that he *is* often drunk and that allows you to get my intention.

Finally, it is obvious that the notion of generalized conversational implicature is important to certain semantic debates and, in particular, that the cancelability of conversational implicatures provides a means for adjudicating these debates. The contexts that Grice cites in which the suggestion normally carried by *A tried to do x* is canceled *really do* provide at least some evidence that the suggestion isn't part of the semantic value of the sentence. And the explanation of how conversational participants' ability to follow the maxims allows a speaker to use the sentence to convey the suggestion seems to provide a good deal more.

The reason we've been examining Grice's notion of implicature is the role it plays in the Millian account of meaning. If, as I've argued in Chapter 3, that account is correct, then the different information conveyed by sentences that contain distinct but co-referring names will have to result from what utterances of such sentences generally implicate rather than from what they say. But now that we have some idea about how conversational implicature works, it still seems incredible that the different information conveyed by, for example, *Superman flies* and *Clark Kent flies*, should result from their carrying different generalized conversational implicatures. Granted, the three obviously correct features of Grice's account listed proved an account of the information conveyed by *some* sentences; but it still doesn't seem at all plausible that the difference between *Superman flies* and *Clark Kent flies* can be explained in this way because these two sentences just seem to obviously mean different things.

However, it isn't just that there are problems with the Millian's use of conversational implicature; though the three features of Grice's account seem obviously correct, a little reflection reveals that there is something paradoxical about conversational implicature itself. And, though the resolution of the Gricean paradox doesn't by itself solve the problem for Millianism, it does clarify what the problem is and point the way towards the solution.

3. The Gricean paradox and two ways of generating it

Grice himself recognized the paradoxical aspect of conversational implicature. To quote:

[I]n order that a nonconventional implicature should be present in a given case, my account requires that a speaker shall be able to utilize the conventional meaning of a sentence. If nonconventional implicature is built on what is said, if what is said is closely related to the conventional force of the words used, and if the presence of the implicature depends on the intentions of the speaker, or at least on his assumptions, with regard to the possibility of the nature of the implicature being worked out, then it would appear that the speaker must (in some sense or other of the word *know*) know what is the conventional force of the words which he is using. This indeed seems to lead to a sort of paradox: If we, as speakers, have the requisite knowledge of the conventional meaning of sentences we employ to implicate, when uttering them, something the implication of which depends on the conventional meaning in question, how can we, as theorists, have difficulty with respect to just those cases in deciding where conventional meaning ends and implicature begins? (1989, 49)

The *sort of paradox* that Grice is referring to results from the last of the obviously correct features of his account listed above: the fact that it seems obvious that conversational implicature as characterized by Grice has relevance to certain semantic debates. Consider, once again, the conclusions concerning the sentence *A tried to do x*.

(1) The existence of contexts in which *A tried to do x* isn't used to convey the information that A failed to do x is evidence that the information is not part of the sentence's semantic value.

(2) The fact that we can use the conversational participants' mutual knowledge of the maxims to explain why *A tried to do x* can be used to convey that A failed to do x (when it is used communicate it) provides important further evidence for the claim that the information is not part of the sentence's semantic value.

But part of the Gricean explanation of why *A tried to do x* often carries the implicature that A failed to do x involves conversational participants' knowledge of the semantic value of the sentence. Recall that the explanation is that listeners assume that speakers are trying to be as informative as the circumstances require. And, in most circumstances in which *A tried to do x* would be uttered, listeners won't merely be interested in whether A tried to do x; they'll also want to know whether A did do x. So, if A in fact did do x, the listeners assume that the speaker would have just said that A did x. Since the speaker instead said that A tried to do x, the listeners assume that A didn't do x. And, since the speaker and his listeners mutually know all of the above, the speaker can intend his utterance to convey the information. So the inferential process by which the listeners calculate the implicature appears to require that they know that the semantic value of the sentence *doesn't include* the information that A failed to do x. And, since the speaker uses the common knowledge of the conversational maxims to convey the implicature, he too must know that the semantic value of the sentence doesn't include all of the information he means to convey. But, if anyone competent to use the sentence to convey that A failed to do x must know that this isn't part of its semantic value, then how is it possible that there is a dispute about whether this information is part of its semantic value? In short, the paradox arises because the way in which conversational implicature serves as a means to adjudicate the dispute concerning the semantic value of *A tried to do x* seems to imply that there shouldn't have been any such dispute in the first place; for inferring what's implicated from what's said seems to obviously *require* distinguishing what's implicated from what's said.

But why does this requirement seem so obvious? That is to say, why does it seem impossible that you should be able to infer what's implicated by an utterance without being able to distinguish it from what's said? Well, one reason is that it's somewhat natural to understand Grice's talk of inference as talk of *conscious* inference. And, if Gricean inferences are *conscious,* then it seems utterly trivial that competent language users will have to tell the difference between what's said and what's implicated.

Now, though it's somewhat natural to take Gricean inferences to be conscious inferences, just a little attention to the phenomenon shows that, even if we really do calculate implicatures in the way that Grice suggests, we don't do so consciously. Consider once again the sentence *Fergie was sober today* and the implicature that it would sometimes carry. If you were to use the sentence to convey that Fergie is often drunk, you wouldn't have any explicit thoughts about conversational maxims or inferences that listeners will make; rather, without any explicit thinking, you would immediately know that the sentence will convey the information you intend it to. And, when I understand that your utterance is intended to convey that Fergie is often drunk, I don't have any explicit thoughts about conversational maxims, nor do I perform any explicit inferential reasoning; rather, I immediately know what information you mean to convey. And, though speakers often use a sentence to convey information that is not a part of its semantic value, it is *almost never* the case that anyone explicitly uses his knowledge of the sentence's semantic value and the maxims to calculate what the information is. Indeed, how could Grice's account of conversational implicature be a profound philosophical discovery—which, if true, it certainly is—if everyone was engaging in such explicit reasoning all of the time? Students have to be *taught* the distinction between the semantic value of an utterance and what it implicates, and the relevance of the conversational maxims to this distinction; and in my experience they usually find it to be one of the more interesting distinctions in the philosophy of language. But how could either fact be true if they were explicitly reasoning from the semantic values of utterances to what they implicate all of the time? So it's absolutely clear that we don't consciously calculate implicatures in anything like the way that Grice's account might suggest that we do.

Moreover, though it may be somewhat natural to understand Grice as meaning the inferences to be conscious, he does not ever say they are. The closest he comes is when he says "[T]he presence of a conversational implicature must be capable of being worked out" (1989, 31); but, at most, this merely seems to require that it's in some sense *possible* to consciously calculate any implicature. The quoted sen-

tence certainly doesn't require that any implicature actually is consciously calculated or even that it is ever easy to do so; perhaps one needs to know a substantial
part of Grice's theory in order to manifest the capability. So there's no textual reason to think that Grice takes implicatures to be consciously calculated and, given
that the idea that they are turns out to be completely and obviously at odds with the
phenomenon, it's almost impossible that Grice would have assented to it. To the extent that the Gricean paradox depends upon taking inferences from what's said to
what's implicated to be conscious inferences, it depends on an idea that any reasonable person who reflected on the phenomenon would reject.

However, the paradox doesn't seem to depend on the idea that inferences from
what's said to what's implicated are consciously worked out. It does seem true that,
if these inferences are conscious inferences, then conversational participants would
have to know the distinction between what's said and what's implicated; but, importantly, this isn't the only way that conversational participants might have to
know this. Perhaps it's simply part of the nature of conversational implicature that
conversational participants must always be able to tell the difference between
what's implicated and what's said whether or not they consciously infer the former
from the latter. This seems to be how François Recanati understands conversational
implicature. Recanati (1993, 245) claims that a speaker has conversationally implicated that P only if he would recognize that he has done so.

So far we've discussed the Gricean paradox and seen that there are two ideas
that might lead to it: the first is that inferences from what's said to what's implicated
are conscious inferences. Going through such an inference seems to require knowing the difference between what's said and what's implicated and, hence, if a
speaker consciously goes through such an inference, he should be conscious of the
distinction between what he has said and what he has implicated. The second idea
that might generate the Gricean paradox is simply that the distinction between
what's said and what's implicated must itself always be consciously accessible to
conversational participants *independently* of whether the entire inference from the
former to the latter is. The first idea that we consciously infer what's implicated
from what's said is so obviously at odds with the phenomenon that the reader might
fairly wonder why it is even worth discussing. Since no one could reasonably take
such an idea seriously and since there's no reason to think that Grice did, it can't be
relevant to the Gricean paradox. As I've indicated above, one motive for making it
clear that Gricean inferences are not conscious is that a naive reading of Grice
might somewhat naturally leave the impression that they are. However, there's another, more important motive. For, despite appearances, the second idea, that the
distinction between what's said and what's implicated should always be accessible,
is not in fact independent of the first. Once we abandon the completely implausible idea that Gricean inferences are conscious, we should also abandon the less implausible idea that conversational participants must always know the distinction between what's said and what's implicated.

4. The accessibility of Gricean inferences

As we've seen, it's sufficient to generate the Gricean paradox that the distinction between what's said by an utterance and what it implicates must always be known to speakers. For, if the distinction must be known, then speakers shouldn't be capable of confusing what's said by an utterance with what it implicates. But Grice intends his account of implicature to show that many semantic disputes—for example, whether the semantic value of *A tried to do x* includes that A failed—involve just such a confusion.

As mentioned above, Recanati believes that a speaker must always know the difference between what he says and what he implicates. According to Recanati, a speaker has said that P by uttering some sentence only if he would recognize that he has said it. For example, it is usually thought that the semantic value of the sentence *John has three children* does not include the proposition that John has *exactly* three children but, rather, that the latter is merely a generalized conversational implicature carried by the sentence; the semantic value of the sentence is only that John has *at least* three children. However, Recanati (1993, 249) claims that because "the speaker would not recognize the proposition that he has at least three children as being what he has said," the usual thought is wrong; the proposition that John has *exactly* three children *is* part of the semantic value of the sentence rather than merely being implicated by it.

It's important to see that Recanati's requirement isn't the apparent triviality that a speaker must in some sense know what he's said. Usually, if someone uses a sentence *P* to say something, he will know that he has said that P; and Recanati is not merely claiming that the speaker must know this. Rather he's claiming that, for *any proposition that P*, a speaker must know whether or not he's said that P by uttering some sentence. The difference here is somewhat subtle, but it is important. If someone assertively utters the sentence *Steve tried to pass the test*, it may be trivial to claim that he must know that he has said that Steve tried to pass the test. And this apparent triviality won't generate the Gricean paradox. But there is another question here: has he also said that Steve has *failed* to pass the test? And Recanati is claiming that if the speaker has also said this he must know that he has. If Recanati is right, then Grice's use of conversational implicature to adjudicate semantic disputes is, as Grice worried, somewhat paradoxical. For Grice claims that you *don't* say that Steve failed by uttering the sentence *Steve tried to pass the test*; and if Recanati is right, this means that anyone who utters the sentence must know that he hasn't said that Steve has failed and, hence, he shouldn't think that he has said this. More generally, if Recanati is right, then conversational implicature can't help adjudicate semantic disputes in the way that Grice envisioned because on Recanati's account it's built into the notion that a speaker always knows whether or not he's saying something by uttering a sentence and, hence, it's not possible to confusedly think that you're saying what you're really only implicating.

If Recanati is right that the distinction between what's said and what's implicated is always accessible to speakers, then the solution to the paradox is that the apparently paradoxical cases of conversational implicature turn out *not* to be cases of conversational implicature at all; and, hence, Grice's account has far less application and philosophical import than he took it to have. For example, since many ordinary speakers would be inclined to say that in uttering the sentence *A **tried to do** x* they have said that A failed to do x, on Recanati's view the latter *is* part of what they say by uttering the sentence. Jenny Saul (1998, 368) has pointed out that Recanati's requirement seems to yield the wrong result for the sentence ***John has three children*** because someone who utters this sentence "might reasonably continue *in fact he has four.*" But, if Recanati is right that the speaker has said that John has exactly three children, then the continuation would be inconsistent with the initial assertion. The continuation appears to *cancel the implicature* that John has exactly three children and, hence, that John has exactly three children appears to go beyond what the speaker has said. And Saul's point generalizes; there are many cases in which a speaker would take some piece of information to be part of what he has said by an utterance but in which this piece of information can be canceled. For example, someone who utters the sentence ***The burglar entered and I screamed*** is likely to think that he has said that the burglar entered and *then* he screamed. However, the suggestion of temporal order would be canceled if the speaker were to continue ***but not in that order***.

Indeed, what a speaker would take himself to have said by uttering some sentence is a perfectly empirical question, and the answer is likely to vary from speaker to speaker and context to context. Given that people have to be *taught* the distinction between what is said and what is implicated, it wouldn't be surprising if cases that even Recanati would want to classify as implicatures turn out not to be on his account. For example, it wouldn't be at all surprising if many ordinary untutored speakers would think themselves to have *said* that Fergie is often drunk by uttering ***Fergie was sober today***. Moreover, a speaker rarely thinks to himself *I've said P but not Q*; just as speakers almost never consciously work out what implicatures their utterances carry, they almost never explicitly think about the distinction between what they've said and what they've implicated. So the question of what a speaker takes himself to have said by some utterance will have to depend upon the answer he *would* give if he *were* asked. And it's very likely that in many circumstances there won't be a single answer, that the answer will differ depending on how the question is put. It's also very likely that the answer will vary from circumstance to circumstance. The person on trial for perjury is likely to think that he has said very little whereas the student defending his incomplete exam answer is likely to think that he has said quite a lot. The temptation here is to think that these contexts are *abnormal* contexts and, hence, that they aren't relevant. But it seems impossible to specify which contexts count as normal and to defend the claim that a speaker's answer in such contexts (however specified) must be authoritative. There is a very general point here: prior to learning the distinction between what's said and what's implicated, ordinary speakers don't at all have a clear conception of the distinction between the two. But, absent a somewhat clear conception of the distinction, it can't be required that they be able to infallibly distinguish them.[11]

Moreover, there is also an even more fundamental problem here. Once we give up on the idea that the inferential processes posited by Grice are conscious, there's no longer any motivation whatsoever to hold that conversational participants should be able to consciously recover *any aspect* of these processes. If we're willing to grant—as we obviously must—that even noncontroversial cases of implicature aren't consciously worked out by language users, what possible reason could there be for thinking that people must in all cases be able to distinguish what is said from what is implicated? Once you've allowed that some psychological process is unconscious, you've got to allow that a person who undergoes it needn't be able to consciously know that he does. Perhaps he must be able to bring it to consciousness with appropriate training or reflection—though it's not even clear that this should be so—but he needn't be able to do so in the ordinary course of things. There are some cases—for instance, the *Fergie is sober today* example—in which it's undeniable that there's a distinction between what's said and what's implicated. But, as emphasized above, in virtually none of these cases will either the speaker or the listeners engage in any conscious reasoning from what's said to what's implicated; so, to the extent that something like the Gricean inferential processes occur in such cases, they can't be conscious processes. But, once this is acknowledged, whether or not conversational participants can distinguish what's said from what's implicated is obviously an open question; and this is why the answer is likely to vary depending on the person and the circumstances. Indeed, there are cases—for example, *A tried to do x*—in which we *know* that intuitions about what is exactly said by a sentence differ. And, if we require what's said by an utterance to be consciously accessible to the speaker, different speakers will turn out to say different things *whenever* they disagree about what's said. But, once we see that speakers needn't consciously calculate what they will implicate from what they will say, there's no reason to think that their conscious opinions about these matters will be in every case authoritative.

5. The underdetermination of the inferences

So far I've emphasized that once we abandon the idea that conversational participants consciously calculate what's implicated from what's said, there's no reason to think that they should always have the ability to consciously distinguish the former from the latter and, indeed, plenty of reason to think that they shouldn't. Hence, we can resolve Grice's paradox without giving up on the idea that there can be disputes about what a particular sentence says. However, something much stronger than this is true: even if it turned out that we do explicitly calculate what an utterance implicates, it *still* needn't be the case that we can distinguish it from what it says. For it turns out that how a subject infers what's implicated from what's said is, in a certain sense, underdetermined. And, even if such inferences are in all cases conscious inferences, whether or not you can distinguish what's implicated from what's said will depend upon the precise inference you make. Moreover, once this dependence is brought out, it becomes clear that determining what is implicated by an utterance doesn't in fact require any calculation, whether conscious or unconscious.

To see what I'm getting at here, let's consider one of Grice's examples. Suppose you receive a letter of recommendation from me for someone applying for a philosophy job that merely says, *Mr. X's command of English is excellent and his class attendance has been regular*. You would immediately believe that my intent is to convey that Mr. X is philosophically inept. But what Gricean chain of reasoning underwrites this belief? Well, one of the maxims is that speakers should give whatever information is required to fulfill the purpose of the conversational exchange and, in this example, your belief that I intend to convey that Mr. X is philosophically inept seems to result from the fact that I haven't said enough to provide the requisite information for a letter of recommendation. If I don't mean to convey more than what I've literally said, then I'm violating Grice's (1989, 26) first *maxim of quantity*: I'm not "making [my] contribution as informative as is required (for the current purposes of the exchange)." So one way that you may have calculated the implicature is as follows: you believe that letters of recommendation are supposed to say more than what I've said; *because* you believe that I also believe this and that I believe that you do, you believe my intent must be to convey information that I'm reluctant to write down; and, *because* you also believe that I wouldn't be reluctant to write down good things about the candidate, you believe that I must intend to convey that Mr. X is bad at philosophy. This is in fact Grice's explanation of how the inference goes and, if you were to consciously calculate the inference in this way, you would need to know that what I've implicated (that Mr. X is no good at philosophy) is not what I've said (that Mr. X's command of English is excellent, etc.). For part of Grice's explanation is that you know that what I've said *doesn't* supply the required information: that if I don't mean to convey more than I've said I'm flouting the first maxim of quantity. However, though even if the maxim of quantity is involved in how I've conveyed more than I've said, *your calculation needn't appeal to this maxim*.

Recall that the maxim of quantity, like all of Grice's maxims, is supposed to follow from the more general Cooperative Principle: "Make your conversational contribution such as is required, at the stage at which it occurs, by the accepted purpose or direction of the talk exchange in which you are engaged" (Grice 1989, 26). But, because each of Grice's specific maxims is supposed to follow from the Cooperative Principle, a violation of the maxim of quantity, like a violation of *any particular maxim*, will also be a violation of the more general maxim to cooperate. But this means that your calculation of my intended meaning could appeal to the more general Cooperative Principle rather than the more specific maxim of quantity. You *might* reason, as in Grice's explanation given above, that if I don't mean to convey that Mr. X is bad at philosophy I'm not giving the required amount of information. But your reasoning might instead be more general; you might simply reason that if I don't mean to convey that Mr. X is bad at philosophy I'm being uncooperative, without any reference at all to the specific way in which I'd be being uncooperative: that is, without thinking at all about which particular maxim I'd be flouting.

Now it might seem that the more general pattern of reasoning wouldn't suffice to calculate exactly what I intend to get across. After all, the mere fact that I'd be being uncooperative if I didn't mean to get across more than I've said doesn't specify exactly *how* I'd be being uncooperative: it doesn't specify whether I'd be violating one of the maxims of quantity (whether I'd be giving too much information or not enough), or one of the maxims of quality (whether I'd be saying something I believe to be false or for which I lack adequate evidence), or one of the other maxims. The maxims that are supposed to follow from the Cooperative Principle tell us the specific ways in which speakers are supposed to cooperate. And the general fact that I wouldn't be cooperating if I meant to get across only what I've said doesn't tell you what I must mean to get across if I *am* cooperating. But then how could you tell what I mean to get across—namely, that Mr. X lacks philosophical ability—without knowing that my potential uncooperativeness would consist in not giving enough information about Mr. X's philosophical ability?

Surprisingly enough, the answer here is that you just would and that there can't be any reason to think that the inference itself has to provide you with the ability to determine what's implicated. No matter what story we tell about the precise nature of your inference, at some point we will have to appeal to some ability of yours that isn't grounded in an inference. For example, on the account that Grice gives of how you would determine my intended meaning, you need to explicitly know the distinction between what I've said and what I've implicated: that is, you need to know

(a) I haven't said anything about Mr. X's philosophical ability.

And, like any of the premises in Grice's account of the inference, one can ask, How is it that you know (a)? But here, and likewise for any of the other premises, an appeal to some inference from other facts you know won't ultimately help; for such an appeal will just leave open the question of how you know these other facts. At some point, we'll have to suppose that you have a *noninferential ability* to determine the premises that go into your inference. And, assuming that Grice's account of the inference is meant to be complete, on his account (a) is such a fact; to make the inference you'll need a noninferential ability to determine what it is that I've said. But, if noninferential abilities must figure into the account somewhere—for example, if it's legitimate to suppose that you can figure out what it is I've said without making any inference—then there's no reason that you shouldn't have a noninferential ability to tell that, if I'm being cooperative, I must mean that Mr. X is bad at philosophy.

It's important to be clear on what is and isn't being claimed here. I am claiming that your inference to my intent could appeal to the more general Cooperative Principle rather than the more specific first maxim of quantity. But I am *not* claiming that my potential failure to cooperate doesn't involve a potential violation of the first maxim of quantity. If I intended to convey only what I've said, then my uncooperativeness would certainly consist in having not given the information required in a letter of recommendation; the point here is only that your calculation of what I meant to convey needn't appeal to the precise maxim that I've potentially violated. That the implicature carried by an utterance depends upon a certain maxim *underdetermines* exactly how you might calculate the implicature; for you might calculate it by appealing to the more general Cooperative Principle rather than the specific maxim that is relevant.

Two points emerge from the way in which particular Gricean inferences are underdetermined. First, even it turned out that such inferences must in all cases be conscious, it doesn't follow that conversational participants must in all cases be able to distinguish what's said from what's implicated. Any Gricean chain of reasoning will, at some point, have to rely on an ability that isn't an inferential ability; and, while it might be that you have a noninferential ability to know what's said and you infer from this knowledge what's implicated, in which case the inference requires that you can distinguish what's said from what's implicated, it might instead be that you have a noninferential ability to know what the speaker means if he is cooperating, in which case the inference doesn't require that you can distinguish what's said from what's implicated. For example, in the case of the letter of recommendation, if you simply reason that I'd be being uncooperative if I didn't mean to convey that Mr. X is bad at philosophy, you needn't know that I haven't said that Mr. X is bad at philosophy. For one way of being uncooperative is to say something that's false and you might think that my potential uncooperativeness consists in my having said something false if X isn't bad at philosophy; that is to say, you might think that I've simply said that he's bad at it. In the previous section we saw that, since implicatures are rarely if ever consciously worked out, there's no reason to suppose that what's said by an utterance should be consciously accessible. But the point here is that, even if all implicatures were consciously calculated, Recanati's requirement that what is said be accessible to conversational participants still needn't hold.

But there's also a much more important point here: namely, that there's no reason to suppose that our ability to determine what is implicated by an utterance depends on *any inference whatsoever, either conscious or unconscious.* Though Grice is right that the presence of a conversational implicature depends upon the fact that linguistic communication is governed by maxims of cooperative activity, it doesn't follow that our ability to determine what is implicated by some utterance results from our making inferences that involve these maxims. As language users we have some understanding of what it takes to be cooperative in a conversational exchange; but there's no reason this understanding shouldn't be grounded in a noninferential ability to cooperate. Grice's account of how we determine what's implicated from what's said suggests that we have a noninferential ability to determine what is said; but perhaps, instead, we have a noninferential ability to determine what is implicated and, hence, don't need to consciously or unconsciously know what's said by any particular utterance. Upon hearing me say something, you have the ability to determine what I mean to convey; more generally, we both have the ability to engage in the cooperative, rational activity that is linguistic communication. But this ability needn't depend on some antecedent ability to consciously or unconsciously determine the difference between what's said and what's implicated; for our ability to act in accordance with the Cooperative Principle needn't be grounded in any conscious or unconscious knowledge of this principle.

6. Dispensing with the inferences

Whenever you successfully follow a rule, your behavior accords with it. But, as is well known and often discussed, the converse doesn't hold. There are various distinctions that one might draw to bring this out, but the most helpful for our purposes is that between *merely* acting in accordance with a rule and doing so because of some thought that involves the rule. You act in accordance with a rule whenever your behavior conforms to it, regardless of whether the rule plays any role in your thoughts that motivate the behavior. But sometimes you act in accordance with a rule because of some thought about the rule: the rule guides your actions because of this thought. So, for instance, you probably act in accordance with the rule *Don't go to the supermarket in a helicopter* since your behavior is probably perfectly consistent with this rule. However, even though your behavior accords with it, it doesn't do so because of some thought involving this rule. Insofar as your thoughts are concerned, it's a kind of *accident* that you never take a helicopter to a supermarket.

Now it might seem that any case in which one acts in accordance with a rule without thinking about the rule must be a case of accidental accordance. After all, if you have no thoughts at all about the rule, how could the fact that your behavior accords with it be anything but accidental? It seems as if the only way a rule could play a role in guiding your behavior is if your behavior results from a thought involving the rule. And, insofar as things seem this way, it will also seem that, if Grice's Cooperative Principle and its attendant maxims are to play any part at all in how we come to know what others mean to convey, they will have to play an inferential part: at a minimum we must *unconsciously* use the maxims to infer what's implicated from what's said. For, if the maxims don't even guide us unconsciously, how could they guide us at all? And the fact alluded to in the previous section—namely, that the particular inference used to calculate what's implicated from what's said is always underdetermined—doesn't yet show that the dilemma between using the maxims unconsciously or there being no maxims at all is a false one.

As we saw, any particular case of calculating what's implicated from what's said is underdetermined because making any such inference requires that you have a *noninferential* ability to determine its premises. For example, many of the particular inferences that Grice cites, if they are to be the whole inferential story, require that conversational participants have a noninferential ability to determine what is or would be said by an utterance. But, as we also saw, given that noninferential abilities are required at some stage, there's no reason they shouldn't come in at the very beginning: no reason that language users shouldn't simply have the noninferential ability to determine what's implicated upon hearing what's said. And the fact that we don't consciously make any such inferences suggests that we do have this ability. But to say this is not yet to explain how the Cooperative Principle and its attendant maxims could be relevant to a noninferential ability, to an ability that involves neither conscious nor unconscious appeals to these maxims. If there is a distinction between what's said and what's implicated, then it seems that our ability to determine the former from the latter may be noninferential. But the distinction between what's said and what's implicated seems to involve the Cooperative Principle and its attendant maxims. And how could they possibly explain the distinction if we don't even unconsciously use the maxims to determine what's implicated from what's said? How can rules that we don't think about nonetheless play a role in our acting in accordance with them? There is an answer here, and it lies in commonplace facts about *abilities*.

To begin with, an ability is, obviously, always an ability to do something; you have the ability to drive a car, to solve mathematical problems, etc. But, just as obviously, when you have the ability to do a certain thing, exercising this ability involves doing many other things. For example, suppose that, for whatever reason, you decide to type Aristotle's *Nicomachean Ethics* into your computer and you set about doing this. Doing it will involve striking every key on your keyboard that corresponds to some letter in any word that occurs in the *Nicomachean Ethics*. But, of course, unless you're a pretty bad typist, you won't have to think about striking a key each time you need to do so. The activity of typing the *Nicomachean Ethics* into your computer is a complex activity that involves literally tens of thousands of more simple things; but you have the ability (if you're even a halfway decent typist) to type the *Nicomachean Ethics* into your computer without having to think about typing each letter into the computer. More generally, many of the things we are able to do consist in doing lots of other things; but we have the ability to do something without thinking about doing all of the things it consists in. As I say, there's nothing at all startling here. However, the obvious fact that we can perform a complex action without having to think about performing its more basic constituent actions explains how Grice's rules can be relevant to our ability to determine what's implicated, even though this ability does not involve a conscious or unconscious appeal to these maxims.[12]

Our communicative use of language involves an ability to do something: namely, an ability to convey and receive information by using language. But, just as typing a book into a computer consists in doing lots of other things, conveying and receiving information by using language also consists in doing other things. Some of these other things are (in the case of spoken language) things like pushing air through your vocal cords, moving your mouth in certain ways, etc.; conveying information via language in part involves uttering sentences, and there are various actions or bodily movements that uttering sentences consists in. But conveying and receiving information via language is, as Grice points out, a cooperative and rational activity and, hence, using language in these ways also consists in engaging in a cooperative and rational activity; that is to say, it consists in following certain maxims that constitute any such activity. And, just as you have the ability to type a book into a computer without having to think about all of the things that constitute doing so, you have the ability to intend to communicate information via language without having to think about all the things that constitute doing so. Striking keys with your fingers *is part of what it is* to type a book into a computer, and following the conversational maxims *is part of what it is* to engage in linguistic communication; and, as examples like typing illustrate, we can exercise an ability to do something without thinking about all its constituents.

Now it might seem that there is an important disanalogy between the ability to perform actions like typing and the ability to communicate via language. The latter involves following certain rules and, hence, if one can intend to communicate via language without thinking about the rules that constitute such communication, then one can follow a rule without thinking about it. But, as mentioned earlier, it seems that the only way your acting in accordance with a rule could be anything but accidental is if your behavior accords with the rule *because* you are thinking about the rule. Striking a key on a keyboard seems a perfectly physical thing, so it's no mystery that you can do so without having to think about doing so, but how could you count as following a rule if you aren't thinking about the rule?

The first thing to notice here is that striking a keyboard might in some sense be a perfectly physical event, but it is something more than a mere bodily movement. My hitting the *k* key on my keyboard is not like a muscle spasm or some other involuntary movement; it's not merely something that happens to my body. Rather, it's something that, in some sense, I *do*. Striking the *k* key in the course of typing something might or might not count as a full-fledged *action*, but it is more robust than a mere bodily movement. And this is true in part because, like linguistic communication, it involves engaging in behavior that nonaccidentally accords with a rule. When you successfully copy a book into a computer, your behavior accords with the rule *If a letter appears in the book, strike the key with that letter on it*. And, even though there's no reason to think that you unconsciously appeal to this rule each time you strike a key, the rule is nonetheless relevant to your typing behavior in a way that the rule *Don't take helicopters to the supermarket* isn't relevant to your shopping behavior. Indeed, each time you strike a key you follow the rule *If a letter appears in the book, strike the key with that letter on it*. So I think it's clear that we do have the ability to follow a rule without consciously or unconsciously appealing to it, because we have the more general ability to do something without consciously or unconsciously thinking about all the things that constitute doing it.

Now there is one difference between typing and linguistic communication that may be relevant here. Before you learn to type well, it may be that you have to think about the rule *If a letter appears in the book, strike the key with that letter on it.* It's important, however, not to overstate the role this rule will play for the novice typist. It's not that the novice typists thinks to himself: *If a letter appears in the book, I will strike the key with that letter on it. The letter k appears in the book. So I will strike the key with the letter k on it,* and so on for every other letter he types. Even the worst typist in the world is unlikely to have to make an inference involving the rule each time he strikes a key; at worst, the novice typist will likely have to think to himself: *There's a k, so I should strike the k key* or, if he's learning the standard method of touch typing, *There's a k, so I should strike the key my right middle finger is hovering over.* Even the most pathetic typist is likely to have the ability to follow the rule *If a letter appears in the book, strike the key with that letter on it* without thinking about following the rule each time he strikes a key. At most, in learning to type the novice typist must at *some point* think to himself *If a letter appears in the book, I will strike the key with that letter on it,* but he needn't go on to think about the rule each time he strikes a key. However, if one needs at some point to have explicitly thought about following the rule in the typing case, this makes it different than the linguistic case; for it's very implausible that at some time or another before learning a language every speaker forms an explicit thought about following Grice's maxims. Our ability to type doesn't show that you can follow a rule without ever thinking about it; rather, it merely shows that a particular bit of behavior that counts as following a rule needn't involve an appeal to the rule. The worry here is that striking a particular key counts as following the general rule only because at some earlier point you explicitly thought about the general rule and this thought played a role in your learning to follow the rule; and, since the same isn't true about language acquisition, the only way we could turn out to be following Gricean maxims is if we unconsciously appeal to them when we determine what's implicated by an utterance.

There is a genuine disanalogy between typing and language here, but it isn't generally true that if your behavior is to nonaccidentally accord with a rule you need at some point to have had an explicit thought involving the rule. For example, a few years ago I decided to learn to skip rope. There are various patterns of skipping; for example, you can skip so that both feet jump and land together, or you can skip so that only one foot is on the ground at any given time. After I learned to somewhat competently skip in the latter way, I noticed that there are two asymmetrical ways of doing it; and, though I was able to skip both ways and even switch back and forth between them, it took me about a month to be able to identify the difference between them. One way is to step over the rope with your left foot; and, as the rope passes over your head, lift your left foot, put your right foot down, and then step over the rope with your left foot again. The other way is just the reverse: step over the rope with your right foot; and, as the rope passes over your head, lift your right foot, put your left foot down, and then step over the rope with your right foot again. So, before I was able to identify the rule associated with either way of skipping, I was able to skip both ways; that is, my behavior non-accidentally accorded with one or the other of the rules, even though I couldn't at first tell what these rules were. Now, had I known the rule associated with each way of skipping prior to learning them, my knowledge would no doubt have facilitated my learning to skip each way: I would have caught on faster. But following the rules didn't require me to think about them, since I was able to do so before having the faintest idea of what they even were. When, on a particular occasion, I decided to skip one of the two ways, I decided to engage in an activity that is constituted by following a certain rule; and I was able to engage in this activity without knowing what the rule is and, hence, without appealing to it with each skip.[13]

And the same thing seems to occur in the typing example. Learning to type is facilitated by explicitly forming the intention to follow the typing rule; indeed, maybe, unlike rope-skipping styles, the *only way* to learn to type is to at some point explicitly think about the rule. But the fact that you had this thought at some point isn't what makes it the case that you're following the rule each time you strike a key; rather, you have the ability to engage in an activity that is constituted by following a certain rule without having any knowledge of what the rule is, and you have this ability because you have the ability to do something that is constituted by doing certain other things without thinking about its constituents. And linguistic communication is likely the same. I don't consciously calculate what you've implicated from what you've said by appealing to Grice's maxims, nor is there any reason to think that I unconsciously do so. Still, in virtue of being able to communicate via language, and in virtue of the fact that such communication consists in following the maxims, my knowing what you've implicated is a result of following the maxims.

Several points need to be made here. First, though I've claimed that one can follow a rule without having any conscious or unconscious thought about it, the general point here doesn't really depend upon this strong a claim. It's possible that one doesn't strictly speaking *follow a rule* unless one at some time or another has some conscious or unconscious thought about the rule. So perhaps it's wrong to say that, prior to knowing the different rules involved in the different ways of skipping rope, I followed either rule. Be that as it may, the rule certainly wasn't irrelevant to my skipping behavior in the way that the rule *Don't take helicopters to the supermarket* is irrelevant to my shopping behavior. While skipping in one of these ways, I was exercising an ability to do something that involves acting in accordance with the relevant rule; and, because of this, my behavior's accordance with the rule was nonaccidental, whether or not it strictly speaking counted as following the rule. Similarly, insofar as you exercise your ability to communicate via language, you're doing something that involves acting in accordance with Grice's maxims and, as such, your communicative behavior isn't in mere *accidental* accordance with the maxims. Upon hearing someone say something, you have the ability to know what they mean to convey and this ability involves acting in accordance with these maxims, whether or not, strictly speaking, you can be said to be appealing to them. Thus the maxims are relevant to your ability to work out what someone implicates, even though you need neither consciously nor unconsciously appeal to them, nor even consciously or unconsciously have any knowledge of them whatsoever.

Second, though I find the suggestion that any case in which some behavior non-accidentally accords with a rule is a case in which the subject must at least unconsciously have some thought about the rule absurd, I have no doubt that lots of philosophers won't find it so absurd. Some will be inclined to reject the idea that you can successfully engage in some rule-governed activity without at least unconsciously representing the rules: even prior to consciously knowing the relevant rules in the jump-rope case, I must have unconsciously known them as soon as I was able to act in accordance with them. However, though I think this view is deeply wrong (and, to be honest, kind of silly), for the purposes at hand it doesn't matter if it's correct or not. For, if you think that I unconsciously followed the relevant jump-rope rule, then you should have no problem in thinking that we unconsciously follow Grice's maxims. And, though I do hope to have shed some light on how the Gricean rules figure into linguistic communication, my main concern is to show that there's no reason to expect these rules, and the semantic values of sentences that are their input, to be consciously accessible to language users.

I think the fact that speakers almost never consciously engage in anything like the inferences that Grice describes means that our ability to determine what's implicated from what's said isn't an inferential ability. We don't consciously think about the semantic values of our utterances or about the Gricean maxims, and saving Grice's account by claiming that we unconsciously do this is a desperate and ill-motivated move. Grice is right that linguistic communication is a rational, cooperative endeavor, and he is right that, as such, it is governed by certain rules; if we succeed at this endeavor, then we must act in accordance with these rules, since acting in accordance with the rules is part of what constitutes the endeavor. But our ability to act in accordance with the rules doesn't require that we have any conscious or unconscious thoughts about them. Riding a bicycle requires that you take advantage of the laws of physics, but it's absurd to suggest that doing so requires that you have thoughts about these laws. And, similarly, communicating requires that you follow certain rules that govern cooperative endeavors, but it doesn't require that you do so by thinking about these rules.[14] The fact that you don't consciously do so suggests that you don't do so at all. There is certainly a distinction between what someone says and what he implicates; and something is certainly right about Grice's account of this distinction. But we say more than we need to and more than is plausible when we suppose that the inferential processes that Grice posits occur.

It is hard to imagine abandoning the distinction between the semantic value of an utterance and what it conversationally implicates, and something does seem right about the Gricean account of the distinction in terms of maxims that govern cooperative activity. There is undoubtedly a distinction between the semantic value of *Fergie was sober today* and the information that he is often drunk, which it can sometimes be used to convey. And it is hard to doubt that, when the sentence is used to convey this information, it does so because of the conversational participants' ability to act in accordance with the maxims. But this ability almost never involves a *conscious* inference; we are generally consciously aware only of what a speaker intends to convey. And, even if we follow Grice in thinking that inference is involved, we have to admit that such inferences are unconscious and, hence, that there's no reason that conversational participants should have conscious access to the semantic values of their utterances. However, I'm suggesting that we should abandon the idea that there are generally any inferences, conscious or unconscious, involved in conversational implicature. To the extent that we intend to communicate, we must act in accordance with the maxims, but we can have the ability to do so without consciously or unconsciously thinking about these maxims. At some point, we have to suppose that our ability to know what's implicated involves some noninferential ability; and there's no reason to suppose that the noninferential ability doesn't come in at the very beginning and that our ability to know what an utterance implicates is itself noninferential. And, if this is right, we have even less of a reason to suppose that the distinction between the semantic value of an utterance and what it is used to convey needs to be consciously accessible to conversational participants. We are, for the most part, consciously aware only of the information conveyed by an utterance. And, though semantic values will play a role in any sensible account of how such information is conveyed and how speakers can intend it to be conveyed, semantic values are *theoretical entities*; that is to say, they are *theoretical postulates* of the theory of linguistic communication. Our students have to be taught the distinction between a sentence's semantic value and its implicature, and they have to be taught that the information that Fergie is often drunk is not part of the semantic value of the sentence *Fergie was sober today*. What is implicated by an utterance is almost always apparent, but in some cases—for example, *A tried to do x*—it is quite difficult to work backwards to what its semantic value is.

7. Semantic value as a theoretical entity

So far I've argued that once we recognize that Gricean inferences are almost never conscious, there's no reason to require that the processes by which implicatures are worked out be accessible and every reason to think that the requirement should be abandoned. I've tried to show that Grice's rules can be relevant to our ability to determine what's said from what's implicated without our unconsciously thinking about these rules and, hence, that we needn't have any unconscious knowledge of an utterance's semantic value either. In having the ability to nonaccidentally act in accordance with the maxims, we have the ability to determine what's implicated when presented with what's said, but we needn't unconsciously think about what's said and, hence, we needn't even be able to unconsciously distinguish it from what's implicated. However, if you think that the fact that someone's behavior nonaccidentally accords with a rule requires that they have at least unconscious thoughts about it, then you should also think that we unconsciously follow Grice's maxims; hence, you should have no problem thinking that the semantic value of an utterance needn't be consciously accessible to someone in order for him to know what it implicates. Either way there's no reason to think that semantic values are consciously accessible, and this is enough to discharge the Gricean paradox. For the paradox assumes that the processes by which we work out implicatures are accessible to us and, hence, that conversational participants must be able to tell whether something is part of an utterance's semantic value or merely implicated by it. But these processes are almost never conscious and, hence, there's no reason to think that they should always be accessible. It is implicature and not semantic value that we are for the most part consciously aware of. Sometimes, as in the case of *Fergie was sober today*, it is easy to consciously distinguish a sentence's semantic value from its implicature; but, other times, as in the case of *A tried to do x*, it can be quite difficult.

The points emphasized above can be put succinctly as follows:

> *The information an utterance is used to convey is an observational entity of linguistic theory and the semantic value of an utterance is a theoretical postulate of that theory.*

According to some of our intuitions about meaning, the meaning of a sentence is determined by the meaning of its constituent words and (together with the way the world is) determines its truth-value. The term *semantic value* is used to refer to the entity that corresponds to these intuitions about meaning. Furthermore, the semantic values of sentences play a crucial role in linguistic communication. But, in the vast majority of conversational exchanges in which an utterance conveys an implicature, the participants are not consciously aware of the utterance's semantic value; rather, they are directly aware of the information conveyed by it, and it is this information that they consciously reason with and use in conscious decisions about which actions to take.

It is often not sufficiently recognized how much of the information speakers intend to convey in normal conversations goes beyond the semantic values of their utterances. *Smoking is bad for you* is usually intended to convey that you shouldn't smoke; *Suzette lives somewhere in Los Angeles* is usually intended to convey that the speaker doesn't know exactly where in Los Angeles she lives; *It's three in the morning* is often intended to convey that the speaker thinks it is time for you to go home; *I'm a vegetarian* is sometimes intended to convey that the speaker prefers that pepperoni not be on the pizza; *Do you mind if I ask whether P* usually is intended to convey that the speaker would like his interlocutor to tell him whether P; *I believe that P* is usually intended to convey that the speaker isn't certain that P;

I don't believe that P is usually intended to convey that the speaker *does* believe the negation of P; and so on *ad infinitum*. In none of these cases is the information that the sentence is used to convey a part of its semantic value, and it's safe to say that a sentence used to convey something besides its semantic value is the rule rather than the exception. The gap between a sentence's semantic value and the information it is used to convey is not merely some interesting anomaly; it is a crucial part of our day-to-day conversations and, hence, a crucial part of any adequate theory of linguistic communication. Moreover, in none of the above cases would the speaker or listener consciously work out what the information conveyed is; hence, the theoretical nature of semantic values is no anomaly either.

It is worth noting that strictly analogous points hold for Kaplan's notion of *character*. According to some of our intuitions about meaning, the word *I* means the same thing in everyone's mouth. But, as we have seen, this implies that this notion of meaning isn't *semantic value*, and we use the term **character** to refer to it. Though the semantic value of *I* differs depending on who the speaker is, its character is a function from linguistic contexts to referents and it remains the same. We must, in some sense, *know* the character of *I*; but, when the word is used in a sentence, we do not consciously reason from its character to its referent. If you were to utter the sentence *I am tired* in my presence I would have no conscious thoughts about the character of *I*; rather, I would immediately know that you were claiming that *you* are tired. And, as in the case of Grice's maxims, there seems to be no reason to think that I *unconsciously* calculate the referent of *I*. The same is true of utterances containing other indexicals. Moreover, just as we are apt to confuse the semantic value of a sentence with its implicature, we are apt to confuse its semantic value with its character. Before Kaplan (1989), most philosophers thought that the contribution of the word *I* makes to the truth-conditions of sentences in which it occurs is the same as the contribution that *the speaker* would make. Just like the distinction between semantic value and information conveyed, the distinction between semantic value and character constituted an important philosophical *discovery*. And character, just like semantic value, is a theoretical postulate of linguistic theory.

The recognition that semantic value is a theoretical postulate of linguistic theory provides an explanation of why the semantic values of some sentences are more transparent to us than the semantic values of others. In some cases it is obvious that some piece of information that an utterance is used to convey isn't part of its semantic value. For example, we have no temptation to think that the truth of *Fergie was sober today* requires that Fergie is often drunk. The reason that we have no temptation to confuse the implicated information with the sentence's semantic value is that there are many everyday contexts in which sentences containing the word *sober* are *not* intended to convey any such information. For example, the sentences *Fergie's sober, so he should drive* and *You shouldn't make any important decisions when you're not sober* are perfectly commonplace sentences in which the word occurs and which would not be used to convey anything about anyone's often being drunk. Although *information conveyed* rather than semantic value is the observational entity of linguistic theory, the fact that *sober* *usually isn't* used to convey the information that the person described as *sober* is often drunk forestalls any confusion about its semantic value.

However, when some sentence is usually used to convey some piece of information, it is difficult to work out that the information isn't part of the sentence's semantic value. For example, because uses of the word *tried* *usually are* used to convey that someone failed to do something, it is a genuine issue whether this is part of the semantic values of sentences in which the word occurs. With a bit of ingenuity, however, one can think of contexts in which the sentence is not used to convey such information, and the existence of these contexts provides evidence that it is *not* part of the semantic value of *tried*. The cancelability of a generalized conversational implicature is a means for using the observational entity of *the information conveyed by a sentence* to determine the theoretical entity of *the semantic value of a sentence*. By trying to find contexts in which a sentence is not used to convey some piece of information, we can determine whether this information is likely to be part of its semantic value. But the harder it is to find a context in which the information that the sentence can be used to convey is canceled, the harder it will be to determine that it is not part of the sentence's semantic value.

Again, it is important to note that strictly analogous points hold for character. Because an assertive utterance of, for example, *I am tired* always conveys that the speaker is tired, we are apt to think that the word *I* makes the same contribution to the truth-conditions of the sentence as the phrase *the speaker* would, and it takes a great deal of careful thought to see that this isn't in fact so. Very few of the entities posited by our theory of linguistic communication are transparent to us in the way that our use of the term *meaning* to refer to them suggests they are.

8. The opacity of semantic value

So far I have suggested that semantic values are *theoretical postulates* of linguistic theory: our intuitions about the truth-conditions of a sentence are intuitions about the truth-conditions of the *information it is used to convey in particular contexts*; and, though semantic values play a role in the communication of information, determining a sentence's semantic value involves using the cancelability of information that it can be used to convey but that isn't a part of its semantic value. Given these facts, it is not so far-fetched to claim that a competent language user might not know the semantic value of an utterance. However, this way of formulating Millianism's claim about the opacity of semantic value can't be quite correct; for, as noted in Section 4, it seems that in some sense the semantic value of any sentence must be known to any competent speaker (of the sentence's language; henceforth, I will take this qualification to be understood). After all, even if pure Millianism about belief is correct, isn't the semantic value of *Lex believes that Superman flies* simply the proposition that Lex believes that Superman flies and the semantic value of *Lex believes that Clark Kent flies* simply the proposition that Lex believe that Clark Kent flies? In some sense, knowing a sentence's semantic value appears to be an utterly trivial matter and, hence, our formulation of the point against Millianism appears to be somewhat imprecise. How then should the point be put?

What's really at issue isn't whether or not speakers know the semantic values of particular sentences; what's at issue is whether speakers know that the semantic value of *one sentence* (for example, *Lex believes that Superman flies*) is the same as the semantic value of *another* (for example, *Lex believes that Clark Kent flies*). And, similarly, it seems that the semantic value of *A tried to do x* must also be known to competent speakers: it's simply the proposition that A tried to do x. Again, the real issue is whether or not the semantic value of *A failed to do x* is included in the semantic value of *A tried to do x*. It may be a trivial matter to specify the semantic value of any sentence by embedding it in a *that*-clause; however, since language users are consciously aware only of the information an utterance can be used to convey, it can be a nontrivial matter to determine whether the semantic values of two sentences are the same or whether the semantic value of one sentence is included in the semantic value of another.

Of course, the claim that any competent language user must trivially know the semantic value of any sentence does not imply that, if two distinct sentences have the same semantic value, he must know that they do. For, obviously, you can know who the super-powered protector of Metropolis is (everyone knows he is Superman) and know who the bespectacled *Daily Planet* reporter is (everyone knows he is Clark Kent) without knowing that the super-powered protector of Metropolis *is* the bespectacled *Daily Planet* reporter. In general, the fact that you know what the F is and what the G is doesn't imply that you know whether the F is the G. And note that the precise formulation of the Millian's claims concerning the opacity of semantic value greatly weakens the case against Millianism.

The case against Millianism rests upon the idea that, whenever two sentences have the same semantic value, a competent speaker will know that their semantic values are the same. But, as we have just seen, the demand being made here is that when the semantic value of *P* is the same as the semantic value of *Q*, competent speakers should know they are the same. And, of course, it isn't at all true that one must know that the F is the G if in fact the F is the G; Frege's puzzle is about co-referring *names*, but the reason that descriptive Fregeanism is a possible solution to the puzzle is that there isn't any similar puzzle for descriptions, since it's obvious that you don't need to know when two co-referring definite descriptions do in fact co-refer. So why should anyone demand that such knowledge obtains when the descriptions concern the semantic values of sentences? I think that the plausibility of such a demand depends upon thinking that the semantic value of a sentence is just *its meaning*. After all, if you are competent in the use of two expressions, then it seems that you should know that they have the same meaning if in fact they do. However, we've already seen enough to recognize that one of the most important lessons to be learned from recent philosophy of language is that *there simply isn't any such thing as the meaning of a sentence.*

As stressed above, intuitively, the meaning of a sentence has many features, some of which are as follows:

(1) It is determined by the meaning of the sentence's constituent words and (together with the way the world is) determines the sentence's truth-value.
(2) Different utterances of the same sentence have the same meaning.
(3) The meaning of a sentence is what's communicated to listeners when the sentence is uttered.

However, as was also stressed above, it is crucial to recognize that there isn't anything that shares any two of these features. A proper understanding of indexicals shows that there's nothing that shares (1) and (2): if different utterances of, for example, *I am tired* have the same meaning (as (2) claims they do), then it is clear that meaning can't determine truth-value (as (1) claims it does). And Grice's discussion of conversational implicature shows us that there isn't anything that shares features (1) and (3), or (2) and (3). Since, intuitively, linguistic meaning has all three features, there simply can't be any such thing as linguistic meaning. The situation here isn't that different from the one that leads us to distinguish between weight and mass. Pre-theoretically, we have two distinct options of *how much an object weighs* that are inconsistent with each other. On the one hand, how much an object weighs doesn't seem like it should depend upon whether it's on the earth or the moon but, on the other, how much an object weighs does seem like it should depend on this. Obviously nothing can meet both criteria but it turns out that something does meet each one. We have two distinct things here; the first gets called *mass* and the second gets called *weight*. Similarly, we can distinguish distinct things that correspond to (1)–(3), and we have distinct terms to refer to them: *semantic value* is what we call the thing that has feature (1), *character* is what we call the thing that has feature (2), and *information conveyed* is what we call the thing that has feature (3). Now, perhaps when two sentences convey the very same information anyone competent in their use must know that they do. But, once we recognize that there really isn't any such thing as meaning and clearly distinguish the distinct things speakers intend to be getting at by using the word, and once we realize that *semantic values* are theoretical postulates of linguistic theory, there is in fact no reason to suppose that the fact that two sentences have the same semantic value is always known to competent speakers and every reason to suppose that it isn't.[15]

I pointed out above that it seems that competent speakers must trivially know a sentence's semantic value. However, we are now in a position to see that, in this regard, appearances are somewhat deceiving. Semantic values are theoretical postulates of linguistic theory, and once we see that a sentence's semantic value isn't its meaning, it becomes clear that most speakers will have nothing close to a clear and distinct conception of what semantic values are and, as a consequence, won't have a clear and distinct conception of what the semantic value of any sentence is. It's crucial that we explicitly recognize how far our discussion has moved beyond intuitive ideas that anyone is capable of having. A theorist about language may be in a position to trivially know that the semantic value of *P* is the proposition that P, but an untutored speaker simply lacks the conceptual resources to know these apparently trivial facts.

Millianism is usually indicted for having the consequence that competent speakers sometimes fail to know the meaning of certain very ordinary sentences. We have already seen one way in which this charge is inaccurate. Millianism's claim about the opacity of semantic values isn't that competent speakers don't know the semantic values of certain sentences; rather, it's that they sometimes don't know that the semantic value of one sentence is the same as that of another. And, in general, competent speakers needn't know when two co-referring descriptions do in fact co-refer. However, the observations of this section reveal another way in which Millianism is innocent of the charge.

Contrary to the charge, *Millianism makes no claims about the meaning of sentences*; it only makes claims about their semantic values: about what (together with the way the world is) determines their truth-value. The term *meaning* simply shouldn't occur in an even moderately sophisticated account of linguistic communication. Of course, this isn't a reason to stop using the term in ordinary conversations, just as the heliocentric theory of the solar system is no reason to stop saying *The sun has risen* in ordinary conversations. But when a speaker untutored in the complexities of linguistic theory says that *Lex believes that Superman flies* and *Lex believes that Clark Kent flies* mean different things, there's no reason to think he intends to say anything more than that the two sentences always convey different information; and in this regard he is correct. Normal language users aren't confused about the *semantic values* of these sentences any more than they are confused about whether Newton's formula for adding velocities or Einstein's is correct; and the fact that they can use language is no more reason to claim that they must know of semantic value than the fact that they can catch a football is reason to claim that they must have views on how to add velocities. Insofar as Millianism is committed to competent speakers' having some ignorance about the semantic values of the belief ascriptions, the view is on firm ground; for the vast majority of competent speakers don't have any views about semantic values at all.

So the plausibility of the standard charge against Millianism depends upon not realizing exactly what Millianism's claims about the opacity of semantic values really are and not realizing that these claims are theoretical claims about theoretical entities. However, there is a charge against the view that survives even once the above confusions are cleared up. As we've seen, one way to determine a sentence's semantic value is to think of what the truth-value of the information it is used to convey is in various contexts. However, even when we are clear on the theoretical nature of semantic value, this method doesn't seem to be of much help in determining that, for example, the semantic values of *Lex believes that Superman flies* and *Lex believes that Clark Kent flies* are the same. But why should this method fail for such sentences? The recognition that semantic values are theoretical entities provides the beginnings of an answer.

Even if you're wise to the complexities of linguistic communication, you'll still be aware only of the information a sentence is used to convey and, hence, you'll have to use the cancelability of its implicature to determine how much of what it conveys is part of its semantic value. Hence, even for such a person, intuitions about a sentence's truth-value aren't a sure means for determining its semantic value. As we have seen in the case of *A tried to do x*, sometimes it can be very difficult to determine that what is implicated by a sentence isn't part of its semantic value. The relevant sentences are simply another case in which it is difficult to separate a sentence's implicature from its semantic value. *C'est la vie.*

However, as things stand, the *C'est la vie* is more than a bit cavalier. After all, even though it's difficult to determine whether or not the semantic value of *A tried to do x* includes that A failed to do x, neither position runs completely against our intuitions about the information the sentence is used to convey. But the sentences *Lex believes that Superman flies* and *Lex believes that Clark Kent flies* are *always* used to convey different information. And if their semantic values really are the same, shouldn't there be some contexts in which each is used to convey only its semantic value and, hence, in which the identity of their semantic values seems intuitively correct? To put the point another way, the semantic value of *A tried to do x* may be somewhat opaque, but it isn't completely opaque; we have conflicting intuitions about what the sentence's truth-conditions are, and cancelability is merely a tool for settling which intuitions are correct. Yet, if Millianism about belief is correct, the semantic values of some belief reports are *completely* opaque, and nothing said so far has explained how this could be so. Is it really plausible that two sentences could have the same semantic value and yet never convey the same information?

I think that it is not only plausible that the semantic values of the relevant sentences should be completely opaque; it is also *entirely predictable* that they are. To see why it is predictable, we need to take a closer look at what makes it the case that the semantic values of some sentences are more opaque than those of others.

9. Trivial but informative sentences

So far, we have discussed two clear examples of conversational implicature: in many contexts *Fergie was sober today* is used to convey the information that Fergie is often drunk; and in many contexts *A tried to do x* is used to convey the information that A failed to do x. As we saw, despite the fact that each sentence carries a certain implicature in many contexts, there is an important difference between them. Even though there are many contexts in which the sentence *Fergie was sober today* carries the implicature that he is often drunk, the semantic value of the sentence is still pretty transparent: no one who understands the distinction between the semantic value of an utterance and what it implicates would be tempted by the view that part of the semantic value of the sentence includes that Fergie is often drunk. However, the semantic value of *A tried to do x* is a good deal less transparent, as witnessed by the fact that people *have* been tempted by the view that its semantic value includes the information that A failed to do x. As we also saw, the fact that semantic values are theoretical entities and the role that cancelability plays in how we use intuitions about the truth-value of a sentence to determine its semantic value provide an explanation for the difference between the two sentences. There are many more everyday contexts in which the first sentence isn't used to convey the information that Fergie is often drunk than there are in which the second isn't used to convey that A failed to do x; hence, it is easier to think of a context that cancels the first sentence's implicature than it is to think of one that cancels the second sentence's. And being able to think of such a context is crucial to successfully using intuitions about how a sentence is used to determine its semantic value.

So far I have been speaking as if the semantic value of a sentence is always at least *part* of the information it is used to convey; but, of course, this isn't the case. Whenever irony, sarcasm, metaphor, or hyperbole are present, the semantic value is *no part* of the information the speaker intends to convey. Were I to utter the sentence *Adam is as big as a mountain*, I could not intend to convey that Adam is *literally* as big as a mountain since my listeners would know that no person is that big (and no mountain is that small). The fact that sometimes the semantic value of an utterance is no part of the information that it is intended to convey is important to our discussion. For this fact, combined with the role that cancelability plays in the way intuitions about a sentence's use can help determine whether something is merely an implicature of a sentence or part of its semantic value, makes it entirely predictable that we should be confused about the semantic value of identity statements and belief ascriptions containing them, as the Millian claims we are.

To see this, suppose that there is a sentence S that has the following features:

(1) The semantic value of S constitutes information such that no speaker in any context would intend to convey it alone; that is to say, in any context in which S is uttered the speaker will intend to convey more information than the semantic value of S.
(2) There are plenty of contexts in which S can be used to convey information that a speaker might intend to convey.

Let's call any such sentence *trivial but informative*.[16] Since the semantic value of a trivial but informative sentence constitutes information that is never, by itself, conveyed, there will be no contexts in which a speaker uses S to convey just its semantic value. But, given that we are aware only of what S conveys in a given context, this means that our intuitions about contexts in which S is used will be misleading. Since there is no context in which the semantic value of S alone is conveyed, we won't be able to find a single context that cancels out all of the information it conveys so that all that remains is its semantic value; and, since there are plenty of contexts in which S can be used to convey information that a speaker might intend to convey, it will seem that its semantic value is such that speakers might want to convey it alone. So a proper understanding of conversational implicature implies the possibility of a sentence such that our intuitions about its use in various contexts would be a somewhat misleading means for determining how much of the information it normally conveys is part of its semantic value.

Now, though Millianism is committed to our intuitions about the use of certain sentences misleading us about their semantic values, the problem with the view isn't that we confuse the semantic values of these sentences with what they implicate. As we saw in the previous chapter, the relevant information a sentence containing a name is used to convey is—as Frege saw—descriptive; and, though this makes it tempting to think that the sentence's semantic value is descriptive, we know that descriptive information has the wrong modal properties to be the semantic values of sentences containing names. And, perhaps even more importantly, we know that there isn't any description that someone needs to associate with a name in order to competently use it. The Millian's problem is that, even after we recognize that the descriptive information can't be the semantic value of a sentence containing a name, our intuitions about use still incline us to think that $a=a$ doesn't have the same semantic value as $a=b$, even when a and b co-refer. However, triviality but informativeness still has a role to play in making the Millian's claims more plausible; for, if two sentences have the same semantic value and one of them is trivial but informative while the other is just trivial, it should be the case that our intuitions about their use will be somewhat misleading as a means for determining that their semantic values are the same. This should be the case because though the trivial but informative sentence can often be used to convey information, we won't be able to think of a context in which it is used to convey *only* its trivial semantic value; and, hence, there will be *plenty* of contexts in which the sentence is used informatively but *no* context in which its semantic value is—so to speak—laid bare. But, as we will next see, identity statements, negated identity statements, belief ascriptions involving identity statements or negated identity statements, and negated belief ascriptions involving identity statements or negated identity statements are all *trivial but informative*.[17]

10. True identity statements, belief ascriptions containing true identity statements, etc.

Let's begin with true identity statements that contain distinct but co-referring names. Suppose that $a=b$ is such a sentence. According to Millianism, this sentence has the same semantic value as the sentence $a=a$; that is to say, its semantic value is the utterly trivial information that a is identical to itself. Hence, the sentence would never be used to convey just its semantic value. However, given that the speaker and his listeners believe that the thing called *a* is D and the thing called *b* is D', and given that they have common knowledge of these beliefs, the former sentence, but not the latter, can be used to convey the information that the thing that is D is D'.

To bring the point home, consider the names *Brad* and *Ski*. Each of these names refers to a friend of mine, but (presumably) you are not familiar with my use of either. Suppose I now tell you that Brad is Ski. What information have I conveyed to you that could be part of the semantic value of the sentence? I've certainly conveyed that the person I call *Brad* is the person I call *Ski*, but we can explain how this information is conveyed without claiming that it is part of the semantic value of the sentence. Moreover, this metalinguistic information is only contingently true while the sentence *Brad is Ski* is necessarily true (if true at all) and, hence, we know the metalinguistic information can't be part of the sentence's semantic value. The sentence will also convey to you the related information that I call someone *Brad* and that I call someone *Ski*; but, again, this information clearly isn't a part of the sentence's semantic value. The sentence does convey some nontrivial information to you that isn't metalinguistic: namely, it conveys to you that Brad exists. But the information that Brad exists—though implied by the sentence's semantic value—obviously isn't its semantic value. And the sentence conveys nothing to you aside from the information that Brad exists and the relevant metalinguistic information.

The reason that the sentence conveys nothing to you aside from this information is that you don't associate any descriptive content with the names and, hence, putting aside the information that Brad exists and the metalinguistic information the sentence conveys, *Brad is Ski* can't have any more significance to you than the proposition that someone is self-identical. Because you don't associate any descriptive content with the names, you have no way of distinguishing the subject of the proposition from anyone else. There may even be a sense in which the information that Brad is Ski and the information that someone is self-identical *are the same* information; for neither will have any effect on your reasoning or on your actions that the other doesn't have. Moreover, since you already know that someone is self-identical, the proposition expressed by *Brad is Ski* can't constitute new information to you. Indeed, aside from the information that Brad exists and the relevant metalinguistic information, the sentence *Brad is Ski* conveys exactly the same thing to you that the sentence *Brad is Brad* does; *both convey nothing*. Since the semantic values of true identity statements containing co-referring names constitute trivial information, our intuitions about contexts in which such sentences are used will tend to mislead us about their semantic values; for the semantic values of such sentences are never by themselves conveyed and, hence, no single context cancels all of the implicated information so that only the semantic values remain.

Thus, our intuitions about the truth-value of the information the sentence *Fergie was sober today* is used to convey in various contexts easily tell us that the information that he's often drunk isn't part of the sentence's semantic value; we have a bit more trouble using such intuitions to determine whether the information that A failed to do x is part of the semantic value of the sentence *A tried to do x*; and our intuitions about the truth-value of the information conveyed by *a=b* (when the sentence is true) can be a misleading means for determining that its semantic value is the same as that of *a=a*. And the same is true for negated identity statements containing co-referring names, except that their semantic values constitute the trivially false information that something is distinct from itself.

It is important to notice that our intuitions about the use of *a=b* (when the sentence is true) can be misleading because there are no contexts in which the sentence is used to convey only its semantic value and, hence, we won't be able to determine that the sentence has the same semantic value as *a=a* by considering the information it is used to convey in *any single context*. However, our intuitions are not entirely useless as a means for determining that *a=b* has the same semantic value as *a=a*. As we saw above, by considering contexts in which the listener associates no descriptive content with either name (and, hence, in which the sentence would not be used to convey information), we can see that the two sentences have the same semantic value. And, by considering what information nonsarcastic, nonironic, etc. assertive utterances of the sentence *a=b* can be used to convey in different contexts, we can see that the information it is used to convey varies depending on the descriptions that conversational participants associate with the names and, hence, that (putting aside the metalinguistic information we know isn't part of the sentence's semantic value) there is no single piece of information that a sincere utterance of the sentence is used to convey. Hence, *a=b* doesn't differ from *a=a* in the context-invariant information it is used to convey.

As in the case of true identity statements containing distinct but co-referring names, a proper understanding of the theoretical nature of semantic values predicts that our intuitions concerning the semantic values of belief ascriptions involving such statements will also be misleading. For on the Millian view, such sentences are also trivial but informative, though their triviality doesn't consist in their being trivially true or false. To see this consider the sentence *Suzette believes that Brad is Ski*. If I were to utter this sentence to you, I would, again, convey metalinguistic information; for example, I would convey that Suzette believes of the person I call *Brad* and the person I call *Ski* that they are identical. But, again, none of this metalinguistic information is the semantic value of the belief ascription; and, once we factor out all of the information conveyed by the sentence that clearly isn't part of its semantic value, the sentence conveys no more than the sentence *Suzette believes that Brad is Brad*; that is to say, the information conveyed by the belief ascription amounts to the trivial information that Suzette believes that Brad is self-identical. Now, this information isn't exactly as trivial as the information that Brad is Brad, since knowing that Suzette believes that Brad is Brad implies the nontrivial information that she has beliefs about Brad. However, no one would use the belief ascription to communicate this information when they could use the sentence *Suzette has beliefs about Brad*. Hence, again, given that our ability to determine a sentence's semantic value depends upon how easy it is to cancel any implicatures so that only its semantic value is conveyed, our intuitions about truth-value will be a misleading means for determining that the semantic value of *Suzette believes that Brad is Ski* is the same as that of *Suzette believes that Brad is Brad*. And a similar story explains why belief ascriptions involving negated identity statements that contain co-referring names, negated belief ascriptions involving identity statements that contain co-referring names, and negated belief ascriptions involving negated identity statements that contain co-referring names are also trivial but informative.

Notice that, as in the case of true identity statements, our intuitions aren't entirely worthless as a means for determining that (when a is b) the semantic value of *S believes that a=b* is the same as that of *S believes that a=a*. Again, by considering contexts in which the listener doesn't associate any descriptions with the names (and, hence, contexts in which the sentence wouldn't be used to convey information), we can see that the two sentences have the same semantic value. And, again, considering what information the first sentence would be used to convey in different contexts reveals that (putting aside metalinguistic information that we know isn't a part of its semantic value) there is no context-invariant information that the sentence would be used to convey and, hence, that its semantic value is the same as that of the second sentence.

So, for any utterance of any of the types of sentences discussed above, its semantic value constitutes information that the speaker could not, by itself, intend to convey; hence, if the speaker is cooperating, he must mean to convey information involving the descriptive content that both he and his listeners associate with the names. Perhaps, as I've suggested, our ability to get the implicature doesn't depend on any unconscious representation of its semantic value and the cooperative maxims; or perhaps this ability is grounded in unconscious representations of them. But, in either case, the conversational participants won't have any conscious knowledge that the semantic value of the sentence is trivial. And, since there are no contexts in which a speaker would merely wish to convey the uttered sentence's semantic value, we cannot think of any single context that shows its semantic value is identical to that of the obviously trivial sentence obtained by substituting one of the names for the other. And this is why our intuitions concerning the use of such sentences are a very unreliable means for determining their semantic values.[18]

We now see how we can be as confused about the semantic value of identity statements and belief ascriptions as the Millian must claim that we are. However, the account in the last section goes no way toward explaining our confusion concerning certain nonidentity statements and belief ascriptions involving them. We explained our confusion about identity statements and belief ascriptions containing them in terms of the fact that such sentences are trivial but informative. However, even on the Millian view, the semantic values of the sentences *Superman flies* and *Clark Kent flies* and belief ascriptions involving them are anything but trivial. After all, the semantic value of each sentence represents that a certain individual flies; and belief ascriptions involving these sentences attribute to their subjects a belief that represents that a certain individual flies. Hence, triviality and informativeness can't be used to explain our confusion about nonidentity statements. So how can our confusion about such sentences be explained?

11. A kind of conventional implicature

The first thing we need to note is a point made in Chapter 3: our confusion concerning the semantic values of such sentences doesn't run nearly as deep as many philosophers seem to think. The sentences *Grice is coming, Paul Grice is coming, Professor Grice is coming, Paul is coming, He is coming* (said while pointing to a picture of Grice), *You are coming* (said while talking to Grice), and *I am coming* (said by Grice) all convey roughly the same information. I say *roughly* the same information because there are some differences: using *Paul* suggests that the speaker is relatively well acquainted with Grice, while using *Professor Grice* suggests that he isn't. Using the indexical *he* while pointing to Grice conveys to listeners that the person to whom you are pointing is coming, using *you* conveys that the person to whom you are talking is coming, and the use of *I* by Grice conveys that the speaker is coming. However, none of these differences in information conveyed is very mysterious, and none threatens Millianism at all. The differences in information conveyed between using *Professor Grice* and *Paul* are easily explained in terms of conversational participants' understanding of conventions involving use of titles and first names; and the different information conveyed by using *he, you,* or *I* is easily explained by conversational participants' understanding of the character of such indexical terms: that is to say, how context determines the referents of such terms. For example, any intuition we have that *Grice is coming* and *He is coming* (said while pointing at a picture of Grice) have different semantic values is easily explained by the fact that the latter sentence conveys the information that the person in the picture is coming. And, since whenever you point to someone and say *He is F* you will convey the information that the person you are pointing to is F, this information conveyed by using the term *he* can't be canceled; hence, Grice's method for determining that the semantic values of the two sentences are different will be somewhat misleading. A similar story holds for sentences containing other indexicals. For example, an utterance of *You are F* will always convey that the person being addressed is F.

The same is true for belief ascriptions involving such sentences; whatever differences in information conveyed there are among *Tony believes that Grice is coming, Tony believes that Paul Grice is coming, Tony believes that Professor Grice is coming, Tony believes that he is coming* (said while pointing to Grice), *Tony believes that you are coming* (said while talking to Grice), and *Tony believes that I am coming* (said by Grice) can easily be explained by common knowledge of conventions involving names and common knowledge of the characters of indexicals. And, again, the differences in information conveyed between the use of an indexical and the use of a name are not cancelable, so we should expect that our intuitions about the truth-value of the information conveyed by these utterances will be a somewhat misleading means for determining whether they have the same semantic value. Indeed, we should be more impressed that co-referring names and indexicals almost always seem substitutable *salva veritate* in belief contexts than we are by the few examples in which they do not that have captured the attention of philosophers. But how do we explain our intuitions about the cases in which it seems that co-referring names aren't substitutable *salva veritate*?

As we saw in Section 7 of the previous chapter, the Fregean intuition that a name *a* can't generally be substituted *salva veritate* for a co-referring name is far stronger than the Millian intuition that it can only in a very few cases: namely, those in which there is some descriptive content that most speakers associate with *a*. The two most common examples of pairs of co-referring names for which the Fregean intuitions dominate are *Hesperus/Phosphorus* and *Superman/Clark Kent*, and I want to suggest that these names—and other names for which the Fregean intuitions dominate—have something like a conventional implicature associated with them. To see what I'm getting at, suppose that someone has the descriptions associated with the names *Superman* and *Clark Kent* reversed: like most other people, this person falsely believes that the super-powered protector of Metropolis and the bespectacled *Daily Planet* reporter are distinct, but he also believes that *Superman* is the name of the bespectacled *Daily Planet* reporter, and that *Clark Kent* is the name of the super-powered protector of Metropolis. It seems to me that such a person doesn't really know how to use the names *Superman* and *Clark Kent*; that is to say, such a person suffers from *linguistic confusion* about the names. Likewise, someone who has the descriptions associated with *Hesperus* and *Phosphorus* reversed, or who simply doesn't know which description is associated with which name, seems to me to suffer from some linguistic confusion or ignorance about these names (at least as they are used in philosophical examples).

Now, because of these facts, the names *Hesperus/Phosphorus* and *Superman/Clark Kent* are quite different from ordinary names. There are many descriptions that are true of Paul Grice; and, as Kripke (1972/1980) has famously pointed out, I need not associate any of these descriptions with any of the names I use to refer to Grice in order to competently use them. But which descriptions one does or doesn't associate with *Hesperus/Phosphorus* and *Superman/Clark Kent* do affect one's competence in using these names. It seems to me that the right conclusion to draw is that these names have a descriptive content as part of what they *conventionally* implicate. This descriptive content doesn't affect the truth-conditions of sentences that contain them: *Hesperus is a planet* is true in just those possible worlds in which *Phosphorus is a planet* is. However, if competence with the name *Hesperus* requires that one associate a certain description with it, then a sentence of the form *Hesperus is F*, besides conveying to listeners that Hesperus is F, also conventionally implicates that the thing that satisfies the description is F; and sentences of the form *S believes that Hesperus is F*, besides conveying that S believes that Hesperus is F, may also convey that S believes that the thing that satisfies the description is F.[19] We have seen that the sentences philosophers use to illustrate Frege's puzzle are special, since most names are substitutable *salva veritate*. And the specialness of these names is that, unlike most proper names, they have some descriptive content conventionally associated with them.[20]

Another example of co-referring names that philosophers often use is *Cicero/Tully*; for example, it is often claimed that someone can believe that Cicero was a great orator without believing that Tully was. But, as pointed out in Chapter 3, unlike the *Superman/Clark Kent* example, it doesn't seem to me to provide very good evidence for the Fregean position. While I wouldn't balk at saying the person in the example has the one belief and not the other, it seems equally intuitive to say that such a person *does* believe that Tully was a great orator; he just doesn't know that Cicero was called *Tully*. So the Fregean and Millian intuitions are equally compelling in this case; and, as pointed out in the previous chapter, this is because the names don't have distinct descriptive contents that most people familiar with the names associate with them. The only names for which the Fregean intuitions dominate—and, hence, the only ones that provide an argument for a Fregean solution to the puzzle—are ones in which the relevant descriptions are so closely associated with the names that they become part of what's conventionally implicated by sentences containing the names.

If *a* and *b* co-refer but carry distinct conventional implicatures, then the fact that *a is F* and *b is F* seem to express different propositions is easily explained. Since we determine the semantic value of a sentence by trying to come up with contexts that cancel out what's implicated by it, when a sentence carries a conventional implicature, it will be difficult to see that it is merely a conventional implicature and not part of the sentence's semantic value. So, if *a is F conventionally* implicates that the G is F, there won't be any contexts in which the sentence conveys its semantic value without conveying that the G is F and, hence, we won't be able to separate the semantic value from the conventional implicature by finding contexts that cancel the latter. However, there can be other evidence that the descriptive content is not part of the semantic value of the sentence. If the sentence seems to be true when evaluated in a possible circumstance in which a isn't the G—in which the descriptive content conventionally associated with the name isn't a property of the name's referent—then this is a reason to think that the descriptive content is not part of what is said by the sentence. For example, if *Hesperus is a planet* is true when evaluated at a world in which it's a planet but *not* first seen in the evening, then the descriptive content conventionally associated with the name isn't part of the name's semantic value.[21, 22]

12. Conclusion

In Chapter 3, I argued that pure Millianism must be correct and, in this chapter I argued that the apparently unacceptable consequences of Millianism are due to thinking that the semantic value of a sentence is just its meaning. There is no such thing as a sentence's meaning; semantic values are theoretical entities that correspond to some of our intuitions about meaning and that play a role in an explanation of linguistic communication. And, once we see the precise role they do play and the precise claims that the Millian must make about the opacity of semantic values, it turns out that these claims can easily be explained.

Recall that one of the reasons for thinking that the belief that Superman flies must be distinct from the belief that Clark Kent flies is that the sentences *Lex believes that Superman flies* and *Lex believes that Clark Kent flies* convey different information. But this way of making the point is in a way much too weak: it isn't just that the two sentences convey different information; it seems obvious that the sentences *mean different things*. With regard to this reason for holding that the beliefs are distinct, my point so far has been that, once we recognize that semantic values are theoretical entities, there isn't any reason to suppose that we have any privileged epistemic access to the identity of the semantic values of the sentences. An analogous point emerges when we stop talking about philosophy of language and start talking directly about beliefs. For someone might object to the conclusions of this chapter as follows:

> You have presented various ways of generating Frege's puzzle, and in doing so you have presented various *arguments* for a distinction between the belief that a is F and the belief that b is F. Now it may be that non-descriptive modes of presentation don't really help in addressing these arguments, and it may be that, since these arguments depend upon intuitions about semantic value, the theoretical nature of semantic values makes them weak. However, these arguments are really only a part of the motivation for positing non-descriptive modes of presentation. The main reason for positing non-descriptive modes of presentation is that it's just obvious that the belief that a is F is sometimes distinct from the belief that b is F even if *a* and *b* co-refer. Since we know descriptivism about names is false, the only way to individuate the beliefs is in terms of non-descriptive modes of presentation. All this talk about information conveyed obscures the real reason for positing non-descriptive modes of presentation, the real reason being that it's just crazy to suppose that the belief that a is F can't be distinct from the belief that b is F when the names co-refer, and descriptions can't be what individuates them.

There are two points that need to made in response. First, if your goal is to capture every one of our intuitions about belief individuation, then maybe this can be done by claiming that some beliefs contain more than what they represent. However, if this fact doesn't connect to the information conveyed by simple sentences and belief ascriptions that figure in generating Frege's puzzle, any proposal for what these constituents of beliefs might be is entirely arbitrary. Since non-descriptive modes of presentation can't do any work in solving Frege's puzzle, we might as well conclude that the belief that Superman flies and the belief that Clark Kent flies are distinct because the first contains the planet Mercury while the second contains my cat. If it is to be at all plausible, a proposal for what entities distinguish the beliefs has to explain some role these entities play in generating Frege's puzzle. And we have seen in the previous chapter that non-descriptive modes of presentation can play no such role.

But, second, why should we take our intuitions that the beliefs are distinct to be so reliable? In Chapters 1 and 2, we saw that many views on perceptual representation are motivated by an attempt to understand cases of unsuccessful representation as special cases of successful representation: those who hold that the defining feature of mental representation is its intentionality claim that even when we misperceive the material world we do so in virtue of accurately perceiving an intentional object; and the sense-data theorist holds that any misperception of the world occurs in virtue of accurately perceiving sense-data. The idea that if two beliefs are in fact identical we must know that they are is a similar kind of thought; for it is the thought that we have a privileged epistemic relation to beliefs insofar as we can't think that two beliefs that are in fact identical are distinct. But there is no more reason to hold this kind of thought in the case of belief than there is in the case of perception. Indeed, given that we have no perceptual access to our beliefs and, hence, that our only insight into their nature can come from theorizing, a privileged access thesis is, if anything, less plausible in the case of beliefs than it is in the case of perception. If we can make surprising and substantive discoveries about planetary bodies, why shouldn't we be able to make surprising and substantive discoveries about belief?

There is one final, simple objection to Millianism that's important to consider. If the sentence *Lex believes that Clark Kent flies* is true, it is intuitively tempting to think that, since it's true, it must be appropriate to assert it. However, once again, the temptation of intuition leads us astray. Whether or not it is appropriate to assert a sentence depends entirely upon the information it conveys and not at all on its truth-value. Though the semantic value of the belief ascription is true, uttering it would be misleading in almost any context.

Suppose that Batman (who knows Superman's secret identity) is worried that if Lex Luthor knows his secret identity, Lex may attack Superman's parents. He might consult a semanticist, and the semanticist might tell him that, given that Lex has any beliefs about Superman, it is trivially true that Lex believes Superman to be identical to Clark Kent. But, of course, the question the semanticist answers is not the question Batman asked. Batman wanted to know whether Lex believes that his super-powered enemy is the bespectacled *Daily Planet* reporter and not whether Lex bears the belief relation to the proposition

<Superman, =, Superman>.

And the sentence *Does Lex believe that Superman is Clark Kent?* is, and continues to be, a perfectly good way to ask for the information he wants. It is crucial to recognize that, insofar as language is a vehicle for conveying information, the point of speaking isn't at all to utter true *sentences*; rather, the point is to convey true *information*. Because of this, Millianism implies no absurd prescriptions for the way we should speak.

5

Black-and-White Mary

0. Introduction

In Chapter 3, we saw that the apparent distinction between, for example, the belief that Superman flies and the belief that Clark Kent flies provides no motivation for triadism about belief and hence—since descriptive Fregeanism is false—that only pure Millianism about belief can provide a solution to Frege's puzzle. And, in the previous chapter, we learned that the consequences of Millianism are not nearly as bizarre as they might at first appear to be and indeed that, properly understood, they are both acceptable and predictable. It's now time to turn our attention back to perception, where these earlier results and clarifications will play an important role in establishing the view of perception introduced in the first chapter.

In Chapter 1, we saw how the possibility of spectrum inversion might provide an argument for the qualia freak's view that perceptions cannot be adequately distinguished by *what* they represent and, hence, must also be distinguished by *how* they represent. However, against this, we also saw that appealing to a difference in the intrinsic qualities of things that mediate Norm's and Abnorm's visual perception of the world ultimately cannot account for their relative spectrum inversion. So, if spectrum inversion is possible, the difference between Norm and Abnorm must be a difference in *what* their respective visual perceptions represent: vision must represent objects as having properties distinct from but corresponding to the colors, and it is representation of these properties that will account for the subjective difference between Norm's and Abnorm's experiences.

Finally, recall that, in Chapter 1, we also saw that the heart of the argument from spectrum inversion is a clash of internalist and externalist intuitions: mental representation of color is externally determined, but it seems that something about our visual perception of color must be internally determined. And, since it also seems

true that mental representation of shape, distance, and other properties and relations that are plausibly represented by vision is externally determined, and since it
also seems true that something about visual representation of such properties must
be internally determined, there is an equally good argument that vision must represent objects as having properties distinct from but corresponding to shape properties, distance relations, etc.

Although I think that this view of perception is correct, the argument given in
Chapter 1 is not decisive. For, as pointed out at the end of that chapter, if, on the one
hand, you're convinced that mental representation of color, shape, distance, etc. is
externally determined, then you have a reason to doubt that there is some aspect of
the way things perceptually seem that is internally determined. After all, the recent
discovery that some mental content is externally determined was surprising, and the
philosophical community is, no doubt, still digesting the lessons of externalism. So,
though it seems plausible that there is something about perception that is internally
determined, perhaps this plausibility results from a failure to understand how far
the lessons of externalism extend. If, on the other hand, you remain convinced that
there is some aspect of the way things perceptually seem that is internally determined, you'll have a reason to doubt that mental representation of color, shape, distance, etc. is externally determined. After all, if some aspects of perceptual representation are internally determined, then why shouldn't Norm and Abnorm mean
different things by their color, shape, distance, etc. terminology? Perhaps this internally determined aspect of the way things perceptually seem just is representation of color, shape, distance, etc.

Now that the discussions in Chapters 2, 3, and 4 are in place, we can see that
there are more decisive considerations for the view of perception introduced in the
first chapter. These considerations revolve around the case that Frank Jackson
(1982, 1986) uses in his famous *knowledge argument* against physicalism about the
mental. The case involves Mary, a brilliant neuroscientist and psychologist who has
spent her entire life in a room in which everything is either black, white, or some
shade of grey. We are to suppose that Mary has learned all of the physical truths
about vision—where the physical truths include the chemical, biological, and functional truths—but that she has learned these truths from a black-and-white television and equally drab books. The point is that while Mary knows all of the physical truths about vision, she has never seen any colors besides black, white, and
shades of grey. We are next asked to suppose that Mary is set free from her prison
and that the first object she sees is red: say, it's a fire engine. Jackson claims that
upon seeing the fire engine Mary will learn a new truth: namely, *what it is like to
see red*. Since Mary *learns* this truth upon leaving the room, she couldn't have
known it while in the room. So, while in the room, Mary knew all of the physical
truths but did not know what it's like to see red. Jackson concludes that what it's like
to see red is not a physical truth and, hence, that physicalism about the mental is
false.

Since Jackson presents the Mary case as an argument against physicalism, the commentary about the case has focused on what, if anything, it establishes about physicalism. However, much as the focus on functionalism obscured the real import of the case of spectrum inversion discussed in Chapter 1, this focus on physicalism has obscured the real import of the Mary case; its real import, like the real import of spectrum inversion, lies in what it tells us about perceptual representation.

1. A first pass at the argument

Consider Mary once again, and suppose that, while in the room, she is shown a red object but not told that it's red and that she has no information from which she could infer anything about its color. When Mary looks at the red object, it appears to have a certain intrinsic property: namely, the property in virtue of which, other things being equal, it would seem more similar to an orange object than it would to a blue one. This is the property picked out by the expression *the way that red things look*, which was introduced in Chapter 1. It may seem obvious that this property is redness—that the way that red things look is simply red—but, for now, let's remain neutral about this. Suppose that Mary decides to use R as a predicate to pick out the property. Let's follow Mary in this usage. Both of the following claims are now true:

(P1a)   Mary believes that the object is R.

(P2a)   Mary doesn't believe that the object is red.

But to someone philosophically unsophisticated this would seem to imply

(C1a)   R-ness and redness are distinct properties.

After all, how could Mary believe that the object has the one property and not believe that it has the other if they are in fact the same property?

If the above argument does in fact establish that R-ness isn't redness, then it establishes the view of color perception suggested in Chapter 1. On this view, there is a way that red things look to us: that is to say, a property that is perceptually associated with redness. It is the property in virtue of which, other things being equal, a red thing appears to be more similar to an orange thing than it does to a blue thing.[1] We ordinarily take this property to be redness, but we are mistaken. And likewise for the other colors.

But, of course, the argument just presented for this view involves a version of Frege's puzzle and so, if you've read the previous chapters or have a marginal acquaintance with the puzzle, you'll know that such arguments generally aren't sound. However, there are, of course, *reasons* that such arguments generally aren't sound and, as it turns out, it isn't immediately obvious that these reasons apply to the

Mary argument presented above. But, before considering what they are and whether or not they do, it should be noted that the conclusion of the argument extends further; for, like the argument in the first chapter, the argument here does not depend upon any facts peculiar to colors.

Suppose that Vladimir is a blind expert geometer. He knows all there is to know about the mathematics of shapes and he has felt the shape of many objects; but, since he's blind, he has never seen any shapes. Suppose further that Vladimir becomes able to see and that the first object he sees is square but that he is not told this. When Vladimir sees the object he will notice that it has a certain intrinsic property in virtue of which, other things being equal, it seems more similar to a (non-square but otherwise) rectangular object than it does to a circular one; this property is *the way that square things look*. Suppose that Vladimir uses the predicate *S* to pick out the property. By now it should be pretty obvious where this is heading. Vladimir believes the object to be S, but he doesn't believe it to be square, so S-ness and squareness are different properties. There is a property that is picked out by *the way that square things look*; and we commonly suppose that this property is just squareness, but we are mistaken. And it should be clear that the argument can be revised so that it applies to any property that we refer to by means of a public-language predicate and that is plausibly represented by vision or any other perceptual modality.

However, we can determine the shape of objects by different sense modalities; you can tell that objects are square by seeing them or by feeling them. And this means there's a question, first raised by William Molyneux (see Locke [1690] 1975: II.ix.8), as to whether a person blind at birth who later becomes sighted would immediately be able to visually recognize the shape of objects. And it's bound to be objected that applying the argument to shapes depends upon the answer to Molyneux's question. For, if the answer to Molyneux's question is *yes*, then it appears that, contrary to what I've said above, Vladimir *would* immediately know that the thing he sees is square. And, if this is right, then there's no argument that S-ness is distinct from squareness.

Now, one reason we might not have to worry about the answer to Molyneux's question is that it is an empirical question. So it could be argued that, even if it turned out that the recently sighted can recognize shapes, it still seems possible for Vladimir to be deficient in this regard. However, this isn't an answer that I'd be very happy with; if the answer to Molyneux's question is *yes*, we would need to know a lot more about why the answer is *yes* before being entitled to declare that it's only contingently *yes*.

However, Molyneux's question has been answered and, rather than showing that the case is impossible, the answer provides empirical evidence for the view that I'm claiming follows from the Vladimir case. There have been people who were born blind but who later had their vision surgically repaired. And *not one* of these people was immediately able to visually recognize the shape of an object; and, indeed, some of them *never* gained the ability to do so. Hence, the Vladimir case is not merely possible; similar cases have actually occurred. Moreover, those who did eventually gain the ability to visually recognize the shape of an object did so only after a long process of learning (see von Senden 1960). And, if the view of perception argued for here is correct, then there is a simple explanation for this: the recently sighted have difficultly correlating S-ness with squareness and, likewise, for other shapes.

The conclusion I want to draw is extremely counterintuitive, and our discussion of Frege's puzzle in Chapter 3 suggests reasons that the argument might not establish it. In discussing the argument, I'll focus for the most part on its application to color. But it should be clear that what follows applies to the argument when it is revised to apply to shape, distance, or any other property or relation that is expressible by a public-language predicate and that is plausibly represented by some perceptual modality.

2. A response to the argument

Recall that we're considering the case of Mary, who has spent her entire life without having seen any colors except black, white, and shades of gray but somehow has managed to acquire all the physical truths about vision. At some point, Mary is shown a red object but not told its color. Using *R* as a predicate to pick out the intrinsic surface property that the red object will appear to have to Mary—to pick out *the way that red things look*—we have the following argument:

(P1a)   Mary believes that the object is R.

(P2a)   Mary doesn't believe that the object is red.

Therefore

(C1a)   R-ness and redness are distinct properties.

As things stand, so far so bad. For, if you've gotten anything at all out of the previous chapters, you're going to think I must be joking, since the argument will seem laughably unsound. And the reason you'll be on the verge of laughter is that we've just spent a couple of chapters trying to account for why the conclusion of the following similar argument is clearly—obviously, definitely, no question about it—*false*.

(P1b)   Lex Luthor believes that Superman flies.

(P2b)   Lex Luthor does not believe that Clark Kent flies.

Therefore

(C1b)   Clark Kent is not Superman.

And there's no way around it: (C1b) is as false as false can be. But before you fall off of your chair laughing at the equally bad Mary argument, let me ask a question: what exactly is wrong with the Lex Luthor argument? Sure, it's got a false conclusion, so *something's* got to be wrong with it; and, as we learned in introductory logic, there are only two options: either it's got a false premise or it's invalid.[2] But which is it and, whichever it is, why is it that? There are answers to these questions and, before you mock this poor little Mary argument out of consideration, you'd better make sure these answers apply to it.

As we saw in Chapters 2 and 3, one answer to the question of what's wrong with the Lex Luthor argument is that the belief that Superman flies and the belief that Clark Kent flies are distinct because they contain distinct non-descriptive modes of presentation of Superman. On this proposal, Lex's having the first belief doesn't imply that he has the second; for, since the beliefs are distinct, Lex can believe one without believing the other, even though Clark Kent is Superman. So, according to this answer, the argument turns out to be invalid. However, in Chapter 3, I argued that non-descriptive modes of presentation can't help to solve Frege's puzzle. And the reasons for this are, of course, reasons for believing that the Mary argument and the Lex Luthor argument are both valid.

But, as also argued in Chapter 3, since non-descriptive modes of presentation can't be of any help in solving Frege's puzzle, pure Millianism about belief is correct. And, while Millianism implies that the Lex Luthor argument is valid, it also implies that it has a false premise: there is nothing to distinguish the belief that Superman flies from the belief that Clark Kent flies—they're the very same belief— so, since Lex has the first belief, he has the second and, hence, the second premise is false.[3] But, if this is right, then shouldn't we say that Mary's belief that the object is R is the same as her belief that it is red and, hence, that the second premise of the Mary argument is also false? More generally, there's obviously *some* problem with the Lex Luthor argument, since Clark Kent is Superman; the Millian diagnosis is that it has a false premise, and the Fregean diagnosis is that the two beliefs (that Superman flies and that Clark Kent doesn't) present the same person via distinct modes of presentation and, hence, that the argument is invalid. So, even if Millianism is false and, hence, the second premise that Mary doesn't know the object is red is true, doesn't this just mean the argument is invalid and that the belief that the object is R (which she has) and the belief that it's red (which she doesn't) present the very same property via distinct modes of presentation? Can't we start laughing now?

Well, not yet. For, though both the Mary argument and the Lex Luthor argument involve, so to speak, an exploitation of Frege's puzzle, it's not so obvious that the diagnoses for the latter can be applied to the former. Let's begin with the Millian diagnosis. Millianism implies that Lex Luthor *does* in fact believe that Clark Kent flies and, hence, that the second premise of the Lex Luthor argument is false; but this isn't all there is to the Millian diagnosis, since it's obvious that there's still *some* relevant belief that Lex lacks. According to *descriptive* Fregeanism:

(1) Lex doesn't believe that the bespectacled *Daily Planet* reporter flies

and

(2) the belief that the bespectacled *Daily Planet* reporter flies just is the belief that Clark Kent flies.

Now Saul Kripke ([1972] 1980) drove a stake through the heart of descriptive Fregeanism, and Scott Soames (1998a) cut off the head and stuffed its mouth full of garlic. So descriptive Fregeanism is out of the picture. But, as we saw in Chapter 3, descriptive Fregeanism wasn't all bad. A sensible Millianism should reject only (ii); the descriptive Fregean is obviously right that Lex doesn't believe that the bespectacled *Daily Planet* reporter flies and he's even right that the second premise of the Lex Luthor argument—*Lex doesn't believe that Clark flies*—conveys that Lex doesn't believe that the bespectacled *Daily Planet* reporter flies. The Millian and descriptive Fregean diagnoses part company only with regard to whether what the belief ascription conveys is part of its semantic value.

But suppose Lex hears someone utter the sentence *Clark Kent flies* and, upon hearing this, Lex proceeds to utter the sentence *My God, Clark Kent flies*. Lex's utterance will clearly convey some belief he has just acquired; and, though the Millian thinks that Lex already believed that Clark Kent flies (since that's just the belief that Superman flies), if Millianism had to deny that Lex's utterance fails to convey any new belief of his, then the view really would be absurd. But, as we have seen, Millianism can and should agree with dearly departed descriptive Fregeanism that when Lex utters *My God, Clark Kent flies* he conveys to listeners his new belief that the bespectacled *Daily Planet* reporter flies. Descriptive Fregeanism was perfectly right about what's conveyed by the sentence and its sin was over-reaching: claiming that the information the sentence conveys is part of its semantic value.

Turn your attention back to the Mary case. Mary is shown a red object but doesn't know its color and she calls the relevant intrinsic property that the object appears to have *R*. Upon first seeing the object, Mary has a belief that she conveys by uttering *The thing in front of me is R*; but, not knowing its color, she doesn't believe it to be red. Now suppose someone tells her it's red and she then utters *So the thing in front of me is also red*. This sentence clearly conveys a belief she has just acquired and if, as in the Millian diagnosis of the Lex Luthor argument, her belief that it's R is just the belief that it's red, then the new belief is not the belief that it seems to be: namely, the belief that the thing is also red. But, as in the Lex Luthor case, we still need some account of the new belief she gets upon being told that the thing is red: some account of what she conveys by uttering *So the thing in front of me is also red*. And the same would be true for descriptive Fregeanism were it not a corpse, except that, according to the corpse, this new belief *is what's expressed* by her utterance, *So the thing in front of me is also red* rather than merely what's conveyed by it.

The second premise of the Mary argument presented above is *Mary doesn't believe that the thing in front of her is red* and this sentence certainly conveys something that's true: there is *some belief* that Mary doesn't have prior to being told the object is red, and this sentence conveys that she doesn't have it. And the general point here is that, whether you're a Millian or a descriptive Fregean, you've got to give some account of what that belief is. Moreover, these points don't in fact depend on anything about Millianism or descriptive Fregeanism. They also apply to non-descriptive Fregeanism. Recall that in Chapter 3 I fired the following silver bullet into the heart of non-descriptive Fregeanism.

The New Information Principle
Whenever someone gets new information in virtue of accepting some sentence, he also gains a belief that differs from any of his old beliefs with respect to its *what*.

But suppose that, contrary to the arguments of Chapter 3, there's some way to dodge the bullet, some way to salvage non-descriptive Fregeanism that is consistent with The New Information Principle. Upon hearing me utter the sentence *Clark Kent flies*, Lex says *My God, Clark Kent flies*, and his utterance clearly conveys some belief that he has just acquired in virtue of accepting my utterance. Now, if non-descriptive Fregeanism is right, then the belief that Clark Kent flies and the belief that Superman flies are distinct in virtue of containing distinct non-descriptive modes of presentation; so Lex's belief that Clark Kent flies is a new belief. However, though the belief is new, *what* it represents is the same as what Lex's old belief that Superman flies represents. Both represent that the very same individual flies; it's just that they present this individual by means of different non-descriptive modes of presentation. And, as pointed out in Chapter 2, Section 15, a difference in non-descriptive modes of presentation is *not* a difference in what is represented.

But The New Information Principle *still* implies that Lex must get some belief that is new with respect to *what* it represents when he hears me say *Clark Kent flies*, since, upon hearing me say it, he'll certainly get new information. And one such belief will be (at least part of) what he conveys by uttering *My God, Clark Kent flies*. And, since on non-descriptive Fregeanism *what* the belief that Clark Kent flies represents is the same as *what* the belief that Superman flies represents, Lex's acquiring the former belief isn't the belief he acquires that is new with respect to *what* it represents. So, even though the non-descriptive Fregean claims that the Lex Luthor argument is invalid, he still needs to explain which new belief Lex gets that is new with respect to its *what* in order to account for the fact that Lex gets new information.

And the same holds for the Mary argument. The non-descriptive Fregean will claim that it's also invalid because the belief that the object is R and the belief that it's red both represent the object as having the same property, but they do so via distinct non-descriptive modes of presentation. However, as in the Lex Luthor case, Mary clearly gets some new information when she is told that the object is red and, hence, she must acquire some belief that is new with respect to *what* it represents. But, though the non-descriptive Fregean claims that the belief that the thing is R and the belief that it's red are distinct, on his view *what* each represents is the same; each represents that the very same object has the very same property, and they differ only because they present the property via distinct non-descriptive modes of presentation. So her belief that the thing is red can't account for the fact that she gets new information; to account for this, the non-descriptive Fregean still needs to explain what belief Mary acquires that is new with respect to *what* it represents. That is to say, even the non-descriptive Fregean needs to explain what new information Mary conveys when she utters *So the thing in front of me is also red*.[4]

The general point here is that, regardless of what the exact solution to Frege's puzzle is, there are some basic undisputable facts: to wit,

(1) Upon hearing the sentence *Clark Kent flies*, Lex Luthor gains some descriptive beliefs like the belief that the bespectacled *Daily Planet* reporter flies.

(2) And it is these descriptive beliefs that account for the new information that Lex gets.

Though I've argued that pure Millianism gives the best account of these facts, regardless of what you want to stick into the propositions—descriptive modes of presentation, non-descriptive modes of presentation, little bits of food to help you survive the coming winter—these *are* the facts that need to be accounted for. And, similarly, since Mary gets new information when she finds out the object is red, she must acquire some belief that's new with respect to *what* it represents. I'm going to continue to assume that I've established that Millianism is true (since I have). But, if you're unconvinced and want to go digging around in graveyards trying to revive the dead, you can simply take my talk of *Mary's new belief* as talk of Mary's belief that is new with respect to *what* it represents; and, regardless of what view you take, you need some explanation of what this new belief is. According to the Mary argument presented above, R-ness is distinct from redness and, hence, what the belief that the thing is R represents is distinct from what the belief that it's red represents; so Mary's new belief is just that the object is red.

However, now that you've seen what needs to be done to make it plausible that the Mary argument presented above is unsound, you can start laughing again; for it turns out not to be so difficult. What we need to do is come up with some plausible candidate for the new belief she conveys by uttering *So the thing in front of me is also red*, and there are in fact plenty of other plausible candidates for what this new belief is besides the one that the thing in front of her is red: that is, plenty of candidates that don't require that R-ness is distinct from redness. After all, Mary has plenty of beliefs involving the property red that she would express via sentences containing the word *red*. For example, since she's an expert on color perception, she believes that red things have such-and-such surface reflectance properties. And, when she's told that the thing in front of her is red, some of the new beliefs that she will acquire will be that the thing in front of her is the same color as objects with such-and-such surface reflectance properties. And, if Lex's utterance of *My God, Clark Kent flies* conveys his new belief that the bespectacled *Daily Planet* reporter flies, why shouldn't Mary's utterance of *So the thing in front of me is also red* convey her new beliefs that the thing in front of her is the same color as things with such-and-such surface reflectance properties?

3. A qualification: Conveying vs. registering

There is something to this objection to the version of the Mary argument presented in Section 1, but it is important to see exactly what this something is. And, to do so, the description of the case needs to be qualified a bit. Consider once again the Lex Luthor case. According to Millianism, when Lex utters the sentence *My God, Clark Kent flies* the proposition he expresses isn't something he has just learned, since the proposition expressed by his utterance is just the proposition that Superman flies, which Lex has known all along. Lex's new belief is a descriptive belief, something like the belief that the bespectacled *Daily Planet* reporter flies; and, since his utterance of *My God, Clark Kent flies* doesn't *express* this new belief, and since the notion of an utterance's *conveying* a proposition that it doesn't express ran throughout the previous chapter, I have been talking about the relationship between Lex's utterance and his new belief by saying that the utterance *conveys* his new belief. However, though the truth of Millianism implies that the sentence doesn't *express* his new belief, to say that it *conveys* it isn't, or at least needn't be, the right characterization of the relationship either.

Begin with a triviality: if someone uses an utterance to convey information, then there must be someone to whom he intends to convey the information. When you try to convey information, you try to convey it *to someone* and normally that someone is not yourself. Of course, there can be cases in which the person to whom you're giving information to is yourself. For example, you might leave a note for yourself containing some information that you know you're likely to forget; and such cases do seem to have all of the essential features of more standard cases of communication in which two people are involved. You intend what you say in the note to get certain information across to your future self, and you might even take advantage of the conversational maxims in your note so that when you read it something will be implicated to you that you haven't, strictly speaking, said. However, there are other cases in which you might utter a sentence with no other person in mind, but in which you are not conveying information to yourself; sometimes we use an utterance as a vehicle to represent some belief even though there is no communicative intention involved whatsoever. For example, suppose you see someone in the street and, though the person looks familiar to you, you cannot recall who she is. This might bother you throughout the rest of the day and, upon realizing who she is, you might say to yourself *My God, that was the former Prime Minister of England Margaret Thatcher*. You might utter the sentence out loud, or you might utter it to yourself, so to speak, *sotto voce*, producing in yourself a kind of auditory image of the sound of the sentence so that you almost seem to hear it. In either case, you have used the sentence to represent some proposition without having any communicative intention.

Examples of this kind abound and they're not restricted to times when you've figured out the answer to some problem that's been exercising you. Much of our mental lives involves such internal monologue*s*; and, though like the case of leaving a note to yourself such episodes involve no one beside yourself, if we understand them as on a par with what happens when you leave a note to yourself, then we *misunderstand* them. When you use a sentence to convey some piece of information, whether to someone else or to yourself at some later time, your intention is to tell the relevant person something you believe he may not know, or remember, or be sure of, or appreciate, etc. But when you realize that the person you saw was Margaret Thatcher and say to yourself *My God, that was Margaret Thatcher*, or when you go to the market and say to yourself *I need to buy milk*, you aren't attempting to tell yourself something you don't know, or don't remember, or aren't sure of, or don't appreciate, etc. By the time you're in a position to utter the sentence to yourself, you must already have the relevant information. In such cases, you don't use the sentence to communicate something new to yourself, and in fact the sentence serves no communicative function at all; rather, you use the sentence to, so to speak, *think* some thought to yourself: you use the sentence, as I will call this phenomenon, to *register* the relevant belief. Ordinarily, having a belief doesn't involve any kind of phenomenology; it doesn't involve being aware of any sentence that represents the belief to you. You've consistently believed for a long period of time that 2+2=4, and, unless you bother to register this belief by saying (either aloud or to yourself) *2+2=4*, there is nothing that it's like to have this belief. But, if you want to use some belief in a train of explicit, conscious reasoning, there needs to be some object of your awareness that represents the belief. And one function of registering a belief is to make it available for conscious reasoning in which it is involved.

To return again to the Lex Luthor case, suppose someone assertively utters the sentence *Clark Kent is Superman* in Lex's presence and that Lex trusts this person. Sometime after hearing this sentence, Lex utters the sentence *So Clark Kent is Superman*. At the time of Lex's utterance, there needn't be any others present and, even if there are, Lex may not be uttering the sentence with them in mind. Indeed, even if there are others present, that the sentence begins with the word *so* might indicate that, rather than using the sentence to communicate his new belief to them, he is using it to register it for himself.

Now, the proposition that is expressed by the sentence is the triviality that Superman is Superman and, hence, when Lex uses it to register his belief that the bespectacled *Daily Planet* reporter is the super-powered protector of Metropolis, what it registers is more than its semantic value. But, even though the same is true when the sentence is used to implicate this descriptive information—that is to say, even though the implicature it carries is not a part of its semantic value—it's important to recognize that the way in which a sentence can be used to *implicate* more than it says is different than the way it can be used to *register* more than it says. When the sentence **Clark Kent is Superman** is used to convey the information that the bespectacled *Daily Planet* reporter is the super-powered protector of Metropolis, supposing that this extra information is a *conversational* implicature, it is carried in something like the following manner. Both the speaker and the listener associate the relevant descriptions with the names and each understands that the other does. And, if the speaker doesn't mean to convey more than the trivial proposition that the sentence expresses, he is providing no nontrivial information and, hence, not cooperating. So the conversational participants' ability to cooperatively exchange information via language allows the speaker to use the sentence to convey the descriptive proposition even though this proposition isn't part of the sentence's semantic value. When a sentence containing a name is used to implicate some descriptive proposition, it's crucial that both the speaker and the listeners associate some description with the name and that each at some level understands that the other does. When you use a sentence to implicate something, you at some level *intend* that your listener gets the information and that he at some level understands that this is your intention. And, if there were no such mutual understanding about the descriptive content associated with the name, then there could be no such intention.

However, when someone uses a sentence containing a name to register some descriptive proposition, the sentence serves no communicative function and, hence, there's not even any room for some criterion concerning mutual understanding that the name is associated with the descriptive content. If you think of the person you call *Dave* as the dangerous maniac who has threatened your life, you can use the sentence *Dave is out of town* to register that the dangerous maniac who has threatened your life is out of town; unlike the case of conversational implicature, no one else need believe that Dave is a dangerous maniac who has threatened your life, nor need you believe that anyone else does. When a sentence is used to implicate more than its semantic value, it carries the implicature it does because of the conversational maxims, but these maxims play no role when a sentence is used to register more than its semantic value. Conversational implicature involves an intention to communicate based on a certain mutual understanding; registration doesn't involve communication at all and, hence, what anyone else does or doesn't believe is entirely irrelevant to what you can register by uttering a sentence.[5]

According to the Mary argument presented in Section 1, upon seeing the red object and not being told its color, Mary knows that the object is R and, upon being told its color, she learns that it's red; so the argument concludes that redness isn't R-ness. I've noted that there's a response to the argument along the lines of the Millian response to the parallel Lex Luthor argument: R-ness *just is* redness, so when Mary sees the object and learns that it's R, she thereby learns that it's red. But, after being told the object's color, when she says to herself *So the thing in front of me is also red*, since she associates certain descriptive content with the word *red*—for example, that objects that are rightly called *red* have such-and-such surface reflectance properties—this utterance might involve the new information that the thing in front of her is the same color as objects with such-and-such surface reflectance properties.

However, if this response is correct, the utterance doesn't involve this new information by *conveying* it, since we are, by hypothesis, not talking about a communicative situation. Rather, if the response is correct, Mary uses the utterance to *register* her belief that the thing in front of her is the same color as objects with such-and-such surface reflectance properties. And, since she does associate this descriptive content with the term *red*, it's very plausible that she is using the utterance to register this belief. Moreover, since registration is not a species of communication, it's not at all relevant whether anyone else associates this descriptive content with the term. So long as Mary believes that objects that are rightly called *red* have such-and-such surface reflectance properties, she might be using the sentence *So the thing in front of me is also red* to register her new belief that it is the same color as objects with such-and-such surface reflectance properties. Just as Lex's belief that the guy called *Superman* is the super-powered protector of Metropolis allows him to use the sentence *Superman flies* to register that the super-powered protector of Metropolis flies, the descriptive content that Mary associates with the word *red* would allow her to use the sentence *So the thing in front of me is also red* to register her new belief that it is the same color as objects with such-and-such surface reflectance properties.

The only difference between the cases is that the first concerns a name while the second concerns a predicate. In the first case, the fact that Lex thinks of the person he calls *Superman* as the super-powered protector of Metropolis allows him to use the name to register a belief containing the descriptive content *the super-powered protector of Metropolis*, and in the second, the fact that Mary thinks of the property she calls *red* as the color of objects with such-and-such surface reflectance properties allows her to use the predicate *is red* to register a belief containing the descriptive content *the color of objects that have such-and-such surface reflectance properties*. And, since Mary might be using *is red* in this way, there's no reason to think that her new belief is that the object is red and, hence, no reason to think that her prior belief that it's R isn't just the belief that it's red: that is, no reason to think that R-ness isn't just redness.

There is no way to defend the above argument against these considerations.

When someone tells Mary that the object she's seeing is red, because there's plenty of descriptive content that she associates with the term *red*, there are plenty of new beliefs about the object that she'll acquire, that she might use the sentence *So the thing in front of me is also red* to register, and that wouldn't be the belief that the object is red. So we don't need to suppose what she learns when she's told that the object is red is that it's red. And this means her initial belief that the object is R might just be the belief that it's red and, hence, contrary to the argument, that R-ness just is redness. However, though the initial Mary argument can be rebutted in this way, the case can be altered so that there's no way to account for her new belief without supposing that R-ness is distinct from redness.

4. Reformulating the argument

Take 2: suppose again that, prior to leaving the room, Mary is shown a red object without having any information from which she could infer its color. Now, there are many things that Mary might wonder while she gazes at the object. She might, for instance, wonder what color the object is. But she also might stare at the object and say, *I wonder if fire engines have that property?* where her use of *that property* picks out the property we earlier called *R*, the way that red things look. Suppose that later Mary hears someone utter the sentence *The thing you're seeing is red* and that Mary trusts this person. Since Mary knew lots of things about red while imprisoned in her room, we can suppose she also knew that fire engines are red. So, upon being told that the thing she's seeing is red, she will now have the answer to her question about fire engines, which she can register by uttering the sentence:

So fire engines have that property! (uttered while looking at the red thing)

where Mary takes *that property* to refer to what it referred to when she said to herself *I wonder if fire engines have that property*: that is, to refer to the intrinsic surface property of the red thing she's looking at. But the belief that Mary registers by uttering this sentence is clearly a belief about what fire engines are like and Mary already knows that they are red; so if R-ness just is redness what new belief could Mary be registering by saying to herself *So fire engines have that property*?

On the original version of the argument, Mary registers a new belief by uttering *So the thing in front of me is also red*. And, since Mary had plenty of ways of thinking of redness that she associated with the word *red*, there were plenty of plausible candidates for the belief she registered that didn't require that R-ness and redness be distinct properties; for she could be using the sentence to register her belief that the thing in front of her is the same color as objects with such-and-such surface reflectance properties. So, on the original version of the argument, the registered belief needn't be that the thing in front of her is red and, hence, her initial belief that the thing in front of her is R might *just be* the belief that the thing in front of her is red. But notice that it seems that the belief that Mary registers by uttering *So the thing in front of me is also red* in some way ascribes redness to the thing in front of her; and the plausible candidate for her new belief is plausible only *because* there is a way in which it ascribes redness to the thing in front of her. It does so by ascribing the property of being the color of objects with such-and-such surface reflectance properties, which is the color red, to the thing in front of her; her new belief does ascribe redness to the thing in front of her, but it does so via the descriptive mode of presentation *the color of objects with such-and-such surface reflectance properties*. Just as Lex can use the name *Superman* to register a belief about Superman that contains a descriptive mode of presentation of Superman that he associates with the name, Mary can use the predicate *is red* to register a belief that predicates redness of something by containing a descriptive mode of presentation she associates with the term *red*: for example, *the color of objects with such-and-such surface reflectance properties*.

But, on the revised version of the argument, Mary uses the sentence *So fire engines have that property* to register a belief and this belief is clearly a belief that ascribes to fire engines the intrinsic property visually presented to her when she looks at the red thing. Now, since we're supposing that Mary already knows that fire engines are red, if the property she ostends by the phrase *that property* just is redness, the new belief that she registers will have to present this property via some descriptive mode of presentation that, prior to finding out that the object is red, she did not associate with the term *red*. But, prior to finding out that the object is red, the only properties that Mary believes the intrinsic property she ostends to have (and that she doesn't associate with the term *red*) are things like *being the intrinsic surface property of the thing she's seeing*. So, if the property she's ostending just is redness, the new belief that Mary registers by uttering the sentence *So fire engines have that property* will have to be something like the belief *that fire engines have the intrinsic surface property of the thing she's seeing*.

Now I don't actually want to deny that Mary *might* be registering some such belief when she utters the sentence *So fire engines have that property*. But I do want to deny that any such belief can fully account for the content of the new belief that she registers. When Mary looks at the red object, she directly sees a way that red things appear to be: an intrinsic surface property they appear to have. And, on the basis of seeing this, she can see certain things about the property; for example, she can see that it's a surface property and that it's dissective (that, if a thing has it and you cut the thing up into parts, the parts will also have it). And, though she may acquire the belief that fire engines have *the intrinsic surface property of the object she's seeing*, there's no denying that this property is *visually* represented to her without any such descriptive mode of presentation and that she uses the sentence *So fire engines have that property* to ascribe this property to fire engines by simply ostending it, without any such descriptive mode of presentation. As I say, perhaps part of what Mary's utterance registers is her belief that fire engines have the intrinsic surface property of the object she's seeing. But it may not register this belief and, even if it *doesn't*, it still registers a belief that ascribes this property to fire engines; and it does so on the basis of her ability to visually ostend the property.

To better explain this, we can suppose that Mary is looking at the object on a black-and-white monitor and that she has already been told that it's red. Suddenly, the screen becomes colored. Since she already knows that fire engines are red, Mary will acquire a new belief that she can register by pointing to the colored screen and uttering the sentence *So fire engines have that property*. But, since on the version of the case we're now considering, Mary knew that the thing was red before the screen became colored, she also knew before the screen became colored that fire engines have the intrinsic surface property of the object on the monitor. More generally, because she knew before the screen became colored that the object was red and that fire engines are red, if the property she ostends when the screen does become colored just is redness, there will be no descriptive content F that picks out a property such that Mary doesn't already know that the object has the property that's F and, hence, that fire engines have that property. Because Mary already knew the object was red, there is nothing for her to learn about it or about fire engines when the screen becomes colored if the intrinsic surface property visually represented to her just is redness. And, hence, if the intrinsic surface property she ostends with *that property* just is redness, Mary gains no new information when the screen becomes colored. But this can't be right.

Look at a red thing and focus on the intrinsic property in virtue of which it seems similar to orange things. Now say to yourself *Red things have that property*. Is it at all plausible that Mary doesn't learn anything when the screen becomes colored and, in particular, is it at all plausible that she doesn't learn that the object she's seeing has *that property*—the one you ostended while looking at the red thing—and, hence, that fire engines have that property? If the intrinsic surface property that red things appear to have just is redness, then, given that Mary is told that the object is red before the monitor becomes colored, there's nothing at all that she can learn when it becomes colored. But of course Mary does learn something about the object when the screen becomes colored and, in particular, she learns that it has (look at some red thing) *that property*; and, since she knew that fire engines are red, she also learns that fire engines have (look at it again) *that property*. But, since this is new information for her, the relevant property cannot be redness. In short, I'm claiming that Mary definitely does acquire new information when the screen becomes colored but that there's no new information for her to acquire if the property she ostends just is redness.

More generally, I'm claiming that the only way to account for Mary's new knowledge is to suppose, as claimed in Chapter 1, that vision represents objects in the world as having properties distinct from but corresponding to colors, shapes, distances, etc. and that the same holds, *mutatis mutandis*, for other aspects of conscious experience; for the above argument can obviously be modified to show that C-sharp and loudness aren't represented in hearing, that sweetness and saltiness aren't represented in taste, or that hurtfulness is not represented in pain.[6] However, as stated in the introductory section of this chapter, Jackson uses the Mary case to draw quite different conclusions. According to Jackson's *knowledge argument*, since Mary knew all of the physical truths about perception before seeing the red object but learned what it's like to see red upon seeing it, physicalism about the mental is false. And most of the commentary on the Mary case concerns what, if anything, the Mary case tells us about physicalism.

Now, though the Mary argument presented and defended above doesn't involve physicalism, some of the physicalist criticisms of the knowledge argument, if correct, do undermine the conclusions about perception that I wish to draw from the argument and, hence, must be considered. And, importantly, though these criticisms ultimately aren't right, they do contain important insights about the Mary case; these insights help to sharpen how the Mary case establishes the conclusions about perception argued for above and, in the process, help to show that these conclusions don't really depend upon the case at all. The bizarre counterfactual case of Mary is just a way to make vivid a puzzle about perception that doesn't depend at all upon the strange circumstances that Jackson asks us to imagine.

5. First response: Mary gains only non-propositional knowledge

As we've seen, Jackson himself argues that what it's like to see red isn't a physical truth and, hence, that physicalism about the mental is false. So, obviously, if his argument is sound, what it's like to see red has to be a truth; and, since Jackson concludes that what it's like to see red isn't a physical truth, because Mary couldn't have known it while in the room, clearly his argument requires that to learn what it's like to see red is to learn a truth. But to learn a truth involves acquiring a belief in a true proposition, so for Jackson's argument to succeed, Mary's new knowledge must be *propositional knowledge.*

But there are other types of knowledge besides propositional knowledge. People can know how to ride a bicycle, how to construct an argument, and how to fill out a grant application. In each of these cases, having the relevant knowledge amounts to having an ability: the ability to ride a bike, construct an argument, and fill out a grant application, respectively. Call such knowledge *know-how.* David Lewis (1983, 1990) has responded to the knowledge argument by claiming that Mary gains no new propositional knowledge when she sees the red object; rather, her new knowledge is know-how. (Nemirow [1990] gives the same response to Jackson). According to Lewis (1983, 131), "knowing what it's like is the possession of abilities: abilities to recognize, abilities to imagine, abilities to predict one's behavior by means of imaginative experiments." And Lewis claims that this kind of know-how is the only knowledge Mary acquires when she sees the red thing.

Now, just as Jackson's argument requires that knowing what it's like to see red is propositional knowledge, the Mary argument presented and defended above requires that when Mary utters *So fire engines have that property* (while looking at the red thing) she registers a proposition that she has come to believe. After all, if it turns out that she hasn't registered a new *belief*, then I can't argue that, since she already believes that fire engines are red, the property picked out by her use of *that property* must be distinct from redness. So, if Lewis is right that the only kind of knowledge that Mary gains upon seeing the red thing is know-how, the Mary argument presented and defended above fails. Though there are several problems with Lewis's response, it also contains insights about the Mary case. Let's begin with the problems.

The first problem is that Lewis's response is open to counterexample. Consider Leon, who has a normal visual system and is raised in a normal environment until the age of 18 and, hence, has seen colored objects. Upon turning 18, Leon moves into Mary's black-and-white room and stays there until the age of 50. It is perfectly possible that throughout his stay in the room Leon maintains the abilities to recognize red, imagine red, and predict his behavior concerning red things on the basis of imaginative experiments—that he retains all of the abilities in Lewis's analysis of what Mary learns—but that, while in the room, he never bothers to exercise any of these abilities. Suppose that at age 50 Leon leaves the room and sees a red object. At this point, given that Leon hasn't bothered to imagine redness for thirty-two years, he might truthfully say *My God, I'd forgotten what it's like to see red*. So, prior to leaving the room, Leon no longer knows what it's like to see red even though he meets all of Lewis's criteria.

It's very doubtful that adding more abilities to Lewis's list will yield an account of knowing what it's like. For any added ability, we can always hypothesize that Leon has the ability but never bothers to exercise it while in the room; and, since it's hard to see how any *unexercised* ability would block him from forgetting what it's like to see red, after leaving the room he might recall what it's like to see red without there being any change in his abilities. One might be tempted to add the condition that the relevant abilities are exercised by the subject. The problem with this is that prior to the age of 18 Leon *did* exercise the abilities. So the emendation would have to be that the abilities must have been exercised not too long ago. But this response seems hopeless. Any choice of a precise amount of time is arbitrary. More importantly, why couldn't someone forget what it's like to see red if he fails to exercise the relevant abilities for even a few minutes? Such a person would be cognitively deficient, but why should this cognitive deficiency be ruled out? There is no reason to rule it out as long as we distinguish between *having the ability* to imagine or see redness and *knowing what it's like to exercise these abilities*. Knowing what it's like to exercise these abilities requires actually having exercised one of them, whereas simply having them doesn't.[7]

Contrary to Lewis, knowledge of what it's like can't be analyzed as know-how; but the crux of Lewis's response is that knowing what it's like isn't propositional knowledge, and mightn't this be true even if his particular analysis of knowing what it's like fails? And, indeed, the crux of Lewis's response to Jackson is correct. For the sentence *Mary knows what it's like to see red* doesn't relate Mary to a proposition. After all, the standard form for a propositional-knowledge ascription is *S knows that P* and there is no *that*-clause in the sentence *Mary knows what it's like to see red*. Moreover, the only part of it that might name the proposition known is *what it's like to see red*. But it makes no sense to say *Mary knows THAT what it's like to see red*. So the general idea behind Lewis's response is certainly right.

However, while Jackson's argument explicitly involves knowing what it's like to see red, the argument presented and defended above doesn't; rather, it involves the claim that Mary acquires a belief that she registers by uttering *So fire engines have that property* or simply *Fire engines have that property*, where she uses *that property* to pick out the intrinsic surface property of the red object she's looking at. And it is very implausible that her utterance fails to register a proposition. After all, when the sentence is embedded in a belief ascription—for example, *Mary believes that fire engines have that property*—the ascription does have the standard form of a sentence that relates its subject to a proposition. Moreover, as Peter Geach (1965) pointed out, the semantic value of the truth-functional connectives requires that the sentences on which they operate be truth-apt. Hence, if the result of placing a phrase in the scope of a truth-functional connective is truth-apt, then the phrase must be truth-apt. But upon leaving the room Mary might say *If fire engines have that property, then they are similar to orange things* or *If fire engines have that property, either blood isn't red or it has that property*. And these sentences are clearly truth-apt. So *Fire engines have that property* must also be truth-apt and, hence, it must express a proposition.[8]

Upon leaving the room, Mary doesn't just learn what it's like to see red. Upon leaving the room and seeing the red object, Mary might say *So fire engines have that property* (while looking at the fire engine). Mary clearly registers a new belief by uttering this sentence, so despite the fact that knowing what it's like to see red isn't propositional knowledge there is still some propositional knowledge that Mary acquires.

So far we've seen that Lewis is right that knowing what it's like to see red isn't propositional knowledge, that he's wrong that it's the acquisition of abilities, and that in any case Mary does acquire propositional knowledge upon seeing the red thing. However, though knowing what it's like to see red isn't propositional knowledge, it doesn't seem to be entirely unrelated to the propositional knowledge that Mary acquires. And, if Lewis is wrong that knowing what it's like to see red is know-how, what kind of knowledge is it and how is it related to the relevant propositional knowledge?

6. The relation between Mary's new propositional and non-propositional knowledge

The general problem with Lewis's analysis of knowing what it's like to see red is that it seems to glide over the distinction between *having the ability* to imagine or see redness and *knowing what it's like to exercise such an ability*. If you know what it's like to exercise one of the abilities that Lewis mentions, then it's true that you'll know what it's like to see red. But to know what it's like to exercise one of these abilities you must have actually exercised it, whereas you can simply possess the ability without ever exercising it and, hence, without knowing what it's like to exercise it. The general point here is this: merely having an ability is not an occurrent event, whereas exercising an ability is. The relation between having an ability and exercising it is like (and may even be a special case of) the relationship between a disposition and its manifestation. The glass's fragility is not some occurrent event involving the glass; rather, it consists in the fact that the glass will be involved in some occurrent event—namely, its breaking—under certain circumstances. And, similarly, your ability to, for example, imagine redness is not some occurrent event in which you are involved; rather, it consists in the fact that you will be involved in some occurrent event—namely, your imagining redness—in circumstances in which you attempt to do so and in which nothing blocks you from exercising your ability. If you actually do at some point exercise your ability to imagine redness, then you'll know what it's like to see red; and the general problem with Lewis's analysis is that your knowing what it's like to see red requires that some occurrent event like imagining redness or seeing a red object (in normal circumstances) occurs, whereas the mere having of an ability doesn't require this, since it's possible to have an ability that you never exercise.

But why is it that in order to know what it's like to see red you have to undergo some occurrent event like imagining or seeing something red? Well, this is because of what *knowledge of what it's like to do something* is; whenever you know what it's like to do something, your knowledge amounts to the fact that you've done something similar in the past and in some sense remember what that was like. If you know what it's like to jump out of an airplane, then the experience of jumping out of an airplane is familiar to you: you won't be surprised as to what the experience is like if you do jump out of an airplane because, in one way or another, you've had a similar kind of experience—maybe you've jumped out of an airplane, or jumped out of a helicopter, or been in some kind of wind tunnel that simulates free-fall— and you in some sense remember what that was like. And, if you know what it's like to smoke a cigarette, then the experience of smoking a cigarette is familiar to you: you won't be surprised as to what the experience is like if you do smoke a cigarette because, in one way or another, you've had a similar kind of experience—maybe you've smoked a cigarette or smoked a pipe or cigar—and you in some sense remember what that was like. And, similarly, to know what it's like to see red is to have had some kind of experience that's sufficiently similar to the experience of seeing red so that, if you remember what this experience was like, you won't be surprised when you see something red. More generally, when you know what it's like to do something, it's because you've done something in the past that's sufficiently similar to doing that thing so that doing it won't seem unfamiliar.

Now, for each of the abilities on Lewis's list what it would be like to exercise it is sufficiently similar to what it's like to see red so that, if you had exercised it and remembered what it was like to do so, you'd know what it's like to see red: if you've exercised the ability to recognize red, then you've actually seen red; if you've exercised the ability to imagine red, then you've done something that's very similar to seeing red (namely, imagining red); and, if you've exercised your ability to predict your behavior by means of imagining red, then you've thereby once again imagined red. Exercising any of the abilities that Lewis analyzes what it's like to see red in terms of requires that you either see or imagine red; and, if you've done either and remembered what it's like, then the experience of seeing red will be familiar. In short, knowing what something is like is being familiar with what it's like and, while this isn't propositional knowledge, it also isn't know-how; rather, it's the kind of knowledge that is alleged to breed contempt: namely, *familiarity*. As the counterexamples to Lewis's analysis show, Mary's ignorance of what it's like to see red isn't ignorance of how to do something. It's not that she lacks know-how; rather, her ignorance is a lack of familiarity with what seeing red is like, and she lacks this familiarity because she hasn't had an experience that's sufficiently like seeing red. But what is it to *see red* and what does it take for an experience to be sufficiently like seeing red so that in being familiar with it you'll be familiar with what it's like to see red?

7. Seeing objects vs. seeing properties

The first thing we need to note is that *red* refers to a property rather than a particular and, because of this, *seeing red*, in the relevant sense, is not the same thing as *seeing a red object*. If you are looking at an object that happens to be red, you are *seeing a red object*, but the fact that the object you're seeing is red doesn't imply anything about the way the object *perceptually seems* to you; though the thing you're seeing is red, it may appear to be blue or green or yellow to you. Nothing about the nature of the object seen implies anything about your phenomenology, about the way things perceptually seem to you. But *seeing red,* in the relevant sense, *is* supposed to imply something about the phenomenology of the perceiver. If you're seeing *a red object* and I'm seeing an otherwise identical *blue object*, nothing is implied as to whether there is any subjective difference between our experiences, as to whether things perceptually seem different to us. Even though the objects seen differ, it may be that my visual perception *misrepresents* the thing I see so that it looks the way red things look; and, if this is the case and if your perception is accurate, there will be no subjective difference between our experiences. But, if you're seeing *red* and I'm seeing *blue*, then this implies that things do perceptually seem different to us. When we talk of seeing *properties*, we're talking about something that determines aspects of the perceiver's phenomenology, but when we talk of seeing *objects*, we are not. But, if seeing red isn't the same thing as seeing a red object, then what is it?

Well, as emphasized in Chapter 2, Section 9, perception does represent objects as being certain ways, and this means that perception does involve a relation to a proposition. If your visual experience represents a as being F—if it relates you to the proposition that a is F—then you count as *seeing a* and *seeing F-ness*. More generally, for any object or property x, you count as *seeing x* if x is a constituent of the proposition to which you are visually related (or if x is one of the things determined by those constituents if, contrary to Chapters 3 and 4, Millianism is false).[9] But, as emphasized above, it matters very much whether x is an object or property. If x is an object—if it is, so to speak, the subject of your visual experience—then the fact that you're seeing x has no phenomenological implications. On the other hand, if x is a property, then the fact that you're seeing x *does* have phenomenological implications.

So, though seeing a red object isn't the same thing as seeing red, if your perception of the object is veridical and it represents that object as red, then we will describe you both as *seeing red* and as *seeing a red object*. For talk about what property someone sees when he sees an object is talk about what property his visual perception represents the object as having. And this is why the fact that you see a property, unlike the fact that you see an object, implies something about your phenomenology. If we would describe you as *seeing red* and as *seeing an object that's red*, then the object is visually represented to you as having the intrinsic surface property that we intuitively take to be redness; that property is a constituent of a proposition to which you are visually related. And this explains what *what it's like to see red* is and its relation to the propositional knowledge that Mary acquires when she sees the red thing.

As I set up the Mary case in Section 4, upon seeing the red thing Mary registers a belief by uttering the sentence *So fire engines have that property*, where *that property* picks out the intrinsic surface property that the red object has and that we intuitively take to be redness. Because we intuitively take this property to be redness, we describe you as *seeing red* when your visual perception represents some object as having that property. And our talk of *what it's like to see red* is talk of what it's like for someone to have a visual perception that represents that property; we say that you *know what it's like to see red* when having a visual perception that represents that property is familiar. One way it may be familiar is if you've had such visual perceptions in the past. But, since the property can also be represented when you have a mental image, we'd also describe you as knowing what it's like to see red if you've had a mental image with the property as a constituent. So the question of what it's like to see red is just the question of what this intrinsic surface property that red objects appear to have is, and the knowledge Mary gains when she knows what it's like to see red is just familiarity with this property.

I've been careful to say that we *describe* someone as seeing red when the proposition to which he is visually related represents some object as having the relevant property and this is, of course, because, contrary to what we intuitively take the property to be, I don't believe it to be redness. Hence, since seeing a property is being visually related to a proposition that contains that property, if the view of perception argued for here is correct, what we describe as *seeing red* is not in fact seeing red; rather, it's seeing some other property that we mistake for red. But the important point here is that, although knowing what it's like to see red isn't propositional knowledge, the question of whether someone knows what it's like to see red is just the question of whether they've had a visual perception or mental image that represents the intrinsic property that is a constituent of the proposition that Mary registers when she says *So fire engines have that property*. The question of what knowledge Mary gains when she learns what it's like to see red is just the question of what that property is. And the Mary argument presented and defended above is supposed to establish that it isn't redness.

8. Second response: Mary learns about red'

I've just claimed that the question of what knowledge Mary gains by learning what it's like to see red is just the question of what intrinsic surface property she sees upon seeing her first red object. And, assuming that the property is not presented to her by some mode of presentation, this is correct. However, the qualia freak thinks that properties represented in consciousness *are* presented via modes of presentation: when you see some property, you do so in virtue of being aware of some property of your visual experience. And, if this view were right, the question of what Mary learns when she learns what it's like to see red, rather than being a question about the nature of the property, might be question of how that property is presented to her.

Jackson takes the Mary case to establish that physicalism is false *and* that there are qualia. And, though Jackson is not very forthcoming about why he takes the Mary case to establish the latter, we can now see why he might think that it does. Jackson might claim that the property that Mary's visual experience represents the red object as having is just redness, and Mary learns what it's like to see red, not simply because she has had a visual experience that represents redness, but rather because this experience represents redness by having a red' quale. On this line of thought, the property that Mary becomes familiar with when she learns what it's like to see red is, as I have claimed, distinct from redness; but it is a quale, a property of her own visual experience. And, of course, if this is the right account of what Mary learns when she learns what it's like to see red, then the conclusion of the Mary argument presented and defended above isn't correct.

I've claimed that the property Mary refers to by *that property* when she utters *So fire engines have that property* is the intrinsic surface property of objects that red things appear to have and that, since Mary knew all along that fire engines are red, this property can't be redness. However, if Mary's new knowledge comes from the fact that she has become acquainted with the quale red', there are two distinct ways I might be mistaken. On the one hand, I might be correct that Mary is referring to the intrinsic surface property of objects that red things appear to have, but this property might just be redness; and the reason Mary's utterance registers a new belief is that the property is being presented to her in a new way, via an experience with a red' quale. On the other hand, maybe Mary *doesn't* use *that property* to refer to rednesss via the mode of presentation red'-ness; maybe she uses it to refer to red'-ness, and her perception mistakenly projects red'-ness—which is a property of her experience—onto the object she sees and, hence, she mistakenly comes to believe that fire engines are red'. On the first account, Mary's belief is new because it attributes redness to fire engines via a red' experience; on the second, it is new because it (mistakenly) attributes red'-ness itself to fire engines.

I think we've already seen enough to know that if either of these accounts of the Mary case is correct, it'll have to be the second one according to which Mary's belief mistakenly projects the red' property of her experience onto the red object she sees. When Mary registers her new belief by uttering the sentence *So fire engines have that property*, it's clear that what she has come to believe is that *fire engines* have the property with which she became visually acquainted upon seeing the red thing, and that it is *the red thing* that will appear to her to have this property. This is just Moore's point about the diaphanousness of perception discussed in Chapter 1, Section 7 again. When, while looking at a red thing, you try to focus on the intrinsic properties of your perception, the only properties that are there for you to focus on seem to be properties your perception represents objects in the world as having. Upon seeing her first red thing, Mary's visual perception certainly acquaints her with a new property, but this property will seem to her to be a property of the red thing, not a property of her visual experience.

To return to the case of spectrum inversion, it's the tomato that seems different to Norm and Abnorm and, in any sense in which it's true to say that *their experiences seem different to them*, this is just another way of saying that the *tomato* seems different to them. And, similarly, the property with which Mary becomes visually acquainted upon seeing the red thing will appear to her to be a property of that very thing, and her utterance of *So fire engines have that property* will register her belief that *fire engines* have the property with which she has become visually acquainted. So, if it turns out that this property is actually a property of her experience, her visual experience mistakenly represents the thing she sees as having one of its properties—it mistakenly represents the object as being red'—and Mary's utterance of *So fire engines have that property* registers the false belief that fire engines have the relevant property of her visual experience: namely, that they are red'. Mary's use of *that property* refers to the quale red' and she is wrong that the object in front of her and fire engines have it. This account of the Mary case is, of course, well known as the view that perception involves the *projective error* of mistakenly attributing its own properties onto the things we see. And, given that the new property with which Mary becomes visually acquainted will appear to her to be a property of the red thing she sees, and that the belief she registers by uttering *So fire engines have that property* will attribute this property to fire engines, the only way that qualia might help to explain the Mary case presented is if perception involves a projective error.[10]

The view that perception involves such a projective error can be cashed out in two different ways. On the first way, it might be that the primed-properties of experience red', green', blue', etc. are actually just the colors red, green, blue, etc. and likewise for the primed-shapes, primed-distances, etc. On this way of cashing out the projective error, the intrinsic properties of experience that experience projects onto objects in the world are just the colors, shapes, and distances that we take objects in the world to have and to bear to one another. However, this way of cashing out the projective error can't help to solve the Mary case presented above. For the point of that case is that Mary already believes the fire engine to be red; so, if the intrinsic property of experience red' just is redness, then the property with which Mary becomes visually acquainted upon seeing the red thing just is redness. And, hence, the belief that Mary registers by saying *So fire engines have that property* just is her old belief that fire engines are red. So, if an appeal to the projective error is going to explain the new information that Mary gets, red' will have to be distinct from red; this is the second way of cashing out the projective error.

Now, one thing to note is that this account of the Mary case is, in some ways, not so different than the one argued for above. On both views, Mary's new belief attributes the intrinsic surface property that she sees to fire engines; and, on both views, this property is not redness. However, the projective error account differs from the one given above in that it takes the property to a property of Mary's visual experience and, since it doesn't seem that objects in the world could have such properties, it implies that perception of objects as having these properties is illusory and that Mary's new belief about fire engines is, accordingly, false. The qualia freak assumes that experiences are internal states of subjects and, if these internal states are immaterial states (as, for example, Block [1978] suggests), then it seems impossible that the material objects we see should have these properties. On the other hand, if experiences turn out to be states of the brain (as, for example, Harman [1973, 1990], Tye [1995], and numerous other philosophers believe), then it's still unlikely that any material objects we see will have their properties. Whichever brain-state property red' turns out to be, it's hard to see how ripe tomatoes and fire engines could have it. Regardless of what experiences turn out to be on the qualia freak's view, the objects in the material world we see won't have their properties; and this is why experience projecting its own properties onto the objects in the world would be a projective *error*.

In Chapter 1, Section 6, I made the point that if the existence of qualia is to account for how things perceptually seem to us, then we will have to be aware of our experience *as having* qualia; that is to say, our experiences will have to be represented to us as having qualia. And, once this is granted, whether or not they do have the qualia turns out to be irrelevant to how things perceptually seem. To consider our spectrally inverted pair again, so long as Norm's experience of the tomato *seems* red' to him and Abnorm's *seems* green' to him, there will be a subjective difference between their experiences of the tomato. But, given that even the qualia freak will have to account for subjective differences in terms of representational differences, and given that the phenomenology of perception doesn't seem to present our own visual experiences to us, why not respect the phenomenology of perception and hold that the relevant properties are represented as properties of objects in the world?

However, the qualia freak's account of the Mary case, according to which perception involves a projective error, offers a compromise; the qualia freak respects the phenomenological facts by saying that perception ascribes the relevant properties to objects in the world but still maintains that they are in fact properties of experiences. Now one problem with this compromise, noted above, is that it implies that our experiences of objects as having the relevant properties are always illusory. Since the properties are really properties of our perceptual experiences, it seems that the objects in the world that we see won't actually ever have these properties; when your experience projects its own properties onto some object in the world, it does so erroneously.

As pointed out in various places above, there is no reason to restrict the qualia freak's conclusions to color, so aside from there being primed-colors there will also be primed-shapes, primed-distances, etc. And, if the qualia freak adopts the projective error compromise, he's going to have to say that perception mistakenly projects all of these properties onto objects in the world and, hence, is completely illusory. There would have to be pretty strong reasons to accept even the restricted claim that our experiences of things as having color are essentially illusory; and they'd have to be overwhelmingly strong if we're to accept that our experiences of things having *any property whatsoever* are essentially illusory and that nothing in the world is anything at all like the way we perceive it to be.

But, once we recognize that we are not aware of our own experiences, there is no motivation at all for maintaining that perception projects properties of those experiences onto the things of which we are aware; once we see the mistake that the qualia freak is making, total abandonment rather than compromise is what's called for. As pointed out in Chapter 1, the qualia freak's view is a descendent of the Lockean theory of ideas and the sense-data theory of Russell and Moore. According to these theories, we immediately see certain kinds of objects that mediate our visual perception of objects in the world and it is these intermediaries that bear the sensible properties like color and shape that the objects we see intuitively appear to have. Almost nobody holds these theories anymore and the qualia freak discussed in Chapter 1 makes two concessions to the obvious realities of perception. First, he admits that it is objects in the world that we *see* and, hence, that our relation to these perceptual intermediaries can't be that we *see* them; rather, it must be that we have some more general kind of *awareness* of them. And, second, he admits that the properties of these intermediaries that we're aware of aren't color or shape; only objects in the world have these properties. The qualia freak we're now considering takes the first concession a bit farther. He admits that not only do we not *see* the alleged perceptual intermediaries, we are not even *aware* of them. However, we are aware of their properties and somehow perception mistakenly attributes these properties to the objects in the world that we do see.

This extension of the first concession is, in many ways, more bizarre than the two concessions themselves. It concedes the phenomenological fact that the *objects* of which we're perceptually aware aren't perceptual intermediaries but rather are things in the world like tomatoes and tables; but it holds on to the idea that the *properties* of which we're perceptually aware are properties of perceptual intermediaries. Somehow, we are perceptually aware of the properties of our experiences without being aware of the experiences themselves, and somehow perception mistakenly attributes these properties to the *objects* in the world of which we are aware: to things in the world like tomatoes and tables. This is a bizarre view; and, once it's recognized that we are not aware of our own perceptual experiences, why maintain that we are still aware of their properties and that it is these properties that perception mistakenly attributes to objects in the world? Once we recognize that we have no awareness of our own visual experiences and that, instead, perception represents objects in the world as having certain properties, there's no reason to think that these are in reality properties of experience.

One reason you *might* think that they are properties of experience is the need for some explanation of how we, so to speak, *latch onto* these properties, of how it is that our experiences represent objects as having them. This is, of course, a real and difficult problem. However, it's not as if positing that these properties are in fact properties of our experiences provides any answer to it; for it's no more obvious how we could latch onto properties of our experiences than it is how we could latch onto properties of objects in the world. Indeed, given that we are not aware of our experiences but are aware of objects in the world, if anything it is more puzzling how we could latch onto properties of the former. In any event, if the argument for projectivism is going to be that it does provide some explanation of how we latch onto the properties which is unavailable if they aren't properties of experience, we'd need some indication of what that explanation is.

Now some qualia freaks have attempted to preserve the idea that experiences and their intrinsic properties have a role to play in accounting for the phenomenology of perception while denying that this requires that we have any awareness of their intrinsic properties. For example, Block (1990, 74) says that what is really at stake between the intentionalist and the qualia freak is whether "*there are* intrinsic mental features of experience" (original emphases), not whether we are aware of them (see also Block forthcoming). The phenomenological facts seem to be that we aren't aware of our experiences, and this would seem to suggest that there's no reason to suppose that we're aware of their properties. And Block's suggestion seems to be an attempt to make the qualia freak's view consistent with both these facts. However, it's hard to see how the suggestion is supposed to work.

It's not clear what exactly Block means by a *mental feature*; but, if he means merely something that can be a property of a mental thing, then, contrary to his intention, he has no argument with the intentionalist. For the experiences he posits are supposed to be particulars that carry the representational content of our perceptions, so they are clearly mental entities. And all of the intentionalists hold that they exist but are just states of the brain (see, for example, Harman 1973, 1990, and Tye 1995). Hence, according to the intentionalists, there are perceptual intermediaries; and, of course, if they exist, they will have lots of intrinsic properties. Moreover, Block takes his view to be inconsistent with functionalism. But it is part of the definition of functionalism that experiences are internal states of perceivers that play a certain causal role; and, as internal states of perceivers, they'll certainly have lots of intrinsic properties. So, by *mental feature*, Block can't simply mean *property that can be an intrinsic property of a mental particular*.

If Block is to have any disagreement with intentionalism or functionalism, then a *mental feature* had better be something like a property such that anything that has it is necessarily a mental particular or a property that necessarily is instantiated only in mental particulars. But the intuition that qualia are mental properties in either of these senses is an extremely complex intuition, and how could imagining spectrum inversion or the Mary case establish it?[11] Even if imagining these cases convinced you that we are aware of certain intrinsic properties of our experiences (which, of course, it shouldn't), what reason would you have to think that either of these complex modal facts is true of these properties? Indeed, there seems to be good reason to think they are not. Suppose there are qualia and consider a single quale instantiated in something that bears no mental relations to any subject and represents nothing. The thing in which the quale is instantiated has no representational properties and plays no role in any mental life, so is there any reason to think that this thing is a mental particular? Of course, it may be that a quale can be instantiated in an object only when the quale is being perceived; and, hence, it may be that the case described above isn't possible. But notice that I am trying to establish only that it isn't an optional feature of the qualia freak's view that we are aware of qualia. Hence, to appeal to *esse est percipi* in order to block the argument is just to concede the larger point.

And note that the point isn't merely a verbal one about what properties we call *mental*. As Block (1980a, 172) himself has pointed out, functionalism isn't an attempt to reduce the mental to the physical; it's an attempt to reduce the mental to the *functional*. Indeed, one alleged virtue of functionalism is that, since it allows that mental state tokens might be nonphysical, it can capture the intuition that the mental might not be physical (see Lewis [1978] 1980). So, even if Block could establish that qualia are properties of nonphysical things, he *still* wouldn't establish that they're *mental properties* in any of the relevant senses. And, if he can't establish this, he has no disagreement with intentionalism or functionalism unless he claims that we are aware of our experiences or of their properties.[12]

Moreover, if we aren't aware of our experiences or their properties, there is no role for them to play in accounting for the phenomenology of perception. As we saw in Chapter 1, Section 6, one way the qualia freak can use qualia to account for the way things perceptually seem to us is to say that we are aware of our experiences as having qualia. But, since we clearly aren't aware of our experiences, the qualia freak might instead take the projective error line introduced in this section: we're aware of *objects* in the world, we're aware of the *properties* of our experience, and perception mistakenly projects the latter onto the former. But, if we have no awareness of the properties of our experiences—if these aren't the properties that perception ascribes to objects in the world—the properties our experiences have are entirely irrelevant the phenomenology of perception; for, as pointed out in Chapter 1, Section 6, the phenomenology of perception is that objects seem to be— *are represented as being*—certain ways. So, once the qualia freak sees that we aren't aware of our experiences, if qualia are to play any role, he must embrace the projective error; the objects of which we are perceptually aware are objects in the material world, but the properties of which we are aware are properties of our experiences and, somehow, perception attributes the latter to the former.

But, as we've seen, such maneuvers are attempts to respond to problems with the earlier views concerning perceptual intermediaries, like the Lockean theory of ideas and sense-data theory, without fully recognizing the source and extent of these problems. As Gilbert Harman (1990) and Michael Tye (1994) have pointed out, and as mentioned in Chapter 1, Section 8, the temptation to think that when looking at a ripe tomato you *see* a *red* representation of the tomato arises from the natural inclination to confuse a representation with what it represents and the properties of a representation with the properties of what it represents: from what I've called *generalized use-mention confusion*. The problems that the qualia freak's emendations attempt to address aren't simply that we aren't aware of perceptual intermediaries and their properties. That the Lockean theory of ideas and sense-data theory make the mistake of thinking we see such things arises from a natural predilection to confuse representations with what they represent. And, once this is recognized, the proper response is not to tinker with the earlier views so that some kind of awareness of something about perceptual intermediaries can still play some role in the phenomenology of perception; the proper response is to abandon the idea that there is anything about them that has any role to play. Indeed, once we recognize the full extent of the errors that lead to the Lockean theory of ideas and sense-data theory, the proper response is to abandon the idea that there *even are* perceptual intermediaries.

One mistake the qualia freak makes is not seeing that the problems with the ancestors to his view all arise from generalized use-mention confusion. The qualia freak takes our perceptual experiences of objects in the world to be particulars that represent these objects and confusedly thinks that awareness of these representations or their properties must play some role in accounting for the phenomenology of perception. However, before you can make this mistake, you need to make another mistake: namely, the particularizing fallacy discussed in Chapter 2. The notion of *experience* according to which an experience is a perceptual intermediary is a philosophical invention; on our ordinary notion of experience, an experience is merely an interaction between a subject and the world. The experience of being a bank teller isn't some internal mental state shared by all and only bank tellers; rather, to have had a bank teller's experience is to have done the things that bank tellers do. And visual experiences are likewise experiences of seeing. An experience is the instantiation of a relation between a subject and things in the world, not a particular. Not only are we not aware of mental intermediaries, there is no reason to believe that there even are such things so long as we're careful not to make the natural mistake of taking the *instantiation* of a relation between things to be *some particular* in virtue of which they are related. So long as we're careful (in the terminology of Chapter 2, Section 5) not to confuse *instantial states* with *internal states*, there's simply no motivation for thinking that experiences are internal states of subjects with intrinsic properties.

When Mary looks at her first red object, it is the object and not something that mediates her perception of the object that appears to have a certain intrinsic surface property. There's no reason to think that there even is any such perceptual intermediary and, even if there were such a thing, there would still be no reason to think that the intrinsic surface property the red object appears to have is in fact some property of a perceptual intermediary. Once we see how and why the qualia freak's view is mistaken, we cannot explain what this property is—nor can we explain Mary's new knowledge—in terms of qualia. Mary comes to believe that fire engines have *that property* and not that her experience has it; and, once we've completely put generalized use-mention confusion aside, there's no motivation for thinking it's actually a property of her visual experience.

I've argued that this property cannot be redness because Mary learns that fire engines have it but already knew that they're red. And nothing about qualia can help to explain Mary's new knowledge. However, once we abandon the idea that qualia are relevant, there does appear to be another possible problem with the Mary argument presented and defended above. Perhaps, contrary to the argument, the intrinsic surface property of the red object is simply redness and what Mary *learns* is that fire engines are red. The reason this is supposed to be ruled out is that we're assuming that Mary believed that fire engines are red before seeing her first red object. But is it so plausible that prior to seeing a red object Mary can have beliefs about redness? Maybe the property is redness and, in order to have beliefs about redness, you must first be visually acquainted with redness. This response to the Mary argument presented and defended above certainly needs to be considered and it is in fact how Gilbert Harman (1990, 43–46) responds to Jackson's original argument against physicalism.

9. Third response: Mary lacks the concept red

The first thing that we need to note is that the case that Harman considers is not Mary's. Harman asks us to consider someone blind from birth—call him *Homer*—who like Mary is a brilliant and nearly omniscient neuroscientist and psychologist. In Harman's version of the knowledge argument, Mary is replaced by Homer. Homer, like Mary, knows all of the physical truths about perception; but, since he's blind, he doesn't know what it's like to see red. So, the argument concludes, what it's like to see red isn't a physical truth. Harman responds that Homer can't have the concept red and, hence, *can't* really know all of the physical facts. However, Harman explicitly takes himself to be responding to Jackson, so he must think that Mary also lacks the concept red and, hence, can't know all of the physical facts. But what does it exactly mean to say that someone *possesses* or *lacks a concept*? Though the answer to this question is so obvious to philosophers that it rarely gets an explicit answer, it's worth being explicit about what a philosopher means when he talks about concept possession.

One reason that it's worth being explicit is that this philosophical talk of concepts and what it is to possess or lack them has little or nothing to do with ordinary, non-philosophical talk in which such expressions occur. If Bruce believes that marriage doesn't require monogamy, an ordinary speaker might say that *he doesn't have the concept of marriage*; and here the speaker would simply mean that Bruce lacks certain beliefs about marriage that the speaker takes to concern central and perhaps even essential aspects of what marriage is. And, if Amity thinks that the role of government is to defend private property while Sam thinks its role is to redistribute wealth, we might say that they have different *concepts* of government; and here we'd mean that they have different beliefs about what's central and perhaps essential to government. Our ordinary talk of the concept of X generally refers to properties of X that we take to be central and perhaps essential to what X is; and to possess the concept of X, lack the concept of X, or have a different concept of X than someone else is to believe that X has the relevant properties, fail to believe that X has the relevant properties, or have different beliefs about what the relevant properties are than someone else does. Our ordinary talk of concepts is very much like our ordinary talk of *ways of thinking about things*. A way of thinking about something, in our ordinary talk, is a collection of properties that the thing has; for example, one way of thinking about Superman is as the super-powered protector of Metropolis, another is as the last son of Krypton, and another is as Lex Luthor's archenemy. In our ordinary talk, *your way of thinking about X*, like *your concept of X*, is a collection of properties you believe X to have, except that *the concept X is* generally some way of thinking about X that we think captures some very important or essential features of it.

Now properties can, of course, be constituents of propositions. However, on the philosophical use of *concept*, concepts needn't be properties and *being a concept* is more tightly bound up with being a constituent of a proposition; indeed, what it is to be a concept is just to be a constituent of a proposition. (For example, Peacocke [1992] and Rey [1994] use *concept* in this way.) On this philosophical usage, *the concept X* is the constituent of a proposition expressed by a sentence containing the word *X*: namely, the constituent that's associated with the word *X*. For example, the proposition that Alec Guinness was the twentieth century's greatest actor attributes a certain complex property to Alec Guinness; and, as discussed in Chapter 2, Section 7, as such it contains constituents that determine Alec Guinness and the complex property of being the twentieth century's greatest actor. On the philosophical usage, these constituents are *concepts*: for example, the constituent that determines Alec Guinness is the *concept of Alec Guinness*. That is to say, concepts are what we've been calling *semantic values*. And to *possess* a certain concept is to be capable of having thoughts with that concept as a constituent, whereas to lack the concept is to be incapable of having such thoughts. For example, on the Millianism argued for and defended in Chapters 3 and 4, philosophical talk of the non-complex concept X is simply talk of X itself, and philosophical talk of possessing the concept X is simply talk of being capable of having *de re* thoughts about X.[13]

But, whatever the constituents of propositions turn out to be, there will be some constituent in, for example, the proposition that ripe tomatoes are red that picks out redness. And Harman's claim that Homer lacks the concept red is simply the claim that Homer is incapable of having beliefs with that concept as a constituent—he can't, for example, believe that fire engines are red, that red is his wife's favorite color, that red objects have such-and-such surface reflectance properties, or anything that is, in the relevant sense, *about* redness.[14] Because he thinks Homer can't have any such beliefs, and because some such beliefs will be included in the physical truths about color perception, Harman thinks Homer can't know all of the physical truths about color perception and, hence, that the argument against physicalism has a false premise.

Harman's reason for thinking that Homer can't have beliefs that are, in the relevant sense, about redness begins with the claim that *functionalism* is true. Recall that functionalism can be seen as the combination of two ideas. The first idea is that mental state types are defined by their function, by what they do. The second idea is that what a particular mental state type does is defined by its *causal role*, by the kinds of things it causes and is caused by, where these include other mental states. For example, a functionalist might say that what it is for a particular mental state to be pain is for it to be caused by certain kinds of things like bodily damage and to cause certain kind of things like panic and movement away from the source of the pain. According to Harman, functionalism has the consequence that *concept possession* is dependent on functional role; that is to say, what thoughts you are and aren't capable of having depends upon the causal facts about your internal brain states which relate you to these thoughts. And one result of this dependence is, according to Harman, that in order to have thoughts that contain the concept red you must be disposed to form thoughts containing that concept as a natural and immediate consequence of being in front of red things. Since Homer is blind, he isn't so disposed and, hence, according to Harman, he can't have thoughts that contain the concept red. And, since Harman is explicitly responding to Jackson's Mary case, he must think that the same is true of Mary before she has seen her first red object.

The Mary argument presented and defended above is not at all concerned with physicalism; so, insofar as Harman's response is meant to defend physicalism, it's entirely irrelevant to our concerns. However, if Harman is right that Mary can't have thoughts that ascribe redness to anything, then the Mary argument presented and defended above has a problem. For the argument depends upon the idea that, prior to seeing the red thing, Mary already believed that fire engines are red and, hence, that the property that Mary refers to when she registers a new belief by saying *So fire engines have that property* can't be redness. But, if prior to seeing her first red object Mary can't have beliefs that ascribe redness to anything, then prior to seeing the red thing she couldn't have believed that fire engines are red. Of course, prior to seeing the red thing, she can assertively utter the sentence *Fire engines are red* to register *some* belief; but, if she doesn't have the ability to have thoughts with the concept red as a constituent, then the belief she registers can't be that fire engines are red. And, if Mary doesn't have this belief prior to seeing her first red thing, then the new belief she registers by uttering the sentence *So fire engines have that property* might simply be the belief that fire engines are red; that is, contrary to what I've claimed, the intrinsic surface property she refers to by the words *that property* might simply be redness. But has Harman shown that Mary can't have thoughts that contain the concept red?

One possible problem with Harman's response is that it depends upon functionalist assumptions that might be questioned. Indeed, as mentioned in Chapter 2, Section 5, functionalism presupposes that the reality of the mental requires that there be *internal*, as opposed to mere *instantial*, mental states and, hence, since there's no reason to think that mental states are internal states, the mind-body problem it's intended to address and the view itself are both nonstarters. However, we don't need to worry about functionalism to see that Harman hasn't established that *Mary* can't have thoughts that contain the concept red. Even assuming that blind people lack dispositions necessary for having such thoughts, Mary, unlike Homer, *isn't* blind; it's just that she has been cruelly imprisoned in a nonchromatic environment. We're considering the possibility that the Mary argument presented and defended above is unsound because Mary couldn't believe that fire engines are red prior to seeing a red object and, hence, that the intrinsic surface property represented in her first visual experience of a red thing is, contrary to the argument presented above, simply redness. But, if the argument presented above is unsound and colors *are* represented in vision, then Mary *is* disposed to form thoughts involving the concept red as an immediate consequence of being in front of red things in normal circumstances; her only problem is that she hasn't been in front of any red things.

It shouldn't be surprising that Harman's response fails; for, at heart, his response to Jackson isn't any different from Lewis's response discussed in Section 5. Lewis gives an analysis of knowing what it's like to see red in terms of abilities and thus claims that Mary gains no propositional knowledge, whereas Harman gives an analysis of what it is to possess the concept red in terms of dispositions and claims that Mary lacks this concept and, hence, doesn't know all of the physical facts. However, despite the fact that they deny different premises of Jackson's knowledge argument, the idea behind Lewis's response is that Mary lacks an ability, whereas the idea behind Harman's is that she lacks a disposition. And, as discussed in Section 5, neither abilities nor dispositions are occurrent events and Mary's ignorance ultimately *does* reside in the fact that she hasn't been involved in a certain occurrent event: namely, seeing a red thing. Lewis's response is in some ways better than Harman's, since Mary, unlike Homer, doesn't even lack the dispositions that Harman adverts to, whereas she at least does lack the abilities that Lewis adverts to; and Harman's response is in some ways better than Lewis's, since Harman at least does recognize that Mary acquires a new belief. But in essence, they make the same kind of claim as to what it is that Mary ultimately lacks and, hence, in essence, make the very same mistake.

However, though Harman has provided no reason to think that prior to seeing her first red object Mary couldn't have thoughts containing the concept red, this, of course, does not mean that she could. And it doesn't seem so implausible that someone who has never seen any colored objects couldn't have any beliefs that attribute redness to anything. So it doesn't seem implausible that the belief that Mary registers by saying *So fire engines have that property* is simply the belief that fire engines are red: that, contrary to what I've argued, the intrinsic surface property that the red object Mary sees appears to have just is redness. However, why does it seem plausible that, prior to seeing her first red thing, Mary couldn't have any beliefs about redness? Consider the following argument that she can.

Suppose that someone telephones Mary while she's in the room and utters the sentence *All fire engines are red* and that Mary trusts this person and forms the belief that she would register by the sentence. Suppose further that, when Mary leaves the room, the first colored object that Mary sees is a fire engine and she recognizes it as such. At this point Mary can and will come to believe that the thing she is seeing is red. How does she come to believe this? The obvious explanation is that when she heard *All fire engines are red* while in the room, she came to believe that all fire engines are red and, recognizing that the thing she sees is a fire engine, she concludes that it must be red. But, on this explanation, Mary must believe that all fire engines are red *before* seeing her first red thing. What explanation is available if Mary can't have beliefs about redness before this?

The only available explanation would be something like the following. When Mary hears the sentence *All fire engines are red* she comes to believe that the sentence is true, and she knows that *red* refers to some property. From this she concludes that all fire engines have some property called *red*. Upon seeing the fire engine she acquires the ability to have beliefs about redness and, hence, comes to know that *red* refers to redness. Since she knows that the thing she sees is a fire engine, she knows that it has the property called *red*; and, since she knows that *red* refers to redness, she concludes that the thing she sees is red.

Though I've put this explanation of how Mary might come to believe that the thing she sees is red in terms of a rather complicated inference, it needn't be put this way. Mary probably won't consciously go through any such inference involving these beliefs and, of course, given the discussion in Chapter 4, Sections 3–6, I think it's dubious to suppose that she does so unconsciously. Mary's having the beliefs that figure into the inference described above may cause her to believe that the thing she sees is red without her going through any inference to this conclusion which involves these beliefs. So the inferential processes posited are inessential to the response and, hence, don't present a serious problem for it. However, there are two other problems for it that are serious.

First, prior to leaving the room Mary will have some belief that she can register by uttering the sentence *All fire engines are red*. Indeed, since she's an expert on vision she'll have lots of beliefs that she would register by uttering sentences containing the word *red*. But it won't seem to her that any of these beliefs are merely about *the word red*. If I tell you that *grogon* refers to a property, and that all fire engines are grogon, the most that you can come to believe is that all fire engines have a property called *grogon*. But it won't seem to Mary that she is being exposed to a word whose meaning she doesn't know. Moreover, after leaving the room, it won't seem to Mary that the word *red* has acquired a *new* meaning.[15] Thus the line of response under discussion attributes two sorts of errors to Mary. While in the room, she misconstrues the logical structure and content of some of her thoughts, and after leaving the room, she falsely believes that some of her current thoughts have the same logical structure and content as some of the thoughts she had while in the room. Now, if you've gotten this far, you'll know that I'm the last person in the world to make any broad indubitability claims concerning our knowledge of the content of our own thoughts, but any view that attributes this much error to Mary had better have some motivation. And the second problem with this response is that its only motivation involves a mistake.

The only reason that Mary might not be capable of having beliefs containing the concept red while in the room is that she hasn't been visually or imaginatively acquainted with the property redness. But we know that perceptual or imaginative acquaintance isn't generally a requirement for having the concepts associated with names and predicates, so why should it be a requirement for having color concepts? Admittedly, it's natural to think that color properties differ from most other properties insofar as visual or imaginative acquaintance with a particular color *is* required to have beliefs about that color (for example, Jackson and Pargetter [1987] claim that this is so); and this is why it seems plausible that Mary can't have thoughts containing the concept red prior to seeing some red thing. But, despite its naturalness, this thought depends upon a false picture of the way we think about colors.

As Wittgenstein (1953, §604, among other places) famously pointed out (or at least gestured toward), contrary to what we are prereflectively inclined to think, you don't conjure up a red image whenever you think about redness. Even when you occurrently form the belief that (for example) fire engines are red, your occurrent thought almost certainly won't be accompanied by a mental image of a red surface. But this means that there needn't, and very likely won't, be any difference between Mary when she believes a proposition as a result of hearing you utter *All fire engines are red* and you when you occurrently believe the proposition that all fire engines are red. So why should the mere fact that you are *capable* of forming an image of a red surface imply that your belief is about redness if Mary's belief can't be?

Indeed, things are a good deal worse than this; for many normal perceivers don't have the ability to form colored images. My own ability to conjure up images is so deficient that I feel lucky if I can get a black-and-white one going. I am not alone in this deficiency, and those like me aren't in worse shape than Mary with regard to our ability to imagine a red-colored surface. Indeed, it isn't at all incoherent that Mary *would* be able to form an image of a red surface if she tried. Perhaps Mary is constructed in such a way that if she thinks to herself *I want to imagine a red thing* she will. This would, of course, make Mary very unusual, but nothing about the case or our knowledge of the way images are formed makes it impossible. So the only difference that there must be between Mary and you is that you have seen red things and she hasn't; and why should this fact imply that you can have beliefs about red when Mary cannot?

To bring the point home, suppose that tomorrow you become blind and also completely lose your ability to form mental images. If this were to happen, you would have more difficulty in forming images than Mary does. But it isn't at all plausible that under such unfortunate circumstances you would be unable to remember that you liked the color red or to regret that you can no longer see it. Hence, it isn't at all plausible that you would have lost the ability to have thoughts about redness and, hence, it also isn't at all plausible that Mary lacks this ability. Once it is recognized that the link between having red images and having beliefs about redness is much weaker than we are prereflectively inclined to think, there is no reason to deny that the belief that Mary comes to have upon hearing *All fire engines are red* isn't simply the belief expressed by the sentence. For the link isn't just weak; it is, in fact, nonexistent.

And, indeed, our prereflective thought on the subject doesn't unambiguously favor the view that having beliefs about redness requires seeing something that's red. Remember, as Jackson describes the Mary case, we're supposed to suppose that she knows *all of the psychological facts about color perception*; and in order to know all of these facts, she'll need to have lots of beliefs about redness. Indeed, as Jackson sets up the case, Mary probably knows much more about redness and the other colors than you or I do. And, when the case is first presented, it doesn't seem at all implausible that Mary should have such beliefs. It comes to seem implausible only when we adopt the intuitive picture of thinking about color criticized by

Wittgenstein. But Wittgenstein is obviously right and the picture, though intuitive, is obviously wrong. Visual or imaginative acquaintance with the intrinsic surface properties of objects we take to be their colors is not a requirement of having thoughts about colors any more than such acquaintance is a requirement of having thoughts about Aristotle or shapes. Mary *can* have beliefs that ascribe redness to objects prior to leaving her prison and, hence, the property she comes to learn that red things have can't be redness.

10. Toward the heart of the argument: Dumbing Mary down

So far I've presented and defended an argument, which spins off of Frank Jackson's Mary case, for the view of perception introduced in Chapter 1. However, what Jackson asks us to imagine is pretty wild. We're supposed to imagine what it would be like for someone who has been imprisoned and reared in an entirely nonchromatic environment but somehow has managed to become completely omniscient about any and all physical truths relevant to visual perception. And, regardless of how persuasive a case I've made for the conclusions I think follow from the Mary case, it's doubtful that anyone's going to be convinced of any controversial conclusions that depend upon this kind of unfettered exercise of imagination. As Daniel Dennett (1991, 400) has pointed out in response to Jackson's knowledge argument, it's hard to see how we could be entitled to any confidence about what someone who is completely omniscient about any and all physical truths relevant to visual perception would or wouldn't know. You may be able to imagine that, whatever these truths are, Mary knows them, but it's really impossible to imagine what it would be like to really know them, since you don't have any idea of what most of them even are. So, for all we know, if Mary somehow managed to know all of the physical truths relevant to perception, she would know what it's like to see red.

Dennett's response to Jackson's argument is part of a general skepticism about drawing conclusions solely on the basis of trying to imagine fantastic circumstances and, as suggested in Chapter 1, Section 4, I think such skepticism is more than warranted and, indeed, admirable. When we're asked to imagine far-out counterfactual circumstances, who knows what it is we're actually imagining, what the consequences would be if what we're imagining were actual, or whether what we're imagining is really even possible? No serious person would draw any conclusions *entirely* on the basis of imagining that there's a world in which water is replaced by some unknown substance that does exactly what H_2O does or that there's some person for whom red things look green, green things red, blue things yellow, yellow things blue, etc. If philosophy constitutes an attempt to understand certain phenomena rather than a display of inventiveness and cleverness more appropriate for a game that mentally gifted children play, then such cases by themselves establish nothing. However, while the deliverances of unrestrained imagination won't by themselves establish any substantive point, they can serve to make vivid a point that really doesn't depend on being ridiculously optimistic about the epistemic power of your imaginative faculties. And I think our discussion of the Mary argument presented above, besides defending the argument from possible objections, shows that its conclusion isn't dependent on imagining Jackson's Mary. Mary serves to highlight a problem about the nature of conscious experience, and the conclusion of the Mary argument presented above is the only plausible solution to this problem.

The first point to remember here is that Jackson's initial Mary case was supposed to show that there are qualia *and* that physicalism is false. In Section 8, I argued that qualia can't really help to solve the problems that arise from the Mary case, but it's also true that nothing about the case has any obvious connection to physicalism. Many philosophers, including Jackson himself, construe physicalism as the thesis that the mental *supervenes* on the physical: that is, as the thesis that any two possible circumstances that differ with respect to any of the mental facts must also differ with respect to some of the physical facts.[16] However, as is by now well known, the fact that someone can't deduce the A facts from the B facts doesn't at all show that the A facts don't supervene on the B facts.[17] The water facts clearly supervene on the chemical facts: any two possible circumstances that differ with respect to the amount of water there is or where there's water have to differ with respect to the arrangement of atoms and molecules. But, of course, this doesn't mean that if you know the arrangement of all the atoms and molecules you'll know all the water facts; for knowing all about the arrangement of atoms and molecules doesn't even imply that you have the concept water.[18] So, besides having nothing to do with the Mary argument presented and defended in this chapter, concerns about physicalism have nothing to do with the Mary case at all.[19]

But notice that the assumption that Mary is omniscient about the physical truths relevant to perception is necessary only *because* the case is supposed to provide an argument against physicalism; since Mary knows all of these truths but doesn't know what it's like to see red, we're supposed to conclude that what it's like to see red isn't a physical truth and, hence, that physicalism is false. And the assumption of Mary's omniscience about the physical truths about perception plays no role in the Mary argument presented and defended above; that argument assumes that she can know some things about redness while in the room, but it doesn't require that she know all of the physical information relevant to visual perception of redness, let alone all of the physical truths relevant to all perception. So the Mary argument presented and defended isn't affected by Dennett's perfectly reasonable point that we're not entitled to any confidence about what it would be like for someone who knew *all* of the physical truths about perception or how much else such a person would know. It's impossible to imagine in any detail someone who knows all the things that Jackson's Mary is supposed to know, but my Mary needn't know very much at all; hence, she is easily imagined. However, though Mary herself is easily imagined, the circumstances she finds herself in are still pretty bizarre.

Detaching the Mary case from any worries about physicalism gets rid of the wildest part of Jackson's original case: namely, Mary's omniscience about the physical truths relevant to perception. However, the Mary argument presented and defended above still depends upon a pretty wild case. We've still got some poor woman trapped in an entirely nonchromatic environment from the earliest years of her life. And, though it's easier if we also don't have to think of her as somehow acquiring all the physical truths that there are about perception, it's still pretty ridiculous to rest any substantive conclusions about perceptual representation on something that sounds like an episode of *The Twilight Zone*. However, it isn't just that the conclusion of the Mary argument presented and defended above doesn't depend upon Mary's unimaginable omniscience about the physical truths of visual perception; it also doesn't depend on her cruel imprisonment.

11. Toward the heart of the argument: Setting Mary free

In the Mary argument presented and defended above, Mary's imprisonment in the black-and-white room serves only one function: since she has never seen a colored object before, it makes it clear that the belief that she registers by uttering *So fire engines have that property* constitutes new information for her and, hence, constitutes different information than her belief that all fire engines are red. Once we've established that these beliefs constitute different information, we've also established that the intrinsic surface property she picks out by her use of *that property* can't be redness. For the only explanation of the different information is that the beliefs differ with respect to *what* they represent. The belief that Mary registers by uttering the sentence *So fire engines have that property* doesn't differ from the belief that fire engines are red by involving a red' quale, since there's no reason to suppose that Mary has any awareness of her experience or its intrinsic qualities; indeed, there's no reason to suppose that there even are *experiences* in the sense of the term that the qualia freak uses, where experiences are internal states of subjects. The belief that Mary registers by uttering the sentence *So fire engines have that property* simply ascribes to fire engines the property visually presented to her and her old belief that fire engines are red simply ascribes to fire engines the property of redness. If these beliefs really do constitute different information, then they must ascribe different properties to fire engines. As argued in Chapter 3, even if there were non-descriptive modes of presentation in these beliefs, they couldn't explain how the beliefs constitute different information. Just as you don't get new information about snow by learning the German for *Snow is white*, you don't get new information about fire engines by having some property you already knew they have presented to you by a new non-descriptive mode of presentation.

As we saw in Section 9, one possible response to the Mary argument presented and defended above is to deny that Mary really did have the belief that fire engines are red prior to seeing her first red object. I have argued that this response is wrong:

there's no reason to suppose that perceptual acquaintance is required for the possession of color concepts. But the conclusion of the Mary argument presented and defended above doesn't really depend on the strong claim that someone who has seen no colored objects could still have beliefs about redness. The conclusion can be established without imprisoning Mary in the black-and-white room.

The general conclusion about colors that I want to draw from Jackson's Mary case is that they aren't represented in visual perception. But the specific conclusion of the argument I've given is that when you look at a red object (in normal circumstances), the intrinsic surface property that it appears to have is not in fact redness. Now, the first thing to notice is that the general conclusion about colors and the specific conclusion about red aren't as related as they first appear. The general conclusion about colors is bizarre and shocking and, though the specific conclusion about redness seems the same, it is, if you think about it a bit, completely mundane and obvious. For it's completely obvious that, even if contrary to the general conclusion colors *are* represented in visual perception, the color red—or, for that matter, blue, or green, or yellow, etc.—is never represented in visual perception; rather, objects are visually represented as being *some determinate shade* of red, or blue, or green, or yellow, etc. Even if the intrinsic surface property that is ascribed to some red object by the proposition to which you're visually related is its color, that object will be represented as having a far more determinate color than red: it will be represented as being a certain shade of red. If redness is represented in vision, then vision at least always represents some very determinate shade of red with some determinate level of saturation and brightness.

Now, when we first realize that redness is more indeterminate than any intrinsic surface property represented in perception, this seems to provide an alternative and better account of the Mary case than the one suggested above. I've claimed that the intrinsic surface property that the red object is represented as having in Mary's visual perception isn't red and, in fact, isn't a color at all. But, given that it's actually rather obvious that red is too indeterminate to be the intrinsic surface property that the object is visually represented to have, why say that the property represented isn't a color? It's less counterintuitive—and, indeed, completely intuitive—to say that Mary's perception represents the object as being *some specific shade* of red. And this perfectly intuitive fact is sufficient to explain why her belief that fire engines are red and the belief she registers by saying *So fire engines have that property* constitute different information. *That property* isn't redness; it's a particular shade of redness. So the two beliefs ascribe different color properties to fire engines and, hence, constitute different information.[20] In short, once could—and, indeed, independently of Mary *should*—accept that the relevant intrinsic surface property isn't redness; but this doesn't imply that it isn't a color and, hence, contrary to what I've argued, we needn't say anything shocking to account for the Mary case presented above.

But, though this way of accounting for the Mary case already presented above does initially sound promising, it can't ultimately work. Many determinate shades of color have been categorized (see MacAdam 1985). So we can suppose that the first red thing Mary sees is, say, red_{17}, and that Mary knows of the categorization of shades of red while in the room and believes that fire engines are red_{17}. The argument can be run as before. Of course, to run this version of the argument, we have to assume that Mary knows a bit more about the colors than the average person does; indeed, perhaps to make it plausible that Mary does have concepts corresponding to each of the determinate shades of red we'll have to assume that she knows a bit about the kinds of surface reflectance properties that correspond to these shades. But such knowledge nowhere near approaches the kind of omniscience about perception that Jackson supposes her to have and, indeed, could be acquired by reading a bit of color science. However, we don't need to get into whether or not it's plausible that Mary should be capable of having thoughts about specific shades of red. For the reason I've brought up the issue of determinate color shades is not to tinker with the Mary case; rather, my reason is that it allows us to dispense with the case altogether.

Chartreuse is a determinate color shade and I know some things about chartreuse; for example, I know it's a shade of yellow. And I've even seen chartreuse objects in the past and believed that they were chartreuse; in fact, I currently believe that the couch in my house on Olive Street—henceforth, simply *my couch*—was chartreuse. But I don't remember what it was like to see a chartreuse object; that is to say, I don't remember what my couch looked like when it was visually represented to me as having the intrinsic surface property that chartreuse objects have. Suppose I am now presented with two objects that are each a distinct shade of yellow and told that one of the objects is chartreuse but not told which is. I could focus on the intrinsic surface property of the first object and ask *I wonder whether my couch had that property* . . . and then, focusing on the intrinsic surface property of the second object, continue . . . *or whether it had that property?* And upon being told that the object on the left is chartreuse, I could register the answer to my question by focusing on the intrinsic surface property of the first object and uttering the sentence *So my couch had that property*. The belief I would register by uttering this sentence clearly is an answer to what I had wondered; that is to say, it clearly constitutes new information for me.

The case just presented exactly parallels the Mary case presented before it. Assuming that Mary already believed that fire engines are red, if the belief she registers by uttering *So fire engines have that property* is new information for her, then redness must be distinct from the intrinsic surface property she ostends; and, assuming that I already know that my couch was chartreuse, if the belief that I register by uttering *So my couch had that property* constitutes new information for me, then chartreuse must be distinct from the intrinsic surface property that *I* ostend. However, the case just presented, unlike the Mary case, doesn't involve any potentially problematic exercises of our imaginative faculties. The case concerns me as I really am and my couch as it really was; the only counterfactual supposition is that I'm shown two color samples one of which is chartreuse. I could get someone to present me with two such samples to make the case entirely actual, but I trust that this isn't necessary since the counterfactual supposition is completely mundane and ordinary.

I argued above that the link between thoughts about color and visual or imaginative acquaintance with color is, contrary to what we're pretheoretically inclined to think, nonexistent and, hence, that Mary can have beliefs about redness prior to leaving the room. But I also noted that the Mary case is pretty wild and, hence, in the end, who knows what its consequences would be? But it's absolutely clear that I can have beliefs about chartreuse; I've seen chartreuse objects and can even identify chartreuse as a shade of yellow. I cannot call up a mental image of something that's chartreuse, but I can't call up any images that are in color; I can barely imagine in black and white. And, again, I'm not alone in this deficiency; many people can't form images in color, but this doesn't prevent us from having beliefs about red, green, blue, and other colors. So what motivation could there be for denying that I can have beliefs about chartreuse? The only possible motivation is that, though I can identify which objects are red, green, blue, and other colors, I cannot identify which yellow objects are chartreuse. Now this is a pretty slim reed on which to rest that denial; indeed, given the lack of connection between our beliefs about color and visual or imaginative acquaintance with color, I think it's a nonexistent reed.

But suppose that we tweak the example a little bit. I'm relatively sure but not entirely certain that the first object is the chartreuse one; that is to say, I do have the ability to identify which yellow objects are chartreuse, but I'm not entirely confident in my ability. Surely this is enough to allow me to have thoughts about chartreuse. But in such circumstances I might say to myself *I'm pretty sure that my couch had that property* (focusing on the intrinsic surface property of the first object) *but I'm not entirely sure that it did; it might have had that property* (focusing on the intrinsic surface property of the second object). And, upon being reassured that it is indeed the first object that is chartreuse, I might say to myself *Okay, the couch definitely had that property* (focusing on the intrinsic surface property of the first object). But I already believed that the couch definitely was chartreuse, so the belief I register with this sentence constitutes new information; and, again, the only explanation of this new information is that the intrinsic surface property that the first object appears to have is not chartreuse.

12. At the heart of the argument

The point of imprisoning Mary in the black-and-white room, of denying me the knowledge of precisely which yellow objects are chartreuse, or of making me not quite sure which are, is in each case to establish that the belief the subject registers by using *that property* to pick out the relevant intrinsic surface property is *new information* and, hence, different information than the relevant belief about color. And, once we have established that it is new information, we have also established that the intrinsic surface property ostended is not the relevant color property. But we don't really need to deny the subject the relevant knowledge to see that beliefs about colors and beliefs that involve ostending the intrinsic surface properties of objects must constitute different information: that the intrinsic surface properties vision presents to us, which we intuitively take to be the colors, aren't in fact the colors.

If I'm incapable of identifying which yellow objects are chartreuse, then, when presented with the two yellow objects, I might focus on the intrinsic surface property of each in turn and wonder whether my couch has it. Since I've wondered this, it's clear that when I find out my couch had *that property* (I'm now looking at a chartreuse object), I've acquired new information, since finding this out has settled the question I was wondering about. However, suppose I am perfectly capable of identifying which yellow objects are chartreuse and am entirely and justifiably confident in my ability to do so. There is a belief that I can register by saying *My couch had that property,* where I use *that property* to ostend the intrinsic surface property of some chartreuse object I'm looking at. And, if I'm neither visually nor imaginatively acquainted with this intrinsic surface property, then this is a belief that I cannot have. This belief ascribes a certain property to my couch, and the heart of the argument of this chapter is that there's no way to explain the difference between this belief and the belief that the couch is chartreuse without supposing that this property *isn't* chartreuse. If we ignore the issue about determinate shades of color in order to avoid having to talk of obscure colors like chartreuse, at its heart the argument is merely a challenge to explain what distinguishes a belief that an object is red, or yellow, or blue, etc. from a perception according to which it *looks* red, or yellow, or blue, etc. My answer is that the two are distinguished by what they represent, and the argument for this is really that there isn't any other remotely plausible way to answer the challenge.

It won't do to say that seeing the tomato is perceptual and believing it's red is *cognitive.* For it is precisely the distinction between conscious experience and cognition that needs explaining. And, similarly, it won't do to suggest that perception involves *non-cognitive* concepts or *phenomenal* concepts and belief doesn't; these are merely ways of naming the distinction masquerading as explanations of it.

As pointed out in various places above, your perception of the tomato seems to present only the tomato and the qualities it perceptually seems to have; hence, an appeal to qualia can't explain the difference. You might try to claim that perception differs from belief in the modes of presentation of what it represents—that is to say, in *how* it represents—but that these modes of presentation are not qualia. But then you have to explain what they are, how they are individuated, and how they account for the way things perceptually seem. And it is very doubtful that this is possible. How can perceptual *hows* explain the way things seem when (as argued in Chapter 1) a difference in the way things seem always turns out to be a difference in what is represented? And how can you posit perceptual *hows* and stay true to the fact that perception seems to represent only objects in the world as having properties? A proper appreciation of Moore's point about the diaphanousness of perception seems to rule out that the difference between perception and belief is anything but a difference in *what* they represent.

The distinction between perception and belief also cannot be explained by appealing, as Tye (1995) and others do, to the representational richness of perception. It's true that it would take me ages to describe the scene currently before my eyes by citing my beliefs about it, but if colors are represented in perception, then this needn't be the case. Imagine that you are looking at a completely smooth and uniformly red surface that extends as far as the eye can see both vertically and horizontally. In this case, your perception isn't very representationally rich at all, but it is still completely different from any belief you might have that you would register by a sentence containing the word *red*. Moreover, attempting to explain the distinction between perception and belief in terms of perceptual richness doesn't account for certain beliefs that aren't so dissimilar from perceptions. Look at some thing and focus on the property it has that you would normally take to be its color. Now say to yourself *sotto voce* **The thing I'm looking at has that property**. Aside from the voice you seem to faintly hear, your having this belief is similar to having a perception. But the belief is no richer than any other belief. And doesn't it seem plausible that having this belief is similar to having a perception because it represents the very same property that is represented in perception? The view of perception argued for here explains this difference and similarity nicely: the difference between the perception and the belief is that the belief represents only one of the many properties represented in your perception and the belief is accompanied by faintly hearing the sentence that registers it; the similarity is that there is a common property that both represent.

Finally, it is sometimes suggested that perception differs from belief in that perceptual representation is like pictorial representation, whereas belief representation is like sentential representation. But, as pointed out in Chapter 2, Section 9, this contrast can't bear the slightest scrutiny. It's true that *seeing* a flower can be very much like *seeing* a picture of a flower; but this is a reason to think that the picture and the flower are similar rather than a reason for thinking that seeing is like a picture. *Petting* a dog can be very much like *petting* a cat, but no one would infer from this that petting is like a cat. And, as pointed out in the same section, beliefs are supposed to be like sentences because both have syntactic structure. But talk of the syntactic structure of a belief is really just a way to make the point that the belief relates its constituents in certain ways. For example, the belief that Aristotle was a philosopher ascribes the property of being a philosopher to Aristotle; and the so-called *syntactic structure* of the belief amounts to nothing more than this. But perceptual representation clearly does represent objects as having properties; hence, in whatever the sense the belief that Aristotle was a philosopher has a syntactic structure, perceptual representation also has a syntactic structure.

If you want to reject the account of perception offered here, you need to answer the challenge in a different way. And, ultimately, the argument is that you can't. If

I am right that you can't, belief and perception really constitute a single phenomenon; both perception and belief are truth-normed relations that we bear to propositions. As mentioned in Chapter 2, Section 9, perception, unlike belief, is also object-detecting-normed: one function of perception is to detect objects in your immediate environment. But the distinction between perception and belief that accounts for the consciousness that comes along with perception involves the properties it attributes to objects; *consciousness is just the representation of certain properties*. We can sometimes have beliefs that attribute perceptual properties to objects; for example, you can focus on some property visually presented to you and ascribe it to, say, fire engines by using the sentence ***Fire engines have that property*** to register the belief. But having a belief that ascribes a perceptual property to an object requires a certain kind of phenomenological episode; that is, it requires that the property be visually (or imaginatively) presented to you. And what makes up the phenomenology of consciousness is just the properties it presents to us. Given Moore's point about the diaphanousness of perception, there isn't really anything else that could make it up.

13. Why we can't name the properties represented in perception

Recall that, in Chapter 1, we saw another argument for the view that vision represents objects as having properties distinct from but corresponding to the colors. Representation of color is externally determined, but there seems to be something about the way colored objects seem that is internally determined. At least one of the reasons to think that representation of color is externally determined is that we refer to colors using public-language terms and, hence, it doesn't seem as if the content of your color terminology should depend entirely upon what you're like. Though the argument presented in this chapter makes no mention of externalism, it also depends upon our referring to colors via public-language expressions. For the heart of the argument in this chapter is that any belief you could register by a sentence that contains some color term is in some way completely different from your perception of the intrinsic surface property you would take to be its color. But this isn't true for your beliefs about these intrinsic surface properties that are expressible by certain sentences that contain demonstratives. As mentioned in the previous section, if you point to an object, focus on the intrinsic surface property you would take to be its color, and say *sotto voce* to yourself ***The thing I'm looking at has that property***, aside from the fact that you dimly seem to hear the sentence, the belief you express is not so different from your perception of the object. So the very different observations of the first chapter and this one both point to the same conclusion.

However, the way in which these quite different observations point to the same conclusion raises an apparently troubling aspect of that conclusion.[21] The conclusion is that the intrinsic surface properties represented in vision that we take to be colors are not in fact colors; color terms like *red*, *blue*, *green*, *chartreuse*, and *teal* don't pick out any properties that are represented in vision. But, granting this conclusion, we should be able to coin words that pick out these properties; for example, in the initial flawed version of the Mary argument presented above, Mary looks at a red object and dubs its intrinsic surface property *R*. But, given that this is possible, the kind of argument that the relevant intrinsic surface property isn't red (or a more precise shade of red) will also show that it isn't R. For, if *R* is a public-language predicate that refers to the property, someone could always believe that some object is R without having the belief they would register by pointing to the object and saying *It has that property*. More generally, there is some difference between the belief that it's R and the belief registered by this sentence; and, if the arguments presented above are correct, this shows that R isn't the relevant intrinsic surface property. As soon as we come up with a public-language predicate that picks out the relevant property, the kind of arguments presented above, if sound, will show that the predicate *doesn't* pick out the property. So it seems that we can't coin a predicate to refer to these properties. The arguments presented above depend upon the assumption that we can use public-language predicates to pick out the colors but we can't use them to pick out the intrinsic surface properties that we mistake for the colors. Why isn't this completely arbitrary?

The appearance of arbitrariness depends upon not fully seeing what the view of perception defended here really is. The view takes Moore's diaphanousness point seriously; perceptions are distinguished by what properties they represent objects as having and that's all there is to the phenomenology of perception. But, given this, what distinguishes perception from belief is that these properties aren't available in belief except by demonstrating them while perceiving them. What makes a perception a perception—and what makes it a conscious episode—is the properties it represents and, importantly, representation of these properties is internally determined. To have a perception that represents an object as having one of these properties essentially involves having a perception with a certain phenomenology; for example, if some object is visually represented as having the intrinsic surface property we mistake for red (or some particular shade of red) at some particular time, then this property must be visually represented to you at that time. One of the lessons of the Wittgensteinian observations cited in Section 9 is that *red*, *blue*, *chartreuse*, and other public-language predicates don't pick out the properties they do because your utterances of them visually or imaginatively acquaint you with some property. But, in order for some object to be represented as having one of the intrinsic surface properties we mistake for the colors, such acquaintance is required; *what it is for one of these properties to be represented to you is for you to be visually or imaginatively acquainted with it.*

Hence, coining a word to pick out one of these properties would require coining a word such that someone's uttering it causes him to be visually or imaginatively acquainted with the relevant property. That someone used the word to register beliefs about the property would require that his use of the word be accompanied by a certain kind of phenomenological episode. Now the first point here is that this implies that if such a predicate were coined one couldn't run the kinds of arguments above to show that it doesn't pick out the relevant intrinsic surface properties of objects. Suppose that you've managed it so that whenever you utter *R* you become visually acquainted with the intrinsic surface property that corresponds to some shade of red; for example, suppose that whenever you utter *R* there appears to be a disc that you would describe as red somewhere in front of you. Under these circumstances, you might then be able to use, for example, *Fire engines are R* to register a belief that fire engines have that property. But, in doing so, you'd be registering the very same belief you'd register by focusing on the property and saying *Fire engines have that property*. So there couldn't be an argument that R-ness isn't the relevant intrinsic surface property, since there could be no case in which you'd have the one relevant belief without having the other. Indeed, if you did manage to make your utterance of *R* cause visual acquaintance with the relevant property and, in doing so, managed to arrange it so that your utterance of *Fire engines are R* registers a belief that ascribes the property to fire engines, this wouldn't make *R* a public-language predicate; for you couldn't use *R* in a sentence to convey the relevant belief to me unless it's also true that your utterance of *R* causes *me* to be visually acquainted with the property. And, even if we managed to arrange it so that hearing or saying *R* causes everyone to be visually acquainted with the relevant property, this still wouldn't make *R* a public-language predicate that refers to the property.

Under these circumstances, your utterance of *R* serves two distinct functions, a causal function and a registrative function: (i) hearing or saying *R* causes you to be visually acquainted with the property, and (ii) you use *R* to register a belief that ascribes the property to fire engines. But the Wittgensteinian observations from Section 9 are precisely that public-language words don't serve the causal function alluded to in (i). Because, in the case we're considering, the utterance of *R* causes the visual acquaintance, it might seem that the word picks out the property in the way that public-language predicates pick out properties. But, instead of having utterances of a word cause the visual acquaintance with the property, we might install a button on everyone's temple so that when someone pushes the button he becomes visually acquainted with the relevant property. Pushing the button would serve the same causal function as saying or hearing *R*, and this makes it clear that serving this function doesn't make *R* anything like a public-language predicate that refers to the relevant property.

If anything makes *R* a public-language predicate it's the second function: namely, since it fulfills the first causal function of visually acquainting you with the relevant property, you can use it to register a belief that ascribes the property to something. But notice that the mere fact that uttering *R* serves the causal function isn't sufficient for it to have the registrative function. The fact that your utterance of *Fire engines are R* causes you to be imaginatively acquainted with the relevant intrinsic surface property isn't by itself sufficient for your utterance to register a belief that attributes this property to fire engines. If, by some quirky neurological accident, your utterance of the words *is prime* caused you to be visually acquainted with some property, this wouldn't mean that when you utter *2 is prime* the belief you register attributes this property to 2. The mere fact that the utterance of some word would cause some kind of phenomenological episode in you would be an interesting and perhaps annoying fact, but it wouldn't mean that when you used this utterance as a predicate the property presented in the phenomenological episode is attributed to the subject of your sentence by the belief you register. If your utterance of *Fire engines are R* is to register a belief that ascribes the relevant intrinsic surface property to fire engines, it isn't sufficient that uttering *R* causes you to be visually acquainted with the property; you're also going to have to focus on the property and make a conscious effort to use the predicate to ascribe the property to fire engines when you utter *Fire engines are R*. And, if you succeed, then *R* serves a linguistic function only because you're using it as a *demonstrative*: only because you utter the word to yourself while focusing on the intrinsic surface property you see in attempt to get the word to register this property. There's no difference in the belief you would register if you used *R* to serve both the causal and registrative function, if you pushed a button on your temple to cause visual acquaintance with the relevant property and then uttered *Fire engines are R* in an attempt to ascribe the property to fire engines, or if you pushed the button and uttered the sentence *Fire engines have that property* while focusing your attention on the property. If an utterance of *R* causes you to be visually acquainted with the relevant property, then you may be able to use the *R* to register that something has this property; but this is just to use *R* demonstratively to refer to the property. In the case we're considering, the causal function and registrative function of *R* are entirely distinct; and if *R* can have the latter function, this is because you can also use it to demonstrate the intrinsic surface property with which it visually acquaints you.

The reason we cannot coin a predicate to refer to one of these properties is that the phenomenology of your conscious experience *just is a matter of* having these properties represented to you. Their representation is internally determined and, hence, essentially different than the way we use public-language predicates to register beliefs that represent certain properties. The difference between consciousness and cognition is a difference in the kinds of properties that the propositions to which they relate us ascribe to objects. And representation of the these two kinds of properties is grounded in radically different facts: representation of the properties represented in consciousness is internally determined, whereas representation of the properties generally represented in cognition is externally determined. I say *generally*, because we can focus our attention on the properties represented in perception and, by the use of demonstratives, make them available to cognition.

14. Looking some color

I've argued that vision represents objects in the world as having properties distinct from but corresponding to colors, shapes, distances, etc. and that the same holds, *mutatis mutandis*, for other modes of conscious experience; for the above argument can obviously be modified to show that C-sharp and loudness aren't represented in hearing, that sweetness and saltiness aren't represented in taste, and so on. But, as I've implicitly indicated in various places, the considerations above not only establish these conclusions; they also establish that colors, shapes, distances, etc. *are not* represented in vision and, likewise, *mutatis mutandis*, for other perceptual modalities. For example, when you look at a ripe tomato there's only one relevant intrinsic surface property it appears to have. You will naturally take this property to be a color; but if, as I've argued, it isn't a color, then there isn't some other property that is represented in the proposition to which you're visually related and which could be a color. It's *that* intrinsic surface property that you're inclined to think is red (or some shade of red); and, if it turns out not to be, then colors aren't represented in the propositions to which you are visually related and, likewise, *mutatis mutandis*, for any other properties that might at first seem to be represented in some perceptual modality but can figure in an argument like the one presented above.[22]

The idea that colors, shapes, distances, etc. aren't represented in visual perception, besides being extremely counterintuitive in its own right, has certain counterintuitive consequences about our talk of an object's *looking* to be some color. And addressing the latter counterintuitive consequences first will help clear the way for addressing the former.

It is widely thought that certain uses of the word *looks* are essentially tied to the phenomenology of visual perception. Philosophers generally take the word *looks* to be ambiguous; when the word is followed by a color (or shape, or distance) term, as in *looks red* or *looks blue*, it has one meaning, but it has quite another in phrases like *looks tired* or *looks old*. For example, Frank Jackson (1977, 30) has called the first alleged sense of *looks* the *phenomenal sense* and the second sense the *epistemic sense*.[23]

If you are a qualia freak and accept that *looks* is ambiguous in the ways described above, then it is natural to think that something's looking red (or green, or blue) amounts to something like the fact that your current perceptual intermediary has the kind of intrinsic quality that those that represent redness (or greenness, or blueness) normally have: that is to say, something looks red to you when your experience has a red' quale. However, once you recognize that the qualia freak's view isn't correct, there is another natural proposal for what the phenomenal sense of *looks* is: to say that something looks red (or green, or blue) to you is to say that it is represented as being red (or green, or blue) to you. But, on the view of perception presented here, vision doesn't represent objects as having colors and, hence, if there is such a phenomenal sense of *looks*, the view argued for in this chapter implies that nothing ever looks any color to anyone, which, needless to say, is not a consequence I'd be happy with.

However, in our ordinary use of *looks c*, where *c* is some color term, *c* is almost never some specific determinate shade of a color; we often say that something looks red, or blue, or yellow, and it's rare that we say that it looks *fuchsia*, or *teal*, or *chartreuse*. And, hence, even if the intrinsic surface properties of objects that vision represents are determinate shades of color, if to say that something *looks c* is to say that it's visually represented as c, then most of our ordinary *looks* talk is false anyway. Regardless of what exactly the determinate intrinsic surface properties represented in vision turn out to be, our talk of things *looking to be certain colors* isn't as tied to the phenomenology of perception as those who advocate a phenomenal sense of *looks* take it to be.

I've been claiming that if the intrinsic surface properties represented in vision are colors, then they are determinate shades of color and, hence, that colors like red, blue, and yellow are not represented in visual perception. It might seem that this claim is false: that vision's representing a determinate shade of, say, red, is not inconsistent with—and, indeed, even implies—its representing red itself. There are two possible grounds for making such a claim, and it's important to distinguish them. The first is simply confused, while the second actually further discredits the idea that there is some special phenomenal sense of *looks* according to which saying that the tomato looks blue to Bob is saying that the proposition that he's visually related to represents it as blue.

The first reason for thinking that if the proposition to which you're visually related represents some object as being, say, chartreuse, then it thereby represents it as yellow is just that chartreuse is a shade of yellow and, hence, that being chartreuse is simply a way of being yellow. So, if something is represented as chartreuse, in order for it to be represented accurately it has to be yellow. Since accurate representation of something's being a particular shade of some color requires that it be that color, it can seem that when it's represented as being that shade of the color it's represented as being that color. However, this line of reasoning isn't at all correct. Being divisible by 4 is a way of being even, but the belief that 8 is divisible by 4 does not represent that 8 is even. Yes, if the former is true, then the latter must be true; but this does not imply that, if the former is represented, then the latter is. If something is represented as being divisible by 4, it's true that there is a property such that, if something has it, it is even and the thing is represented as having that property. But evenness is not a constituent of the proposition that 8 is divisible by 4; rather, a particular way of being even—namely, being divisible by 4—is a constituent. Likewise, if something is represented as chartreuse, then there's a property such that, if something has it, it is yellow and the thing is represented as having that property. So we might say that if something is represented as chartreuse it is in some sense *de re* represented as yellow. But yellow is not a constituent of the proposition that my couch was chartreuse; rather, a particular way of being yellow—namely, chartreuse—is a constituent. This is similar to the point against

Stalnaker's possible worlds analysis of propositions discussed in Chapter 2, Sections 7 and 8: that two propositions each necessarily entail the other does not imply that they represent the same thing. So it certainly isn't true that if the necessary entailment goes in only one direction—if only the first entails the second—then the second represents whatever the first does. In more formal terminology, representation is *not* closed under necessary entailment. So the fact that being chartreuse implies being yellow doesn't imply that when something is represented as being the former it's thereby represented as being the latter.

The second reason for thinking that if something is represented as being some particular shade of a color it's represented as being that color is that we are immediately inclined to make judgements about an object's general color on the basis of the determinate intrinsic surface property it appears to have. So, if, contrary to the view of perception advocated here, we understand these intrinsic surface properties to be particular shades of color, then we'll understand this to be an immediate inclination to judge something's general color on the basis of the determinate shade it's represented as having. Importantly for the point at hand, to describe this propensity as an *inclination to immediately judge* an object to be, say, yellow on the basis of the determinate intrinsic surface property it appears to have is to not do sufficient justice to this inclination or its immediacy. Of course, you do not take the determinate intrinsic surface property presented to you and think to yourself, *Hmm, given that the thing I'm seeing has that property, it must be yellow*; that is to say, you don't make any conscious inference from the determinate intrinsic property the object appears to have to its yellowness. But to merely say that you don't run through a conscious inference of this sort thoroughly understates the sense in which your judgment that the object is yellow follows immediately from your perception of its intrinsic surface property. Indeed, the idea that there is a *judgment* involved by itself substantially understates the immediacy.

It isn't just that you don't focus on the intrinsic surface property, register some belief linking it to yellowness, and then judge that it's yellow. You don't even focus on the intrinsic surface property and then judge that it's yellow without registering the bridge premise; in the normal case there won't even be any *focusing* or *judging* at all. When you see a yellow object (in normal circumstances), your visual perception represents it as having various determinate intrinsic surface properties; but, unless the object is a Jackson Pollack painting or some other piece of abstract art, you're unlikely to focus at all on these intrinsic properties. And, in most cases, you also won't bother to make any kind of explicit judgment as to what general color the thing you're seeing is. And, if you do decide to register or convey its color by uttering a sentence, you still won't do any focusing or thinking about what its color is given that it's got the determinate intrinsic surface property it appears to have. When you see an object (in normal circumstances), you just immediately know its general color without focusing your attention, making any inference, or registering any thought at all. In the normal case, there are no steps whatsoever between seeing the object as having some determinate intrinsic surface property and obtaining the information about its color; in the normal case, we get this information immediately upon, and in virtue of, seeing it as having some determinate intrinsic surface property.

Because of this immediacy we're inclined to think that, in representing an object as having a determinate intrinsic surface property, the proposition to which you're visually related also represents it as having some general color. However, there are any number of other cases of such immediacy that make it clear that it doesn't imply that the relevant property is represented to you in vision. For example, if you were to see me, you'd immediately know on this basis that I'm more than 2 years old; you wouldn't have to focus your attention on any aspect of me, make any inference, or utter any sentence that would register this information in order for you to have it. You get the information that I'm more than 2 years old merely in virtue of how I'm visually represented to you. But it's obvious that the property of being more than 2 years old isn't a property that's represented in vision. Likewise, if you were shown a sample of your handwriting, you'd likely immediately know it's a sample of your handwriting without any focusing, inferring, or registering; you get this information merely in virtue of how the writing on the page is represented to you. But, again, it's obvious that being a sample of your own handwriting isn't a property that's represented in visual experience. And, just as obviously, there are an endless number of examples of information that is, so to speak, carried by what's represented in vision without being represented in it.[24] Moreover, it isn't as if in such examples the information is any less immediate than the information about an object's color is. Upon seeing me in a red shirt, you'll get the information that I'm more than 2 years old and that my shirt is red; but the former information won't be any less immediate than the latter. Neither will require focusing on any of the properties that the proposition to which you're visually related represents, making any inference from these properties, or uttering a sentence that registers a belief that ascribes these properties to objects. In both cases the information comes along with what's represented in vision without being part of what's represented in vision.

If, as I'm claiming, saying that something *looks* red and saying it *looks* like a sample of your handwriting involve exactly the same sense of the term *looks*, then there is no special phenomenal sense that the term *looks* has when it's applied to colors: no sense of the term according to which the color an object looks to you to be is the color it's represented as having in the proposition to which you're visually related. We've already seen one reason that the claim that there is such a sense of *looks* is false: namely, that, even if colors are represented in visual perception, it is determinate shades of color that are represented rather than general colors like red, blue, yellow, etc. Hence, even if colors are represented in visual perception, our ordinary talk of objects looking red, blue, yellow, etc. doesn't refer to the properties these objects are represented as having. On any reasonable view, to say that something looks red to you is to go beyond the content of your visual experience of it. However, even if color properties as general as red, yellow, blue, etc. were represented in visual perception, there are other reasons to be dubious about the philosophical tendency to find multiple senses of the term *looks*.

Suppose you are looking at a tapestry in bad light so that you are not sure that the information you glean from your visual perception of the object is accurate. In these circumstances, you might utter the sentence *It looks red and very old* to describe the tapestry. But, if *looks red* is ambiguous in the ways described above, then the sentence should seem ill-formed or at best false. For, given the ambiguity, *looks* as it occurs in the sentence must refer to the *phenomenal* sense, since this is the sense the word has when it is followed by a color term. But the sense anaphorically referred to in the sentence's second conjunct must be the epistemic sense, since the property of being old isn't directly represented in vision. And, given the way the sentence is constructed, the sense tacitly adverted to in the second conjunct must also be the *very same sense* that is explicitly adverted to in the first. So, if *looks* has these two senses, something about the sentence should seem wrong. This is a perfectly standard test for the presence of an ambiguous word. For example, the sentence *I went fishing at one bank and cashed a check at another* does seem wrong. And it seems wrong because (if the sentence is to be true) *bank* must refer to a money bank and *another* must refer to a river bank. But *another* must anaphorically refer to the same thing that *bank* does; hence, if you try to interpret the sentence in a way that makes it true, it winds up making no sense. (See Zwicky and Sadock's [1975] *identity test* for ambiguity.)

On the alleged epistemic sense of *looks*, the semantic value of *a looks x to me* is something like that of *my visual perception of a gives me a reason to think it is x*. This may not be exactly right, but the important point is that, on any reasonable attempt to define the alleged epistemic sense, if something *phenomenally* looks x to me, then it will *epistemically* look x to me; for example, if vision represents something as being red to me, then I will have a reason to believe that it's red. Since the alleged phenomenal sense—whatever it exactly is—is closely tied to the phenomenology of perception, and the epistemic sense—whatever it exactly is—is closely tied to evidence, and since the phenomenology of perception gives evidence, the epistemic sense, so to speak, *includes* the phenomenal sense. And, because the epistemic sense includes the phenomenal sense, there is no need to bifurcate the word's semantic value; there is only one sense of *looks*, and it is the epistemic sense. We do not mean two different things by *looks* when we say that something looks red and that something looks old.

However, given that there aren't two distinct senses of the term *looks*, what explains the philosophical tendency to think that there are? The explanation is our tendency to think that colors like red, blue, yellow, etc. are represented in the proposition to which you're visually related. Given that we're inclined to think that these properties are the intrinsic surface properties that the proposition to which you're visually related represents objects as having, and given that something generally looks to be some color because it is visually represented as having some intrinsic surface property that we would intuitively take to be that color, it's natural to think that there's a special sense of *looks* when the term is applied to color. *Looks red* suggests something different than *looks old* because normally there is a single property that something is represented as having in virtue of which it looks red, and it's a property we intuitively take to be redness. Normally you'll be able to focus on a single property represented in the proposition to which you're visually related in virtue of which the object looks red; and, moreover, you'll think this property just is redness. But there isn't any single property represented in the proposition to which you're visually related in virtue of which something looks old to you. And this is why there seem to be different senses of *looks* associated with *looks red* and *looks old*.

However, though *looks red* normally suggests something that *looks old* doesn't, this needn't be the case and, hence, it isn't due to the semantic value of the phrase. The sentence *x looks red to S* does normally carry the suggestion that S's evidence for x's being red involves some particular property with which he's visually acquainted and which we would take to be redness. But we can imagine that someone has only black-and-white vision but is in an environment in which, for the most part, all and only red things have a peculiar grainy surface that is difficult, but not impossible, to visually detect. Upon being told the correlation between redness and graininess, and upon learning to recognize the graininess of red things, the person may truthfully come to say of something that appears grainy that it *looks red* to him. Hence, *looks* doesn't have a different semantic value merely in virtue of being followed by a color term. And the view of perception advocated in this chapter doesn't imply that nothing ever looks to be any color.

15. The intuition that colors are represented in perception

The issues raised by the philosophical tendency to bifurcate senses of the word *looks* come directly from the fact that the arguments presented and defended above imply that colors aren't represented in perception. Because the only plausible candidate for the phenomenal sense of *looks* is one according to which *x looks red to S* expresses that the proposition to which S is visually related represents x as red, if colors are never represented in the propositions to which we're visually related, then nothing looks to be any color to anyone. And, indeed, to deal with the linguistic issue about the word *looks* without addressing the problem of why it seems so counterintuitive to claim that colors aren't represented in vision is to avoid the real problem.

Though I think the arguments presented and defended above are sound, I also recognize that the conclusion that colors are not represented in the propositions to which we're visually related is extremely counterintuitive and hard to swallow. Something needs to be said about why it's so intuitive to think that colors are represented in those propositions and why, despite the intuitiveness of the idea, they aren't. And the arguments presented and defended above don't offer any explanation of why and how we go wrong in thinking that colors are represented in visual perception; and, likewise, *mutatis mutandis*, when these arguments are modified to show that shape, distance, pitch, tone, and other properties expressible by public-language predicates aren't part of the representational content that accounts for consciousness.

We've already discussed a number of times one way in which our intuitions that color is represented in vision shouldn't be taken at face value. The claim that vision does not represent objects as being red will strike most philosophers as extremely implausible; but, as pointed out above, it's actually pretty obvious that vision doesn't represent objects as being red, blue, or yellow. Even if color properties are represented in vision, they are always far more determinate shades of color than red, blue, or yellow. The intrinsic surface property you become acquainted with upon seeing a ripe tomato certainly isn't red; at best, it's some particular shade of red. Now, I think our inclination to be prereflectively certain that the property is red should, by itself, make us less confident about our intuitions that vision represents objects as being colored. However, to say this is certainly not to say where our intuitions go wrong; and some explanation of this must be given if we're to accept the conclusions about perception drawn above.

When you look at a red object (in normal circumstances) your vision represents it as having a certain intrinsic surface property; you are very inclined to think that this property must be redness and the question is, if it's not redness, why you are so inclined to think that it is. The discussion of *looks* in the previous section might seem to make this question even more difficult to answer. As pointed out in that section, if you were to look at me, you would, without any focusing or conscious thought, immediately get the information that I *am more than 2 years old* even though this property clearly isn't visually represented to you; and, if you were to look at a sample of your own handwriting, you would likely, without any focusing or conscious thought, immediately get the information that it *is a sample of your own handwriting* even though this property clearly isn't visually represented to you. Now I'm claiming that your immediate knowledge that some object you're seeing is yellow or even some specific shade of yellow such as chartreuse is like these cases; though, on the basis of your visual experience, you immediately get the information that the object is yellow and maybe even, if you're knowledgeable about colors, that it's chartreuse, neither property is represented in the proposition to which you're visually related. But, if this is right, why are we inclined to think that one of these color properties is represented in vision but completely disinclined to think that *being more than 2 years old* or *being a sample of your own handwriting* is? The fact that we can immediately get the information that an object has these latter properties by seeing it does show that not all of the information we immediately acquire about an object in virtue of seeing it is information that is visually represented to us. It isn't just that we immediately acquire information about an object's color in virtue of seeing it; we are strongly inclined to think that, unlike these other properties, colors *are* represented in vision. But, if the—so to speak—visual status of colors is instead like that of the properties *being more than 2 years old* and *being a sample of your own handwriting*, why don't we realize this?

When you immediately acquire the information that someone is more than 2 years old by seeing him, or immediately acquire the information that something is a sample of your own handwriting by seeing it, there is no single property that the relevant thing is visually represented as having that gives you this information. Suppose, after looking at a sample of your own handwriting, you are asked whether it appears to be a sample of your own handwriting; you immediately reply that, yes, it does appear to be so. However, if you're then asked to focus on some *one* property visually represented to you in virtue of which it appears to be a sample of your own handwriting, you would reply that there isn't any single such property to focus on. You might be able to focus on what you'd describe as the shape of certain letters, the spacing between words, and the ways the *i*'s are dotted and *t*'s are crossed as being relevant to why this appears to be a sample of your own handwriting, but there isn't any single property, which what you see or any part of what you see is visually represented as having, that is responsible for its looking to be a sample of your own handwriting. And, similarly, there isn't any single property which I'm visually represented as having when you see me in virtue of which you know me to be more than 2 years old; there are various properties visually represented to you on which you might focus, any one of which inclines you to think that I'm more than 2 years old, but there isn't one particular property visually represented to you that stands out as being relevant. It's, as it were, the whole picture that makes the handwriting sample look to be one of your own and that makes me look to be more than 2 years old.

However, if you look at some red object and are asked to focus on a single property in virtue of which the thing looks red to you, unlike the cases just discussed, *there is* a property to focus on; you would focus on the intrinsic surface property the object appears to have. And, because there is a single property that is visually represented to you in virtue of which you get the information that the object is red, you'll be naturally inclined to think that this property is red. Of course, as noted many times above, upon reflection this property isn't red; at best it's some particular shade of red. But, because it's solely on the basis of this property's being represented to you that you judge the object to be red, you're mistakenly inclined to think that the property is redness. It is, upon reflection, as implausible that redness is represented in vision as it is that *being more than 2 years old is*. But the difference between these two properties that inclines you to think that the former is visually represented is that you get the immediate information that the red object is red in virtue of its being represented as having a single property; whereas there isn't any single property that I'm visually represented as having in virtue of which you get the immediate information that I'm more than 2 years old.

More generally, the information we get about a thing's color by looking at it is entirely due to what intrinsic surface property it's represented as having. Hence, whether or not these intrinsic surface properties are colors, we'll be inclined to think that they are. Granting that the view of perception argued for above is correct, it's predictable that we'd confuse the relevant intrinsic surface properties with the colors. However, though this does explain why our intuitions that these properties are color properties are wrong, it also raises another question. On the basis of some object's being visually represented as having a certain intrinsic surface property, you get the information that it's red. However, if this property isn't redness, how could the information that it is red be justified? What entitles you to the belief that the object is red based on being visually related to a proposition that represents it as having some property that isn't red?

Now, one way to answer this question would be to point out that precisely the same questions can be asked about any properties whose representation is, so to speak, carried by visual representation. If you were to look at me, on the basis of how I'm visually represented to you you'd get the information that I'm *more than 2 years old*. But this property clearly isn't a property that's represented in the proposition to which you're visually related, so there's a question about what entitles you to believe that I'm more than two years old on the basis of being visually related to a proposition that doesn't represent me as having this property. Indeed, on any reasonable view about the content of perception, almost all of the beliefs we acquire and judgments we make based on perception go beyond its content, so the same question could be asked about almost any empirical belief.

And, in such cases, one answer to the question is that the property you believe or judge the object to have is well correlated with its having the properties your vision represents it as having. When you look at me, the proposition that you're visually related to represents me as having any number of properties and some collection of these properties is well correlated with a person's being more than 2 years old. Similarly, the answer as to what justifies or entitles you to believe that an object is red on the basis of its being visually represented as having a certain intrinsic surface property might just be that being red is well correlated with that surface property. Of course, if the question is how your belief that it's red could be *guaranteed* to be true given that the object has the relevant intrinsic surface property, or if the question is how you could know that the property *is* correlated with redness and, hence, how you could *know that* you're entitled to your belief that it's red or *know that* the belief is justified, then the correlation between the properties won't answer it. But, if these are the questions, then we're well into the territory of general skepticism about empirical knowledge.[25] And this is, of course, a very general philosophical problem about all empirical knowledge, and there's no reason to think that there are any special problems associated with the view of perception argued for above. In short, the answer to the question of how your belief that an object is red could be justified given that the proposition that you're visually related to doesn't represent it as being red might be: *the same way most of your other empirical beliefs are justified.*

I think this would be a perfectly acceptable answer to the question, but there is a more specific and intriguing answer available. In this section I've explained why it's so intuitive that colors are represented in perception even though they aren't; however, the intriguing answer to the question about justification shows that, in some ways, it's also intuitive that colors *aren't* represented in vision.

16. Perceptual representation and dispositionalism about color

It is very natural to think that colors are represented in vision. Boghossian and Velleman (1989) are two prominent philosophers who think they are. Indeed, Boghossian and Velleman define the colors as those intrinsic surface properties that are visually represented to us. And they use this fact to argue against *dispositionalism about color*, according to which each color property is identical to a disposition to cause the type of perception that is standardly caused by things of that color. Now, dispositionalism about color is a very intuitive view; many philosophers have thought that some version of it is true, and something seems right about the claim that what it is to be (for example) red is intimately tied to something about the type of perceptions that red things standardly cause (see, for example, Evans 1980, McGinn 1983, McDowell 1985, and Johnston 1992). But Boghossian and Velleman recognize that dispositionalism about color is inconsistent with the claim that objects are represented in vision as having particular colors. For they rightly point out that if red is to be identified with a disposition to cause a certain type of perception, then the relevant type of perception must be specified. But, if *red* is the way that red objects are normally represented in vision, the only available type would seem to be something like the type of perception that represents its object as red; and any definition of red in terms of the type of perception that represents things as being *red* is clearly circular.[26]

So, while it may seem very intuitive that vision represents objects as being red, this intuition is inconsistent with the intuition that the nature of a particular color is tied to the type of perceptions it typically causes; the intuition that colors are dispositions to appear certain ways presupposes that the relevant way objects appear isn't as being some color. Now perhaps the intuition that vision represents objects as being colored is the stronger of the two, but it isn't so much stronger than the other that no argument against it should be considered and, as we saw in the last section, there is an explanation of why it should seem that colors are represented in vision. Moreover, as continually emphasized above, the most basic intuition that very general colors like, red, blue, and yellow are represented in vision turns out to be false on any reasonable view. So there is at least as good a reason to maintain the intuitive idea that colors are dispositions to appear certain ways as there is to maintain the contrary idea that they are represented in vision. And the view of perception argued for here is perfectly consistent with the idea that colors are dispositional properties. Since, according to the view here, the property that red objects are normally represented in vision as having isn't red, there is no problem about defining red in terms of representation of this property. And, likewise, for the other colors; each color C can be defined as a disposition to cause a representation involving the property perceptually correlated with C. Moreover, that the view of perception advocated here is consistent with dispositionalism offers a more specific reply to the worry about justification raised in the previous section.

It is clear that we sometimes justifiably infer that an object is some color on the basis of perceiving the object. If perception represents objects as having colors, there is no mystery about how this can be so. But, if perception doesn't represent objects as having colors, how could we justifiably infer the color of an object on the basis of the way vision represents it as being? The move from perceptual representation to belief representation will be a move from one property to quite another one. Now, as mentioned in the previous section, this is a perfectly general problem about the justification of our empirical beliefs and, as such, there's no reason to think it presents any special difficulties for the view of perception advocated here. But, with that said, if a particular color property *just is* the property of causing the kind of perceptual representation that objects of that color normally cause (for example, if redness just is the property of causing a perception that represents its object as having the property perceptually correlated with redness), then there is no mystery as to how such inference from perception to belief can be justified. For, if circumstances are normal and an object is represented in your visual perception as having the property perceptually associated with redness, then the object will be red. Hence, if you have reason to believe that circumstances are normal, your perception of an object as having the property perceptually associated with redness will justify your belief that it's red.

17. Conclusion

In Chapter 1, we saw another argument for the view that vision represents objects as having properties distinct from but corresponding to the colors. Representation of color is externally determined, but there seems to be something about the way that colored objects seem that is internally determined. At least one of the reasons to think that representation of color is externally determined is that we refer to colors using public-language terms and, hence, it doesn't seem that the content of your color terminology should depend entirely upon what you're like. And, as we've seen in Section 13, though the argument presented in this chapter makes no mention of externalism, it also depends upon the fact that we refer to colors via public-language terms. For the essence of the argument in this chapter is that your belief about an object's color is in some way completely different from your perception of it. But this isn't true for your beliefs about colors that are expressible by sentences containing demonstratives. If you look at some object and, while focusing on the intrinsic surface property it appears to have, say *sotto voce* to yourself **The thing I'm seeing has that property**, aside from the fact that you dimly seem to hear the sentence, the belief you express is not so different from your perception of the object. So the essence of the argument from spectrum inversion considered in the first chapter and the essence of the Mary argument considered in this one both lead to the very same conclusion.

Moreover, the observations of the first chapter also seem to imply that color is not represented in vision. After all, it isn't just that there is something about the way colored objects seem that is very plausibly internally determined; *everything* about the way things visually seem is very plausibly internally determined. Contrary to what some have claimed, I find it very hard to imagine that there could be *any* phenomenological difference between your physical duplicate and you. But it is quite easy to imagine environmental differences that seem to imply that your and your physical duplicate's respective perceptions *can't* be representing the same colors. We need only imagine that, for whatever reason, visual experiences of red things have the same effect on him as those of green things have on you, and so on. So the observations of the first chapter *also* suggest that colors aren't represented in vision.

In Chapter 3, I argued that non-descriptive modes of presentation do not essentially figure into the belief relation. Much of that argument essentially depends upon the observation that, insofar as beliefs figure into practical and theoretical reasoning, non-descriptive modes of presentation are irrelevant to their nature. And, again, these observations support the view of perception defended in this chapter. For perception also figures into such reasoning, so non-descriptive modes of presentation are irrelevant to perception as well. I've also stressed that, besides their role in reasoning, we want our perceptions and beliefs to be true. But non-descriptive modes of presentation are irrelevant to this feature of belief and perception as well. Indeed, the role that belief and perception play in reasoning depends on the fact that they are truth-apt, since to be the kind of thing that plays the role in reasoning they play is to be the kind of thing that's truth-apt. A banana or a cigarette can't play anything like the role in reasoning that belief does, but a sentence can.

But a sentence plays this role only because it can register or express a belief; and it's important not to think that for every belief you have there must be some internal state of you that is a vehicle that represents the belief. Because we can use sentences as vehicles to register and to express beliefs, there's a danger of thinking that the essence of belief resides in the existence of such vehicles. It's tempting to think that consciousness and cognition both fundamentally involve *internal mental states* and that questions about the nature of consciousness and cognition are questions about the nature of certain particulars that relate us to the representational content of our perceptions, sensations, and beliefs. But this conception of consciousness and cognition is badly confused. The fundamental nature of these phenomena is not that they are internal states of subjects; rather, it is that they are relations we bear to things in the world.

However, even once we recognize that the essence of the phenomena lies in their being relations, it's still tempting to suppose that these relations are mediated by relations to entities to which we have some kind of privileged epistemic access. Part of the motivation for positing non-descriptive modes of presentation is to adequately distinguish belief from perception. As we have seen, this is a job that they cannot do. But, as we've also seen, another (sometimes hidden) motivation for positing mental intermediaries is the thought that our fallible epistemic access to the stuff in the world is grounded in a less fallible access to some other kind of thing. Sense-data and intentional objects are always as they seem to be; and, when two sentences express the same Fregean proposition, if you understand them you will know that they do. Though it would in some ways be comforting to think that we had access to a realm of things that wasn't as fallible as our access to the stuff in the world, what you've just read has, in part, been an attempt to show that the thought can't be sustained.

Moreover, if there were entities that mediated our cognitive relation to the world, it would be a mixed blessing at best. For we would be less fallible about these entities at the cost of bearing no direct mental relation to the things in the world that we actually care about. Consciousness and cognition are relations we bear to propositions that consist entirely of stuff in the world. And part of the essence of both relations is that they are truth-normed: their function is to get us on to the world as it really is. And, though much more needs to be said about these relations, my intent here has been to convince you that, contrary to orthodoxy, they aren't brokered.

Notes

Chapter 1

1. Some form of intentionalism is advocated by Harman (1990, 1997), Lycan (1996), and Tye (1994, 1995). Qualia freaks include Block (1990), Jackson (1977, 1982), Loar (1990), McGinn (1991), Peacocke (1983), and Chalmers (1996). Sydney Shoemaker was once something of a qualia freak but has more recently advocated a view of color perception that is similar to the one presented in this chapter (compare Shoemaker 1982 and Shoemaker 1994b). Though the basic idea behind Shoemaker's view is ingenious and correct, ultimately his view cannot account for color perception in the way that he wants it to. Shoemaker's view is discussed in Section 10 of this chapter.

2. According to *commonsense functionalism*, the functional-state types will be given by common-sense or folk psychology, whereas, according to *psychofunctionalism*, they will be given by theoretical psychology. The example in the text is what a common-sense functionalist, not a psychofunctionalist, might say. For the varieties of functionalism, see the essays collected in Part 3 of Block (1980b, vol. 1).

3. See, for example, Putnam (1975) and Burge (1979a, 1982). These, and other papers on the subject, are collected in Pessin and Goldberg (1996).

4. Notice that *I am not* assuming that the fact that something *looks* a particular color to someone amounts to the fact that his visual experience *represents* it as being that color to him. Though most philosophers do assume this, in chapter 5 I will argue that it is in fact false: the color a thing looks to have should *not* be explained in terms of the color it is represented as having.

5. Notice that there is no argument that the primed-property terminology should mean the same thing in everyone's mouth. You use *red′* as shorthand for the description **the intrinsic quality that my visual experience has when something seems red to me**. Hence, your use of *red′* and the other primed-property predicates involves a description that is explicitly tied to qualities of your visual experiences of red, and my use of these predicates is similarly tied to my experiences. So, while general externalist considerations may establish that you and I mean the same thing by **Apples are red**, they can't establish that we mean the same thing

by *Visual experiences of apples are red*'; but, of course, if there are such properties as red' it may turn out that we do mean the same thing.

6. Many philosophical arguments presented as pertaining only to colors in fact have nothing in particular to do with colors. For example, Boghossian and Velleman (1989) argue that, since after-images can be colored, yet no object is represented as being colored when one has an after-image, color must be a property of experiences rather than a property of objects in the external world. But, of course, in whatever sense in which they can be colored after-images can also have shape, size, etc.

7. Though Locke thought that primary qualities, unlike secondary qualities, resembled qualities in objects, this is not a characterization of what the distinction amounts to. In an excellent paper, Margaret Wilson (1992) makes a convincing case that the distinction amounts to that between those sensible properties that will figure into mechanistic explanations of perception (the primary ones) and those that won't (the secondary ones). Hence, Wilson also makes a good case that the distinction is a vestige of seventeenth-century assumptions that are no longer held and, hence, is no longer a relevant distinction. But, even if there is some way to resuscitate the distinction, there's no reason to think it will yield a reason to restrict the qualia freak's view to color.

8. Note that while the representational content of a belief is, according to the picture, given by a thought, the picture does not depict the representational content of a perception as residing in thoughts; indeed, thoughts are not part of the picture of perception at all. Of course, in order to see why this might be so we would need to know much more about thoughts. This is discussed in Section 9 of Chapter 2.

9. I take this to be part of what Wilfred Sellars ([1956] 1997) means to be getting at in his attack on *the myth of the given*.

10. Of course, there isn't any single way that red things look. For example, besides the surface property that red things look to have to Norm and green things look to have to Abnorm, red things look like material objects. *The way that red things look* is an improper definite description, like *the table*. In this context, it should be clear which property it is intended to pick out.

11. If the property that visual experiences represent ripe tomatoes as having and that we take to be redness isn't redness, then what property represented in visual experience is redness? In Chapter 5 I will argue that the answer is that visual experience *does not* represent objects as having colors. Rather, visual experience represents objects as having properties distinct from but corresponding to the colors, and on the basis of this we form beliefs about the colors of objects, and likewise for shapes, distances, etc. Thus, contrary to Jackson (1977), the word *looks* is univocal in *looks red* and *looks like it's going to rain*. All of this is discussed in Chapter 5 where a different (and, for reasons that will emerge, better) argument for the view of perception suggested in this chapter is presented.

12. Block makes this observation in a discussion of mental imagery and his point is that our tendency to talk of mental images as having color properties isn't a reason to think that they are literally colored; rather, when we speak of a mental image as being red, we really mean to be saying that it represents something as red.

13. Michael Tye (1995, 111–16) uses phantom limb pain in an argument that pain is representational, but I think he interprets the significance of phantom limb pain incorrectly. Tye claims that when Steve has an experience as if there were pain in a limb that has been removed—say, it's a left leg—the sentence *Steve has a pain in his left leg* is true. But, since the sentence *There is something such that Steve has pain in it* is clearly not true, Tye concludes that existential generalization on terms governed by the word *pain* is invalid and, hence, that pain is intentional. There are several problems with this argument. First, failure

of existential generalization is only one criterion of intensionality. The invalidity of substitution of co-referring terms is the other and *pain* does not meet this criterion of intensionality. If *Mary has a pain in her right index finger* is true and *Her right index finger is where she wears her graduation ring* is true, then it follows that *Mary has a pain where she wears her graduation ring* is true. Second, there are well-known terms that appear to set up intensional contexts but that do not stand for intentional phenomena: for example, *necessary* and *possibly*. Indeed, Terence Parsons (1982) and Paul Pietroski (2000, 59, and n.3) have suggested—and it is almost certainly correct—that the appearance that *believes*, *desires*, and other propositional-attitude terminology set up intensional contexts is illusory; what's really setting up the intensional context in these cases, and in the case of modal terminology as well, is the word *that*. Finally, it doesn't at all seem that *Steve has a pain in his left leg* is true when Steve has no left leg; if Steve doesn't know he has no left leg he may think the sentence is true, but I think one would be inclined to say to Steve that he doesn't really have a pain in his left leg since he has no left leg. And, indeed, not only is the sentence not true, if anything it is actually the *falseness* that establishes that pain is representational. For, as pointed out in the text, since he doesn't have a pain in his left leg Steve's sensation is nonveridical: it misrepresents something as going on that isn't.

14. Shoemaker's reason for thinking that the relevant properties are properties of causing certain sorts of visual experiences is that this is the only way that he can see to avoid an error theory about the relevant properties. I am not entirely sure why he thinks this. If you think (as Boghossian and Velleman [1989, 1991] do) that the relevant properties are properties of experiences that could be instantiated only in something mental, but that ordinary experience represents the properties as being instantiated in something physical, then you're stuck with an error theory. But once one abandons the first idea (which Shoemaker does) I don't see why avoiding an error theory requires that the properties turn out to be relational.

15. I present more arguments for this in Thau (2000).

Chapter 2

1. See Brentano ([1874] 1995). Gilbert Harman (1990) and Michael Tye (1995) are two contemporary intentionalists who adopt Brentano's views. Unlike Harman and Tye, many philosophers claim that mental representation has *intentionality* without committing themselves to Brentano's doctrines on the aboutness relation or intentional objects. Indeed, many philosophers seem to use *has intentionality* and *is intentional* as synonyms for *is representational*. I think that, since this use of *intentional* and its cognates has caused a lot of people to think that there must be *something* about Brentano's views on mental representation that is correct, the use of *intentional* to mean *representational* has not been harmless. And, as we will see in Sections 1 and 2 of this chapter, those who use the terms synonymously have tended to follow Brentano in focusing on the wrong feature of mental representation. In any case, I'm not sure what the point of introducing a strict synonym for *representational* could be and, since I need some convenient way of referring to Brentano's doctrines, I will use *intentional* and its cognates for this purpose.

2. Though some who claim that mental representation is intentional claim that (A2) is intuitively true, and though I will assume in the text that it is, it doesn't seem intuitively true to me at all. It seems to me that if my belief is about the Irish pub at 1214 Sansom Street and if that is the pub owned by the waterslide champion of Wildwood, then my belief *is* about the pub owned by the waterslide champion of Wildwood (though I don't know that it is). Indeed, as Steven Davis has suggested to me, the idea that the belief is about the Irish pub

at 1214 Sansom Street without being about the pub owned by the waterslide champion of Wildwood seems to arise from *de re/de dicto* confusion. As is well known, sentences of the form *S believes the F is G* sometimes convey that S has the *de re* belief of the F that *it* is a G and sometimes convey that he has the *de dicto* belief that the F (whoever or whatever it is) is the G; and sometimes such sentences convey that S has both the *de re* and the *de dicto* belief. But, once these two types of beliefs are clearly distinguished, the case for (A2) seems rather weak. The pure *de dicto* belief plausibly isn't about the F at all, since a subject's merely having this belief doesn't imply that he has any idea of who or what the F is, whereas the *de re* belief is clearly about the F and, if the F is also the H, about the H as well; for example, my belief of the Irish pub at 1214 Sansom Street that it's a good pub is about the pub at 1214 Sansom Street even if I don't know that it is the pub at 1214 Sansom Street. So it's also about the pub owned by the waterslide champion of Wildwood whether I know this about the pub or not. However, I will give those intentionalists who hold (A2) the benefit of the doubt and assume that there is some sense of *about* according to which my belief isn't about the pub owned by the waterslide champion of Wildwood.

3. Some caveats: Brentano ([1874] 1995, 88–94) and Harman (1990, 34–38) commit themselves only to (A3) and the fact that there can be nonexistent intentional objects, whereas Tye (1995, 95–96) commits himself to (A1)–(A3) and says that the commitment to nonexistent intentional objects makes Brentano's view obscure. This suggests that Tye may wish to deny that there are nonexistent intentional objects. However, Tye (ibid., 95) does say that, despite the obscurity, "Brentano did succeed in drawing to our attention an extremely interesting fact about a wide range of our mental states . . . , namely, their capacity to represent or be about things that do not exist." And I am not sure how one can deny that there are nonexistent intentional objects yet claim that subjects can bear relations to them. Second, it should be noted that Tye seems to interpret Brentano as holding that intentional objects *never* exist, whereas in the text I interpret him as holding that intentional objects *can* fail to exist. I think that Tye's interpretation of Brentano is correct; however, in the text I adopt the weaker (and thus more plausible) interpretation. Finally, each of the above-mentioned authors says that one thing that makes some particular mental phenomenon intentional is that it relates its subject to something that *does not* exist and that this is one peculiar feature of at least some mental phenomena. But, as Nathan Salmon (1987, 1998) has pointed out, there isn't anything so odd about bearing a relation to things that *don't exist*: Socrates doesn't exist, but he did exist at one time and his prior existence is sufficient for me to bear some relation to him when I think about Socrates. But there is something paradoxical about thinking that one can bear a relation to something that doesn't exist at any time; hence, I have put the point about intentional objects by saying that an intentional object needn't *ever* exist. Since most examples in the literature on nonexistent objects of thought are also (very likely) examples of never-existing objects of thought, and since philosophers often use *x exists* to mean *x exists at some time or other*, my way of putting the point is probably what many prior authors meant.

4. In some supplementary remarks, Brentano ([1874] 1995, 271–94) recognizes that there really couldn't be any relation that has relata that never exist. But his response is to call aboutness a *quasi-relation* rather than a *relation*. He says that a quasi-relation is like a relation, except that the former can have relata that never exist. Aside from this, he doesn't explain what a quasi-relation is or how it can have never-existing relata. Since the introduction of unexplained terminology does nothing to explain the paradox, I have omitted the change in terminology.

5. One of Austin's points is that, though it is called *the argument from illusion*, the case it concerns involves hallucination (which he calls *delusion*) rather than illusion.

6. Of course, one way to resolve the paradoxes might be to explain how there can be objects that don't exist. For example, such a theory is offered in Parsons (1980). However, as we will see, the paradoxes of intentionality can be addressed if we take a different approach toward belief and perceptual representation.

7. I use the words *true* and *false* to apply respectively to accurate and inaccurate beliefs and perceptions. If the reader objects to applying these words to perceptions, at this stage *accurate* and *inaccurate* will do just as well. It might be thought that truth is a special kind of accuracy that applies only to *propositions*—the things we believe and express by our sentences—whereas the more general notion of accuracy applies to perceptions, which are non-propositional. However, as discussed in Section 9, the idea that perception is non-propositional stems from a misunderstanding about what propositions are.

8. The fact that utterances are governed by norms of communication rather than norms of truth will be very important later in the discussion. In Chapter 4 we will see how focusing on the truth and falsity of utterances yields confusion about belief ascriptions and, hence, confusion about belief itself.

9. If we view our conceptual and perceptual faculties as providing us with the *ability* to get on the the world accurately, then the mistake at the heart of Brentano's view and sense-data theory is an instance of an even more general error. As Jim Pryor (1997) points out, the idea that your fallible knowledge of the external world rests upon infallible knowledge of sense-data depends at least in part upon the more general idea that your fallible ability to do something is grounded in an infallible ability to do something else. And, as Pryor also points out, this more general idea is wrong; my ability to, for example, skip rope is fallible—sometimes I miss—but I don't exercise my fallible ability to skip rope by exercising some other ability infallibly. However, even here there is some temptation to think that there really *is* something I do infallibly when I fallibly skip rope: namely, I skip rope by first *trying* to skip rope and, though I might fail to skip rope, I can't fail to try. Besides the delusion of essential infallibility, one mistake here is to think of *trying* as a special kind of action: to think of the trying, which is a *relation* to some activity, as being itself an activity, only one that you can infallibly perform. And here the qualia freak makes the same general error by thinking of a perception, which is a relation to an object one perceives, as itself a special kind of object of perception. In both cases a *relation* a subject can bear to some sort of thing (in the case of trying, a relation to an activity; and, in the case of perception, a relation to an object) is confused with the sort of *thing* to which a subject can bear the relevant relation (in the case of trying, an activity; and, in the case of perception, an object). This fallacy of particularizing a relation is discussed in Section 6.

10. Thanks to Mark Kalderon for helping me to see this point.

11. Of course, there are things to which subjects can bear the belief relation that no one ever has believed or ever will believe. Hence, if something's being a belief requires that someone bears the belief relation to it, then some propositions *aren't* beliefs and, in this respect, they will differ from Frege's conception of what a thought is. However, it doesn't in fact seem wrong to call an unbelieved proposition a *belief*. For example, I'm certain that no one has ever had the belief that Nixon ate forty-two penguins the first time he was in the White House. But, if that's a *belief* that no one has ever had, then there are unbelieved beliefs. With this said, even if it is wrong to call an unbelieved proposition a *belief*, all that follows is that some propositions aren't beliefs; it doesn't follow that some beliefs aren't propositions. Rather, the natural view to take would be that a belief is a proposition to which someone *does* bear the belief relation, just as a husband is a man to whom some woman bears the marriage relation. Thus *proposition* would be a general term for the kind of thing to which a subject can bear the belief relation, and *belief* would be reserved for a proposition that is believed. Since this usage is terminologically easier, it's the one I'll adopt.

12. Many philosophers think that possible worlds are mysterious entities and are thus suspicious of their existence. But as Robert Stalnaker (1984, 46) has pointed out, if possible worlds are ways the world might have been, then it is natural to think that possible worlds are properties. My car has the property of being maroon, but it might have had the property of being yellow. Likewise, *the concrete world* has the property of being the way that it actually is, but it might have been some different way and thus had some different property. *Possible world* is an unfortunate name for such entities, since they are not particulars but rather are properties. The term *the actual world*, as it is ordinarily used, picks out a particular, the thing that is constituted by everything there is. But, if possible worlds are properties and if we mean to use *the actual world* to pick out something that is ontologically on a par with the other possible worlds, then we will have to use the term in a very unnatural way: namely, to refer to a property *possessed by* what we would normally call *the actual world*. Also, if possible worlds are properties, then philosophical talk of things happening *in* possible worlds is, to put it mildly, a highly misleading metaphor.

13. Lewis (1986, 57–58) also presents the view that propositions are functions from possible worlds to truth-values; however, Lewis accepts that there is a legitimate sense of *proposition* according to which propositions are structured entities.

14. For expositional ease, I'm ignoring context-dependence. If the proposition to which *S believes that P* relates *S* can vary depending on the context, then there won't be any single thing that is the belief that *P*. There will be such context-dependence whenever *P* contains indexicals, but on some accounts of belief ascription—and, because of his remark about context-dependence quoted in the last section, Stalnaker's appears to be one of them—which proposition *S believes that P* relates *S* to varies depending on context and, hence, belief ascriptions are *always* context-dependent (see, for example, Crimmins 1992). So, in order to account for the possibility of context-dependence, we should say that, in any given context, *the belief that P* refers to the proposition to which *S believes that P* relates *S*.

15. The nature of these intuitions will take center stage in Chapter 4.

16. Depending on what the constituents of propositions are, it may be possible that they sometimes fail to determine an object (or property). If such cases occur, then a proposition with a constituent that fails to determine an object (or property) is not true, but is it false? And, if it is neither true nor false, does it have some third truth-value? These questions are, of course, well known and they do not affect my concerns. However, it should be noted that, if it turns out (as is likely) that propositions can be neither true nor false, this doesn't undermine the point that belief and perception are truth-normed relations to propositions. To believe a proposition that isn't true is to have a belief that's flawed, though maybe not as flawed as a false belief.

17. The structured account of propositions has been well worked out in the literature. Salmon (1986) offers one among many detailed versions. However, Salmon is a Millian and, hence, he takes the constituents of the proposition that a is F to simply be a and F-ness. A more neutral account would take the constituents to be something that determines a and something that determines F-ness. Since a determines a and F-ness determines F-ness, such an account allows that Millianism may be correct but doesn't imply that it is. Millianism and Fregeanism are discussed later in this chapter.

18. Of course, even though the proponent of the possible worlds account must use the resources of the structured account to explain how mathematical sentences express necessary truths, there may still be reasons for accepting the possible worlds account. Stalnaker (1984) offers at least two such reasons. First, Stalnaker argues that other accounts can't give a *naturalistic* explanation of how subjects come to be related to propositions. However, he considers only two proposals for how other accounts might give a naturalistic explanation and

admits to having no general argument that no other account can give one; and he admits that his own naturalistic account is incomplete. Moreover, by **naturalistic** Stalnaker seems to mean something like **materialist**, and it seems legitimate to say that, even if his argument that only the possible worlds account can give a naturalistic explanation of our relation to propositions is correct, so much the worse for materialism.

Stalnaker's other argument for the possible worlds account involves the fact that when my cat Shasta scratches at the rug, we can have reason to say **Shasta believes there's a mouse under the rug**, but since Shasta lacks the concept *rug* we also have good reason to deny that Shasta has the same belief that I do when I believe there's a mouse under the rug. According to Stalnaker, if propositions are functions from possible worlds to truth-values, we can preserve both intuitions because the domain of the relevant function is contextually determined and, when a belief is ascribed to Shasta, the context picks out a different domain than it does when the belief is ascribed to me. But, even if the structured account is correct, each proposition still determines a function from possible worlds to truth-values. So, if Stalnaker's solution works, a proponent of the structured account could also adopt it by claiming that a belief ascription relates a subject to a structured proposition *and* a domain of possible worlds. Hence, Stalnaker has given no reason to favor the possible worlds account over the structured account.

But should we accept that the constituents of propositions should be supplemented with domains of possible worlds in order to account for belief ascriptions to animals? It seems to me that we shouldn't. First, while Stalnaker's proposal does yield a difference between Shasta's belief and mine, what possible reason is there to think that it is the right difference? Second, Shasta doesn't have the concept *rug*, so literally speaking she doesn't believe that there is a mouse under the rug. When we say that Shasta has that belief, we speak falsely, but we convey the information that she has some belief or other that explains her rug-scratching behavior. We often make false ascriptions of attitudes to things in order to communicate explanations or descriptions of their behavior (for example, **The sun is trying to come out**, **The computer doesn't know there's a disk in the drive**), and this seems to be the best explanation of why ascribing beliefs to animals can be appropriate even when the belief ascriptions used are false.

19. Maybe the structure that realizes the syntactic structure of propositions is some set-theoretic structure. But then the question is, which set-theoretic structure? And it's crucial to realize that the answer can't be *It makes no difference, so we can arbitrarily pick one*. We might choose some set-theoretic structure to represent the structure of propositions and, for certain purposes, it may not matter which we choose. But, if there really are propositions and they really have a syntactic structure, either some particular kind of structure realizes their syntactic structure or it is unrealized.

20. I'm construing the *structure* of a proposition as that which determines what the proposition, so to speak, says about the objects, properties, and relations determined by its constituents. But the dominant conception of syntax is that it is in no way the handmaiden of semantics; on the dominant conception, the syntax of a language provides the rules that determine whether an arrangement of words counts as a grammatical sentence rather than providing rules by which the semantic values of those words combine to form a meaningful proposition. But it's doubly hard to see how this semantics-free conception of syntax can be applied to propositions. First, this conception of linguistic syntax obviously requires that the words be arranged in some way; so it's hard to see how this notion of syntactic structure can be applied to a proposition without any sense of what the relations between its constituents that determine their *arrangement* amount to. But, second, if the structure of a proposition isn't what determines what it says, then it seems to me that we have no idea whatsoever about what this structure is.

21. An existential proposition will have to contain something corresponding to the existential quantifier as a constituent (or at least something that determines such a thing). Again, the details have been worked out in the literature. See Salmon (1986) for one version. It should also be noted that, in the end, I don't think that perception *ever* represents an object as being colored. Rather, perception represents that objects have properties distinct from but corresponding to the colors, and on the basis of this we form beliefs that represent objects as being colored. In Chapter 1 reasons were given for thinking that vision must represent objects as having properties distinct from but corresponding to the colors, but in the end I did not take these reasons to be decisive, and *no reason* was given for thinking that vision doesn't also represent objects as colored. In Chapter 5 I will present decisive reasons for thinking that vision represents objects as having properties distinct from but corresponding to the colors *and* that vision doesn't represent objects as being colored (likewise, for shapes, distances, etc.). However, for now, the obvious line to take is that when Eloise is hallucinating a brown and green object, her perception relates her to an existential proposition that there is a brown and green object before her.

22. According to Russell's (1905) analysis of definite descriptions, the proposition that the G is F is the existential proposition that there is a unique G that is F. So, on Russell's analysis, the proposition doesn't attribute a property to an object. However, Russell introduces a defined operator that allows one to represent the proposition that the F is G in a way that mirrors the surface grammar of the sentence and, hence, allows us to recover the properties that determine which object the proposition is intuitively about. Kaplan (1972) offers good reasons for maintaining that, even if Russell's analysis gets the truth and falsity of descriptive propositions right, it should be rejected in favor of an analysis that gets their truth and falsity right *and* preserves the surface grammar of sentences that express them.

23. I have formulated the puzzles of intentionality using beliefs that are expressed by sentences containing definite descriptions, but these puzzles can also be formulated using beliefs that are expressed by sentences containing names: for example, some will think that a subject's belief that Hesperus is far away is about Hesperus without being about Phosphorus, and a child's belief that Santa is coming seems to be about a nonexistent object. But, in the case of names, the puzzles of intentionality merely present arguments that names have senses as well as referents and that a subject bears the aboutness relation to the former rather than the latter. What it might mean to say that names have senses is discussed later in this chapter, and whether or not they do is discussed in the chapters 3 and 4.

24. Actually, this is just one among many reasons that Fregeans give for distinguishing the propositions. All of the reasons will be discussed in the next chapter. It should also be noted that, of course, Superman doesn't exist. However, as many philosophers who work on Frege's puzzle have noticed, the fictional example of Superman provides a nice illustration of the Fregean considerations for distinguishing certain beliefs, and for the sake of the example we will pretend that the Superman fiction is true. Finally, it should be noted that most philosophers use Lois Lane as an example of a person who is ignorant of Clark Kent's dual identity. However, as the Superman fiction currently stands, Lois is married to Clark Kent and *does* know that he's Superman. Happily, Lex Luthor remains ignorant of Clark Kent's dual identity.

25. Descriptive Fregeanism is often defined as the view that each name is synonymous with some definite description. However, this is an overly restrictive definition. The essential feature of the view is that, like a definite description, each name picks out its referent by being associated with a collection of properties that its referent uniquely satisfies; that is to say, the essential feature is that names function like definite descriptions, *not* that each name has to be synonymous with some definite description. Hence, the term *descriptive Fregeanism*

is in some ways misleading. However, it is so standard a name for the view that to adopt any other would invite more confusion than it would forestall.

26. I say that the Fregean *may* wish to hold that the proposition that the G is F contains some mode of presentation of F-ness rather than F-ness itself because I do not think that Frege himself should be interpreted as holding this view. In "Concept and Object," Frege ([1892] 1984b) thinks that the referent of a predicate is what he calls a *concept*, a function from objects to truth-values. For example, the concept *red* is the function that takes the value true when the argument is a red thing, and false when it's a non-red thing. Frege says in "Concept and Object" that concepts are properties, but they clearly aren't *properties* in our sense of the word, since co-extensional predicates needn't express the same property (in our sense of the word). With regard to the senses of predicates, Frege thinks that the sense of a predicate is something that determines its referent: that is, something that determines the relevant function from objects to truth-values. But then the most plausible way of understanding Frege's proposal is that the sense of a predicate *just is* the property expressed by the predicate; for what else is there that determines which objects in the actual world satisfy the predicate?

27. Anyone who proposes that modes of presentation are discriminatory abilities must have something to say about (i) how they work, (ii) how they are individuated, and (iii) how their individuation allows one to get the intuitive individuation of belief that's supposed to follow from Frege's puzzle cases (for example, the belief that Superman flies is distinct from the belief that Clark Kent flies). I find it very difficult to understand Evans (1982/1995) on modes of presentation and don't feel that any of these requirements are met. It should also be noted that by categorizing all proposals according to which modes of presentation are non-descriptive together, I do not mean to imply that there aren't important differences between specific proposals. However, I will argue that, regardless of exactly what non-descriptive modes of presentation are, they are importantly different from descriptive modes of presentation.

28. I am defining descriptive Fregeanism as the view that *every* mode of presentation is merely a collection of properties that uniquely determines the object presented (if such there be) and non-descriptive Fregeanism as the view that *every* mode of presentation is merely some non-descriptive entity. There are other possible Fregean positions, but discussing them in the text would complicate matters in a way that would make it very difficult for the reader to get the upshot of dividing Fregeanism in two. For those interested, they are as follows. First, one might hold a hybrid position according to which modes of presentation are sometimes descriptive and sometimes non-descriptive. As will become apparent by the end of this chapter, views according to which there are *sometimes* non-descriptive modes of presentation in belief should be grouped together, whereas views according to which there are *never* non-descriptive modes of presentation in belief should be grouped together. Hence, the hybrid position should be grouped with non-descriptive Fregeanism. Another possible hybrid position would be that a mode of presentation of an object is a non-descriptive way of determining a property (or collection of properties) that then descriptively determines the object. Like the first hybrid view discussed, this view should be categorized with non-descriptive Fregeanism since it claims that there are non-descriptive modes of presentation. Moreover, since the non-descriptive Fregean will need to say that properties as well as objects are presented non-descriptively, the second hybrid view discussed will agree with non-descriptive Fregeanism about propositions expressed by sentences of the form *The G is F*. Of course, other hybrid Fregean positions are possible, but they are so baroque as not to even warrant discussion in a footnote. It should also be noted that on some views non-descriptive entities are constituents of propositions but do not by themselves determine the objects they

present. For example, according to Richard (1990), the constituent of the proposition that a is F that corresponds to the name *a* is an ordered pair consisting of the name and the object to which it refers. Hence, on Richard's view, the name *a* does not by itself determine the object a; rather, the object is determined because it too is a constituent of the proposition. Since I am taking the non-descriptive mode of presentation a to determine the object a, on a view like Richard's, a will be the ordered pair <*a*, a> rather than just the name itself. Richard's view will be discussed in chapter 3.

29. To say that Salmon holds that non-descriptive modes of presentation are an essential part of *the belief relation* is a slightly inaccurate way of putting the point. According to Salmon, the belief relation is a *two-place* relation between subjects and propositions; however, it is definable in terms of a three-place relation among subjects, propositions, and non-descriptive modes of presentation. Hence, a more accurate way of bringing out the similarity between the guise Millian and non-descriptive Fregean positions would be to say that both hold that the belief-relation is *definable* in terms of a three-place relation involving (i) subjects, (ii) non-descriptive modes of presentation, and (iii) *what* is represented by a belief. The guise Millian—like the pure Millian—claims that the belief relation *itself* obtains between (i) and (iii), while the non-descriptive Fregean claims that it obtains between (i) and (ii). However, again, there is no dispute between the guise Millian and the non-descriptive Fregean about the ontology of mind, although there is such a dispute between the guise Millian and the pure Millian. For expositional ease, in the text I will continue to use the slightly inaccurate formulation.

30. Of course, pure Millianism cannot avail itself of Salmon's explanation of why it seems wrong to say that Lex believes that Clark Kent flies. Just how the pure Millian can explain this will be discussed in Chapter 3. It should also be noted that—as in the case of Fregeanism —certain possible positions are not discussed in the text. For example, a Millian might hold that *descriptive* modes of presentation mediate the belief relation. As far as I know, no one holds such a view.

31. I take it that Quinean arguments against quantifying into opaque contexts have been decisively refuted in Kaplan (1986).

32. Salmon doesn't endorse this argument. His response is to argue that *de re* belief attributions commit us to accepting singular propositions. However, he doesn't rebut the initial argument.

33. Or indexicals. There will be more on indexicals in chapter 3.

34. This will be true on the standard version of descriptive Fregeanism that I have been discussing in the text, according to which the proposition that a is F is identical to the proposition that the G is F (for some description *the G*). However, as is now well known, this version of descriptive Fregeanism gets the modal properties of propositions expressed by sentences that contain names wrong (see Soames 1998a for a good discussion), and some philosophers have devised other versions of descriptive Fregeanism to circumvent this difficulty. According to one such version, names are shorthand for definite descriptions whose referents are always the thing at the *actual world* that satisfies them (see Burge 1979b and Evans [1979] 1985). Soames (1998a) offers decisive objections to this view. On this version the content of the relevant description might *appear* not to be part of what is represented. To see this, consider a subject S at some merely possible world w who believes that a is F. If—as the view claims—the proposition that a is F is true at w just in case the thing *at the actual world* that is G is F at w, then the thing needn't be G *at w* in order for S's belief to be true. So S's belief doesn't represent to him that the thing is G *at w*. But his belief still represents to him that the thing is G *at the actual world* and, hence, in general the content of the description is still part of what the belief represents. Finally, in order to get around the fact

that the standard version of descriptive Fregeanism gets the modal properties of *sentences* containing names wrong, Michael Dummett (1973, 110–51) has suggested that names are shorthand for definite descriptions that always take wide-scope over modal operators. Again, Soames (1998a) offers decisive objections, but it should be noted that also on this version of descriptive Fregeanism the content of a description that abbreviates a name is part of what is represented by the belief; for, within the scope of *believes*, the description functions like any ordinary definite description.

35. Since it seems that at least some propositions will have to contain entities corresponding to logical vocabulary, perhaps what I call *the third sort of thing* is really a fourth sort of thing. But perhaps the entities corresponding to logical vocabulary are (higher-order) properties, in which case what I call *the third sort of thing* really is a third sort of thing. In either case, the key point is that what I call *the third sort of thing* is something that stands between subjects and the stuff in the world to which they bear relations.

36. A few points need to be made. First, in Section 2 I pointed out that both sense-data theory and Brentano's view can be seen as attempts to understand unsuccessful representation as a special kind of successful representation. I am inclined to think that something like this is at least part of the motivation behind any philosophical claim that a third sort of thing is essential to belief and perception. The thought that even unsuccessful cases of representation must be cases of successfully latching on to something can—when it lurks in the background—be very seductive. However, once the thought is made explicit, its seductive powers wane. Why should unsuccessful representation be a species of successful representation? And what guarantee could there be that there is a kind of object that we always successfully represent? Of course, there are other reasons to think that belief and perception essentially involve a third kind of thing, but these will be discussed in chapter 3.

Second, it should be noted that my distinction between subjects, the world, and the third sort of thing is *not* Frege's ([1918] 1977) distinction between the first, second, and third realms discussed in Chapter 1. As discussed in that chapter, for Frege these realms were (something like) the physical, the mental, and the abstract, respectively.

Finally, we can now see in exactly what sense perceptions are individuated by *how* they represent on the qualia freak's view. According to the qualia freak, there is a difference between Norm's and Abnorm's respective perceptions of the tomato that isn't a difference in what objects are represented or what properties these objects are represented as having: the things that are alleged—on the qualia freak's view—to mediate their respective perceptions of the tomato differ from each other with respect to the intrinsic qualities in virtue of which they represent the tomato as red. For Norm, a red' perceptual intermediary represents its object as red, whereas, for Abnorm, a red' perceptual intermediary represents its object as green. In short, the primed-colors are non-descriptive modes of presentation of colors.

Chapter 3

1. As noted in n. 26 of chapter 2, on some views non-descriptive entities are constituents of propositions but do not *by themselves* determine the objects they present. For example, according to Richard (1990), the constituent of the proposition that a is F that corresponds to the name *a* is an ordered pair consisting of the name and the object it refers to (see Section 5). Hence, on Richard's view the name *a* does not by itself determine the object a; rather, the object is determined because it too is a constituent of the proposition. Since I am taking the non-descriptive mode of presentation 𝕒 to determine the object a, on a view like Richard's, 𝕒 will be the ordered pair <*a*, a> rather than just the name itself.

2. Though Salmon is right that the puzzle about identity that opens "On Sense and Reference" ([1892] 1984a) doesn't turn on any special problems about identity, Frege was in fact less concerned with this puzzle than he appears to be. See Thau and Caplan (2001).

3. The reason it seems doubtful that the different information conveyed by *Superman flies* and *Clark Kent flies* can be accounted for pragmatically is that assertive utterances of these sentences convey different information in all contexts; and, when an assertive utterance of a sentence conveys information pragmatically, features of the linguistic context are responsible and, hence, one wouldn't expect such information to be conveyed in all contexts. The relationship between the information conveyed by a sentence across all contexts, the proposition it expresses, and the information it conveys pragmaticallly will take center stage in Chapter 4.

4. We've looked at two ways of generating Frege's puzzle that involve belief ascriptions—one that concerns the *information they convey* and one that concerns their *truth-value*—but have only mentioned one way of generating the puzzle that involves simple sentences: it concerns the *information they convey*. Symmetry suggests that there should be a way of generating the puzzle that appeals to the *truth-value* of simple sentences as well; and, as Saul (1997) points out, there are cases in which people have intuitions that two simple sentences have different truth-values even though they differ from one another only by the substitution of co-referring names. For example, if circumstances are such that people intuitively think that *Clark Kent went into the phone booth and Superman came out* is true, they'll be inclined to think that *Clark Kent went into the phone both and Clark Kent came out* is false. And these intuitions also provide an argument that the relevant beliefs are distinct. The arguments below can easily be modified to show that any solution to this way of generating the puzzle implies a solution to the other three ways and *vice versa*; so this way of generating the puzzle also falls under a unified solution. However, I have not included it in the text because the intuition that the above sentences have different truth-values is far less recalcitrant than the intuitions that motivate the other ways of generating the puzzle and, hence, Saul's examples don't provide much of an argument for distinguishing the relevant beliefs. Nor does Saul intend them to; rather, since they don't provide much of an argument for distinguishing the beliefs, her examples are supposed to show—and *do* show—that the intuitions about substitution failure in belief ascriptions don't provide nearly as much reason to distinguish the relevant beliefs as they appear to.

5. The point about there being a unified solution to Frege's puzzle is restricted to cases in which the puzzle involves names (as opposed to indexicals). For, if you think that the proposition expressed by an utterance of *I am F* contains some non-descriptive mode of presentation of the speaker, you're not going to think that *S believes that I am F* expresses that S bears the belief relation to *that* proposition. And Donna's utterance of *I am F* conveys (in part) that the speaker is F whereas *Donna is F* doesn't. But, if you're a pure Millian and think that *this* is the relevant difference in information between the sentences, you're still not going to think that *S believes that I am F* conveys that S believes that the person speaking is F; after all, unless S is present, he won't have any idea that the conversation is even occurring. However, the reason that the point needs to be restricted to sentences containing names is due to something that creates a problem for Fregeanism. According to the Fregean, my utterance of *I am F* expresses a proposition that contains some mode of presentation of me. But, whether this alleged mode of presentation is descriptive or non-descriptive, it clearly won't figure into *anyone else's* beliefs about me. Hence, if my utterance of *S believes that I am F* expresses that S bears the belief relation to the proposition that my utterance of *I am F* would express, the Fregean will have to claim that the belief ascription is, strictly speaking, false but that nonetheless it conveys true information. More generally, as Soames

(1987, 103, 117–19; 1995, 520) and Braun (1998, 557–61) each emphasize, indexicals do seem to be substitutable *salva veritate*; and, besides making Fregeanism an implausible account of indexicals, it also means that there shouldn't be a unified solution to Frege's puzzle applied to indexicals. But, as discussed in the text, to the extent that a unified solution is implausible, Fregeanism is also implausible.

6. See Soames (2002) for a good discussion of Kripke's attack on descriptive Fregeanism.

7. As mentioned in n. 33 of Chapter 2, there have been attempts to revise descriptive Fregeanism so that it is immune to the above criticisms. For example, Burge (1979b) and Evans (1979/1985) suggest that a name is shorthand for a definite description whose referent is always the thing at the *actual world* that satisfies it. However, again, Soames (2002) offers decisive objections against the view.

8. See, for example, Richard (1990). The complexities of interpreting Richard's view are discussed below in n. 10.

9. According to Richard, the constituent of the proposition that a is F that corresponds to the name *a* is an ordered pair consisting of the name and the object to which it refers. Hence, as pointed out in n. 1, on Richard's view the name *Superman* does not by itself determine Superman; rather, Superman is determined because he too is a constituent of the proposition. Since I am taking the non-descriptive mode of presentation associated with a name to determine the name's referent, on a view like Richard's, **Superman** will be the ordered pair <*Superman*, Superman> rather than just the name itself. And likewise for the non-descriptive modes of presentation associated with predicates.

10. Two *caveats* about my presentation of Richard's view should be noted. First, Richard's view is much more complicated than the text suggests. According to Richard, the truth-conditions for a belief ascription involve the subject's *representational system*, or *RS* for short. A subject's RS is obtained by taking all of the propositions he believes on the Millian view and pairing each off with any sentence that he accepts and that (on the Millian view) expresses it. Each of the entities in a subject's RS is called a *Russellian annotated matrix*, or *RAM* for short. RAMs are also *determined by* sentences. For example, the RAM determined by the sentence *Superman flies* can be represented as

<<*Superman*, Superman>, <*flies*, the property of flying>>

and it *is* in Lex's RS, since he accepts the sentence; whereas the RAM determined by the sentence *Clark Kent flies* can be represented as

<<*Clark Kent*, Superman>, <*flies*, the property of flying>>

and it *isn't* in Lex's RS, since he doesn't accept the sentence. According to Richard, the context of a belief ascription provides *correlation functions* that take a RAM to a RAM that contains the same Millian proposition. *S believes that P* is true just in case there is some RAM Q in S's RS such that, for one of the correlation functions f provided by the context of utterance, f(the RAM determined by *P*) = Q. The point is to allow that *S believes that P* can be true in cases where S wouldn't accept the sentence *P* (for example, to allow for a true English belief ascription whose subject is a non-English speaker). So, on Richard's view, *Lex believes that Superman flies* needn't convey that Lex accepts the sentence *Superman flies*; rather, it conveys that Lex accepts some sentence obtainable from one of the functions provided by the context of utterance with the RAM determined by *Superman flies* as argument. However, in some cases the relevant function will simply be the identity function and, since none of this matters to the discussion below in the text, I will assume that the relevant function is *always* the identity function.

Second, in the text I have called Richard a *Fregean*, but in fact, even assuming the classificatory scheme I've adopted, it isn't clear whether he is one. Recall that I classify a view as *Fregean* if it claims that the belief that a is F can be distinct from the belief that b is F even when the names co-refer, and I classify it as Millian if it claims that the beliefs must be identical when the names co-refer. However, Richard is concerned entirely with *belief ascriptions* and he doesn't talk at all about what beliefs themselves are. There are three possibilities, but they all have major drawbacks.

(i) The belief that P is simply the RAM determined by *P*.

(ii The referent of *the belief that P* is context-dependent: in a context c, it refers to the set of RAMs obtainable from the RAM determined by *P* and the functions provided by c.

(iii) The belief that P is the Millian proposition that P.

On proposal (i), Richard is a Fregean. But this proposal has the unacceptable consequences that two subjects who don't speak the same language never have the same beliefs and that substitution of co-referring names in an expression of the form *the belief that P never* preserves its referent. On proposal (ii) Richard is also a Fregean. But this proposal has the unacceptable consequence that the referent of the term *the belief that P* varies from context to context and, hence, questions in the philosophy of mind like *What is the belief that Superman flies?* don't have a fixed meaning. On proposal (iii) Richard is a Millian and, moreover, if this is correct, his attempt to capture the *Fregean* intuitions about the truth-value of belief ascriptions is entirely undermined; for there is little point in capturing these Fregean intuitions if you wind up having to deny the Fregean intuition that the belief that Superman flies is distinct from the belief that Clark Kent flies. I am not sure which of these proposals has the worst consequence, but since the last removes any motivation for capturing the Fregean intuitions about the truth-value of belief ascriptions, and since one main point of Richard's view is to capture them, I assume that he would adopt one of the first two proposals. I think that *any* attempt to get the Fregean intuitions about the truth-value of belief ascriptions right will have the same problems as Richard does in saying what beliefs themselves actually are, but arguing this point would take us too far afield. In any case, as in the case of the kind of view offered by (for example) Crimmins (1992) discussed in section 4, the important point from the perspective of the philosophy of mind is that Richard is a triadist.

11. Of course, it is possible that non-descriptive modes of presentation are not themselves sentences but that they figure into the way information about sentences is conveyed. But, since we are not aware of any non-descriptive entities besides sentences in our ordinary conversations, the view would have to be that we have unconscious knowledge of them. However, I don't see the point of claiming that the relevant information is about sentences but that the *how* of belief is some other kind of thing of which we are at best only unconsciously aware. Once these points are recognized, the motivation for both versions of triadism is seriously undercut on a differences-*about*-the-how proposal. If information about which sentences someone would or wouldn't accept is what's relevant to solving Frege's puzzle, why should the guise Millian claim that the belief relation is *analyzable* in terms of a three-place relation among subjects, sentences, and propositions? That is to say, why should he claim that sentences *necessarily* figure into the relation? All that's required to solve Frege's puzzle is to say that they *sometimes* do; and, since it's obviously true that *sometimes* subjects believe a proposition by coming to accept a sentence, it's obviously true that sentences *sometimes* mediate the belief relation. But in many cases (for example, animal belief and tacit belief) they don't seem to mediate it. If non-descriptive modes of presentation turn out to be unfamiliar entities and if, as a result, we turn out to have no views about when they mediate the belief relation, then I can see why it might be strange to claim that they only sometimes

do. But public-language sentences are familiar entities, and there seem to be cases in which they do mediate the belief relation and cases in which they don't. And there is no reason for the Millian to claim that we are wrong about the latter cases. It might seem that the motivation for non-descriptive Fregeanism *isn't* undercut by a differences-*about*-the-how proposal; after all, the view claims that non-descriptive modes of presentation are *constituents* of beliefs themselves and it would be strange if some beliefs but not others contained them. But the alleged fact that sentences are constituents of beliefs does *no work* in explaining how information about which sentences a subject would accept is conveyed. The utterance of a simple sentence will convey to listeners that the speaker accepts the sentence whether or not the sentence itself is a constituent of the proposition it expresses; and, if it turned out that belief ascriptions generally convey information about which sentences the subject accepts (later in this chapter I argue that they don't), this would be explained by the existence of conventions concerning their use. Now, of course, the non-descriptive Fregean's claim that sentences are constituents of propositions allows him to capture the Fregean intuitions about the truth-value of belief ascriptions. However, since this claim does no work in explaining how the information relevant to solving *Frege's puzzle* is conveyed, it is an entirely arbitrary way of vindicating the Fregean intuitions. So, on either version of a differences-*about*-the-how proposal, it is hard to see what reason there is to believe that sentences are an essential component of the belief relation. Hence, since my quarrel is with triadism about belief, there is perhaps less reason for me to be concerned with this proposal. With that said, I argue below that a differences-*about*-the-how proposal can't solve Frege's puzzle and that the proposal is motivated by a false assumption. These arguments also show that the modification of non-descriptive Fregeanism discussed in this note won't work; moreover, it is important to see the way a differences-*about*-the-how proposal fails if we are to see the right solution to Frege's puzzle.

12. By contrasting an explanation in terms of a subject's reasons with an explanation that is *merely* causal, I do not mean to be implying that reasons are *special kinds* of causes of behavior. I mean to be neutral about whether or not reasons are causes.

13. Richard's correlation functions (see n. 10) are supposed to handle cases in which a belief ascription doesn't convey that its subject accepts the sentence in its **that**-clause. However, they are also supposed to provide information about some sentence (or sentences) the subject would accept. And my point here is that it isn't true that such information is generally conveyed by belief ascriptions.

14. Most commentators believe that Frege's observation that identity statements aren't about language leads him, in "On Sense and Reference" ([1892] 1984a), to reject the view that identity statements are metalinguistic. However, some of Frege's other writings show that this standard way of interpreting "On Sense and Reference" is wrong. See Thau and Caplan (2001) for a discussion of these issues.

15. Recanati (1993, 333) has suggested that the alleged fact that a belief ascription frequently conveys what sentence its subject accepts can be explained in terms of a conversational *Maxim of Faithfulness* that enjoins speakers to report a subject's belief by using words that the subject himself would use. My point in the text has been that in general we don't communicate any such information, but it is worth noting that, even if we did, the communication of such information could not proceed through such a conversational maxim. We could use such a maxim to communicate information about which sentences the subject of a belief report accepts only if there was *already* a convention that when uttering a belief ascription one should use a sentence that the subject would accept; if my listeners didn't know that there was such a convention, then they couldn't infer any information about which sentence the subject accepts from my utterance of the belief ascription. But, once such a con-

vention is in place, there is no need to appeal to any maxims to explain how such information is communicated by a belief ascription; the convention will explain this all by itself. Compare: an utterance of **Professor Grice is coming** will generally convey that the speaker doesn't know Grice very well, whereas an utterance of **Paul is coming** will generally convey that he knows him quite well. But these differences aren't due to conversational maxims; rather, they are due to conventions concerning the use of titles and names. Conversational maxims will be discussed in the next chapter. It should be noted that Recanati also argues that the Maxim of Faithfulness can't explain the alleged phenomenon, but his reason isn't the one given above and he doesn't notice that there really isn't any such phenomenon.

16. Horgan (1984b), Lycan (1996), and Tye (1995) offer three examples of this kind of response. None of these philosophers explicitly claims that the relevant modes of presentation are non-descriptive, but it doesn't seem at all plausible that they are descriptive. In Chapter 5, I consider the Mary case and argue that neither type of mode of presentation can help solve the puzzle it presents (which, it turns out, isn't quite the puzzle Jackson thinks it is).

17. This seems to be related to Evans's idea (discussed in chapter 2) that someone must have individuating knowledge of a thing in order to think about it. Here, the principle would be that someone must have individuating beliefs about x and y if he can think that x isn't y. My suspicion is that the latter idea is more basic and that Evans's idea is some kind of a consequence of it, but to pursue these matters would take us too far afield.

18. Notice that there's no reason that the relevant description has to be a definite description. Soames (1987, 104–5) notes that when conversational participants associate the same descriptive content with a name, the name is a means of conveying information including that descriptive content *whether or not* that content is part of the proposition expressed by a sentence containing that name.

19. Of course, some properties that photographs represent are represented by the instantiation of the very same properties in the photograph itself: for example, color and two-dimensional shape.

20. Of course, he may think (for whatever reason) that it's interesting that this particular sentence expresses the proposition that snow is white. But *what* this belief represents is different from *what* is represented by any of the beliefs he had prior to finding out what the German sentence means.

21. Frege ([1918] 1977, 12) says that "everyone is presented to himself in a special and primitive way, in which he is presented to no-one else" and he suggests that this mode of presentation can be the one associated with a speaker's use of the word *I*. This might be evidence that Frege thought that the word *I* can be associated with a mode of presentation that lacks a descriptive content. However, Frege (ibid., 13) goes on to say that when a speaker uses the word in a sentence that is intended to *convey information* "he must use *I* in a sense which can be grasped by others, perhaps in the sense of *he who is speaking to you at this moment*." Hence, as I say in the text, Frege does seem to have realized that descriptive content is what's relevant to information conveyed. Similarly, in Section 8 of the *Begriffsschrift*, Frege (1879/1972) gives an example of what he calls a *mode of determination* that determines an object "immediately through intuition." Though at that time Frege had yet to fully work out the sense-reference distinction, modes of determination seem to amount to the same thing as modes of presentation (see Thau and Caplan forthcoming). Still, even if Frege continued to hold that some modes of presentation determine their objects immediately through intuition, such modes of presentation would be irrelevant to what's communicated by the utterance of a sentence.

Chapter 4

1. *Grice's paradox* would be better, but it's already used to refer to a puzzle about probability that Grice (1989, 78–85) formulated.

2. I find Grice's introduction and use of the term *implicature* very confusing. It is supposed to be a noun, but he asks us to compare it to *implying*; hence, it would seem that he intends *implicature* to refer to the *act* of implicating. But he seems to usually use the term to refer to *what* is implicated. Moreover, he explicitly introduces (but rarely uses) the term *implicatum* to refer to what is implicated. I will follow what I take to be Grice's normal use and use *implicature* to refer to what is implicated. Furthermore, though Grice talks only of what *speakers* say (or implicate) by uttering sentences, for expositional ease I will often talk of what sentences themselves say (or implicate) when uttered. Obviously, when I say that an utterance of a sentence *says* (or *implicates*) something, I simply mean that this is what the person who utters it says (or implicates). Finally, when the context of utterance is unimportant or understood, I will often not bother to mention the utterance and simply talk of what the *sentence* itself says (or implicates).

3. Some (for example, Bach 1999) have argued that there isn't any such thing as conventional implicature. However, it is uncontroversial that some linguistic expressions convey information conventionally without expressing any proposition at all: for example, 'ouch' (in English) conveys that the speaker is in pain but an utterance of 'ouch' isn't true or false. So expressions like 'ouch' are uncontroversial examples of expressions that carry a conventional implicature: they conventionally convey information that is definitely not part of what speakers say by assertively uttering them, since there *isn't anything* that speakers say by assertively uttering them. Moreover, since such expressions conventionally convey information without expressing any proposition, it's hard to see why sentences that *do* express propositions shouldn't conventionally convey information that goes beyond what they say.

4. Grice (1989, 39) also says that "the truth of a conversational implicatum is not required by the truth of what is said (what is said may be true—what is implicated may be false)." This is further evidence that he intends *what a sentence says* to refer to what (together with the way the world is) determines its truth-value, that is, to the proposition it expresses.

5. For the sake of simplicity, I'm ignoring and will continue to ignore how the time of the utterance figures into whether or not it's true. See Salmon (1986, 24–44) and Kaplan (1989, 500–505) for different views on how the time of an utterance affects its truth-value.

6. In the full quotation, Grice says that what emerges from the above considerations is that "A should not have done x (should have been prevented) *or that the doing of x was something which presented A with some problems, was a matter of some difficulty*." However, taking the sentence to carry the disjunctive suggestion complicates the discussion of conversational implicature without shedding any more light on the phenomenon. Moreover, as Alan Hajek pointed out to me, the sentence *A tried to do x* doesn't seem to normally carry the disjunctive suggestion; rather, it seems usually to suggest that A simply failed to do x. So in the text I'll assume that *A tried to do x* carries only the simpler suggestion.

7. In the relevant section, Grice gives *five* features that conversational implicatures must possess; however, only the first can help to determine whether something is part of the semantic value of an utterance or merely a generalized conversational implicature. The second feature is roughly: (ii) if a sentence S carries a generalized conversational implicature, and the fact that S does so doesn't depend on the particular words in S, then any sentence with a semantic value that is roughly the same as S's should carry the same implicature; in Grice's terminology, the implicature is *non-detachable*. For example, supposing that the information that A failed to do x is merely a generalized conversational implicature of the sentence *A*

tried to do x, the implicature is non-detachable since *A attempted to do x* and *A strived to do x* likewise convey that A failed to do x. However, non-detachability can't help in determining whether some bit of information is part of the semantic value of a sentence or merely a generalized conversational implicature since whatever confusion one has about *S*'s semantic value will carry over to a sentence that has roughly the same semantic value. For example, to the extent that the information that A failed to do x seems to be part of the semantic value of *A tried to do x*, it will seem to be part of the semantic value of *A attempted to do x* and *A strived to do x* as well. The other features Grice lists clearly don't provide any kind of tests for determining whether some piece of information is part of the semantic value of a sentence or merely a generalized conversational implicature. They are as follows. (iii) Conversational implicatures are not part of the conventional meaning of a sentence. (iv) Conversational implicatures are not carried by the semantic value of the uttered sentence but rather by "putting it that way"; that is to say, they are carried by the utterance of the sentence. And (v) the conversational implicature carried by a particular utterance may be highly disjunctive or indeterminate (see Grice 1989, 39–40).

8. In cases of irony, metaphor, hyperbole, and sarcasm the semantic value of a sentence is completely canceled and, hence, the cancelability of a piece of information normally conveyed by a sentence doesn't decisively establish that it isn't part of the sentence's semantic value. Indeed, Grice discusses cases in which part of the semantic value of a sentence is canceled and in which none of the above phenomena is present. For example, he asks us to suppose that

> two people are considering the purchase of a tie which both of them know to be medium green; they look at it in different lights, and say such things as *It is a light green now*, or *It has a touch of blue in it in this light*. Strictly (perhaps) it would be correct for them to say *It looks light green now* or *It seems to have a touch of blue in this light*, but it would be unnecessary to put in such qualificatory words, since both know (and know that the other knows) that there is no question of a real change of color. (1989, 44)

Still, hardly anything is a decisive test for anything else, and the fact that a piece of information that is ordinarily conveyed by a sentence is cancelable provides some evidence that it is not part of the sentence's semantic value. However, as stated in the text, a further crucial piece of evidence is supposed to be provided if conversational participants' mutual knowledge of the maxims explains why the implicature is conveyed by the sentence.

9. This passage occurs before Grice's introduction of the notions of implicature and cancelability, but it is clearly an application of cancelability as a test for the presence of a generalized conversational implicature.

10. There is one important way in which I think it's clear that Grice is simply mistaken. It is natural to understand his work on conversational implicature as fleshing out a branch of linguistics: syntax provides rules that govern what counts as a grammatical sentence; semantics provides rules that govern how the semantic values of words determine the semantic values of sentences in which they occur; and the conversational maxims provide some of the rules of pragmatics, rules that take us from the semantic value of an utterance to the information it conveys. However, Grice often claims that a certain sentence carries the implicature it does because the speaker has *violated* one of the conversational maxims (for example, he thinks that some implicatures are carried because what the speaker says is uninformative); and, since one couldn't form a grammatical sentence by violating the rules of grammar, on Grice's understanding the maxims aren't on a par with the rules of other branches of linguistics. Grice has almost certainly erred in taking some of the maxims to

apply to *what is said* rather than to *what is conveyed*, and construing these maxims in the latter way places them on a par with the rules of other branches of linguistics. Indeed, Grice (1989, 33) says that, when something is implicated because of the violation of a maxim, the listener is entitled to assume that it, or at least the Cooperative Principle, "is observed at the level of what is implicated." But this means that the maxims apply at the level of what's implicated rather than what's said. This doesn't directly affect our discussion, so I'll ignore it in the text.

11. Of course, one might say that what a speaker says by making an utterance is what he would say he said were he to clearly understand the distinction between what's said and what's implicated and sufficiently reflect upon the question of what it is that he said. But this means that a speaker needn't have access to the distinction between what he said and what he implicated; rather, he need only have such access if he knows enough about the relevant linguistic theory, which is precisely what Recanati (1993, 245) wants to deny. More importantly, if speakers needn't have access to the distinction between what they've said and what they've implicated, this means that the Gricean paradox is resolved.

12. Though the distinction I'm making here seems similar to the one in action theory between *basic* and *complex* actions, in fact I am being very careful to avoid this distinction and the surrounding questions because they don't have any bearing on what I say. In action theory, a basic action is one that you don't perform in virtue of performing any other action and a complex action is one that you do perform in virtue of performing some other action or actions (see, for example, Danto 1963, Goldman 1970, and Hornsby 1980). There are two ways in which my discussion has nothing to do with this distinction. First, I'm not assuming that striking a key on the keyboard is something that you do in virtue of doing nothing else; it's perfectly consistent with my discussion that striking a key isn't a *basic* action in the action-theoretic sense. Second, as mentioned below in the text, I'm not even saying that striking a key on the keyboard is an *action*, and it's perfectly consistent with my discussion that it's not. I do talk of striking a key on the keyboard as something you *do,* and here I mean to imply only that it isn't like a muscle spasm or other random bodily movement. Whether or not it is an action and whether or not you intend to do it, it is in some sense *intentional* (or at least in some sense not *unintentional*).

13. Rules and rule-following are of course much-discussed topics in philosophy. The most prominent source of the discussion is Wittgenstein (1953, §§53ff., 82ff.; 1958, 12ff., 98ff.), but Kripke (1982) is another important source. See also Black (1958a and b), Fogelin (1975, ch. 11); and Waismann (1965, ch. 7). However, the focus of such discussions is often a worry about whether the fact that someone follows a rule can be reduced to material, causal, or other sorts of facts, and this is not a problem that I'm concerned with (nor am I concerned with showing that everything is water). Wittgenstein (1953, §§28–29, 84–89,141) seems to be saying that a thought about the rule wouldn't explain how it is that you count as following it. But his point seems to be a metaphysical one about what sort of facts are, so to speak, the truth-makers of rule-following facts. I'm taking it for granted that people sometimes do follow rules or at least that our behavior sometimes nonaccidentally accords with them, and I'm arguing that there's no reason to think this requires that we have thoughts about rules and that our ability to nonaccidentally accord our behavior to a rule results from the fact that doing so is often constitutive of what it is we're doing. I don't see why the fact that a person's behavior sometimes nonaccidentally accords with a rule should be any more unsettling than the existence of atoms or other physical entities that so many philosophers wish to show are the ultimate furniture of the universe. Of course, when one thinks about an atom one is inclined to picture some objects circling around some other collection of objects and to imagine that electrons, protons, and neutrons are like that except for being *really, really small.*

But, of course, they aren't anything like that and, contrary to what we might be inclined to think when we picture them, it isn't that if you could just squint enough you'd be able to see them. Because vision is such an important sense modality, we're inclined to imagine visual models when we try to understand the unfamiliar, and the structure of the atom lends itself to such modeling whereas rules don't. But this doesn't justify an indiscriminate use of the skeptical ax against rules. If you think about it enough, pretty much any phenomenon is deeply puzzling, mysterious, and in need of further explanation; and philosophers, above all, should realize this.

14. It might be claimed that your ability to ride a bicycle is disanalogous in an important way: your ability to ride a bicycle isn't an ability to acquire some propositional knowledge, whereas your ability to know what it is you will convey by uttering some sentence is an ability to acquire propositional knowledge; it's an ability to know *that* you'll convey that P. If this is right, then an inferential account of the latter ability might seem more plausible than an inferential account of the former. However, the alleged disanalogy depends upon a false picture of linguistic communication that we've already rejected. When I use a sentence to convey some piece of information that P, I almost never think to myself: *If I use this sentence then I'll convey that P*. Such cases do sometimes occur; for example, if I'm trying to convey something (say, that A's fly is open, or that B is a Catholic so A shouldn't make any of his usual insulting remarks about Catholics) to A without conveying it to B when both are present, I might consciously try to figure out a way to do this. But normally my use of a sentence to convey some piece of information doesn't involve my forming any propositional judgment about what information the sentence is likely to convey. Nor do listeners usually consciously think to themselves: *He must mean to convey that P*; generally your understanding of what someone else means to convey simply consists in your hearing his utterance and no further conscious thought is required (for more on this, see the discussion of *registration* in chapter 5). Hence, there's no reason to think inferences have any more relevance to my ability to conversationally implicate than they do to my ability to ride a bicycle. Of course, it may be that speakers or listeners make some *unconscious* propositional judgment about what an utterance will or does convey; but then it also may be that bicycle riders make some unconscious propositional judgment about what effect the rotation of their feet will have on the stability of the bike. So far as I can tell, insofar as there is any reason to think that inferences are involved, these two kinds of abilities are on a par.

15. Even though our intuitions about linguistic meaning are inconsistent, it needn't be that there is no such thing as linguistic meaning. For all that's been said above, it's still possible that linguistic meaning is *character* (or *semantic value*, or *information conveyed*) and, hence, that some of our intuitions about meaning, *but not others*, are false. The problem with this suggestion is that there isn't any reason to think that meaning is any one of these things as opposed to another. I suspect that most philosophers would say that *meaning* (as applied to language) is *ambiguous* among character, semantic value, information conveyed, and whatever other theoretical entities there are that correspond to one or another of our intuitions about linguistic meaning. The thought would most likely be that it simply *couldn't* turn out that all of our pretheoretical claims about meaning are false. My own view is that, given how complex the correct theory of linguistic communication turns out to be, it would be pretty surprising if our pretheoretical claims about meaning turned out to be *true*. After all, no one expects the man-in-the-street's claims about *physics* to be correct, and linguistic communication certainly isn't any less difficult a subject than physics is. Of course, the man in the street can use language to communicate, but he's also likely to be able to ride a bicycle. In any case, our ordinary use of *meaning* (as applied to language) *shows* that it isn't ambiguous. Though we've seen theoretical reasons that *The meaning of 'I am tired' determines whether*

the sentence is true or false and it doesn't change from context to context can't be true, pretheoretically it does seem true and, moreover, it seems to be a perfectly well-formed sentence. But, if *meaning* (as applied to language) is ambiguous, then *the meaning of 'I am tired'* must refer to the semantic value of the embedded sentence *I am tired*. So *it* must anaphorically refer to the embedded sentence's semantic value and, hence, the whole sentence shouldn't seem both well-formed *and* true (cf. *He went fishing at one bank and cashed a check at another*). This is a standard test for the presence of an ambiguous expression and *meaning* (applied to language) fails it. (Notice, however, that sometimes *meaning* refers to something nonlinguistic—for example, in *the meaning of life*—and that *this* ambiguity is revealed by the test. The sentence *The meaning of 'Snow is white' determines its truth-value but that of life doesn't* sounds strained at best.) Moreover, my main point is that we shouldn't use the term *meaning* when we theorize about language. And, since our inconsistent intuitions about meaning, like most intuitions, are pretty recalcitrant, so long as we keep using the term while theorizing we'll be prone to error.

16. Obviously condition (1) is the triviality condition and condition (2) the informativeness one. But by using *trivial* to refer to the properties of condition (1), I am not suggesting that a sentence for which condition (1) holds must be trivially *true*. Trivial truth is one way that a sentence's semantic value might be such that no one would ever intend to convey merely it; however, trivial falseness is another and, as we'll see in section 11, there are other properties a sentence's semantic value might have that would make it trivial in the sense of (1).

17. I have claimed that when a sentence is trivial but informative we should have some difficulty determining that it is trivial. Sentences like *War is war* might seem to be counterexamples since they clearly are trivial and clearly can convey information, but we have no difficulty in determining that they are trivial. However, recall that for a sentence to be informative (in the relevant sense) is for there to be *plenty of contexts* in which the sentence can be used to convey information that someone might want to communicate and, though *plenty* is vague, I don't think there are plenty of contexts in which *War is war* can be used to convey information; you would only use the sentence to convey information if your interlocutor has said something like *The Contras committed many atrocious acts*. More generally, a sentence of the form *a=a* (when it does convey information) conveys that some previously stated claim involving a is unsurprising or less objectionable than it might appear to be given the nature of a. Hence, a sentence of this form can be used informatively only when there is a previously stated claim involving a that someone might take to be surprising, and I don't think that we encounter plenty of contexts like this. And, if there aren't plenty of contexts in which the sentence is used to convey information, we will be more inclined to recognize that it is trivial (in the relevant sense), since, if it isn't trivial, there should be lots of contexts in which it can convey information. More importantly, even if sentences like *War is war* are trivial but informative, there is another reason that it shouldn't be difficult to determine that their semantic values are trivial. Recall that *semantic value* refers to an entity that corresponds to some of our intuitions about meaning, among which are intuitions about compositionality; more specifically, the semantic value of a sentence is a function of the semantic values of its constituent words. But *War is war* contains *the same (nonambiguous) term* on both sides of the *is* of identity; hence, it isn't terribly difficult to work out that its semantic value is the proposition that war is identical to itself. So, if it turns out that sentences like *War is war* convey information in enough contexts so that, other things being equal, we should be confused about their semantic values according to the claims in the text, then other things are not equal because—unlike true sentences of the form *a=b*—the triviality of their semantic values obviously follows from the fact that the same term occurs on both sides of the *is* of identity.

18. The recognition that identity statements and belief ascriptions involving identity statements are trivial but informative also answers a problem raised by Mitchell Green (1998) for
the Millian's attempt to explain away our erroneous intuitions about these sentences in terms
of conversational implicature. Green uses Recanati's (1993) observation that when some
sentence *S* carries the generalized conversational implicature p, although the sentence *It is
not the case that S* will obviously convey the information that it is not the case that S, it generally *won't* convey the information that it is not the case that [S *and* p]; and likewise for
other sentential connectives. When a sentence has these features, let's say that its implicature
fails to embed. To focus on an example of Green's taken from Grice (1989), the sentence
Mary lives somewhere in the south of France will generally carry the conversational implicature that the speaker is ignorant of exactly where Mary lives. So, if the implicature embeds, then the sentence *If Mary lives somewhere in the south of France, then I don't know
exactly where* should generally convey the trivially true information that if Mary lives in
the south of France and I don't know exactly where, then I don't know exactly where. But the
above sentence in general clearly *won't* convey trivially true information; and, since the
same phenomenon is true of many sentences that carry generalized conversational implicatures, many implicatures fail to embed. However, it is clear that the implicatures that the
Millian must posit to explain our confusion about the semantic values of belief ascriptions
embed. It isn't just that the sentence *S believes that a=b* can seem false; when it does, the
sentence *It's not the case that S believes that a=b* will seem true. So, if the Millian is correct, the negation of the first sentence must convey the information that what is implicated
by the first sentence is being negated. Green's challenge for the Millian is to explain why the
implicatures of such belief ascriptions embed when implicatures usually don't. (It should be
noted that Recanati claims that implicatures *never* embed and points out that, if Millianism
is to successfully explain our intuitions, the relevant implicatures must embed. Green notices
that implicatures sometimes embed but offers a tentative explanation of why they do that is
unavailable to the Millian for these cases. However, in the end, he recognizes that his explanation may not explain all of the cases in which implicatures embed, so his final argument
against Millianism is just a challenge that the Millian come up with some explanation.)
However, the fact that such sentences are trivial but informative explains why their implicatures embed. As stated in the text, belief ascriptions that involve identity statements containing co-referring names are trivial because their semantic values are (more or less) trivially true. But this means that the negation of such a belief ascription has a (more or less)
trivially false semantic value. Hence, no speaker would intend to convey only the semantic
value of the negated belief ascription, and the implicature of the belief ascription embeds
when the sentence is negated because otherwise the negated sentence won't convey any nontrivial information. Similar stories explain why the implicature embeds when the sentence is
embedded in the scope of other sentential connectives.

19. Whether or not the belief ascription conveys this information by conventionally implicating it is a complicated matter. The issue of whether *S believes that P* relates S to what
is conventionally implicated by P (as opposed to merely what is said by it) is discussed in n.
22 of this chapter.

20. *Superman* and *Batman* may be names that carry a descriptive conventional implicature, but I think that something even stronger is probably true. Although these terms seem
to provide good (imaginary) examples of Frege's puzzle, I doubt that they are names at all.
In the comic books other people beside Bruce Wayne have been Batman, and Bruce Wayne
has even fought his temporary replacement to determine who would be Batman. Similar
things happen in the Superman fiction, and they suggest that terms for superheros are more
comparable to titles like *The Heavyweight Champion of the World* than to names. Indeed,

in the Batman fiction whoever happens to be Batman is often described as *wearing the mantel of the Bat*, which sounds an awful lot like a title.

21. I think that I have adequately addressed any worries that Millianism implies that we don't know the meaning of some very ordinary sentences. However, there are at least two other objections to the view that, though less worrisome, needs to be discussed. First, since Millianism claims that the semantic value of a name is just its referent, the view would seem to imply that sentences containing nonreferring names have no semantic value (or possibly that all nonreferring names are substitutable for one another *salva veritate*). One response to this worry begins with the fact that—like *Hesperus* and *Phosphorus*—one must associate certain descriptions with a name for a fictional entity in order to use it competently (for example, if you think that *Santa Claus* refers to your next-door neighbor who you know has led an unremarkable life, then it doesn't seem that you know how to use the name). Furthermore, names for fictional entities don't seem as vulnerable to Kripke/Kaplan-style arguments as ordinary names are (for example, I'm not sure what to make of the claim that it's possible that Santa Claus exists but that he is your next door neighbor who has led an unremarkable life). These two facts make it very plausible that the semantic value of a name for a fictional entity involves some descriptive content. (Thanks to Ben Caplan for discussion on these points. For other Millian accounts of nonreferring names, see Braun 1993 and Salmon 1998.)

The second objection to Millianism involves the claim that it is *a priori* that, for example, Hesperus is Hesperus but *a posteriori* that Hesperus is Phosphorus. But (assuming that the semantic value of a sentence just is the proposition it expresses) Millianism implies that the two propositions are the same; so how could one be *a priori* while the other is *a posteriori*? But it is well known that this problem is not unique to Millianism. For you might reasonably believe that ZF is incomplete because you were told by a reliable source that it is, while I might reasonably believe that it is incomplete because I've gone through the proof; hence, it seems as if any *a priori* proposition is also *a posteriori*. I think the right response is that *a priority* and *a posteriority* properly apply to *the way in which a proposition is justified for a particular subject* rather than to the proposition *tout court*; that is to say, it is a subject's *justification for a belief* that is *a priori* or *a posteriori* rather than the belief itself. And, once the notions are understood in this way, there is no worry about how my justification for believing some proposition might be *a priori* while yours is *a posteriori*, or about how I might have both *a priori* and *a posteriori* justification for believing a single proposition.

22. If the ***Superman/Clark Kent*** and ***Hesperus/Phosphorus*** examples do involve conventional implicature, this explains why the semantic values of the relevant sentences are opaque. But, unfortunately, it doesn't yet settle the issue of what the solution to Frege's puzzle is: the issue of, for example, whether the belief that Superman flies and the belief that Clark Kent flies are distinct. Recall that the conventional implicature carried by *P* is not part of the proposition it expresses, but this needn't mean that it isn't part of *the belief that P*. For the proposition that P is what someone says when he assertively utters the sentence *P* whereas the belief that P is the proposition that S believes when *S believes that P* is true. And, though it seems trivially true that the proposition that P is the belief that P, in cases where *P* carries a conventional implicature this may not be so trivial. The question is: when *P* has a conventional implicature does *S believes that P* merely say that S bears the belief relation to what's said by *P* or does it say that S bears the belief relation to what's said, *and* to what's conventionally implicated, by *P*? The answer to this question will determine whether the belief that a is F is distinct from the belief that b is F when the names carry different descriptive conventional implicatures.

If what is conventionally implicated is, so to speak, part of what's believed, then the belief that a is F and the belief that b is F are distinct when the names have different conventional implicatures. For, given that the beliefs include what the embedded sentences implicate, to have one of these beliefs not only must you believe the singular proposition that is the semantic value of one of the embedded sentences; you must also believe the descriptive proposition that is its conventional implicature. If the proposition picked out by a *that*-clause embedded in a belief ascription includes what the sentence conventionally implicates, then descriptive Fregeanism is true for the few names that have some descriptive content as a conventional implicature and that figure *too* prominently in discussions of Frege's puzzle.

However, I think that we should take the proposition that P to be the belief that P even when the sentence carries a conventional implicature. For whether or not *S believes that P* conveys that S believes what's conventionally implicated by *P* seems to be highly context-dependent. For example, in some contexts *S believes that A but B* will convey that S finds some tension between the truth of *B* and *A* (or some other relevant truth), but in many contexts it will merely convey that the speaker finds such a tension. The fact that this is heavily context-dependent suggests that it isn't part of the semantic value of a belief ascription that its subject believes what is conventionally implicated by its embedded sentence. And, if this is right, then the belief that a is F is always identical to the belief that b is F when the names co-refer; the conventional implicature of the name, besides not being part of the proposition expressed by sentences containing it, will also not be part of the belief ascribed in a belief ascription that contains it.

Chapter 5

1. The fact that I indicate what the property is by talking of the way things appear should not mislead the reader concerning what is represented in vision. Vision represents objects as *having* the properties perceptually associated with the colors; it doesn't represent objects as *appearing* to have these properties. The distinction here is best brought out by considering the view of perception that I argue against. On this view, vision represents objects as having color properties; but then, for example, objects are represented as *being* red, not as *appearing* red. Rather, we *believe* that an object *appears* red because it is represented to us *as* red. And the same holds, *mutatis mutandis*, if the properties represented in perception aren't colors. The fact that words like *looks* or *appears* are useful in picking out the properties represented in vision makes it easy to confusedly think that perception represents things as *looking* a certain way or as *appearing* a certain way rather than simply as *being* a certain way.

2. If you took Introduction to Critical Thinking rather than Introduction to Logic, you probably learned that thousands and thousands of things could be wrong with the argument, each with some Latin name. This is the old logic, and in the twentieth century they narrowed it down to two. Who says there's no philosophical progress?

3. I am ignoring, and will continue to ignore, the point from Chapter 4, Section 8 that the names *Superman* and *Clark Kent* are conventionally associated with descriptive contents. However, if as claimed in Chapter 4, Section 8, the descriptive content conventionally associated with these names is a result of what sentences containing the names *conventionally implicate* rather than what they say, then the propositions expressed by sentences containing the names won't include this descriptive content. And, if the belief that P is always identical to the proposition expressed by the sentence *P*, then neither the belief that Superman flies nor the belief that Clark Kent flies will contain any descriptive modes of presentation of Superman and, hence, as claimed in the text, according to Millianism they will be the same belief. However, even if it turns out that the beliefs are in fact distinct, the Lex Luthor case is

merely intended to provide a nice example; and the only harm in ignoring the fact that the names have some descriptive content conventionally associated with them is that it makes my case seem *weaker* than it actually is. It does this because, as pointed out in Section 11 of Chapter 4, there are no cases of names that lack a descriptive content conventionally associated with them in which Fregean intuitions dominate Millian ones. Hence, any argument parallel to my Mary argument that (i) has an obviously false conclusion and (ii) involves names that don't have any descriptive contents will also (iii) have a premise that will, at least according to some of our intuitions, seem false. But neither of the premises of the Mary argument presented above is at all intuitively false. Hence, using names that lack a descriptive content in the parallel argument would, if anything, just increase the plausibility that the conclusion of the Mary argument is true.

4. Note that this means that one can't respond to the knowledge argument (as Horgan [1984b], Lycan [1995], and Tye [1995] do) merely by saying that Mary's new belief is the same as one of her old beliefs except that it contains a different non-descriptive mode of presentation. The New Information Principle tells us that, even if this is the case, Mary must get some belief that is new with respect to its what. In any case, this response to the knowledge argument is a bit odd, since, contrary to what many philosophers seem to assume, just because two beliefs have the same truth-value in all possible worlds, it doesn't mean that you need non-descriptive modes of presentation to distinguish them. They might be distinct merely in virtue of having distinct constituents. For example, the beliefs that 2 is even and that ZF is incomplete have the same modal profile, but they are still distinct since they contain (or at least determine) different objects and properties. And, to take another example, even if H_2O and *water* are rigid singular terms, it does not follow that the belief that water is wet just is the belief that H_2O is wet; for H_2O, unlike *water*, is a complex term and it may be that the second belief, but not the first, contains hydrogen, oxygen, and the number 2 as constituents. And, with regard to Jackson's knowledge argument, it doesn't seem at all likely that Mary's new knowledge of what it's like to see red will have the same constituents as any of her old beliefs. At any rate, Jackson would need to give some reason for thinking that this is true.

5. One interesting fact about registration that isn't relevant here is that, when you use a sentence to convey information to someone, your very utterance normally registers some of this information for him. When I assertively utter the sentence *It's raining* you can simply say to yourself *Then I'd better take my umbrella* without having to re-utter the sentence to yourself to register the information that it's raining; my utterance can itself register the information so that you can draw an explicit conclusion from it. So it appears that a sentence can register information for you whether or not you're the one who has produced the sentence and, indeed, that this is what usually happens in conversational exchanges. There's a tendency to think that listeners take a speaker's utterance as *evidence* for what the speaker means to get across and then decide whether or not to believe it. While this may happen in rare cases, in normal conversational exchanges much of what the speaker means to get across seems to be simply registered for the listener by the speaker's utterance: when you say something to me, you normally, so to speak, *directly place a thought in my mind*. (This seems to be part of the reason it's so easy to successfully lie.) Of course, after hearing someone assertively utter a sentence you may think to yourself *that's false*, but you might also say this about some information that you've registered by uttering a sentence to yourself.

We've just seen in the text that a sentence can register more than it implicates. But the fact that a sentence can register for the listener more than it says as well as conversationally implicating more than it says, raises another question: namely, does all that a sentence implicates also have to be registered by it? I think that it most certainly doesn't and, more particularly, that in many cases where the implicature isn't at all a generalized conversational implicature (where the fact that the sentence implicates what it does depends on unique features of the linguistic context) the information implicated by the utterance is not registered for the speaker. For example, though the sentence *Fergie was sober today* will in many contexts conversationally implicate that he's often not sober, it doesn't seem that in such contexts the sentence will generally register this information for the listener; for it would be odd for the listener to say to himself *So I'd better not give Fergie that bottle of wine for his birthday* without first explicitly saying to himself *Fergie must have a drinking problem*. That is to say, in order to consciously draw an inference from the implicated information, the listener probably *will* have to utter a sentence to himself that registers this information. Hence, it's doubtful that the speaker's utterance registers the implicated information for the listener. However, though the phenomenon of registration raises many such interesting questions, they aren't relevant to the concerns in the text.

6. Just as the semantic value of a name is its referent rather than some descriptive content that picks out its referent, the semantic value of a predicate is the property it picks out rather than some descriptive content that picks out this property; predicates, like names, are directly referential. However, if it's possible to introduce a predicate that picks out a property by having some descriptive content as its semantic value, then it's possible for a public-language predicate to pick out the properties represented in consciousness. However, the point is that it's not possible to have a predicate that directly refers to one of these properties, that has one of these properties as its semantic value.

7. It might be claimed that Leon hasn't forgotten what it's like to see red. After all, at any time he can know what it's like to see red simply by imagining redness. And we don't ordinarily say that someone has forgotten something when he can easily remember it. Two points need to be made. First, Leon is able to remember what it's like to see red only by doing something else: namely, by imagining redness. And I might have forgotten what decorates the wall behind me even though I could easily remember by turning around. When my remembering P depends upon my doing something else, I have forgotten P. Second, suppose that while in the room Leon speaks to someone over the phone and says *You know, I've forgotten what it's like to see red*, and his interlocutor replies that he can simply imagine redness if he likes. Leon might respond by saying *But I like not knowing what it's like to see red, since it provides a good philosophical example*. It seems to me that Leon speaks truly.

8. Terrence Horgan (1984b) makes the same point in defense of Jackson's knowledge argument from the claim that Mary acquires no new propositional knowledge. Horgan points out that, besides learning what it's like to see red, Mary learns that (look at some red thing) *this* is what it's like to see red. Horgan's idea is that *this* picks out a quale and, hence, that Jackson's argument does establish that there are qualia. This idea—that the Mary argument presented above is unsound because, rather than learning about a property that red objects appear to have, she learns of a quale that experiences of red have—is discussed in Section 8.

9. There are some cases in which we would describe you as seeing red even though there is no object that is ascribed the property of redness by the proposition to which you are visually related; for example, we would describe you as seeing red if you were hallucinating a red object. However, as suggested in Chapter 2, Section 11, it's plausible that in the case of hallucinations vision represents that *there is something* that has the property: that is, it's plausible that hallucination involves a relation to an existential proposition. And, if this is right, the case in which you count as seeing F-ness because you're hallucinating that something is F will be subsumed by the criterion in the text that seeing an object or property amounts to its being a constituent of a proposition to which you are visually related. We

would also describe you as seeing red if you were undergoing a red after-image. And perhaps in the case of after-images the property is represented to you but is not a constituent of any proposition to which you are visually related; and, if this is right, the criterion in the text would need to be modified. However, it's far from clear that it is right. For, as Mark Johnston has rightly emphasized (in conversation), if you are undergoing a red after-image, *there is* a way the world could be that would seem to make your perception veridical: there might be a transparent roundish red thing floating about wherever you focus your gaze. And, given this, it seems that even after-images involve a relation to a proposition. However, even if they don't and, hence, even if the criterion in the text needs to be modified, there is no particular problem here. The sentence *The apple is red* represents the apple as being red—that is, it expresses a proposition—but it has a constituent (namely, the word *red*) that by itself simply represents a property without expressing a proposition. And, if vision, like sentences, can represent things as having properties, there's no reason that it shouldn't be able to represent a property by itself. When your perception represents something as having the property F, F is a constituent of the proposition to which you are visually related, but there's no reason you shouldn't simply bear some kind of perceptual relation to the property F; this would be somewhat mysterious, but it's no more mysterious than the nature of propositions and the relations we bear to them. The general point here is just that perception represents objects and properties (whether or not this always or only usually involves a relation to a proposition) but that perceptual representation of properties determines phenomenology, whereas perceptual representation of objects doesn't.

10. The projective error is much discussed by philosophers. See, for example, Shoemaker 1996. Boghossian and Velleman (1989) claim that perception does involve a projective error.

11. Indeed, Block (1990, 73) asserts a methodological principle that (in part) says that one *shouldn't* draw complex intuitions from such cases.

12. And, as noted in Chapter 1, Section 2, even if we are aware of the intrinsic qualities of perceptual intermediaries, it's still not clear that this raises any troubles for functionalism. If functionalism can account for our awareness of objects in the world and their properties, presumably it can account for awareness of perceptual intermediaries and their properties.

13. Admittedly, since on Millianism, non-complex concepts just are the things they determine, it's a bit strange to keep talking about concepts once you've accepted Millianism. However, it's worth noting that some of our ordinary uses of *concept* are consistent with the way the Millian would use philosophical talk of concepts if he weren't to simply abandon such talk. For example, the columnist Paul Craig Roberts has written: "Certainly freedom and justice have lost their universal meanings. These concepts have been dramatically narrowed and today are associated with the self-serving demands of victims groups" (see his "Justice Dethroned," which can be found at the following website www.townhall.com/columnists/paulcraigroberts/pcr2000828.shtml.) And he clearly means that *freedom and justice themselves* have been dramatically narrowed and are associated with the self-serving demands of victims groups. And such ordinary uses of *the concept X* to refer to X itself are not at all uncommon, especially when X is some abstract thing like freedom or justice.

14. It should be noted that there is another philosophical use of *concept* and, though Harman's discussion of Jackson's argument seems to be neutral about which philosophical use he's adopting, in other places Harman has adopted this other use (see, for example, Harman 1982). On the use of *concept* described above, a concept is a constituent of a proposition; let's call such concepts *propositional concepts*. The idea that concepts are propositional concepts can be seen as emerging from the idea that concepts are constituents of beliefs; for, if we combine that idea with the natural idea that beliefs are propositions—that is, that beliefs are the things we believe—it follows that concepts are the constituents of propositions. How-

ever, as discussed in Chapter 2, Section 4, though it's natural to think that beliefs are propositions, many philosophers believe that there is another use of the term *belief* according to which it refers to the internal state of a subject that relates him to the proposition he believes. Now many contemporary philosophers will want to claim that these internal belief states are physical states and, in particular, that they are states of the brain: when you believe that Alec Guinness was the twentieth century's greatest actor, there is some state of your brain that (in at least one sense of the term) *is* your *belief* that Alec Guinness was the twentieth century's greatest actor, and this brain state relates you to the proposition that Alec Guinness was the twentieth century's greatest actor. However, if we start with the idea that concepts are the constituents of beliefs but take the term *belief* to refer to internal brain states rather than propositions, then the term *concept* will refer to the constituent of an internal brain state rather than the constituent of a proposition. On this second philosophical conception of what concepts are — let's call them *internal concepts*—the state of your brain that relates you to the proposition that Alec Guinness was the twentieth century's greatest actor is composed of substates corresponding to the words in the sentence **Alec Guinness was the twentieth century's greatest actor** (or to the words in some transformation of the sentence). And your internal concept of *Alec Guinness* is the substate of your brain that, so to speak, *picks out* Alec Guinness rather than the propositional concept that picks him out. However, if you believe that there are internal concepts, it's natural to think that what makes some state of your brain your internal concept of Alec Guinness is that it bears some semantic relation to the propositional concept of Alec Guinness; more generally, some complex brain state B relates you to a particular proposition P because (i) the internal concepts that are the constituents of B bear some semantic relation to the propositional concepts that are the constituents of P, and (ii) the constituents of B are arranged in some kind of syntactic structure. Harman's idea is that Homer lacks the concept red because, being blind, he is not caused to have thoughts with that concept as a constituent when he's in front of a red thing. Harman probably means that Homer lacks the internal concept red (since this is the use of *concept* he adopts elsewhere); but, since on his view lack of the internal concept implies lack of the propositional concept (that is, if you don't have a brain state that semantically gets on to red things, you can't bear the belief relation to a proposition with a constituent that determines redness), and since Harman's point is that Homer can't have beliefs that ascribe redness to anything, we can interpret his claims as being about propositional concepts. I've done so in the text because in Chapter 2, Section 5, I argued that the philosophical assumption that there are internal belief states depends upon confusing the instantiation of a relation with a particular, upon what I called *the particularizing fallacy*. When someone believes something, he bears the belief relation to some proposition and his belief just is the proposition he believes; and so long as we're careful not to confusedly think of the instantiation of this relation as some particular that relates him to the proposition—in the terminology of Chapter 2, so long as we don't confuse instantial states with internal states—there's no prima facie reason to think that there's any sense of *belief* according to which his belief is some internal state of him. And, given that internal concepts are supposed to be the constituents of internal belief states, if we have no reason to believe in internal belief states, we have no reason to believe in internal concepts. Indeed, the idea that there are internal concepts goes well beyond the idea that there are internal belief states since it involves the ideas that (i) there is some heretofore undiscovered taxonomy of the brain that (ii) can be placed in a one-to-one correspondence with the taxonomy of words in a language and (iii) can be given a syntax and semantics. But the brain isn't a stable collection of objects; it's an enormous collection of neurons in constant flux. And we haven't the faintest idea of how these patterns of neuron firings might be individuated so that some event in the brain might count as the tokening of some linguistic item. It seems obvious that beliefs have constituents; but, so long as we avoid the particularizing fallacy, this provides no reason to think that there are structured internal belief states (as opposed to structured propositions). And, given that we don't even have the beginnings of a glimmer of an idea as to what the relevant taxonomy of the brain looks like, at this stage the idea that there are internal concepts looks like the worst case of the kind of *a priori* armchair philosophizing so often derided. And, if we do avoid the particularizing fallacy, there's no reason to think that the reality of believing depends in any way on the truth of what at best can only be described as wild speculation; we don't even know enough about the alleged taxonomy to describe it as a research strategy. Since Harman's argument is neutral about whether concepts are internal or propositional, given all this it seems best to understand them in the latter way.

15. In Chapter 4, I argued that the term *meaning* won't occur in the correct theory of linguistic communication. But Mary's only an expert neuroscientist and psychologist; she is not an expert semanticist.

16. Besides Jackson, David Lewis (1986b, x) and David Chalmers (1996) are among those who take physicalism to be a supervenience thesis. However, there are other versions of the supervenience thesis besides the claim that any two worlds that are physically the same must also be mentally the same. For example, Lewis (1983; 1986b, x) weakens the thesis to hold only for worlds that are sufficiently like the actual world in certain respects, and there are other ways to weaken or strengthen it (see, for example, Kim 1984 and 1987). But the discussion in the text applies equally well to any supervenience thesis and the version in the text is the simplest to state.

17. See Soames (1998b, 1999) for a discussion of epistemic determination, metaphysical determination, and the (lack of) relation between them.

18. There are a number of potential confusions about this point. First, if *Water is H_2O* is an identity statement like *Hesperus is Phosphorus* (and is true), then it might seem as if the Millianism advocated in Chapters 3 and 4 implies that to have the concept *water* just is to have the concept H_2O. However, there are several confusions here. First, H_2O is a complex expression and *water* is a simple one; hence, the concept H_2O is complex while the concept *water* is simple, so even if *Water is H_2O* is an identity statement, Millianism doesn't imply that the concept *water* is the same as the concept H_2O. Similarly, $2^8=256$, but this doesn't mean that the relevant concepts are the same or that anyone who has one of the concepts knows the identity claim. The concepts H_2O and 2^8 are complex and, hence, pick out their referents in something like the way that descriptive modes of presentation do. Second, there is a related and more general point here that's important and often missed: Millianism does *not* imply that when the A facts supervene on the B facts you can deduce the A facts from the B facts. Though it does imply that if x and y are simple, rigid, referring expressions and $x=y$, then the proposition that x is F just is the proposition that y is F, the supervenience of the A facts on the B facts needn't involve the fact that any of the A's are identical to any of the B's. The view that propositions are unstructured sets of possible worlds does seem to imply that metaphysically necessary relations are always known, but one main point of conceding that propositions must be structured is that it avoids such consequences. Finally, thirty years of philosophical discussion notwithstanding, *Water is H_2O* is obviously *not* an identity statement about the abstract kinds water and H_2O. *Water is wet* isn't a claim about the abstract kind water, since it's obviously *samples* of water rather than the *abstract kind* that are wet, just as *Men are mortal* obviously isn't the claim that *the abstract kind man* is mortal. *Men are mortal* is the claim that *all particulars* that are men are mortal, and *Water is wet* is the

claim that all samples of the kind water are wet. Similarly, *Water is H₂O* is the claim that all samples of water are samples of H_2O. Soames (2002) makes this point persuasively in an extended discussion of whether any sense can be made of Kripke's idea that certain kind terms are rigid designators. And Soames points out that because mass terms like *water* are *grammatically* singular terms (that is, they take *is* rather than *are*) has caused philosophers mistakenly think they are *semantically* singular terms (that is, that their function is to pick out objects rather than to predicate properties). It's obvious that, for example, *Tigers are cats* is a tacitly quantified statement concerning all things that are tigers because *tigers* is a count noun and, hence, we say *tigers are* rather than *tigers is*. But, in the case of mass terms, we don't use *are* and, hence, it's easy to confuse their grammatical singularity with semantical singularity. I think that once this point is brought out it's obviously right: *Water is H₂O* is like *Water is wet* and *Tigers are cats* rather than *Superman is Clark Kent* or *Hesperus is Phosphorus*. And it nicely explains why it's true that water is H_2O but false that H_2O is water since H_2O needn't be a liquid: that is, *all instances* of water are H_2O, but *not all instances* of H_2O are water, and these quantified claims are what *Water is H₂O* and *H₂O is water* respectively express.

19. Jackson and Braddon-Mitchell (1996, 132–33) and David Chalmers (1996, 56–71) have attempted to defend his argument against these considerations, but see Byrne (1999, 1998 ms.), and Soames (2002) for refutations. There's a lot wrong with Jackson's and Chalmers's defenses of the knowledge argument, but one obvious problem is the one noted in the text: namely, that knowing all of the chemical facts doesn't even imply that you have the concept water and, hence, can't imply that you know all of the water facts.

20. If this is right, then there's no reason to think that the belief Mary registers by saying *So fire engines have that property* is true since there's no reason that fire engines should happen to be the exact shade of red that, on this response, is the property Mary ostends. But the truth or falsity of Mary's new belief is irrelevant to the argument; all that matters is that it constitutes different information than her belief that fire engines are red.

21. Thanks to Alex Byrne for making me realize the importance of bringing out and answering this worry.

22. The fact that there's only one relevant property represented in perception is discussed more extensively in Thau (2000).

23. According to Jackson, *looks like* is also another sense of the term, the *comparative* sense. Jackson takes the terms *epistemic* and *comparative* from Chisholm (1957, ch. 4), and Jackson's *phenomenal* sense of *looks* is what Chisholm calls the *noncomparative sense*. Chisholm takes there to be a whole class of *appear words*—for example, *appears*, *looks*, *sounds*—that have these three senses. And, given that the arguments in this chapter extend beyond visual perception to other sensory modalities, similar worries as those discussed above will occur for *appear* words that apply to other sensory modalities—for example. *sounds*—if they too have a phenomenal sense. However, the response to the worry about *looks* presented in this section will obviously also apply to any such similar worries involving sensory modalities other than vision.

24. There is a more detailed discussion of this phenomena in Thau (2000), where I draw a distinction between what's represented *in* vision and what's represented *by* it. The intrinsic surface properties that we mistake for the colors are represented *in* vision, whereas the colors themselves are represented *by* vision.

25. There are of course any number of philosophical texts concerned with general skepticism about empirical knowledge. See, for example, Bonjour (1985).

26. The argument in the text differs slightly from that in Boghossian and Velleman (1989).

In Boghossian and Velleman (1989), the authors define dispositionalism about, for example, redness in terms of dispositions to *appear* red as opposed to dispositions to be represented in vision as red. However, in both of their papers on color (Boghossian and Velleman 1989 and 1991) they seem to understand something's appearing red as amounting to its being represented in vision as red. In any case, even putting this apparent identification aside, it isn't much of an intellectual leap from their argument to the argument in the text.

Works Cited

Austin, J. L. 1962. *Sense and Sensibilia*. Oxford: Clarendon.

Bach, K. 1999. The Myth of Conventional Implicature. *Linguistics and Philosophy* 22: 327–66.

———. 1997. Do Belief Reports Report Beliefs? *Pacific Philosophical Quarterly* 78: 215–41.

Bennett, J. 1971. *Locke, Berkeley, Hume*. Oxford: Clarendon.

Berkeley, G. [1710] 1957. *A Treatise Concerning the Principles of Human Knowledge*. Indianapolis, Ind.: Bobbs-Merill.

Black, M. 1958a. Notes on the Meaning of "Rule." *Theoria* 24: 107–26.

———. 1958b. Notes on the Meaning of "Rule" (II). *Theoria* 24: 139–61.

Blackburn, S. 1984. *Spreading the Word*. Oxford: Oxford University Press.

Block, N. forthcoming. Mental Paint. In a *festschrift* for Tyler Burge, ed. M. Hahn and B. Ramberg. Cambridge, Mass.: MIT Press.

———. 1990. Inverted Earth. In *Philosophical Perspectives*, vol. 4. ed. J. E. Tomberlin (Atascadero, Calif.: Ridgeview): 53–79.

———. 1983. Mental Pictures and Cognitive Science. *Philosophical Review* 92: 499–541.

———. 1980a. What Is Functionalism? In *Readings in the Philosophy of Psychology*, vol. 1, ed. N. Block (Cambridge, Mass.: Harvard University Press): 171–84.

———, ed. 1980b. *Readings in the Philosophy of Psychology*. Vol. 1. Cambridge, Mass.: Harvard University Press.

———, ed. 1980c. *Readings in the Philosophy of Psychology*. Vol. 2. Cambridge, Mass., Harvard University Press.

———. 1978. Troubles with Functionalism. In *Perception and Cognition*, ed. C. W. Savage. (Minneapolis: University of Minnesota Press): 261–325.

Boghossian, P. and D. Velleman.1991. Physicalist Theories of Color. *Philosophical Review* 100: 67–106.

———. 1989. Colour as a Secondary Quality. *Mind* 98: 81–103.

Bonjour, L. 1985. *The Structure of Empirical Knowledge*. Cambridge, Mass.: Harvard University Press.

Braun, D. 1998. Understanding Belief Reports. *Philosophical Review* 107: 555–95.
————. 1993. Empty Names. *Nous* 27: 449–69.
Brentano, F. [1874] 1995. *Psychology from an Empirical Standpoint*. New York: Routledge.
Burge, T. 1982. Other Bodies. In *Thought and Object*, ed. A. Woodfield (Oxford: Clarendon): 97–120.
————. 1979a. Individualism and the Mental. In *Midwest Studies in Philosophy*, ed. P. French, T. Uehling, and H. Wettstein (Minneapolis: University of Minnesota Press): 73–121.
————. 1979b. Sinning Against Frege. *Philosophical Review* 88: 398–432.
Byrne, A. 1999. Cosmic Hermeneutics. In *Philosophical Perspectives*, Vol. 13. ed. J. E. Tomberlin (Atascadero, Calif.: Ridgeview): 347–83.
————. Interpretivism. *European Review of Philosophy* 3.
————. 1993. The Emergent Mind. Unpublished dissertation, Princeton University.
Chalmers, D. 1996. *The Conscious Mind*. New York: Oxford University Press.
Chisholm, R. M. 1957. *Perceiving*. Ithaca: Cornell University Press.
Crimmins, M. 1992. *Talk about Beliefs*. Cambridge, Mass.: MIT Press.
Danto, A. 1963. What We Can Do. *Journal of Philosophy* 60: 434–45.
Dennett, D. C. 1991. *Consciousness Explained*. Boston: Little, Brown.
————. 1987. Reflections: Instrumentalism Reconsidered. In *The Intentional Stance*, ed. Dennett. (Cambridge, Mass.: MIT Press): 69–81.
————. 1983. Styles of Mental Representation. *Proceedings of the Aristotelian Society* 83: 213–26.
————. 1981. Three Kinds of Intentional Psychology. In *Reduction, Time, and Reality*, ed. R. Healey (Cambridge: Cambridge University Press): 37–62.
————. 1977. Critical Notice: *The Language of Thought* by Jerry Fodor. *Mind* 86: 265–80.
Dretske, F. 1996. Phenomenal Externalism. In *Perception*, ed. E. Villanueva. (Atascadero, Calif.: Ridgeview): 143–58.
Dummett, M. 1981. *The Interpretation of Frege's Philosophy*. New York: Harper and Row.
————. 1973. *Frege: Philosophy of Langauge*. New York: Harper and Row.
Evans, G. [1982] 1995. *The Varieties of Reference*. Oxford: Clarendon.
————. 1980. Things without the Mind. In *Philosophical Subjects*, ed. Z. V. Straaten (Oxford: Oxford University Press): 76–116.
————. [1979] 1985. Reference and Contingency. In *Collected Papers*. (Oxford: Clarendon): 178–213.
Ewing, A. C. 1940. The Linguistic Theory of *A Priori* Propositions. *Proceedings of the Aristotelian Society* 40: 207–44.
Fodor, J. A. 1987. *Psychosemantics*. Cambridge, Mass.: MIT Press.
————. 1978. Propositional Attitudes. *Monist* 61: 501–24.
————. 1975. *The Language of Thought*. Cambridge, Mass.: Harvard University Press.
Fogelin, R. J. 1975. *Wittgenstein*. London: Routledge.
Frege, G. 1948. Sense and Reference. *Philosophical Review* 57: 207–30.
————. [1918] 1977. Thoughts. Reprint, in *Logical Investigations*, ed. P. T. Geach (New Haven: Yale University Press): 1–30.
————. [1894] 1952. Illustrative Extracts from Frege's Review of Husserl's *Philosophie der Arithmetik*. Reprint, in *Translations from the Philosophical Writings of Gottlob Frege*, ed. P. Geach and M. Black (Oxford: Oxford University Press): 79–85.
————. [1892] 1984a. On Sense and Meaning [On Sense and Reference]. Reprint, in *Collected Papers on Mathematics, Logic, and Philosophy*, ed. B. McGuiness (Oxford: Blackwell): 157–77.

————. [1892] 1984b. Concept and Object. In *Collected Papers on Mathematics, Logic, and Philosophy*, ed. B. McGuinness. (Oxford: Basil Blackwell): 182–94.

————. [1892–95] 1979. Comments on Sense and Meaning. Reprint, in *Posthumous Writings*, ed. H. Hermes, F. Kambartel, and F. Kaulbach (Chicago: University of Chicago Press): 118–25.

————. [1891] 1984. Function and Concept. Reprint, in *Collected Papers on Mathematics, Logic, and Philosophy*, ed. B. McGuinness (Oxford: Blackwell): 137–56.

————. [1879] 1972. *Conceptual Notation and Related Articles [Begriffsschrift]*. Reprint, Oxford: Clarendon.

Geach, P. 1965. Assertion. *Philosophical Review* 74: 449–65.

Goldman, A. I. 1970. *A Theory of Human Action*. Princeton, N.J.: Princeton University Press.

Green, M. 1998. Direct Reference and Implicature. *Philosophical Studies* 91: 61–90.

Grice, P. 1989. *Studies in the Way of Words*. Cambridge, Mass.: Harvard University Press.

Harman, G. 1997. Explaining Objective Color in Terms of Subjective Reactions. In *Readings on Color*, Vol. 1. ed. A. Byrne and D. R. Hilbert (Cambridge, Mass.: MIT Press): 247–61.

————. 1990. The Intrinsic Quality of Experience. In *Philosophical Perspectives*. Vol. 4. ed. J. E. Tomberlin (Atascadero, Calif.: Ridgeview): 31–52.

————. 1982. Conceptual Role Semantics. *Notre Dame Journal of Formal Logic* 23: 242–56.

————. 1973. *Thought*. Princeton, N.J.: Princeton University Press.

Harrison, B. 1967. On Describing Colours. *Inquiry* 10: 38–52.

Heck, R. 1995. The Sense of Communication. *Mind* 104: 79–106.

Hilbert, D. R., and M. E. Kalderon. 2000. Color and the Inverted Spectrum. In *Color Perception*, ed. S. Davis (Oxford: Oxford University Press): 187–214.

Horgan, T. 1984a. Functionalism, Qualia, and the Inverted Spectrum. *Philosophy and Phenomenological Research* 44: 453–70.

————. 1984b. Jackson on Physical Information and Qualia. *Philosophical Quarterly* 34: 147–83.

Hornsby, J. 1980. *Actions*. London: Routledge & Kegan Paul.

Jackson, F. 1986. What Mary Didn't Know. *Journal of Philosophy* 83: 291–95.

————. 1982. Epiphenomenal Qualia. *Philosophical Quarterly* 32: 127–36.

————. 1977. *Perception*. Cambridge: Cambridge University Press.

Jackson, F., and D. Braddon-Mitchell. 1996. *Philosophy of Mind and Cognition*. Oxford: Blackwell.

Jackson, F., and R. Pargetter. 1987. An Objectivist's Guide to Subjectivism about Color. *Review of International Philosophy* 41: 127–41.

Johnston, M. 1992. How to Speak of the Colors. *Philosophical Studies* 68: 221–63.

Kant, I. [1787] 1922. *Critique of Pure Reason*. Reprint, New York: Macmillan.

Kaplan, D. 1989. Demonstratives. In *Themes from Kaplan*, ed. J. Almog, J. Perry, and H. Wettstein (Oxford: Oxford University Press): 481–564.

————. 1986. Opacity. In *The Philosophy of W. V. Quine*, ed. L. E. Hahn and P. A. Schilpp (La Salle, Ill.: Open Court): 229–89.

————. 1972. What Is Russell's Theory of Descriptions? In *Bertrand Russell*, ed. D. F. Pears (New York: Anchor): 277–88.

Kim, J. 1987. "Strong" and "Global" Supervenience Revisited. *Philosophy and Phenomenological Research* 48: 315–26.

————. 1984. Concepts of Supervenience. *Philosophy and Phenomenological Research* 45: 153–76.

Kripke, S. 1982. *Wittgenstein: On Rules and Private Language*. Cambridge, Mass.: Harvard University Press.

———. [1972] 1980. *Naming and Necessity*. Cambridge, Mass.: Harvard University Press.

Lewis, D. 1995. Should a Materialist Believe in Qualia? *Australasian Journal of Philosophy* 73: 140–44.

———. 1990. What Experience Teaches. In *Mind and Cognition*, ed. W. Lycan. (Oxford: Blackwell): 499–519.

———. 1986a. *On the Plurality of Worlds*. Oxford: Blackwell.

———. 1986b. Introduction to *Philosophical Papers*. Vol. 2. (New York: Oxford University Press): ix–xvii.

———. 1983. Postscript to "Mad Pain and Martian Pain." In *Philosophical Papers*. Vol. 1. (Oxford: Oxford University Press): 130–132.

———. [1978] 1980. Mad Pain and Martian Pain. Reprint, in *Readings in the Philosophy of Psychology*, Vol. 1. ed. N. Block (Cambridge, Mass.: Harvard University Press): 216–31.

———. 1969. *Convention*. Cambridge, Mass.: Harvard University Press.

Loar, B. 1990. Phenomenal States. In *Philosophical Perspectives*. Vol. 4. ed. J. E. Tomberlin (Atascadero, Calif.: Ridgeview): 81–108.

Locke, J. [1690] 1975. *An Essay Concerning Human Understanding*. Reprint, Oxford: Clarendon.

Lycan, W. G. 1996. *Consciousness and Experience*. Cambridge, Mass.: MIT Press.

———. 1995. A Limited Defense of Phenomenal Information. In *Conscious Experience*, ed. T. Metzinger (Paderborn: Schoningh): 243–58.

MacAdam, D. L. 1985. *Color Measurement*. New York: Springer.

McDowell, J. 1985. Values and Secondary Qualities. In *Morality and Objectivity*, ed. T. Honderich (London: Routledge): 110–29.

McGinn, C. 1991. *The Problem of Consciousness*. Oxford: Blackwell.

———. 1983. *The Subjective View*. Oxford: Clarendon.

Moore, G. E. 1922. *Philosophical Studies*. London: Routledge.

Nemirow, L. 1990. Physicalism and the Cognitive Role of Acquiantance. In *Mind and Cognition*, ed. W. Lycan (Oxford: Blackwell): 490–99.

Parsons, T. 1982. What Do Quotation Marks Name? Frege's Theories of Quotations and That-Clauses. *Philosophical Studies* 42: 315–28.

———. 1980. *Nonexistent Objects*. New Haven: Yale University Press.

Peacocke, C. 1992. *A Study of Concepts*. Cambridge, Mass.: MIT Press.

———. 1983. *Sense and Content*. Oxford: Oxford University Press.

Perlmutter, D. M. 1992. Sonority and Syllable Structure in American Sign Language. *Linguistic Inquiry* 23: 407–42.

Pessin, A., and S. Goldberg, eds. 1996. *The Twin Earth Chronicles*. Armonk, N.Y.: Sharpe.

Pietroski, P. 2000. *Causing Actions*. Oxford: Clarendon.

Pryor, J. n.d. On Two-Dimensionalism. Unpublished ms., Harvard University.

———. 1997. How to Be a Reasonable Dogmatist. Unpublished dissertation, Princeton University, Princeton, N.J.

Putnam, H. 1975. The Meaning of "Meaning." In *Minnesota Studies in the Philosophy of Science*, ed. K. Gunderson (Minneapolis: University of Minnesota Press): 131–93.

Ramsey, W., S. Stitch, et al. 1990. Connectionism, Eliminativism, and the Future of Folk

Psychology. In *Philosophical Perspectives*. Vol. 4. ed. J. E. Tomberlin (Atascadero, Calif.: Ridgeview): 499–533.

Recanati, F. 1993. *Direct Reference*. Oxford: Blackwell.

Rey, G. 1994. Concepts. In *A Companion to the Philosophy of Language*, ed. S. Guttenplan (Oxford: Blackwell): 185–93.

Richard, M. 1990. *Propositional Attitudes*. Cambridge: Cambridge University Press.

Russell, B. 1905. On Denoting. *Mind* 14: 479–93.

Salmon, N. 1998. Nonexistence. *Nous* 32: 277–319.

———. 1987. Existence. In *Philosophical Perspectives*. Vol. 1. ed. J. E. Tomberlin. (Atascadero, Calif.: Ridgeview): 49–108.

———. 1986. *Frege's Puzzle*. Cambridge, Mass.: MIT Press.

Saul, J. M. 1998. The Pragmatics of Attitude Ascription. *Philosophical Studies* 92: 363–89.

———. 1997. Substitution and Simple Sentences. *Analysis* 57: 102–8.

Schiffer, S. 1992. Belief Ascriptions. *Journal of Philosophy* 89: 499–521.

Sellars, W. [1956] 1997. *Empiricism and the Philosophy of Mind*. Cambridge, Mass.: Harvard University Press.

Shoemaker, S. 1996. *The First-Person Perspective and Other Essays*. Cambridge: Cambridge University Press.

———. 1994a. Self-Knowledge and "Inner Sense." *Philosophy and Phenomenological Research* 54: 249–314.

———. 1994b. Phenomenal Character. *Nous* 28: 21–38.

———. 1982. The Inverted Spectrum. *Journal of Philosophy* 79: 357–81.

Soames, S. n.d. On Two-Dimensionalism. Unpublished ms., Princeton University, Princeton, N.J.

———. 2002. *Beyond Rigidity*. New York: Oxford University Press.

———. 1999. The Indeterminacy of Translation and the Inscrutability of Reference. *Canadian Journal of Philosophy* 29: 321–70.

———. 1998a. The Modal Argument: Wide Scope and Rigidified Descriptions. *Nous* 32:1–22.

———. 1998b. Skepticism about Meaning: Indeterminacy, Normativity, and the Rule Following Paradox. *Canadian Journal of Philosophy*, Supplementary Vol. 23: 211–49.

———. 1995. Beyond Singular Propositions? *Canadian Journal of Philosophy* 25: 515–49.

———. 1987. Substitutivity. In *On Being and Saying*, ed. J. J. Thomson (Cambridge, Mass.: MIT Press): 99–132.

Stalnaker, R. 1984. *Inquiry*. Cambridge, Mass., MIT Press.

Stanley, J. 1997. Names and Rigid Designation. In *A Companion to the Philosophy of Language*, ed. B. Hale and C. Wright (Oxford: Blackwell): 555–85.

Thau, M. 2000. What to Do When Your Relationships Fail. Unpublished paper.

Thau, M. and B. Caplan. What's Puzzling Gottlob Frege? *Canadian Journal of Philosophy* 31.2:159–200.

Tye, M. 1995. *Ten Problems of Consciousness*. Cambridge, Mass.: MIT Press.

———. 1994. Qualia, Content, and Inverted Spectrum. *Nous* 28: 159–83.

———. 1991. *The Imagery Debate*. Cambridge, Mass.: MIT Press.

Von Senden, M. 1960. *Space and Sight*. London: Methuen.

Waismann, F. 1965. *The Principles of Linguistic Philosophy*. London: Macmillan.

Wilson, M. 1992. History of Philosophy in Philosophy Today: And the Case of the Sensible Qualities. *Philosophical Review* 101: 191–243.

Wittgenstein, L. 1958. *The Blue and Brown Books*. New York: Harper.

———. 1953. *Philosophical Investigations*. Oxford: Blackwell.

Wright, C. 1992. *Truth and Objectivity*. Cambridge, Mass.: Harvard University Press.

Yablo, S. 1992. Review of Alan Sidelle, *Necessity, Essence, and Individuation*. *Philosophical Review* 101: 878–81.

Zwicky, A. M., and J. M. Sadock. 1975. Ambiguity Tests and How to Fail Them. *Syntax and Semantics* 4:1–36.

Index

Austin, J. L., 53, 54, 242 n.5

Bach, K., 255 n.3
belief, beliefs
  de re, 88–90, 92, 127, 209, 227, 240, 242
    n.2, 248 n.32
  dyadism about, 96, 97
  as instantial states, 60–62, 207, 210, 266
    n.14
  as internal states, 60–67, 202, 205, 207,
    210, 216, 237, 266 n.14
  triadism about beliefs, 96–98, 108, 137,
    178, 252 n.11
  and truth-aptness, 59, 60, 67, 68, 75, 196
  and truth-normativity, 59, 67, 68, 79,
    222, 238, 244 n.31
Berkeley, G., 36, 38, 39
Black, M., 14, 36, 126, 178, 179, 182, 193,
    195, 213, 216, 217, 219, 231, 257 n.13
Block, N., 15, 35, 36, 55, 195, 202, 204,
    205, 239 nn.1–2, 240 n.12, 265 n.11
Boghossian, P., 235, 240 n.6, 240 n.11, 241
    n.14, 265 n.10, 268 n.26
Bonjour, L., 268 n.25
Braddon-Mitchell, D., 268 n.19
Braun, D., 119, 250 n.5, 261 n.21
Brentano, F., 48, 50, 54, 58, 241 n.1, 242
    nn.3–4, 243 n.9, 249 n.36

Burge, T., 22, 90, 239 n.3, 248 n.34,
    251 n.7
Byrne, A., 66, 268 nn.19, 21

Caplan, B., 250 n.2, 253 n.14, 254 n.21,
    261 n.21
Chalmers, D., 239 n.1, 267 n.16,
    268 n.19
Chisholm, R. M., 268 n.23
color perception, 24, 180, 187, 209, 213,
    239 n.1
Crimmins, M., 116, 244 n.14, 251 n.10

Danto, A., 257 n.12
Dennett, D., 66, 214, 215
Dretske, F., 47
Dummett, M., 72, 248 n.34

Evans, G., 72, 85, 89, 93, 235, 247 n.27,
    248 n.34, 251 n.7, 254 n.17

Fodor, J., 64, 65
Fogelin, R. J., 257 n.13
Frege, G., 28, 36, 59, 100, 125, 135, 168,
    243 n.11, 247 n.26, 249 n.36, 250 n.2,
    253 n.14
functionalism, 17–21, 24, 26, 180, 205,
    209, 210, 239 n.2, 265 n.12

9 780195 141818